The Rational Design of International Institutions

International Organization

Special Issues

Between Power and Plenty: Foreign Economic Policies of Advanced Industrial States, edited by Peter J. Katzenstein. University of Wisconsin Press, 1978.

Nuclear Proliferation: Breaking the Chains, edited by George H. Quester. University of Wisconsin Press, 1981.

International Regimes, edited by Stephen D. Krasner. Cornell University Press, 1983.

Power, Purpose and Collective Choice: Economic Strategy in Socialist States, edited by Ellen Comisso and Laura D'Andrea Tyson. Cornell University Press, 1986.

The State and American Foreign Economic Policy, edited by G. John Ikenberry, David Lake, and Michael Mastanduno. Cornell University Press, 1988.

Exploration and Contestation in the Study of World Politics, edited by Peter J. Katzenstein, Robert Keohane, and Stephen D. Krasner. The MIT Press, 1999.

Legalization and World Politics, edited by Judith Goldstein, Miles Kahler, Robert Keohane, and Ann Marie Slaughter. The MIT Press, 2001.

The Political Economy of Monetary Institutions, edited by William Bernhard, J. Lawrence Broz, and William Roberts Clark. The MIT Press, 2003.

Readers

Issues and Agents in International Political Economy, edited by Benjamin J. Cohen and Charles Lipson. The MIT Press, 1999.

Theory and Structure in International Political Economy, edited by Charles Lipson and Benjamin Jerry Cohen. The MIT Press, 1999.

International Institutions, edited by Lisa L. Martin and Beth A. Simmons. The MIT Press, 2001.

The Rational Design of International Institutions

Edited by

Barbara Koremenos
University of California, Los Angeles

Charles Lipson
University of Chicago

Duncan Snidal
University of Chicago

CAMBRIDGE
UNIVERSITY PRESS

PUBLISHED BY THE PRESS SYNDICATE OF THE UNIVERSITY OF CAMBRIDGE
The Pitt Building, Trumpington Street, Cambridge, United Kingdom

CAMBRIDGE UNIVERSITY PRESS
The Edinburgh Building, Cambridge CB2 2RU, UK
40 West 20th Street, New York, NY 10011-4211, USA
477 Williamstown Road, Port Melbourne, VIC 3207, Australia
Ruiz de Alarcón 13, 28014 Madrid, Spain
Dock House, The Waterfront, Cape Town 8001, South Africa

http://www.cambridge.org

First published 2001 by MIT Press on behalf of The IO Foundation as a special issue of
International Organization, vol. 55, no. 4
This paperback edition first published 2004

Printed in the United States of America

Typeface Times New Roman PS 10/12 pt.

A catalog record for this book is available from the British Library.

Library of Congress Cataloging in Publication data available

ISBN 0 521 53358 9 paperback

Contents

Contributors

Patricia M. Keilbach is Assistant Professor of Political Science at the University of Colorado, Colorado Springs, Colorado. She can be reached at pkeilbach@uccs.edu.

Barbara Koremenos is Assistant Professor of Political Science at the University of California, Los Angeles. She can be reached at koremeno@polisci.ucla.edu.

Andrew Kydd is Assistant Professor in the Department of Government at Harvard University, Cambridge, Massachusetts. He can be reached at akydd@wcfia.harvard.edu.

Charles Lipson is Professor of Political Science and Co-Director of the Program on International Politics, Economics, and Security at the University of Chicago, Illinois. He can be reached at c-lipson@uchicago.edu.

Walter Mattli is Associate Professor of Political Science and member of the Institute of War and Peace Studies at Columbia University, New York. He can be reached at wm62@columbia.edu.

Helen V. Milner is James T. Shotwell Professor of International Relations at Columbia University, New York. She can be reached at hvm1@columbia.edu.

Ronald B. Mitchell is Associate Professor of Political Science at the University of Oregon, Eugene. He can be reached at rmitchel@oregon.uoregon.edu.

James D. Morrow is Professor of Political Science and Senior Research Scientist at the Center for Political Studies, University of Michigan, Ann Arbor. He can be reached at jdmorrow@umich.edu.

Thomas H. Oatley is Associate Professor of Political Science at the University of North Carolina at Chapel Hill. He can be reached at toatley@email.unc.edu.

Robert Pahre is Associate Professor of Political Science at the University of Illinois at Urbana-Champaign. He can be reached at pahre@uiuc.edu.

John E. Richards is an associate at McKinsey and Company, Palo Alto, California. He is also an IGCC Economy Project Fellow and former Director of International Computer Services Research at the Stanford Computer Industry Project. He can be reached at j2richar@yahoo.com.

B. Peter Rosendorff is Associate Professor of International Relations and Economics and Director of the Center for International Studies at the University of Southern California, Los Angeles. He can be reached at bpeter@usc.edu.

Duncan J. Snidal is Associate Professor in the Irving B. Harris Graduate School of Public Policy Studies and the Department of Political Science at the University of Chicago, Illinois. He can be reached at snidal@uchicago.edu.

Alexander Wendt is Associate Professor of Political Science at the University of Chicago, Illinois. He can be reached at awendt@uchicago.edu.

Abstracts

The Rational Design of International Institutions
by Barbara Koremenos, Charles Lipson, and Duncan Snidal

Why do international institutions vary so widely in terms of such key institutional features as membership, scope, and flexibility? We argue that international actors are goal-seeking agents who make specific institutional design choices to solve the particular cooperation problems they face in different issue-areas. In this article we introduce the theoretical framework of the Rational Design project. We identify five important features of institutions—membership, scope, centralization, control, and flexibility—and explain their variation in terms of four independent variables that characterize different cooperation problems: distribution, number of actors, enforcement, and uncertainty. We draw on rational choice theory to develop a series of empirically falsifiable conjectures that explain this institutional variation. The authors of the articles in this special issue of *International Organization* evaluate the conjectures in specific issue-areas and the overall Rational Design approach.

Trust Building, Trust Breaking: The Dilemma of NATO Enlargement
by Andrew Kydd

Barbara Koremenos, Charles Lipson, and Duncan Snidal conjecture that the conditions of membership in international institutions will grow more restrictive as a response to uncertainty about state preferences. Membership criteria will act as a signaling device—states more committed to cooperation will be willing to meet the criteria, whereas those less committed to cooperation will not. The recent enlargement of NATO to include the former Warsaw Pact members Poland, Hungary, and the Czech Republic illustrates this logic. The potential candidates for admission had to meet standards with respect to democratization, civilian control over the military, and the resolution of border and ethnic disputes with neighbors. These criteria served to identify the more cooperative potential members and to encourage cooperative behavior among those who aspired to membership. However, NATO enlargement came at a price. Although trust was built and cooperation fostered between the East European states that gained membership, trust was broken and cooperation harmed between NATO and Russia. This unfortunate outcome represents a dilemma that arises in the expansion of a security community: While expanding the security community enlarges the zone of peace and mutual trust, it may generate fear among those still on the outside, who view it as a potentially hostile alliance. I present a game-theoretic analysis of this dilemma and analyze the conditions under which it arises.

The Optimal Design of International Trade Institutions: Uncertainty and Escape
by B. Peter Rosendorff and Helen V. Milner

International institutions that include an escape clause generate more durable and stable cooperative international regimes and are easier to achieve *ex ante*. The escape clause is endogenous in a model of repeated trade-barrier setting in the presence of symmetric, two-sided, political uncertainty. They permit, along the equilibrium path, countries to temporarily deviate from their obligations in periods of excessive, unexpected political pressure at some prenegotiated cost. The architects of international agreements optimally choose a cost so that escape clauses are neither too cheap to use (encouraging frequent recourse, effectively reducing the benefits of cooperation) nor too expensive (making their use rare and increasing the chance of systemic breakdown). The international institution's crucial role is to provide information, verifying that the self-enforcing penalty has been paid (voluntarily), rather than to coerce payment. Escape clauses also make agreements easier to reach initially. Their flexibility reassures states that the division of the long-term gains from the agreement is not immutable.

Most-Favored-Nation Clauses and Clustered Negotiations
by Robert Pahre

Though substantively important, centralized negotiations have received less theoretical attention than problems of centralized monitoring and enforcement. I address this gap by examining variation in a particular form of centralized negotiations that I call "clustering." Clustering occurs when a state negotiates with several other states at the same time. Clustering enables states to avoid having to make concessions on the same issue to one state after another, and therefore has important distributional advantages. Clustering also centralizes bargaining within a regime, especially when several states cluster simultaneously in a "macro-cluster."

I propose several hypotheses about clustering. First, most-favored-nation (MFN) clauses are a necessary condition for clustering. They link the distributional conflicts among many pairs of countries and make centralized bargaining more likely. Second, increasing membership in the trade regime makes clustering more likely. This relationship between membership and centralization echoes Rational Design conjecture C3, CENTRALIZATION increases with NUMBER, though the causal mechanism differs significantly. Third, clustering provides distributional advantages to those who cluster. A state that clusters, such as France under the Méline tariff or Germany under Chancellors Leo von Caprivi and Bernard von Bülow, will make fewer concessions than one that does not.

Situation Structure and Institutional Design: Reciprocity, Coercion, and Exchange
by Ronald B. Mitchell and Patricia M. Keilbach

States experiencing negative externalities caused by other states' behaviors have incentives to devise international institutions to change those behaviors. The institutions states create to counter incentives to defect vary in whether and how they expand institutional scope to accomplish that goal. When facing symmetric externalities, states tend to devise narrow institutions based on issue-specific reciprocity. When facing asymmetric externalities, or upstream/downstream problems, states tend to broaden institutional scope using linkage strategies. When victims of an externality are stronger than its perpetrators, the resulting institutions, if any are devised, are likely to incorporate the negative linkage of sanctions or coercion. When victims are weaker, exchange institutions relying on the positive linkage of rewards are more likely. We illustrate the influence of situation structure on institutional design with three cases: international whaling, ozone-layer depletion, and Rhine River pollution.

Private Justice in a Global Economy: From Litigation to Arbitration
by Walter Mattli

Drawing on the analytical framework developed by Barbara Koremenos, Charles Lipson, and Duncan Snidal in the Rational Design project, I seek to shed light on the striking institutional differences among the various methods of international commercial dispute resolution for private parties. These methods include recourse to public courts and more frequently to private international courts, such as the International Court of Arbitration of the International Chamber of Commerce or the London Court of International Arbitration, as well as recourse to so-called ad hoc arbitration and alternative dispute-resolution techniques, such as conciliation and mediation. The key institutional dimensions along which these methods of international dispute resolution vary are (1) procedural and adaptive flexibility, and (2) centralization of procedural safeguards and information collection. I explain why different methods of international commercial dispute resolution are selected. I argue that these methods respond to the varying institutional needs of different types of disputes and disputants. Such needs can be explained in terms of the severity of the enforcement problem, uncertainty about the preferences or behavior of contractual partners, and uncertainty about the state of the world.

Multilateralizing Trade and Payments in Postwar Europe
by Thomas H. Oatley

Europe's postwar shift to multilateral trade and payments arrangements was complicated by three factors. Distributional problems and uncertainty about the state of the world made European governments reluctant to adopt multilateral arrangements without financial support from the United States. An enforcement problem made U.S. policymakers reluctant to finance a European multilateral trading system. The severity of these problems was reduced by institutional designs that combined flexibility, centralization, and particular decision rules. Centralization and flexibility reduced uncertainty and softened distributive conflict. Centralization and particular decision rules solved the enforcement problem that U.S. policymakers faced.

The Institutional Features of the Prisoners of War Treaties
by James D. Morrow

During the twentieth century states negotiated and ratified formal treaties on the treatment of prisoners of war (POWs). These treaties have created a system for the treatment of POWs with universal and detailed standards and decentralized enforcement. I explain the form of the POW system as a rational institutional response to four strategic problems the issue of POWs poses: monitoring under noise, individual as opposed to state violations, variation in preferred treatment of POWs, and raising a mass army. In response to these four problems, neutral parties help address the problem of monitoring the standards. The ratification process screens out some states that do not intend to live up to the standards. The two-level problem of state and individual violations is addressed by making states responsible for punishing the actions of their own soldiers. By protecting POWs, the treaties help states raise armies during wartime. The POW case supports many, but not all, of the Rational Design conjectures. In particular, it suggests other strategic logics to explain variation in the membership and centralization of international institutions.

Institutions for Flying: How States Built a Market in International Aviation Services
by John E. Richards

In the aftermath of World War II, states created a complex set of bilateral and multilateral institutions to govern international aviation markets. National governments concluded bilateral agreements to regulate airport entry and capacity and delegated to the airlines, through the International Air Transport Association (IATA), the authority to set fares and the terms of service in international markets. The resulting mixture of public and private institutions produced a de facto cartel that lasted for more than thirty years. Consistent with the Rational Design framework put forth by Barbara Koremenos, Charles Lipson, and Duncan Snidal, I argue that the institutions states created reflect the bargaining and incentive problems generated by international aviation markets. This case provides support for four of the Rational Design conjectures and slightly contradicts three others.

Driving with the Rearview Mirror: On the Rational Science of Institutional Design
by Alexander Wendt

The Rational Design project is impressive on its own terms. However, it does not address other approaches relevant to the design of international institutions. To facilitate comparison I survey two "contrast spaces" around it. The first shares the project's central question—What explains institutional design?—but addresses alternative explanations of two types: rival explanations and explanations complementary but deeper in the causal chain. The second contrast begins with a different question: What kind of knowledge is needed to design institutions in the real world? Asking this question reveals epistemological differences between positive social science and institutional design that can be traced to different orientations toward time. Making institutions is about the future and has an intrinsic normative element. Explaining institutions is about the past and does not necessarily have this normative dimension. To avoid "driving with the rearview mirror" we need two additional kinds of knowledge beyond that developed in this volume, knowledge about institutional effectiveness and knowledge about what values to pursue. As such, the problem of institutional design is a fruitful site for developing a broader and more practical conception of social science that integrates normative and positive concerns.

Rational Design: Looking Back to Move Forward
by Barbara Koremenos, Charles Lipson, and Duncan Snidal

In this article we summarize the empirical results of the Rational Design project. In general the results strongly support the Rational Design conjectures, especially those on flexibility and centralization; some findings are inconclusive (in particular, those addressing scope) or point toward a need for theoretical reformulation (in particular, the membership dimension). We also address the broader implications of the volume's findings, concentrating on several topics directly related to institutional design and its systematic study. First, we consider the trade-offs in creating highly formalized models to guide the analysis. Second, our discussion of the variable control is a step toward incorporating "power" more fully and explicitly in our analysis. We also consider how domestic politics can be incorporated more systematically into international institutional analysis. Finally, we initiate a discussion about how and why institutions change, particularly how they respond to changing preferences and external shocks. We conclude with a discussion of the forward-looking character of rational design.

The Rational Design of International Institutions

The Rational Design of International Institutions

Barbara Koremenos, Charles Lipson, and Duncan Snidal

International institutions are central features of modern international relations. This is true of trade, international debt and financial restructuring, and even national security, once the exclusive realm of pure state action. It was certainly true of the two major military engagements of the 1990s, the wars in Kosovo and the Persian Gulf. As international institutions have gained prominence in the political landscape, they have increasingly become prominent topics for study. The sharpest debate among researchers has been theoretical: Do international institutions really matter? Missing from this debate is a sustained inquiry into how these institutions actually work. We shift the focus by posing researchable questions about how they operate and how they relate to the problems states face.

We begin with a simple observation: major institutions are organized in radically different ways. Some are global, essentially open to all states; others are regional, with restricted memberships. Some institutions give each state an equal vote, whereas others have weighted voting and sometimes require supermajorities. Institutions may have relatively strong central authorities and significant operating responsibilities or be little more than forums for consultation. Some arrangements—

As this project came to fruition, we received valuable input from many sources. We thank Kenneth Abbott, George Downs, James Fearon, Phillip Genschel, Charles Glaser, Lloyd Gruber, Miles Kahler, Robert Keohane, Dan Lindley, Lisa Martin, Ken Oye, Beth Yarbrough, Alexander Thompson, Mark Zacher, and especially Brian Portnoy, who participated in one or more of the conferences leading up to this volume. Jeffrey Smith, Ryan Peirce, Marc Trachtenberg, David Laitin, Joni Harlan, and Jama Adams provided other valuable comments, as did the participants at the Program on International Politics, Economics, and Security (PIPES), University of Chicago, where this project began. Students who participated in Barbara Koremenos' undergraduate seminar at UCLA, "International Cooperation," provided valuable feedback. We also thank the contributors for their efforts, not only on their individual articles but also on the design of the project as a whole. James Morrow, Ronald Mitchell, Peter Rosendorff, Robert Pahre, and especially Andrew Kydd contributed greatly to the project. We received invaluable criticism, prodding, and support from two anonymous reviewers, from the editors of *IO*, and from Lynne Bush. We thank the University of Chicago's Council on Advanced Studies on Peace and International Cooperation for funding support and the Harris Graduate School of Public Policy Studies for hosting the Rational Design conferences. Finally, we thank Loch Macdonald, Barbara Koremenos' neurosurgeon, who was there when we needed him.

International Organization 55, 4, Autumn 2001, pp. 761–799

for example, most bilateral treaties—have no formal organizational structure; these are plentiful because states have a striking tendency to codify their relationships in formal, legal arrangements.[1]

Why do these differences exist? Do they really matter, both for members and for international politics more generally? Do they affect what the institutions themselves can do? We focus on these large questions of institutional design. Our basic presumption, grounded in the broad tradition of rational-choice analysis, is that states use international institutions to further their own goals, and they design institutions accordingly. This might seem obvious, but it is surprisingly controversial.

One critique comes from constructivists, who argue that international institutions play a vital, independent role in spreading global norms. We agree that normative discourse is an important aspect of institutional life (though surely not the whole of it) and that norms are contested within, and sometimes propagated by, international institutions. But it is misleading to think of international institutions solely as outside forces or exogenous actors. They are the self-conscious creation of states (and, to a lesser extent, of interest groups and corporations).

The realist critique is exactly the opposite. For them, international institutions are little more than ciphers for state power. This exaggerates an important point. States rarely allow international institutions to become significant autonomous actors. Nonetheless, institutions are considerably more than empty vessels. States spend significant amounts of time and effort constructing institutions precisely because they can advance or impede state goals in the international economy, the environment, and national security. States fight over institutional design because it affects outcomes. Moreover, the institutions they create cannot be changed swiftly or easily to conform to changing configurations of international power. Japan and Germany play modest roles in the UN today because they have been unable to reverse the decision made in 1944–45 to exclude them from the Security Council. Institutions rarely adapt immediately to states' growing (or ebbing) power. For this reason, and because institutions matter, states pay careful attention to institutional design.

Our main goal is to offer a systematic account of the wide range of design features that characterize international institutions. We explore—theoretically and empirically—the implications of our basic presumption that states construct and shape institutions to advance their goals. The most direct implication is that design differences are not random. They are the result of rational, purposive interactions among states and other international actors to solve specific problems.

We define international institutions as explicit arrangements, negotiated among international actors, that prescribe, proscribe, and/or authorize behavior.[2] Explicit arrangements are public, at least among the parties themselves. According to our definition, they are also the fruits of agreement. We exclude tacit bargains and implicit guidelines, however important they are as general forms of cooperation.

---

1. See Abbott et al. 2000; and Koremenos 2000.
2. For related definitions of international institutions, see Keohane 1984; and Young 1994.

Institutions may require or prohibit certain behavior or simply permit it. The arrangements themselves may be entirely new, or they may build on less formal arrangements that have evolved over time and are then codified and changed by negotiation. The 1961 Vienna Law on Treaties is a good example.

Although in most arrangements negotiators are typically states, this is not part of our definition; it is an empirical observation that may vary across issues and over time. In fact, nonstate actors participate with increasing frequency in institutional design. Multinational firms, nongovernmental organizations (NGOs), and intergovernmental organizations have all shaped international institutions, solely especially those dealing with the world economy, the environment, and human rights.

Thus our definition of international institutions is relatively broad. It includes formal organizations like the World Health Organization and International Labor Organization, as well as well-defined (and explicit) arrangements like "diplomatic immunity" that have no formal bureaucracy or enforcement mechanisms but are fundamental to the conduct of international affairs.

With this definition in mind, we can begin to explore how institutions vary and, later, how that variation may be the product of rational design considerations. Our work emphasizes five key dimensions within which institutions may vary:

Membership rules (MEMBERSHIP)
Scope of issues covered (SCOPE)
Centralization of tasks (CENTRALIZATION)
Rules for controlling the institution (CONTROL)
Flexibility of arrangements (FLEXIBILITY)

These are certainly not the only significant institutional dimensions, but they have several advantages for our research. First, they are all substantively important. Negotiators typically focus on them, and so do analysts who study institutions. Second, they can be measured, allowing us to compare them within and across institutions over time. Third, they apply to the full array of international institutions, from the most formal to the least bureaucratic.

We locate our analysis in the rational regime tradition. We do not present a literature review but rather build on earlier work to develop the underlying parameters of this research project. We also do not counterpose "dueling perspectives" (realism versus institutionalism or rationalism versus constructivism, for example). Instead, we investigate the rational design approach on its own terms by developing a set of theoretically based conjectures, which are then evaluated empirically in the studies in this special issue of International Organization. Our view is that rational design can explain much about institutions, but not everything.[3]

---

3. Martin and Simmons assess past work on international institutions and propose an agenda focused on explaining causal mechanisms and institutional effects. Martin and Simmons 1998. Their framework complements ours and shows how rational choice can address other important empirical questions.

From Cooperation Theory to Rational Design

The postwar study of international institutions is coming full circle, but with a theoretical twist. The early literature focused on the operational details of international organizations. With the notable exception of neofunctionalist integration theory, it was heavily descriptive,[4] neither theorizing institutions nor clarifying their relationships to wider issues of international relations. By the 1980s the literature had turned sharply toward theory under the broad rubric of "regimes."[5] Within regime theory, one important strand built on rational, game-theoretic analysis, especially the idea that the "shadow of the future" can support "cooperation under anarchy."[6]

The study of regimes favored theoretical questions and moved the research agenda away from analyzing specific institutional arrangements.[7] Likewise, the tools of game theory were directed mainly at general theoretical questions, focusing on cooperation, not institutions, as the dependent variable. The overriding question became "How could states and other international actors produce cooperative outcomes by their own, self-interested choices?" Indirectly, however, this work laid the foundation for a renewed exploration of institutions, this time as part of a wider theory of international cooperation. In focusing on how self-interested states could cooperate, it was logical to ask what role institutions could play. Institutions could be reconceptualized and theorized as arrangements that make cooperation more feasible and durable, at least in some circumstances.

Our goal is to close the circle that began with descriptive studies by explaining major institutional features in a theoretically informed way. We first relax some key assumptions of cooperation theory and then bring in institutions directly by incorporating insights from game theory and institutional analysis. In doing so, we pay particular attention to the logic of their development.

Extending Cooperation Theory

The cooperation literature is premised on the "Folk theorem," which shows that cooperation is possible in repeated games.[8] This result has a strong theoretical foundation and can be applied empirically to a wide range of contemporary issues. The density of contemporary international interdependence creates repeated inter-

---

4. The early issues of International Organization, for example, focused on describing newly formed organizations and publicizing their rules and votes.

5. Krasner 1983.

6. See Oye 1986; and Axelrod 1984.

7. Key works are Stephen Krasner's edited volume International Regimes (1983) and Robert Keohane's After Hegemony (1984). An excellent early overview is Haggard and Simmons 1987. Several commentators have noted that the field has had less and less to say about formal international organizations. See Rochester 1986; and Abbott and Snidal 1998.

8. See Friedman 1971; and Fudenberg and Maskin 1986.

action that makes cooperation feasible.[9] In brief, the possibility of cooperation is present in most modern international issues.

If cooperation is within reach, why it is not always grasped? To answer that, we must go beyond any simple, optimistic interpretation of the Folk theorem. Although we assume that the general conditions of international interdependence are propitious, individual issues have features that make achieving and maintaining cooperation more problematic. Moreover, the standard Folk theorem conclusion needs careful refinement when applied to more realistic situations, where competing equilibria are in play, many actors are involved, and uncertainty is high.

Multiple equilibria are a major obstacle to cooperation that was downplayed by the early emphasis on 2 × 2 games. Although these simple games, especially Prisoners' Dilemma, did much to clarify our understanding of enforcement problems, their very simplicity could be misleading. In a simple 2 × 2 Prisoners' Dilemma, there is only one point of mutual cooperation, the unattainable Pareto optimum where both sides choose to cooperate rather than defect. In practice, states have a wide range of choices and many possible cooperative outcomes, often with different distributional consequences.

If actors prefer different outcomes, the range of possibilities creates bargaining problems. Which cooperative outcome should they choose? How, in other words, should they share any mutual gains from cooperation? These distributional questions do not arise in simple 2 × 2 Prisoners' Dilemma games, though they were discussed in some early work contrasting Prisoners' Dilemma and Coordination games.[10] Recent work by Stephen Krasner, James Morrow, and James Fearon goes further, showing how distributional differences can undermine cooperation in significant ways. Hence, distribution problems merit at least as much attention as enforcement problems, which we know hamper international cooperation.[11]

Large numbers also complicate cooperation. Kenneth Oye addresses the collective-action problem primarily by showing how interactions among large numbers can be decomposed into simple bilateral interactions.[12] Some issues, however, cannot be decomposed this way for technical reasons; others should not be decomposed because successful cooperation requires joint action by all (as in the provision of public goods). Large numbers raise questions about how to share both the costs and benefits of cooperation, especially when some actors are richer, bigger, or more powerful than others.

Uncertainty is a frequent obstacle to cooperation, as is "noise," the difficulty of observing others' actions clearly.[13] States are naturally reluctant to disclose vital

---

9. Notable exceptions are crises where immediate incentives overwhelm longer-term considerations. We set such situations aside.
10. See Snidal 1985; and Stein 1983.
11. See Krasner 1991; Morrow 1994c; and Fearon 1998.
12. See Oye 1986; and Lipson 1986 for an application.
13. This point was foreshadowed by Downs, Rocke, and Siverson in their analysis of arms races, and by Downs and Rocke in their game-theoretic analysis of the limits to cooperation. See Downs, Rocke, and Siverson 1986; and Downs and Rocke 1990.

information that could make them more vulnerable. Reducing uncertainty among participants is a major function of institutions.[14]

Taken together, these factors—distribution, enforcement, large numbers, and uncertainty—suggest that cooperation can be very brittle in the real world. As these factors vary, the prospects for cooperation can shift dramatically, making it far more difficult to manage international cooperation than earlier, simplified theories would predict.

Bringing in Institutions

In broad international relations (IR) theories institutions play only a modest role. It is, after all, cooperation under anarchy. The primary reason for emphasizing anarchy is to rule out centralized enforcement, but there is little consideration of the other roles institutions might play. In fact, institutions often help resolve problems of decentralized cooperation.

IR theorists have begun to address problems of cooperation in more complex and realistic settings, where there may be noise and large numbers.[15] It is generally recognized that institutions may make cooperation more likely,[16] and the compliance literature has begun to analyze empirically how regime design promotes effective cooperation.[17] So far, however, this has not developed into a more general theoretical analysis of specific institutional arrangements.

Our work departs significantly from the earlier cooperation literature. Because decentralized cooperation (supported by the Folk theorem) is difficult to achieve and often brittle, states devise institutions to promote cooperation and make it more resilient. But the form these institutions take varies widely. Often the necessary institutions are fairly minimal and simply reinforce the underlying conditions for cooperation, perhaps providing the information necessary for bilateral bargains. Other times, more complex problems may require a larger institutional role—such as when an issue involves actors with very different resources and information. Under these circumstances, institutions can play a major role in facilitating cooperation.

We argue that many institutional arrangements are best understood through "rational design" among multiple participants. This rationality is forward looking as states use diplomacy and conferences to select institutional features to further their individual and collective goals, both by creating new institutions and modifying existing ones. Even trial-and-error experiments can be rational and forward looking in this way. Although we do not argue that all institutional change is the product of conscious design, we do consider it the overriding mechanism guiding the devel-

14. See Keohane 1984; and Morrow 1994c.
15. On noise, see Downs and Rocke 1990. On large numbers, see Pahre 1994.
16. See Keohane 1984; and Axelrod and Keohane 1986.
17. See Chayes and Chayes 1995; and Mitchell 1994.

opment of international institutions.[18] Moreover, though our primary purpose is to explain institutional design, our approach also provides an appropriate foundation for prescribing policy and evaluating existing institutions.[19]

Our argument that institutional design is deliberate is reflected in the difficult process of creating an international institution. The evolution of the General Agreement on Tariffs and Trade (GATT) into the World Trade Organization (WTO) involved extensive rounds of negotiation. The Law of the Sea Treaty was the culmination of protracted debate, including the sharply contested decision not to have stronger centralized institutions. The same process is seen in the development of the UN charter, which involved extensive planning and bargaining and was designed to achieve critical goals amidst great uncertainty. Moreover, its design has been modified over the years as new members have been admitted, the Security Council has changed, and specialized agencies have been created. Continuing calls for change remind us that most institutions evolve as members learn, new problems arise, and international structures shift. But institutional evolution still involves deliberate choices made in response to changing conditions.

Institutional development frequently depends on prior outcomes ("path dependence") and evolutionary forces. As institutions evolve, rational design choices can arise in two ways. First, participants may modify institutions in stages, by making purposeful decisions as new circumstances arise, by imitating features from other institutions that work well in similar settings, or by designing explicit institutions to strengthen tacit cooperation. Second, institutions may evolve as states (and other international actors) select among them over time. States favor some institutions because they are better suited to new conditions or new problems and abandon or downplay those that are not. For example, the obvious place to handle intellectual property rights would seem to be the World Intellectual Property Organization, but the countries that generate most patents chose to move the issue to the WTO because it offered better enforcement mechanisms. Thus the institutionalization of the issue evolved significantly, not because an older institution was modified, but because another one offered a better institutional design.[20]

Even institutions that are not highly formalized and arise through informal and evolutionary processes may embody significant rational design principles. Sovereignty is clearly the result of historical and normative processes, but at important

---

18. Our proposed conjectures are consistent with an evolutionary perspective that treats rational designs as superior in the sense of providing greater benefits to participants, even if participants are unwitting beneficiaries. Miles Kahler provides an excellent overview and discussion of the relationship between evolutionary and rational theories of international institutions. Kahler 1999. The two approaches begin to align through such concepts as "learning" and "imitation" as key factors underlying institutional development.

19. Of course, many efforts at institutional design fail. States may misunderstand the circumstances they face or wrongly anticipate how actors will respond to institutional innovations, or simply make mistakes.

20. See Schrader 1996.

junctures (Treaty of Westphalia, Congress of Vienna, Vienna Convention) it has been the object of rational design through codification and modification.

Thus, our basic strategy is to treat institutions as rational, negotiated responses to the problems international actors face. We can connect our definition of institutions to the language of game theory, where institutions are aspects of equilibria, including the rules of the game and the expectations of the actors.[21] This equilibrium approach has several important implications.[22]

First, institutional rules must be "incentive compatible" so that actors create, change, and adhere to institutions because doing so is in their interests. Consider an institution that can be sustained only through sanctions and whose members must apply these sanctions themselves. This is an equilibrium institution only if the members who are supposed to apply sanctions actually have incentives to do so. Incentive compatibility does not mean that members always adhere to rules or that every state always benefits from the institutions to which it belongs. It does mean that over the long haul states gain by participating in specific institutions—or else they will abandon them.

Second, specifying independent and dependent variables requires special care. An equilibrium is a statement of consistency among its elements. Decomposing an equilibrium into causal statements connecting independent and dependent variables requires looking beyond the equilibrium itself to the sequence of, and reasons for, institutional changes.

Third, the very institutions we seek to explain as "outcomes" may also play a causal role in shaping others, now or in the future. Consider the EU. Is it a "dependent" or an "independent" variable? The answer depends on the question we ask and the time frame we use. If we want to explain why the EU was formed and the features it has, it is a dependent variable (by our own choice). If we want to explain the shape of some subsequent institution, such as the WTO or the European Monetary System, the EU plays a significant causal role as an independent variable in the institution's development. This is particularly important when we look at which actors are relevant to a particular design issue. An outcome (or dependent variable) at one stage—the membership of the EU—may become a causal factor (or independent variable) at another—the number of actors relevant in the design of the European Monetary System.

Dependent Variables

Consider an emerging international issue, such as global warming, the distribution of pirated software, or the sale of cloned human organs. If states want to promote a common interest, what kinds of institutions might they design to aid their efforts?

---

21. The converse is not true, and not all equilibria are institutions as we define them. In particular we exclude equilibria resulting from tacit bargains and implicit arrangements that arise without negotiation.

22. See Calvert 1995; Morrow 1994c; and Snidal 1997.

They might first ask whether they need an international institution at all. Perhaps their national capacities are more than adequate, or they are converging on tacit arrangements that require little elaboration. If they could benefit from explicit cooperation, they would ask whether current institutions could be extended to cover the issue, in whole or in part.

If the issue were novel (such as trade in cloned organs) and no existing organizations were well suited, then diplomats, executives, scientists, policy activists, and other interested parties might well consider creating a new organization. They would immediately confront several major questions. Should the new institution cover only cloned organs or should it also cover health- or trade-related issues? Should membership be limited to countries with advanced medical industries? What about other, less-developed countries? One practical reason for being inclusive is that excluded states might evade or undermine the rules. What about including scientific institutes, biotechnology companies, health advocates, medical ethicists, and other nonstate actors?

What institutional capacities are needed for success? Would a simple agreement suffice? Should the institution be centralized to collect data, monitor compliance, or even enforce some rules? Or should it be more decentralized, serving mainly as a forum for periodic bargaining? Should all actors be given equal voice and vote, or should some have only an informal, consultative role? What about the rules themselves in such a new and rapidly developing area? Should they be clear-cut and firm, or should they be more flexible, allowing easy changes by mutual agreement or opting out by dissatisfied states?

Regardless of the issue, these kinds of institutional choices zero in on our major concerns: how and why are international institutions designed as they are? To make headway on these overarching questions, we need some clear way to mark out major variations in institutional design. The simplest solution would be to use a single measure, one that describes institutions as, say, "stronger" or "weaker." Unfortunately, such measures are misleading because they collapse several important institutional features into one overly simple statement. We could measure many institutional features in great detail, yielding rich descriptions of individual institutions, but this would obscure the most important types of variation among them. We have chosen instead to focus on a few recurrent problems of institutional design, particularly those we can identify theoretically as vital aspects of cooperation and that vary in measurable ways. Our approach highlights five key dimensions: MEMBERSHIP, SCOPE, CENTRALIZATION, CONTROL, and FLEXIBILITY. These are not the only important dimensions of institutions. Others may well prove significant, theoretically and substantively. In some cases, our dimensions must be refined to clarify design issues in specific institutions. Centralization, for instance, is a broad category—perhaps too broad for some cases. Nonetheless, our first effort is to reduce the myriad elements of institutional variation to a few measurable dimensions that show up repeatedly when institutions are designed or modified. We now take a closer look at each dimension and consider how they vary in modern international institutions.

Membership

Who belongs to the institution? Is membership exclusive and restrictive, like the G-7's limitation to rich countries? Or is it inclusive by design, like the UN? Is it regional, like ASEAN, or is it universal? Is it restricted to states, or can NGOs join?

Membership has been one of the most hotly contested issues in recent years. The expansion of NATO into Eastern Europe is a key example. Expansion, for those who favor it, represents a reinvigoration of the alliance, a commitment to the joint defense of Central Europe, and a symbolic inclusion of new members in the "West." For those who oppose it, NATO's movement to the East adds nothing to the defense of Western Europe and needlessly provokes an already humiliated Russia. These issues resonate widely because NATO is such a prominent and consequential institution.

Scope

What issues are covered? In global trade institutions, for example, some of the toughest battles have been over which sectors to include in negotiations. GATT left out several key economic sectors, but the WTO has expanded to incorporate most trade issues, including agriculture and services. It may be expanded further to include cross-border investments. At the other end of the spectrum are institutions like the 1965 U.S.–Canada auto trade deal designed to cover only one or two narrowly defined issues. This agreement, too, was eventually widened when it was incorporated into NAFTA.

Sometimes two seemingly unrelated issues are linked. A trade issue, for example, may be linked to a security issue to facilitate agreement and compliance. Or a side payment may be offered, as when the Nuclear Nonproliferation Treaty offered the transfer of peaceful nuclear technology to states that agreed to forgo nuclear weapons. Such side payments are clear evidence that scope is being manipulated to facilitate cooperation.

There is a continuum of issue coverage. At one end are institutions like the Antarctic Treaty System that cover a range of scientific, economic, and political issues. At the other end are some early environmental agreements that are restricted to a few well-defined issues, such as greenhouse gas emissions.

Sometimes scope is not open to design choice because of technical considerations or shared perceptions. In the Law of the Sea negotiations, for example, jurisdiction over ocean territories could not be separated from coastal environment and fishing rights issues. Technological interactions required that these issues be dealt with together in a comprehensive settlement.[23] But other Law of the Sea issues seemed

---

23. A parallel and important implication within rational institutional design is that all relevant "margins" of choice must be considered. Barzel 1989. In John Richards' analysis of international airline regulation in this volume, for example, effective agreements on airline fares also require that airlines be prohibited from competing on other margins, such as food quality or seat comfort.

to have little in common. Here linkage was more cognitive—a result of how issues were framed, especially under the rubric of the "common heritage of mankind."[24]

One difficulty in analyzing scope is that the issues themselves are not clearly defined. Does trade in all commodities constitute an issue? Or should we distinguish agricultural goods from manufactures? Although there is no general answer to this difficult task of assessing issue scope, focused empirical research can reveal the extent to which actors narrow or broaden the range of matters being addressed. The problem is simplified when negotiations are expanded to cover items that could clearly be dealt with separately or were not previously linked (as occurred with the "baskets" of the Helsinki negotiations). Most important, changes in institutional issue linkage over time indicate changes in scope within an arrangement.

Centralization

Are some important institutional tasks performed by a single focal entity or not? Scholars often misleadingly equate centralization with centralized enforcement. We use the term more broadly to cover a wide range of centralized activities. In particular we focus on centralization to disseminate information, to reduce bargaining and transaction costs, and to enhance enforcement. These categories are not exhaustive, but they cover many important centralized activities found at the international level.

Centralization is controversial, politically and conceptually, because it touches so directly on national sovereignty. According to the traditional view, states reject any form of centralized international authority. International relations is seen as an immutable anarchy. This is a powerful assertion, but it is only partly right. It blends a simplifying assumption (that theory building should begin with states as independent units) with some hyperbole and errant conclusions.

States understandably guard their domestic authority and their control over foreign policy. They are suspicious of encroachments by other states and strongly resist any shift of sovereign responsibilities to superordinate bodies. But saying that states rarely devolve such authority is inaccurate, and it is a misleading basis for constructing theory. After all, European states not only signed the Treaty of Rome but also agreed to the Single European Act, which permits majority voting.[25] They went still further at Maastricht, when they abolished national controls over money.[26] The EU is uniquely powerful as an international institution, but centralized controls are important elsewhere. The dispute-resolution panels of the WTO are a particularly significant example.

The least intrusive form of centralization is information collection, and many international institutions engage in it. Members of the IMF, for instance, need not

24. Haas 1980.
25. Moravcsik 1991.
26. See Kenen 1995; and Moravcsik 1998.

gather their own data on others' balance of payments. Instead the IMF regularly collects, evaluates, and publishes itemized statistics on its members' payments.

Bargaining procedures and rule enforcement can also be more or less centralized. At the World Bank, for instance, specialists negotiate loans for economic adjustment or major infrastructure investments. These packages require collective approval from a centralized body of members. Most international organizations have relatively decentralized enforcement arrangements. They specify possible punishments for rule violations but leave it up to the members to apply them. Because these multilateral sanctions are both limited and well specified, they minimize the chances for disproportionate punishment or cycles of retaliation. Still, the members themselves must apply the decentralized punishments and bear the inevitable costs.

GATT (and now the WTO) have relied on such decentralized sanctions for decades. If a dispute panel found violations of international trade rules, it was up to the injured party to retaliate within specified limits. GATT itself had no centralized power to punish or reward, only to authorize individual members to do so. This also shows how international organizations can combine elements of centralization and decentralization. The WTO's centralized arrangements for judging trade disputes go hand-in-hand with decentralized arrangements for enforcing the judgments.

Control

How will collective decisions be made? Control is determined by a range of factors, including the rules for electing key officials and the way an institution is financed. We focus on voting arrangements as one important and observable aspect of control.

Even if membership is universal, some states may carry considerably more weight than others because of voting and decision-making rules. Two interrelated rules are especially important: whether all members have equal votes and whether a minority holds veto power. If a minority can veto, its votes inherently carry special weight. In the UN General Assembly all members have equal votes. In the Security Council they do not, since only the permanent members can veto resolutions. The IMF and World Bank have explicit weighted-voting rules; the larger economies, which provide capital to these institutions, carry disproportionate votes. Another element of control is whether a simple majority, a super-majority, or unanimity is required. If a super-majority is needed, some state (or combination of states) may be able to block new rules, members, or officers.

Finally, we distinguish control from centralization. While centralization may reduce control in some cases, the two dependent variables generally vary independently. For example, changes in the voting rules within a quasi-legislative component of an international institution represent changes in control that do not affect the level of centralization. Similarly, centralizing information collection usually has little, if any, effect on who controls an institution.

Flexibility

How will institutional rules and procedures accommodate new circumstances? Institutions may confront unanticipated circumstances or shocks, or face new demands from domestic coalitions or clusters of states wanting to change important rules or procedures. What kind of flexibility does an institution allow to meet such challenges?

It is important to distinguish between two kinds of institutional flexibility: adaptive and transformative. "Escape clauses" are a good example of adaptive flexibility. They allow members to respond to unanticipated shocks or special domestic circumstances while preserving existing institutional arrangements. The general goal is to isolate a special problem—such as a spike in steel imports from a few producing countries—and insulate the broader institution (in this case, the GATT/WTO) from its impact. This limited flexibility is designed to deal chiefly with outlying cases, to wall them off from run-of-the-mill issues.

Some institutions have built-in arrangements to transform themselves in ways that are more profound. This deeper kind of flexibility usually involves clauses that permit renegotiation or sunset provisions that require new negotiations and ratification for the institution to survive. The initial terms of commodity agreements, for example, are typically five to seven years, after which they expire and have to be renegotiated. GATT did not have such a provision, but its periodic rounds of trade negotiations facilitated planning for larger institutional changes, leading to the WTO. GATT's existing rules did nothing to block these larger changes, and its regular forums served to promote them.

Independent Variables

To explain variation in institutional design, we focus on the following independent variables: distribution problems (DISTRIBUTION); enforcement problems (ENFORCEMENT); number of actors and the asymmetries among them (NUMBER); and uncertainty about behavior, the state of the world, and others' preferences (UNCERTAINTY ABOUT BEHAVIOR, UNCERTAINTY ABOUT THE STATE OF THE WORLD, and UNCERTAINTY ABOUT PREFERENCES).

Enforcement of agreements is a cornerstone concern in international anarchy. But recent debates have increasingly stressed that to understand which, if any, international institutional bargains are struck, one must examine distributional issues. The number and relative size of key actors has been a long-standing concern in debates about international cooperation, hegemony, and, more recently, the interrelationship of regional and global politics. Finally, uncertainty is the linchpin of traditional security problems and is equally central in economic and environmental issues.

These variables also play a crucial role in game theory. Enforcement and distribution problems emerge in any strategic situation. Number is the central variable of collective-action theory, and we broaden it here to include explicitly the asymmetries that are so important in international affairs. Finally, many important theoretical developments in game theory over the past two decades center on uncertainty.

Since we extend the existing tradition of cooperation theory, it is useful to compare our independent variables with Oye's.[27] After all, institutions to promote cooperation must be designed around the factors that affect cooperation. But we adapt the independent variables to address the particular questions raised by institutional design. Oye focuses on three independent variables. The most important is "shadow of the future." We do not focus on this as a primary source of institutional variation because the general conditions for cooperation are typically met under contemporary conditions of high interdependence.[28] Instead, we emphasize how variation in the significance of enforcement problems across different issues affects institutional design.

Oye's second independent variable is the type of 2 × 2 game being played, though with an emphasis on Prisoners' Dilemma. Simple games have yielded important insights and have been subjected to important criticisms.[29] The most important substantive criticism is that concentration on Prisoners' Dilemma leads to an overemphasis on enforcement and cheating and to an underemphasis on distributional conflicts.[30] This problem can be partially solved by shifting attention to another 2 × 2 game (Coordination, for example), but each new game misses some other salient problem (such as enforcement). We resolve this by looking at distribution problems as a second independent variable.[31]

We use a broader version of Oye's third variable, "number." Looking beyond the raw number of actors relevant to an issue, we include asymmetries that might exist among them due to different capabilities. This consideration was important in the hegemony literature and becomes even more so in understanding how different-sized actors share control in institutionalized cooperation.

Finally, and most important, driven by advances in the economics of uncertainty and game theory we add "uncertainty" as a new category of independent variable. Uncertainty can impede cooperation, but its impact can be managed through institutions. Indeed, one feature common to our independent variables is that

27. Oye 1986.
28. Alternatively, states will not waste time designing institutions that will not be enforced by their own incentives.
29. In particular, once the games are complicated even slightly, the clean distinctions among them break down. When Prisoners' Dilemma repeats through time, for example, multiple equilibria emerge, and the supergame contains distributional problems. Similarly, recurring Battle of the Sexes problems create incentives for some states to shift the prevailing equilibrium.
30. See Krasner 1991; and Grieco 1988.
31. James Fearon makes a parallel argument that, at a sufficiently general level, all problems in international relations have a common strategic structure. Fearon 1998. States must choose among the range of available cooperative arrangements and ensure that participants will adhere to the chosen arrangement. We label these the "distribution problem" and the "enforcement problem," respectively.

game-theoretic logic allows us to connect them to the dependent variables of institutional design.[32]

Distribution Problems

When more than one cooperative agreement is possible, actors may face a distribution problem. Its magnitude depends on how each actor compares its preferred alternative to other actors' preferred alternatives. In a pure Coordination game, where both actors prefer the same coordination point(s), there is no distribution problem. Distribution problems are greater when actors want to coordinate in a "Battle of the Sexes" game according to the intensity with which they prefer alternative coordination points. In Prisoners' Dilemma games where there are multiple efficient equilibria, the distribution problem depends on actors' differences "along the Pareto frontier."[33] Finally, the problem is most severe in a zero-sum game because a better outcome for one leaves less for the others.

Distribution problems are closely related to bargaining costs.[34] In general, where the distributional implications of a choice are small (such as when only one efficient outcome is possible or the shadow of the future is short), bargaining costs will be relatively small. In situations where the distributional implications are large (such as when there are multiple, substantially different efficient outcomes or the shadow of the future is long), bargaining costs will likely be large.

Distribution problems interact with the other independent variables, but they should be kept separate. Most important, distribution problems are not the same as uncertainty. Uncertainty arises when an actor cannot anticipate the outcome that will result from an agreement and knows only the stochastic "distribution" generating the outcome. In their collaborative venture to develop an anti-missile system, for example, Japan and the United States are uncertain whether the research will be successful even though they are sure they will both share fully in the findings. In contrast, a distribution problem refers to selecting one outcome from a range of known possible outcomes. In allocating quotas for harvesting West Coast salmon, for example, Canada and the United States know the total number of fish that will be caught; the problem is determining each country's allotment. Of course, these problems intertwine in many situations where actors choose among agreements characterized by different stochastic distributions. This is true of fishing agreements over time where both the allotments between states and the size of the fish harvest over time are at stake.

---

32. We asked contributors to examine these independent variables but also invited them to consider others; thus the project as a whole is open to a wider set of independent variables, albeit in a more inductive way.
33. Krasner 1991.
34. Fearon 1998.

Enforcement Problems

Enforcement problems refers to the strength of individual actors' incentives to cheat on a given agreement or set of rules. Even if an arrangement makes everyone better off, some or all actors may prefer not to adhere to it because they can do better individually by cheating—the heart of Prisoners' Dilemma and public goods problems.

The enforcement problem arises when actors find (current) unilateral noncooperation so enticing that they sacrifice long-term cooperation. It can be measured by the minimum discount factor (a state's valuation of future, as opposed to current, benefits) necessary to support cooperation. Seen this way, the necessary discount factor is a characteristic of the issue—including actors' payoffs from cooperation and defection and how frequently they interact—but not of how much actors actually value the future. Issues where actors have large incentives to break an agreement require higher discount factors to support cooperation than do issues where the immediate gains from noncooperation are smaller.

Although we focus on settings of high interdependence where cooperation is generally possible, there is significant variation across issues. At one extreme are cases with no enforcement problems, such as agreements to set technical standards where actors have no incentive to defect. Within the context of repeated Prisoners' Dilemma games, self-enforcing agreements may arise if incentives to defect are small relative to the shadow of the future. But if incentives to defect are greater, or interactions are less frequent, enforcement problems emerge.

Most situations contain both distribution and enforcement problems. In efforts to halt stratospheric ozone loss, for example, the ozone regime needed to set targets for reducing global chloro-fluorocarbon (CFC) emissions and establish rules for cutting back CFC production and use. Different rules obviously impose quite different costs on various states. Whatever rules are chosen still have to be enforced. Knowing this, states may choose particular rules partly because they are easy to monitor and enforce. In this way problems of distribution and enforcement are tightly connected.

Distribution and enforcement can be blended in differing proportions. Some problems are more squarely related to enforcement, with distributional considerations clearly secondary. If first strikes can paralyze one's opponent, enforcement of any arms control agreement overwhelms any distributional concerns about armament levels. Other issues present major distribution problems, with enforcement as a secondary issue. Macroeconomic coordination among the G-7 countries seems to have this property.[35] The same could be said of the last three GATT rounds. The critical issue was who would make what concessions, not whether the resulting agreements would be enforced.

Separating enforcement problems from distribution problems is an analytic choice, not a substantive claim. Unlike early work based on Prisoners' Dilemma or more recent work based on Coordination, it enables us to consider the more typical

35. Webb 1991.

case, where enforcement and distribution problems occur simultaneously. It does not capture more nuanced interactions between enforcement and distribution problems, but by first examining the institutional issues raised by these "main effects," we will be better situated to understand the others. Finally, it is necessary to keep enforcement problems distinct from the other independent variables. Uncertainty and large numbers usually aggravate enforcement problems, but enforcement problems can arise even in repeated-game situations with small numbers and no uncertainty.

Number of Actors

Number of actors refers to the actors that are potentially relevant to joint welfare because their actions affect others or others' actions affect them. Sulfur emissions from factories in the U.S. Midwest, for example, cause acid rain in Eastern Canada and New England, an issue involving two countries. Greenhouse gases emitted from the same factories contribute to global warming, an issue affecting more actors because of the large-scale consequences of global climate change. If firms are seen as the relevant actors, then the number of actors is significantly larger in both cases.

The number of actors involved in military issues depends on technology and on states' ability to harm or help one another militarily. Peace in the Middle East now depends on more states than it once did because technological innovations have increased the range of military aircraft and thus the number of states that can affect the military balance. Were Pakistan able to target Israel with nuclear weapons, it, too, would become a key actor.

Number does not depend solely on geographic or technological factors and is often determined by prior political and institutional arrangements. For example, a decision by the EU about monetary union is effectively a fifteen-state decision, regardless of its effects on outsiders, because EU members made a political decision to limit the number of states involved in the process, not because other states are unaffected. Similarly, when NAFTA takes up an issue, only its three members have a voice, whereas the same issue taken up within an expanded hemispheric trade arrangement would involve more states. In effect, the prior institutional membership decision has redefined the range of "potentially relevant" actors for the issue at hand.[36]

Thus it is important to distinguish between the independent variable, number, and the dependent variable, membership. Number is an exogenous feature of the issue context, including prior institutional developments, in which an institution may or may not be established. It includes the set of interested actors and their relative power in and importance to the issue. In contrast, membership is an endogenous design choice made in the course of establishing, changing, and/or operating the institution. It includes, for our purposes, the rules governing who is a member and

36. Snidal 1994.

(if relevant) different classes of membership. Over time, prior membership choices may affect number—that is, endogenous choices become exogenous constraints—because institutional settings, such as the EU or NAFTA, determine which actors will have standing in subsequent institutional negotiations.

Number also includes asymmetrical distribution of actors' capabilities. On some issues many states may be nominally involved, but only a few really drive the issue. Every state has an interest in the international economy, for example, but few have the economic power to determine its course. Similarly, many states produce some oil, copper, or bauxite, but only a few states dominate the global production of each.

The actors involved in an issue are not always the same as those who become members of the final institution. Although the entire EU membership discussed monetary union, only some met the requirements and chose to join. Similarly, while trade affects virtually all states, not all have played an active role in multilateral negotiations, and not all are members of the WTO.

Uncertainty

Uncertainty refers to the extent to which actors are not fully informed about others' behavior, the state of the world, and/or others' preferences. These distinctions correspond to three important elements of any strategic situation: choices, consequences, and preferences, respectively; and they may have different implications for institutional design. For example, uncertainty about behavior makes cooperation more difficult in many cases, but uncertainty about the state of the world may, under certain conditions, make cooperation easier. Therefore, our assertions are not about generic effects of uncertainty but about the different ways states design institutions to cope with specific types of uncertainty.

Uncertainty about behavior.   States may be unsure about the actions taken by others. If states agree not to pursue technologies associated with the development of biological or chemical weapons, for example, some states may have no way of knowing whether others are abiding by the agreement. Similarly, if countries agree to restrict sulfur emissions to reduce acid rain, how can they be sure others are complying with the agreement?[37]

Uncertainty about the state of the world.   Uncertainty about the state of the world refers to states' knowledge about the consequences of their own actions, the actions of other states, or the actions of international institutions. This could be scientific and technical knowledge or political and economic knowledge. Consider the dispute over the Spratly Islands, which lie off the southern coast of China and have been claimed by a number of states. Any agreement governing the dispute would have to take into account that no one knows how much oil is actually there or its future value.

37. Levy 1993.

Uncertainty about preferences.   Governments are often unsure what their counterparts really want. We assume states know their own preferences, but they are often uncertain about the preferences or motivations of others. A key problem underlying arms competition is determining whether another state is simply seeking its own security or is greedy and expansive. Does India's nuclear testing reflect a desire to aggrandize itself at Pakistan's expense or to defend itself against China? Of course, a major problem in determining others' preferences is that states may have incentives to misrepresent their preferences, either verbally or through their actions.

We do not use standard game-theoretic terminology, such as imperfect information or incomplete information, because it would obscure important distinctions.[38] For example, we could capture uncertainty both about the state of the world and about preferences (or type) through games of incomplete information. But collapsing these into one category prevents us from drawing nuanced inferences about institutional design. Foreshadowing the conjectures discussed later, membership rules may mitigate uncertainty about preferences but not about the state of the world. Similarly, flexibility provisions can help states cope with uncertainty about the state of the world but have no effect on reducing uncertainty about behavior.

Although distinguishing among these kinds of uncertainty is useful conceptually, in practice they are often combined. For example, do European efforts to restrict imports of U.S. beef produced with hormone supplements reflect a concern for consumers' health or for local farmers' profits (uncertainty about others' preferences)? Scientific uncertainty (uncertainty about the state of the world) was also present initially but was resolved when a WTO-appointed panel ruled that hormones posed no health threat. An obvious solution would be to label imported beef as such and let individual Europeans make their own choices. Unfortunately, concerns about monitoring such a labeling system (uncertainty about behavior) would frustrate this solution.

Different mixes of uncertainty often characterize an issue. For example, the environmental area is plagued by enormous uncertainty (most of it scientific) about the state of the world and much less uncertainty about preferences. In contrast, there was little uncertainty about force structures during the latter years of the Cold War, but each superpower had significant uncertainty about the preferences of the other. We would expect the design of agreements in these areas to reflect their different circumstances.

Interactions Among Independent Variables

Our research design is quite simple. We have isolated a set of independent variables that we expect will determine the choice of particular institutional design features— our dependent variables. In our conjectures, we focus on "main effects"—that is, the bivariate relationships between the independent and dependent variables.

---

38. We do adopt standard terminology in using the term uncertainty instead of risk. See, for example, Kreps 1990; Hirshleifer and Riley 1992; and Osborne and Rubinstein 1994.

This approach has several advantages. It provides a general framework for a wide range of empirical studies and fosters comparisons across cases while allowing individual analysts to explore the implications of interactions in their particular cases. Moreover, the emphasis on bivariate relationships allows us to connect our conjectures closely to existing theoretical work—which would be possible for some but not all of the more complex interactions. Although simplicity has tremendous advantages, it ignores potential interactions among the independent variables. Enforcement problems may be combined with uncertainty about preferences or actions, as in an arms control context. Or distribution problems may be combined with large numbers, as in environmental public goods contexts. Because our independent variables may combine in many ways, we need to consider the significance of their interactions.[39] For example, when an enforcement problem occurs in a repeated Prisoners' Dilemma, cooperation is possible provided actors are sufficiently patient. But when uncertainty about actions enters the picture, the viability of cooperative strategies declines, since these strategies hinge on actors' knowledge of each other's behavior. Here the combination of two problems is substantially worse than either one alone. Similarly, uncertainty about the state of the world can interact with distributional problems, making cooperation even more challenging.[40]

The interaction of independent variables can also enhance cooperation. While both large numbers and distributional differences typically impede cooperation, sometimes large numbers mitigate distributional problems by easing relative gains concerns or by offering additional ways to balance costs and benefits across actors.

Conjectures About Rational Design

In this section we develop a series of conjectures that connect our independent and dependent variables. We call these "conjectures" to indicate that they represent generalizations based on a common rational-choice theoretical framework, although they are not formally derived here; however, in presenting the underlying logic of each conjecture we identify close variants that have been formally derived by scholars working in the rational-choice tradition. Although the conjectures follow from this general framework, individual conjectures depend on logics that may entail specific substantive assumptions. For example, public goods arguments assume that all actors share the same goals, whereas "screening" arguments suppose

---

39. Interaction effects may be positive, negative, or zero—that is, when two "problems" arise together in a given context, their joint effect may be less than either problem individually (a large negative effect) or more than either problem individually but less than the sum of the two (a small negative effect). Alternatively, the combined effect may equal the sum of the two individual effects (a zero interaction effect) or be greater than the sum of the individual effects (a positive interaction effect).

40. Koremenos 1999a.

that some actors do not.[41] Thus the conjectures need not be fully consistent with one another in this sense. Similarly, not all conjectures will apply to every case— something we leave to the individual case studies to determine. In the volume's conclusion we discuss the empirical and logical relationships among the conjectures. We now address four broad assumptions that underlie our conjectures.

1. Rational design: States and other international actors, acting for self-interested reasons, design institutions purposefully to advance their joint interests.

We thus make standard assumptions: actors have (well-behaved) preferences over various goals; and the pursuit of those goals is guided by their beliefs about each others' preferences and the relative costs and benefits of different outcomes; and actors are constrained by their capabilities.[42] Although the process of institutional design is usually contentious, we do not focus on the bargaining among the participants but on the broad characteristics of the institutional outcomes they select. These outcomes do not simply reflect the preferences of the individual actors but rather represent their joint efforts—and "compromises" among their preferences—to improve their equilibrium outcome given the strategic circumstances they face. That is to say, they concern the equilibrium outcomes that result from the strategic interaction of states, each of which has preferences. Of course, for certain sets of preferences (such as when distributional issues are absent), the strategic aspects of states' interaction are trivial, and institutional design outcomes appear to reflect only preferences.

2. Shadow of the future: The value of future gains is strong enough to support a cooperative arrangement.

Actors have a sufficiently high density of interaction—and a sufficiently high discount factor—that cooperation is potentially sustainable. We take a long shadow of the future to be a general condition of contemporary international interdependence, but one subject to considerable variation across issues. On some issues, actors may not interact with sufficient frequency for future incentives to be strong enough to support cooperation by themselves.[43] On other issues, such as peacekeeping, unilateral incentives to defect or distributive differences may make cooperation difficult. A variety of other circumstances—especially uncertainty and large numbers—may make cooperation not only difficult to achieve but also difficult to enforce. Therefore, general international circumstances may be propitious for cooperation, but the particular circumstances in any issue may be problematic.

---

41. We thank Jim Morrow for this example, which corresponds to a comparison of conjectures M1 and M2.

42. We focus on states as key actors, though most of the analysis can be generalized to nonstate actors.

43. Of course, harsher punishment strategies can be used to support greater cooperation when the shadow of the future is short; however, such strategies are subject to problems of renegotiation proofness. See Downs and Rocke 1995; and Abreu, Pearce, and Stacchetti 1986.

3. Transaction costs: Establishing and participating in international institutions is costly.[44]

When creating institutions, states need, for example, to acquire information about the issue, about each other, and about the likely effects of alternative institutional forms. One way they do this is through negotiations. There are other types of transaction costs as well, such as safeguards to ensure compliance and sustain cooperation.[45] As David Lake explains, these safeguards may include sanctions, hostages, and dispute-resolution arrangements.[46]

An important aspect of our independent variables is that they may raise or lower transaction costs. For example, the larger the number of actors, the slower and more cumbersome the negotiations. Likewise, greater uncertainty may make it more costly to write complete contracts to deal with every contingency. Thus, number and uncertainty operate partly through their impact on transaction costs, which is why we separate out such costs in our assumptions. We focus on these variables rather than on transaction costs directly because they are more readily observable.

4. Risk aversion: States are risk-averse and worry about possible adverse effects when creating or modifying international institutions.

Risk-averse actors prefer a certain outcome to a chancy one when each has the same expected value. This assumption is the bedrock of modern realism, where states' fears of destruction and keen interest in preserving their sovereignty dominate their strategic calculations. However, even realist states may trade off some sovereignty if they reap large enough gains in return.[47] Institutionalists have a broader view of what states value, but they, too, typically assume states are risk-averse.

With these four assumptions in mind, we now turn to specific conjectures about international institutional design. Because our primary purpose is to generate testable propositions that will guide the empirical analysis of international institutions, we frame the conjectures in a general way.

Each conjecture addresses the expected effect of a change in a particular independent variable, such as the level of uncertainty or the severity of the distribution problem, on one of our dependent variables. Thus our logic is that of comparative statics—that is, we ask how a (perhaps hypothetical) change in an independent variable will affect the equilibrium institutional design. For example, if uncertainty about the state of the world increases, will states design more or less

---

44. For a general discussion of transaction costs, see Williamson 1985. For an important application to international politics, see Lake 1996. Unlike Williamson, we do not assume that the presence of transaction costs implies bounded rationality. Transaction costs refers to the costs of making an agreement and operating it, not of doing what the agreement is designed to do (for example, if two states agree to jointly build a dam, the costs of negotiating and administering the agreement are transactions costs, but the costs of building the dam are not).
45. See Williamson 1985; and Yarbrough and Yarbrough 1992.
46. Lake 1996.
47. Morrow 1991.

flexibility into an international institution? In answering this question, we assume that everything else remains constant. We emphasize the "main effects" of individual independent variables rather than more complicated interactions among them. These simplifying assumptions are necessary given the level of theoretical and empirical generality to which we aspire. After presenting the conjectures we will discuss the limitations of both comparative statics and main effects approaches in terms of design interactions.

Conjectures About Membership

Membership rules determine who benefits from an institution and who pays the costs. They work in several ways beyond simply reducing or enlarging size. By setting criteria for inclusion, for example, they affect the group's homogeneity and asymmetries. Not surprisingly, such rules have important consequences for interactions.

Conjecture M1: RESTRICTIVE MEMBERSHIP INCREASES WITH THE SEVERITY OF THE ENFORCEMENT PROBLEM.

The more severe the enforcement problem, the more restricted the membership. When actors face an enforcement problem (that is, when individuals do not have an incentive to voluntarily contribute to group goals), collective action is problematic. Moreover, the severity of the enforcement problem increases with the number of actors, as Mancur Olson demonstrated.[48] For this reason, Oye argues that reducing multilateral interactions to bilateral ones will increase the incidence of cooperation.[49]

The literature on "club goods" shows that a less drastic reduction in membership may be effective in promoting cooperation among somewhat larger groups.[50] If an institutional arrangement restricts the benefits of cooperation to members, actors have an incentive to pay the price of admission to the club. One of the most important features of institutions is to define these boundaries of membership.[51] Furthermore, when uncertainty about a state's capacity to comply is at issue, inclusive membership may be suboptimal because, as George Downs and David Rocke argue, "every time the third state violates the treaty, the other two states are forced to suspend the cooperation between them to punish it."[52]

---

48. Olson 1965.
49. Oye 1986. Pahre points out that under strict public good conditions, such restrictions are suboptimal. Pahre 1994. He demonstrates the possibility of large-n multilateral cooperation under certain conditions. But unlike conjecture M1, his equilibrium is vulnerable to bad information, and it needs other institutional supports that we discuss under conjectures C1–C3.
50. Buchanan 1965.
51. Snidal 1979.
52. Downs and Rocke 1995, 126.

The effectiveness of membership restrictions depends on the specific characteristics of the issue. In issues like CFC emissions, for example, preventing free riding is virtually impossible. Alliance guarantees, however, are usually effective in restricting nonmembers from receiving security benefits. Enforcement is not always a problem, of course. Agreements on international standards are a good example. Under preference configurations like these, where everyone benefits from wider participation, free riding and enforcement are not issues, and membership tends to be inclusive.

Conjecture M2: RESTRICTIVE MEMBERSHIP INCREASES WITH UNCERTAINTY ABOUT PREFERENCES.

Membership enables states to learn about each others' preferences if the membership mechanism can distinguish cooperators from noncooperators. Ideally, a state that values the goals of an organization will want to join, whereas one that wants a free ride will find it too costly to join a regime they intend to violate. In formal terms, membership is a costly signal. Effective membership rules create a separating equilibrium where only those who share certain characteristics will bear the costs necessary to be included in an equilibrium.[53]

The WTO, for example, requires prospective members to bring key domestic economic rules in line with WTO rules—perhaps with phase-in allowances or special considerations for certain categories of states. Similarly, NATO will not accept a new member until it meets certain domestic political requirements and brings its military up to certain agreed-upon levels. By requiring concessions, these organizations ensure that prospective members are willing to bear the necessary adjustment costs and are likely to be cooperating members down the road. When the price of membership is too low, membership is not informative.

When membership rules are a significant hurdle, they say something significant about nonmembers as well. Refusal to sign the Nuclear Nonproliferation Treaty is a strong and clear signal to other states. Again, it is interesting that states unwilling to commit to this regime generally choose not to sign the treaty rather than to sign but disobey.

Conjecture M3: INCLUSIVE MEMBERSHIP INCREASES WITH THE SEVERITY OF THE DISTRIBUTION PROBLEM.

Realists argue that states care not only about their direct outcomes from cooperative interactions but also how well they fare compared with others.[54] These distributional or relative gains concerns create zero-sum considerations that seri-

---

53. Spence 1974 illustrates how education provides a costly signal of the quality of prospective employees to employers. Spence 1974. Fearon applies signaling models to crisis bargaining. Fearon 1994. See also Kydd 2000a,b.
54. See Waltz 1979; and Grieco 1988.

ously impair cooperation in bilateral situations. One remedy is to rearrange the terms of cooperation so that benefits are more equally balanced, but this may be difficult or costly. An alternative captured in this conjecture is to expand the number of states involved in the issue because the zero-sum properties are rapidly attenuated as membership increases.[55]

Including additional members may also mediate distributional problems by expanding the possibilities for tradeoffs among the members. Thus an agreement might give state X the short end of the stick compared with state Y but compensate state X with the long end of the stick compared with state Z and so forth. This is one advantage of multilateral trade agreements. Such possibilities often occur because new members implicitly increase the range of issues included (for example, tradable products). We deal with these considerations in the next section on issue scope.

Conjectures About Scope

International issues do not come as pre-packaged units. Instead, they are constructed and evolve in complicated ways. While the resulting issue scope partly derives from technological, cognitive-ideational, and other factors that are not analyzed here, rational institutional analysis can explain key patterns of linkage within institutions. We focus on the deliberate choices states make about which issues to include in an institutional framework. In particular, when do states bring together issues they might otherwise have dealt with separately? Our first conjecture follows from efficiency considerations:

Conjecture S1: ISSUE SCOPE INCREASES WITH GREATER HETEROGENEITY AMONG LARGER NUMBERS OF ACTORS.

When states are similarly positioned on an issue, they share common interests over a collective international policy (if any is needed), although they may well have difficulties achieving that policy. Moreover, their relative symmetry on the issue may suggest a focal resolution, especially that all adopt a similar national policy. In these cases an issue often resolves on its own.

As the number of actors increases, however, the heterogeneity within the group will typically also increase. This is especially likely in international settings where the additional actors are often qualitatively different from earlier actors (for example, less-developed countries joining a group of developed countries).[56]

55. Snidal 1991.

56. We do not claim that heterogeneity promotes cooperation; in some cases it promotes distributional differences and conflict. Our position is that linkage provides an institutional means to harness these differences in a mutually beneficial way. Also, having a larger number may promote heterogeneity in capabilities (which we do not address here). For an insightful discussion of these points that also relates heterogeneity to institutional design, see Martin 1994.

When actors have heterogeneous interests, issue linkage may generate new opportunities for resolving conflicts and reaching mutually beneficial arrangements. James K. Sebenius demonstrates how adding issues "can yield joint gains that enhance or create a zone of possible agreement."[57] The paradigmatic example is "gains from trade," both in the limited sense of exchanging commodities and in the broader sense of connecting issues. When one actor values issue X more than issue Y, and the other ranks them the opposite way, both can be made better off by exchange, that is, by agreeing to defer to each other on these issues. Environmental issues that are important to postindustrial states, for example, are often linked to issues of development and technology when less-developed states with less intrinsic interest in environmental quality are essential to the arrangement.[58]

Conjecture S2: ISSUE SCOPE INCREASES WITH THE SEVERITY OF THE DISTRIBUTION PROBLEM.

Linkage not only allows states to increase efficiency but may also allow them to overcome distributional obstacles.[59] When the benefits of an issue accrue primarily to a few, and the costs fall disproportionately on others, linkage to another issue with different distributional consequences allows cost-bearing states to be compensated by those who reap the gains.[60] When each state cares relatively more about one of two issues, linking the negotiations may be the mutually preferred option.[61] In particular, the more each state cares about "its" issue, the more essential linkage becomes in an agreement. Howard Raiffa makes an even stronger assertion, arguing that increased scope can transform a zero-sum game with no zone of agreement into a positive-sum game.[62]

Conjecture S3: ISSUE SCOPE INCREASES WITH THE SEVERITY OF THE ENFORCEMENT PROBLEM.

57. Sebenius 1983, 314.

58. In some cases, membership may act as a mediating variable through which number affects endogenous variables such as scope. Even in such cases, number may also have direct effects, perhaps due to asymmetries among the parties, for which member is not a mediating variable. This complexity is typical in a system with multiple dependent (or endogenous) and independent (or exogenous) variables. Our conjectures focus on the impact of individual independent variables' main effects and thus hold the other independent variables constant, but not the other dependent variables.

59. Tollison and Willett 1979.

60. Conjectures S1 and S2, though distinct, share a similar logic. In each case differences among the actors lead them to expand the issue set in order to find a better outcome. In this way, distributional differences (which cause conflict within issues) are the engine of efficiency gains (across issues). For an instructive analogy in the social-choice literature on logrolling, see Mueller 1989. Logrolling, however, occurs within an institutional framework and thus can lead to Pareto-inefficient moves. Riker and Brams 1973. We would not expect this in the design of new institutional arrangements.

61. Busch and Koremenos 2001a.

62. Raiffa 1982.

When the incentives on an issue are insufficient for decentralized enforcement, linkage to other issues can provide enforcement.[63] The logic here is the same as in the shadow of the future conjecture, except that this works across issues rather than over time. The United States might be unable to resist domestic pressures to impose tariffs on European wine, for example, were it not for the realization that such action would invite retaliation from the Europeans on U.S. beef. Lutz-Alexander Busch and Barbara Koremenos show formally that the higher the discount rate required to support cooperation (that is, as the enforcement problem is more severe), the greater the probability of issue linkage.[64]

Since all three conjectures point to advantages of greater scope, the question naturally arises, Why isn't everything linked to everything else? The answer is that increased scope also has costs. These include the extra bargaining costs associated with additional issues and the greater probability that some actor will "hold up" the agreement to gain additional benefits.[65] The risk of unraveling, whereby failure in one issue may lead to failure in all linked issues, is also greater. What our conjectures predict is that, all else equal, as the independent variables increase, the marginal benefits of additional scope exceed the marginal costs. This leads rational states to increase scope until the marginal cost of adding another issue roughly equals the marginal benefit.

Conjectures About Centralization

International institutions can be centralized in a variety of ways. An international agency may have centralized information-gathering capacities, for example, without having centralized adjudicative or enforcement capacities. In the conjectures that follow we emphasize general tendencies of centralization rather than specific combinations.

Conjecture C1: CENTRALIZATION INCREASES WITH UNCERTAINTY ABOUT BEHAVIOR.

The Folk theorem holds that when states interact over extended periods they can achieve cooperative outcomes on a decentralized basis through strategies of reciprocity. But when states are uncertain about others' behavior, they cannot achieve the same mutually beneficial outcomes. Greater noise lowers the joint gains they can achieve.[66] Downs and Rocke show how tacit bargaining and trigger strategies can make the best of this situation.[67] However, centralized information may offer a more

---

63. See Hardin 1982; McGinnis 1986; and Bernheim and Whinston 1990. A more nuanced version of this conjecture would consider the interrelationships among the issues, for example, whether they are substitutes or complements. See Spagnolo 1997.

64. Busch and Koremenos 2001a.

65. Thus our independent variables may affect the costs as well as the benefits of scope.

66. Kreps 1990.

67. Downs and Rocke 1990.

effective alternative if it can reduce uncertainty about behavior to make (otherwise) decentralized cooperation more effective.[68]

The law merchant model illustrates the value of centralization in promoting cooperation when agents are uncertain about one another's past behavior.[69] The law merchant system includes a centralized actor who serves as a repository of information about the past performance of traders. This actor makes the information available to prospective partners, thereby creating a reputational bond that facilitates current transactions. This actor plays a further centralized role in adjudicating disputes and awarding damages as warranted.

Centralized information not only lets states know how others have behaved but also can provide valuable interpretations of that behavior. States will know better whether others' noncooperation is intentional and deserves retaliation or is excusable because of extenuating circumstances. When states retaliate, their targets and third parties will better understand the action as retaliation rather than unilateral noncooperation or error. Under the WTO, for example, retaliation must be centrally authorized, making misinterpretation highly unlikely.

Conjecture C2: CENTRALIZATION INCREASES WITH UNCERTAINTY ABOUT THE STATE OF THE WORLD.

When states are uncertain about the state of the world, all may benefit from joint efforts to gather and pool information. Scientific activity in Antarctica is coordinated, and international economic organizations have substantial research capacities so that states can share the costs of collecting necessary information. In other cases states benefit from collective information sharing but have individual reasons not to share fully or honestly. James Morrow builds on the "cheap talk" literature to show how regimes can structure communication among actors to promote more efficient information sharing in such circumstances.[70]

CONJECTURE C3: CENTRALIZATION INCREASES WITH NUMBER.

As numbers increase, centralized bargaining reduces transaction costs by replacing a large number of bilateral negotiations—or even a cumbersome multilateral negotiation—with an organizational structure that reduces the costs of decision making.[71] Centralization also allows states to coordinate their operational efforts to achieve economies of scale and to ensure that they do not duplicate or work against

68. Axelrod and Keohane 1986.
69. Milgrom, North, and Weingast 1990.
70. See Morrow 1994c; and Farrell and Gibbons 1989. The parallel relationship that centralization increases to resolve uncertainty about other states' preferences or types is also likely to hold. The very willingness to allow centralized inspection by an organization like the IAEA contains useful information about a state's goals even before it generates any information about its behavior.
71. See Keohane 1984; and Martin 1992a.

each other. NATO, for example, provides these advantages through a centralized command structure that allocates tasks.[72]

Centralization of information is also increasingly valuable with larger numbers. Randall Calvert shows how with increasing group size the shadow of the future may not be sufficient to support cooperation.[73] Multilateral communication allows states to achieve decentralized cooperation through an equilibrium where noncooperation is punished by all other states, not just the one that was directly harmed. Because communication is costly, however, this can be substantially improved by a centralized arrangement where a "director" serves as an information clearinghouse. Indeed, the director can even be viewed as "a third-party enforcer . . . [who] in effect pronounces a sentence on the deviant player, a sentence that will then be carried out by rational players."[74]

The International Coffee Organization plays exactly this role in aggregating reports by importing countries on coffee shipments by exporting states.[75] Moreover, because decentralized cooperation typically entails multiple equilibria, centralization is useful in coordinating behavior on an agreeable equilibrium. An important example is standard setting, where intergovernmental organizations (such as the International Telecommunications Union) and private organizations (such as the International Accounting Standards Committee) provide valuable centralized coordination.[76]

Finally, although we are focusing on main effects, there is an interaction between independent variables that supports conjectures C1 and C3. While decentralized cooperation is theoretically possible with large numbers,[77] it becomes much more tenuous when even small levels of uncertainty are introduced. Jonathon Bendor and Dilip Mookherjee show how centralization increases cooperation under such conditions. In their model a central headquarters is effective because it monitors behavior and excludes shirkers from subsequent benefits of the institutional arrangement.[78] Such a centralized arrangement can support higher levels of cooperation than can be supported in any decentralized arrangement.

Conjecture C4: CENTRALIZATION INCREASES WITH THE SEVERITY OF THE ENFORCEMENT PROBLEM.

In the previous conjectures, centralization alleviates cooperation problems created or aggravated by uncertainty and numbers. But enforcement problems also

72. Abbott and Snidal 1998.
73. Calvert 1995.
74. Ibid., 70.
75. See Bates 1997; and Koremenos 1999a.
76. See Genschel 1997; and Abbott and Snidal 2001.
77. Fudenberg and Maskin 1986.
78. Bendor and Mookherjee 1987 and 1997. Bendor and Mookherjee offer a differentiated view of centralization and show how a combination (federalism) of centralized and decentralized arrangements is most effective for the problem they are examining. Ostrom provides evidence of how small levels of centralization can promote otherwise decentralized cooperation. Ostrom 1990.

occur with good information and small numbers. When the payoff from unilateral defection is significantly greater than from mutual cooperation, concern for the future may not guarantee reciprocity-based, self-enforcing cooperation. In such contexts states may find it optimal to delegate power to a third party to adjudicate and enforce mutually beneficial agreements.[79]

Concern for sovereignty, of course, limits the extent to which states will delegate strong coercive capacities to international organizations. But the ability of organizations like the World Bank to withhold resources gives them significant leverage over weaker states. And the informational capacities of international organizations to expose states' behavior can influence the activities of even the most powerful states by imposing international reputational costs or, sometimes, domestic audience costs. Thus states typically obey the findings of WTO dispute-settlement proceedings even though the WTO has no enforcement capacity. Such mechanisms fall far short of coercive enforcement, but they can be valuable in "topping off" the strictly decentralized incentives that support cooperation.

Expanding on Bendor and Mookherjee, Edward Schwartz and Michael Tomz show how centralized arrangements have significant advantages if the central authority has the ability to expel shirkers from the group. High levels of monitoring will encourage contributions from all actors because shirkers are too likely to be detected and expelled and the value of remaining in the group will increase.[80]

Even centralized institutions that have no enforcement or even adjudicative capacities may be effective in resolving enforcement problems. Eric Posner shows that even if courts are "radically incompetent" in determining fault—that is, they can determine only whether a legal agreement existed but cannot verify whether actors obeyed it—formalized agreements can create reputational incentives that enable parties to solve commitment problems.[81] The reason is that the incentive for each party to cheat is reduced by the increased reputational costs of the breakdown of the agreement regardless of who is at fault. In a similar vein Lisa Martin shows that international organizations are instrumental in maintaining support for sanctions partly because states do not want to undermine the other benefits provided through these organizations.[82]

Finally, modest international centralization is sometimes effective because it harnesses domestic enforcement capacities. The 1998 OECD Anti-Bribery Convention relies on domestic legislation for implementation and on domestic court systems for enforcement, but a centralized inspection system ensures that states

---

79. Using similar logic, Lake argues that "the probability that the partner will engage in opportunistic behavior decreases with relational hierarchy." Lake 1996, 14. In other words, as the expected costs of opportunism increase, hierarchy will be the preferred governance structure.

80. Schwartz and Tomz show that the value of centralization does not always increase monotonically with the capacity of the central agent. Schwartz and Tomz 1997. In their model, an intermediate level of monitoring means that some shirking will occur so that less talented actors are detected and excluded from the group.

81. Posner 1999.

82. Martin 1992b.

police their own firms. This reinforces the point that centralization does not require international agents to have an independent coercive capacity to effectively promote cooperation.

Despite the advantages of centralization captured in the conjectures, states retain deep-seated concerns, intensified by their risk aversion, about how international institutions might behave. Will resources be squandered in bureaucratic excess? Even more important, will international agencies expand their authority over time? Consequently, states view centralization warily, and its overall baseline level may remain quite low. Our conjectures only express conditions under which states will increase (or decrease) centralization in response to their environment. For the same reasons, states also are concerned about maintaining tight control over the institutional arrangements, as indicated in the next set of conjectures.

Conjectures About Control

Two conjectures are relevant to the rules chosen to govern institutions:

Conjecture V1: INDIVIDUAL CONTROL DECREASES AS NUMBER INCREASES.

Conjecture V2: ASYMMETRY OF CONTROL INCREASES WITH ASYMMETRY AMONG CONTRIBUTORS (NUMBER).

The first conjecture seems obvious: as the number of actors increases, the control of any one actor or subgroup of actors decreases.[83] For example, as the EU has expanded, the leverage of individual members has steadily decreased.[84] This is because when the number of actors is large, states must sacrifice individual control to achieve collective benefits. Each state may be adversely affected on occasion, and without the veto a state has no unilateral protection—although its ability to withdraw from the institution ultimately limits its vulnerability. States agree to such a scheme because they benefit from others' inability to veto and strategically block group decisions. An important example is the EU's move toward "qualified majority" voting as membership has expanded.[85]

This conjecture follows directly from the social choice literature on voting rules. Brian Barry, for example, shows that for issues that are recurrent and symmetric in

83. Number here refers to members of the institution who are eligible to have a say in its operations. This is a good example of our earlier observation that a prior institutional decision may be treated as exogenous in considering the adoption of other rules. Alternatively, membership and control rules may be determined together such that, for example, a decision to have a large membership is compatible with one set of control rules, and a decision to have a small membership is compatible with another set of control rules.

84. Hosli 1993.

85. A more sophisticated analysis would also consider the policy preferences of governments. Garrett and Tsebelis show how this leads to a consideration of a broader set of control institutions (for example, the Commission and the Council of Ministers) and to rules regarding other forms of control, such as agenda setting. Garrett and Tsebelis 1996.

several senses, majority voting maximizes expected utility.[86] Similarly, the conjecture is supported by analogy to the theory of the core and noncooperative solution concepts, where increased power to subgroups (such as through vetoes) leads to paralysis by eliminating mutually agreeable outcomes.[87]

The second conjecture follows from an intuition that an actor's control over an institution relates to the actor's importance to the institution. This corresponds to cooperative game-theoretic solution concepts such as the Shapley value, which relates what an actor (potentially) brings to different coalitions to the pay-off the actor receives. When some states contribute more to an institution than others—perhaps because they pay more dues or their behavior is vital to the institution's success—they will demand more sway over the institution. Other states will grant this control to ensure their participation—as the UN did to the permanent members of the Security Council, whose military and financial support was considered essential to the enforcement of resolutions.[88] Membership and voting rules typically formalize this control in some way, as is the case in the UN Security Council and in the weighted voting in the IMF.

Conjecture V3: INDIVIDUAL CONTROL (TO BLOCK UNDESIRABLE OUTCOMES) IN-CREASES WITH UNCERTAINTY ABOUT THE STATE OF THE WORLD.

Because states are risk-averse, they design institutions that protect them from unforeseen circumstances. Veto power is a standard design feature that provides such protection, either to individual states or, in the case of super-majority requirements, to groups of states. A parallel in U.S. politics is the institutional norm of universalism, where legislators place a project in every member's district rather than risk being excluded from a (minimum winning) majority program.[89] The "theoretical engine" behind the universalistic result is uncertainty and legislators' risk aversion.[90]

Conjectures C2 and V3 illustrate quite different institutional responses to the problem of uncertainty. For example, centralization of information can be increased to remedy uncertainty about the state of the world, with the level of control unaffected. Or super-majority voting may mitigate uncertainty about the state of the world without changing the level of centralization. In short, control and centralization can be varied independently or together to deal with uncertainty.

86. Barry 1979. See also the Rae-Taylor theorem in Rae 1969; and Taylor 1969. Mueller provides an excellent overview of the issues and a comparison of majority/unanimity rules. Mueller 1989. Buchanan and Tullock argue for the virtues of unanimity in promoting efficient outcomes when there are no transaction costs. Buchanan and Tullock 1962. As decision-making costs increase—including the costs of preference revelation (which corresponds to uncertainty about preferences)—the case for smaller majorities grows.
87. Shubik 1982.
88. Winter 1996.
89. Weingast 1979.
90. Collie 1988.

Other institutional arrangements provide different forms of protection against uncertainty. Escape clauses in effect allow a state to "veto" some institutional dictates only for themselves. Withdrawal clauses allow the more dramatic step of leaving an institution entirely to avoid undesired outcomes. Such control features blend into what we call flexibility.[91]

Conjectures About Flexibility

Uncertainty about the current or future state of the world presents states with a dilemma. Becoming locked into an institution may lead to unanticipated costs or adverse distributional consequences. But by not making a bargain, states might pass up significant benefits from cooperation.

If uncertainty is high and anticipated benefits are low, risk-averse states will avoid committing themselves to rigid institutions. But what if the uncertainty is lower and the potential benefits are higher? Under these more benign conditions, institutional flexibility becomes important. The possibility of adjusting the agreement when adverse shocks occur allows states to gain from cooperation without tying themselves to an arrangement that may become undesirable as conditions change.[92]

Conjecture F1: FLEXIBILITY INCREASES WITH UNCERTAINTY ABOUT THE STATE OF THE WORLD.

Similarly, states may be uncertain about the distributional implications of particular aspects of an agreement. Koremenos develops a model where states plan to renegotiate all or part of an agreement once they have learned from experience which states benefit the most.[93] The desirability of renegotiation (versus a single, longer agreement) increases with uncertainty about the distribution of gains and decreases with the degree of "noise" in the environment from which the effects of the agreement must be distinguished. An example is the Antarctic Treaty. Although it has no expiration date, the treaty was designed to allow states to learn from their experience and modify the agreement over time. One procedure for modification operated during the first thirty years, another during the subsequent period. In the first learning phase, the parties met biannually for consultations, and the agreement could be changed only by unanimous consent. Some changes and extensions were made, such as the follow-on arrangement to ban resource extraction. Now that the initial period has ended, individual states can press for renegotiation, this time under

91. We proposed but later dropped the related conjecture that "individual control (to block undesirable outcomes) increases with the severity of the distributional problem" because it was logically equivalent to conjecture V3. The impact of distribution flowed fundamentally from uncertainty about the distribution rather than from known distributional consequences, which could be dealt with in other institutional ways. The deleted conjecture was strongly supported in the empirical studies, so dropping it does not bias the results in our favor.

92. Downs and Rocke 1995.

93. Koremenos 2001.

majority rule. They do so with more certainty about how the agreement operates and a better understanding of its costs and benefits.[94]

Flexibility need not be so formalized. For example, "soft" international law allows states to respond to uncertainty by designing arrangements that are less formalized than full legalization. Although often seen as a "failure" of international law, soft law may represent a superior institutional adaptation because of its flexibility.[95]

Even when states face no uncertainty about proposed agreements, flexibility may resolve distributional problems:

Conjecture F2: FLEXIBILITY INCREASES WITH THE SEVERITY OF THE DISTRIBUTION PROBLEM.

Fearon argues that when states lengthen the shadow of the future to solve enforcement problems, distributional concerns become increasingly severe. States bargain harder because the results will affect them for a longer period.[96] Koremenos suggests that in this case states may reduce distributional problems, and bargaining costs, by adopting a more flexible agreement structure.[97] Busch and Koremenos show that under certain conditions, a series of shorter agreements still embodies the shadow of the future required for enforcement while avoiding the bargaining costs associated with a single, long agreement in Fearon's model.[98]

Flexibility has a downside. Renegotiation of treaty terms, as well as dealing with unilateral invocations of flexibility such as escape clauses, is costly. Moreover, individual states have incentives to free ride on an agreement by developing self-serving interpretations of escape clauses that are broader than intended. And renegotiation provides an opportunity for states to "hold up" the cooperative bargain in an effort to increase their own share. Such incentives become greater as more states are party to an agreement—for the familiar reasons associated with collective action.[99] Even without these strategic considerations, as more states become involved, modification becomes more difficult and time consuming. This reasoning leads to our final conjecture.

Conjecture F3: FLEXIBILITY DECREASES WITH NUMBER.

All else equal, states will introduce less flexibility into institutions with larger numbers because larger numbers increase the costs associated with flexibility more than they increase its benefits. For example, where flexibility takes the form of

---

94. This kind of flexibility also solved important distributional issues, the subject of conjecture F2.
95. Abbott and Snidal 2000.
96. Fearon 1998.
97. Koremenos 2001.
98. Busch and Koremenos 2001b.
99. Hardin 1992.

periodic renegotiation of the agreement, larger numbers will increase the associated bargaining costs. Koremenos shows formally that as renegotiation costs increase, rational parties to an agreement will renegotiate less often or not at all.[100] Thus commodity agreements involving forty or so countries are renegotiated significantly less often than are monetary agreements involving the G-7. As renegotiation costs rise, other forms of flexibility become relatively less expensive. For example, states may switch to more centralized forms of flexibility, such as escape clauses combined with a centralized monitoring institution to keep the moral hazard problem in check or the creation of a quasi-legislative institution empowered to adjust the terms of an agreement.[101] Such changes are consistent with conjecture C3, that centralization increases with number, which brings up the question of design interactions. Finally, note that for some types of flexibility, such as withdrawal clauses, the effects of number on the form or incidence of the provisions may be minimal.

Design Interactions

Our simple research design has considerable advantages, but it also has limitations. Because our definitions are broad, they encompass significant institutional variation. The best example is centralization, which includes everything from rudimentary forums for bargaining, through information and monitoring functions, to centralized adjudication and enforcement. Such general conceptions are essential for assessing similarities across cases, but finer conceptual distinctions are needed to understand the more detailed workings and differences among institutions. The volume's contributors begin to do precisely that in the empirical studies that follow.

Our bivariate relationships cannot capture more complex interactions among the variables. For example, while both large numbers and increased uncertainty promote centralization, the interaction of their effects may be most significant of all. The most interesting complexities are those that (may) arise because the dependent variables interact among themselves—as "substitutes," "complements," or "conflicts." Institutional features may substitute for one another by offering alternative ways to solve a particular problem. Escape clauses, for example, introduce flexibility to allow hard-pressed states to avoid the full burden of their treaty obligations on a decentralized basis. An alternative arrangement would be to require states facing special difficulties to seek relief from a centralized institution that can decide how rules apply to new situations. Thus institutional design can enable choice among different means toward the same ends—that is, a choice among multiple institutional equilibria.

Design features may also complement one another. Membership rules, for example, provide one means to deal with enforcement problems (conjecture M1),

100. Koremenos 1999a.
101. For a theoretical analysis with corresponding empirical support, see Koremenos 2000.

but these can be enhanced by centralization when incentives to defect are especially large. Centralization may work either directly as a separate source of enforcement capacity (conjecture C4) or interactively in making the membership mechanism more effective by providing information on members' performance.[102]

Design principles may conflict with one another. Consider an issue with both distribution and enforcement problems. When enforcement is problematic, membership needs to be restricted (conjecture M1), but when there are distributional problems, it needs to be more inclusive (conjecture M3). Obviously, membership rules cannot remedy both problems simultaneously. The only way to circumvent this conflict is to move to a more complex design (such as addressing the enforcement problem with membership rules and the distribution problem by increasing scope).[103] Our bivariate analysis cannot fully capture such complex interactions.[104]

Finally, our analysis looks at individual institutional arrangements in isolation. Substitutabilities, complementarities, and conflicts arise not only in the design of individual institutions but also in relationships among them. Just as individual features of institutions can complement each other, so too can different institutions. One way is by vertical nesting, where institutions that deal with one issue or region are situated within a larger global institution. Vinod Aggarwal has analyzed exactly this kind of relationship between GATT and various textile arrangements.[105] Likewise, the policymakers who planned NAFTA made sure it conformed to GATT trading rules, an issue that will remain important as both NAFTA and the WTO evolve.

We have embraced these challenges by asking the authors of the empirical studies to begin from our concepts and conjectures. We also asked them to be critical of the concepts and on the lookout for ways to refine and improve the conjectures. The ultimate value of our conjectures lies less with their individual veracity than with whether they spur our collective effort to systematize and refine our knowledge of institutional design.

Roadmap to the Rational Design Project

The wide range of conjectures (summarized in Table 1) represents our effort to understand the design of international institutions from a rationalist perspective. The ultimate value of our framework depends on its ability to explain phenomena across a range of substantive issues. The articles that follow take up this challenge by

---

102. The choice among alternatives may also depend on interactions with other independent variables. Thus, the WTO's move toward more centralized dispute resolution was related to the large number of states involved.

103. This problem has been central to the analysis of macroeconomic policy in open economies, especially the relationship between the number of policy goals and the number of policy instruments. Mundell 1962.

104. This problem would bias the empirical results against our bivariate conjectures.

105. Aggarwal 1985.

TABLE 1. Summary of Rational Design conjectures

M1:	Restrictive MEMBERSHIP increases with the severity of the ENFORCEMENT problem
M2:	Restrictive MEMBERSHIP increases with UNCERTAINTY ABOUT PREFERENCES
M3:	MEMBERSHIP increases with the severity of the DISTRIBUTION problem
S1:	SCOPE increases with NUMBER
S2:	SCOPE increases with the severity of the DISTRIBUTION problem
S3:	SCOPE increases with the severity of the ENFORCEMENT problem
C1:	CENTRALIZATION increases with UNCERTAINTY ABOUT BEHAVIOR
C2:	CENTRALIZATION increases with UNCERTAINTY ABOUT THE STATE OF THE WORLD
C3:	CENTRALIZATION increases with NUMBER
C4:	CENTRALIZATION increases with the severity of the ENFORCEMENT problem
V1:	CONTROL decreases with NUMBER
V2:	Asymmetry of CONTROL increases with asymmetry of contributors (NUMBER)
V3:	CONTROL increases with UNCERTAINTY ABOUT THE STATE OF THE WORLD
F1:	FLEXIBILITY increases with UNCERTAINTY ABOUT THE STATE OF THE WORLD
F2:	FLEXIBILITY increases with the severity of the DISTRIBUTION problem
F3:	FLEXIBILITY decreases with NUMBER

evaluating our conjectures in the context of many different areas of international politics.

The empirical articles all share our rationalist approach, taken broadly, but they vary widely in other respects. The institutions examined cover the full spectrum of international politics, from environmental protection to national security. Some institutions are highly articulated organizations; others are much more informal arrangements. The cases exhibit considerable variation in key institutional dimensions, such as centralization of information or breadth of membership.

We have deliberately included methodological diversity. Case studies and quantitative approaches are represented. Some analysts develop our conjectures further by using a formal deductive approach to explain the design of institutions that affect specific issues; others use a more inductive and empirical approach to evaluate and extend the theoretical framework. While most of the studies treat states or international organizations as their central actors, others focus on private international actors, such as firms and private courts, or relax the unitary actor assumption to incorporate key domestic political factors. Most of the studies treat institutional design as a deliberate rational choice; one, however, focuses on "indirect" rational design driven by actors' selection among available institutional alternatives. The first three articles develop the theory in specific contexts and enrich it by connecting it to specific empirical cases. The next five articles use the theory as the basis for intensive empirical analysis of a specific issue-area.

Andrew Kydd looks at NATO enlargement and investigates the causes and consequences of NATO's membership criteria. NATO enlargement has built trust among the potential entrants but weakened it between NATO and Russia. The membership criteria are fairly restrictive: new members must have firmly entrenched democracies, civilian control of the military, and no ethnic or border disputes with their neighbors. These restrictive criteria build trust among new members by diminishing uncertainty about their preferences; they also mitigate the distrust generated in Russia, by showing that NATO is not just expanding willy-nilly to include any state that wants to join.

Peter Rosendorff and Helen Milner look at one of the most common and controversial features of trade agreements: escape clauses. This design feature allows states to enter into agreements they might not otherwise accept because of unforeseeable contingencies. But escape clauses must be costly, or else countries might use them cynically to abandon agreements that are merely inconvenient. Rosendorff and Milner develop a formal model that shows how states design escape clauses to balance these considerations and facilitate agreement.

Robert Pahre asks why states often "cluster" negotiations with multiple states at the same time. He develops a model of clustering, which he tests on nineteenth-century trade relations. But his analysis is equally insightful for understanding the use of negotiating rounds in the postwar GATT/WTO. Clustering occurs in other issue areas as well. It is especially important when states are committed to most-favored-nation policies because these exacerbate distributional problems by linking every bilateral trade negotiation to every other negotiation. Clustering is important because it helps states resolve these distributional problems.

Ronald Mitchell and Patricia Keilbach use their study of environmental issues to investigate institutional design when asymmetric relationships exist among actors. Sometimes "upstream" states create pollution, and "downstream" states are its victims. Polluters have no incentive to join an institution to reduce pollutants unless the institution's scope includes issues they might benefit from. Asymmetry occurs in another way as well. Polluting states can be stronger or weaker than the victims. Mitchell and Keilbach show that weak victims seek institutional designs with positive linkages or rewards, whereas strong victims prefer negative linkage or sanctions.

Walter Mattli highlights the growth of private institutions to arbitrate international business disputes. Private tribunals are often faster, more discreet, and less expensive than public courts. They can be designed to focus closely on specific commercial practices within an industry, a kind of expertise courts rarely possess. The demand for arbitration has been so strong that business groups have produced a multitude of arbitration tribunals. The strengths and weaknesses of different designs lead business partners to select a tribunal to handle disputes as part of commercial contracts. Their choice, Mattli argues, depends on the number of parties involved and their uncertainty about the future state of the world and each other's behavior.

Thomas Oatley deals with a very public institution, the system of multilateral trade and payments for Europe's postwar reconstruction. Two major design problems faced Europeans. One was distributional: who would bear the costs of adjustment to trade imbalances? The second was hard-currency reserves. The United States was willing to provide dollars through the Marshall Plan but feared it might lead to bloated debts rather than disciplined development. Oatley shows how the payments union begun in 1950 resolved these issues with a series of interrelated design features: centralized trade and credit balances, flexible administration, and relatively weak enforcement.

When fighting breaks out, enemy soldiers are frequently seized as prisoners of war. States have joint treaties to ensure that prisoners are treated humanely and modify them to cope with new types of war and imprisonment. James Morrow notes that a workable treaty design must affect the behavior of front-line troops who actually capture prisoners; twentieth-century treaties are designed with that in mind. Moreover, because these treaties entail some costs, ratifying them sends signals about national intentions. Standards for treatment are generally straightforward, partly to make them easily understood by soldiers, partly to resolve any wrangling over the distribution of burdens.

John Richards deals with the institutional design of the global aviation regime. States had to decide whether markets or regulation would govern air routes and fares. Their choice of regulation was prompted by national security concerns, which were closely tied to aeronautics and to states' desire to promote high-technology industries at home. Once on the regulatory path, states faced the complicated task of building effective international institutions. Richards shows how the regulatory institutions that emerged were profoundly shaped by the particular features of the industry, including the large number of states involved and their uncertainty about one another's behavior and future conditions.

The volume concludes with two articles. We invited Alexander Wendt to comment on the project from an "external" perspective. Wendt is both sympathetic to our enterprise and skeptical of it. He questions our decision to focus on rational choice explanations without directly engaging either competing approaches or what he believes are complementary but "deeper" explanations. Wendt further argues that our analysis is insufficiently "forward looking" to address important normative concerns. While we do not fully agree with Wendt's critique, his article provides insight for both insiders and outsiders about the limitations of our approach.

In the final article we summarize the findings. We also combine internal and external critiques of what the volume has accomplished and consider how our rationalist approach can be improved by addressing questions raised by alternative perspectives.

Trust Building, Trust Breaking: The Dilemma of NATO Enlargement

Andrew Kydd

What determines the price of membership in an international institution? Barbara Koremenos, Charles Lipson, and Duncan Snidal hypothesize that uncertainty about the preferences of other states will increase that price, as stated in Rational Design conjecture M2, restrictive MEMBERSHIP will increase with UNCERTAINTY ABOUT PREFERENCES. When states are uncertain about the motivations of other states, they will demand costly signals of reassurance before being willing to cooperate fully.[1] In a multilateral context, this may take the form of an institution with a significant barrier to entry, a price of admission. The price of admission serves to separate states who are seriously interested in cooperation from those who have more exploitative motivations. More cooperative states will be willing to pay the price, and this will reveal their cooperative nature to others, facilitating cooperation. Less cooperative states will not be willing to pay the price, and this too will reveal their type, leading others to cooperate less with them.

The case of NATO enlargement is a perfect example of this logic at work. In the recent enlargement round, NATO established an extensive set of criteria to determine who would be admitted and who would not. The criteria included democratization, civilian control over the military, and the resolution of all border disputes and frictions with neighbors over ethnic minority issues. These hurdles served to separate the more cooperative states from the rest, enabling NATO to admit and cooperate more intensively with those states with proven cooperative credentials. At the same time, proponents of NATO enlargement argue that membership encouraged cooperation between the Eastern European states in spite of lingering mistrust.

I thank the participants in the First Annual Conference on EU–U.S. Relations, European Union Center, Georgia Tech, March 1999, where I presented an earlier version of this article. I also thank the participants in the Rational Design project, the editors of *IO,* and two anonymous reviewers for their feedback. I especially thank Stephan De Spiegeleire, Frank Schimmelfennig, Charles Glaser, Barbara Koremenos, Dan Lindley, Charles Lipson, James Morrow, Duncan Snidal, Robert Pahre, David Pervin, and Peter Rosendorff for their comments and suggestions.
    1. Kydd 2000a,b.

Secretary of State Madeleine Albright, for instance, argued that enlargement would expand "the area of Europe where wars do not happen" thereby preventing conflicts that could draw Russia back into the region or necessitate NATO intervention. Proponents of enlargement see NATO as a benign institution representing the Western "security community" that serves to promote trust and foster cooperation among its members.[2]

Critics of NATO enlargement, including many academics, are more dubious of the merits of NATO expansion. John Lewis Gaddis found a near consensus among historians that NATO expansion was "ill-conceived, ill-timed, and above all ill-suited to the realities of the post–Cold War world."[3] They argued that NATO expansion would antagonize Russia, exacerbating its lingering distrust of the West and strengthening anti-Western elements in the Russian political system. This would in turn lead to lower levels of cooperation between Russia and the West.

Thus NATO enlargement poses an acute policy dilemma. NATO can be a benign security community that identifies more cooperative states and promotes cooperation among them and yet be perceived as an expanding alliance that Russia finds threatening. Although expanding the security community enlarges the zone of peace and mutual trust, it may generate fear among those still on the outside. This dilemma presents policymakers with a difficult choice. They can choose to expand the community and secure the benefits associated with greater cooperation among the members, paying the costs of a lower level of cooperation with the outside power. Or they can choose to forgo expansion in an effort to reassure the outside power, and suffer the consequences of greater instability among the excluded potential members.

I present a game theoretic analysis of the conditions that give rise to this dilemma and show how actors will choose to resolve it. To do so it is necessary to go beyond conventional models of alliances, which focus on public goods provision and deterrence. The most common models of alliances are the public goods provision games that have often been applied to the issue of NATO burden sharing.[4] Another important type of alliance model focuses on signaling and deterrence. Typically a defending power is interested in signaling its resolve to defend an alliance partner against a third party, in order to deter an attack.[5] Neither style of model adequately captures what went on during NATO enlargement, because they do not focus on trust. Trust and mistrust are at the core of the NATO enlargement dilemma—the goal of enlargement is to foster trust among the new allies, and the unwanted side effect is to lessen trust with Russia. Thus the model presented here focuses on trust, how it is built and how it is weakened.

---

2. For the origin of the security community concept, see Deutsch et al. 1957.
3. Gaddis 1998.
4. For the origin of this literature, see Olson and Zeckhauser 1966; and for a survey, see Sandler 1993.
5. See Morrow 1994a; and Smith 1995.

The model shows that enlargement poses a dilemma when the levels of trust are middling, and hence the level of uncertainty about preferences is maximized,[6] both between the potential new members and between the community and the outside power. If states are relatively certain about one another's preferences, there will be little reason to have a high entry price for an institution, because state motivations, benign or malign, will already be known. Likewise, if NATO and Russia are relatively certain about each other's preferences, NATO expansion will have no effect on NATO–Russian relations. It is where uncertainty over preferences is maximized that expansion with a high price of admission is valuable in sorting out the cooperative from the noncooperative states, and yet potentially damaging to NATO–Russian relations. Thus Rational Design conjecture M2, restrictive MEMBER-SHIP increases with UNCERTAINTY ABOUT PREFERENCES, is supported by the model.

A further and possibly counterintuitive result of the model is that under certain conditions expansion will actually be reassuring to the outside power, not provocative as most analysts assume. This is also a function of the criteria by which allies are selected. If NATO were to expand unconditionally, admitting anyone who applied, it would be difficult to portray this to the Russians as an effort by a benign security community to foster cooperation, because membership would not be conditional on cooperation. Instead, it would look like an expansionist West attempting to encircle Russia. The more restrictive and demanding the membership criteria are, however, the more support the benign explanation of NATO behavior has, and the less convincing is the alternative explanation that NATO is out to get Russia and is assembling a large anti-Russian coalition. If the criteria are restrictive enough, conditional expansion may actually be reassuring, because it tells the Russians that NATO is not interested in unlimited expansion and that the stated explanation for expansion is probably correct. Thus with adequately restrictive membership criteria, NATO enlargement can be both beneficial in fostering co-operation among the allies and not too harmful or possibly even beneficial for NATO–Russian relations as well, eliminating the dilemma.

In what follows I will first discuss existing explanations of NATO enlargement. Conventional rationalist approaches have proven largely unsatisfactory; consequently, some analysts have turned to a constructivist alternative. I formulate an alternative rationalist approach to the problem, focusing on trust, reassurance, and the enlargement dilemma identified earlier. In the final section I present a game-theoretic model of NATO enlargement and examine equilibria in the model.

The Puzzle of NATO Enlargement

The enlargement of NATO is one of the most important developments in international affairs after the Cold War; it is also one of the most puzzling. Many factors

---

6. See below for the relationship between trust and uncertainty about preferences.

were at work in producing NATO enlargement, from domestic political issues, such as the existence of electorally significant East European émigré communities in the United States, to the personal rapport between U.S. president Bill Clinton and Czech president Vaclav Havel.[7] Yet certain aspects of the enlargement process seem difficult to explain with conventional theories of alliance formation.

The least puzzling part of NATO enlargement is the desire of the East European states to join the alliance. Most analysts interpret this simply as a desire for protection against Russia, which East Europeans still regard as a potential threat to their independence and autonomy. Given such fears, their desire to join NATO is perfectly understandable; NATO's obvious military superiority to Russia and its successful history of resistance to Russian expansion in the Cold War make it an appealing alliance partner. This desire of East Europeans to align with the stronger side, the West, is clearly at odds with Kenneth Waltz's balance-of-power theory, which predicts that states will join the weaker side.[8] However, it is consistent with Stephen Walt's balance-of-threat theory, which argues that states prefer to join the less threatening side, where perceived aggressive intentions is one component of threat.[9] Eastern European states, still feeling a potential threat from the East, turn to a less threatening alliance for shelter.

While the motivations of the new members seem readily comprehensible, the behavior of the existing NATO members seems less so. Why should current NATO members want new alliance partners? The central purpose of alliances is usually taken to be to increase the security of the members by deterring some external power or better preparing them to fight if deterrence fails. Yet three facts about the recent round of enlargement seem problematic in this light. First, the Russian threat is as low as it has been since the 1920s, and it does not seem to be increasing markedly. This diminished threat from the East leads some realists to predict that NATO will eventually cease to exist, at least as a genuine alliance.[10] Second, NATO enlargement will cost current members both in terms of money and in terms of potential involvement in defending the new Eastern European members.[11] Third, it is not clear what the new allies will contribute toward the common defense and deterrence. At a military level, their forces are far below NATO standards; indeed, bringing them up to Western levels is the primary expense involved in enlargement. One could argue that they bring additional strategic depth, yet NATO was able to hold the much more powerful Soviet Union at bay on the old inter-German border. Why spend money to acquire strategic depth that was not necessary when the threat was far greater than it could ever be again? The new allies might contribute to NATO's

---

7. For detailed accounts of the process leading up to enlargement, see Eyal 1997; and Goldgeier 1998.

8. Waltz 1979, 127.

9. Walt 1987, 25.

10. See Mearsheimer 1990, 5; and Walt 1997, 171.

11. On the issue of monetary costs, for the optimistic side, see Asmus, Kugler, and Larrabee 1996; and for the pessimists, see Perlmutter and Carpenter 1998; and Rubinstein 1998.

new mission of out-of-area peace enforcement,[12] but in the most recent case, Kosovo, the chief burden has been borne by the great power members, especially the United States, Britain, and France.

Considerations such as these have led some analysts to despair of explaining NATO enlargement in rationalist terms. In an insightful essay, Frank Schimmelfennig highlights these difficulties for rationalist approaches and then argues for an alternative, constructivist, explanation.[13] According to Schimmelfennig, "In the constructivist perspective, the enlargement of an international organization is primarily conceived of as a process of international socialization."[14] International organizations engage in socialization when they "teach" their set of constitutive norms and values to aspiring new members of the community. New members are graded on how well they have internalized the norms and values and are admitted when they have proven that they have sincerely adopted the new identity. NATO is "best understood" as an "organization of an international community of values and norms;" primarily democracy, liberty, and the rule of law.[15]

Schimmelfennig goes on to show how the process of NATO enlargement seems to conform to this logic. NATO's "Study on NATO Enlargement" outlines the goals that enlargement was to achieve and criteria for entry for potential new members.[16] The goals include not only the traditional aim of "collective defense" but also such things as spreading democracy and civilian control over the military, fostering cooperation, consultation, and consensus building, and increasing transparency in defense planning and military budgets. Membership criteria for potential members are also revealing. Heavily stressed are such attributes as democracy, civilian control over the military, and the resolution of all border disputes and ethnic conflicts.

These criteria might be dismissed as pleasant-sounding verbiage if not for the fact that the countries invited for membership in the first round—Poland, the Czech Republic, and Hungary—met them and the ones put on the slow track did not. Leaving aside the former Soviet Republics, Romania, Bulgaria, and Slovenia were at one time or another mentioned as possible members during the first wave and were all rejected in part because the political goals were not achieved. Hungary's inclusion is striking in this context. Hungary has indeed made much progress on democratization, building a liberal economy and, crucially, peacefully resolving post–Cold War frictions with Romania concerning the Hungarian minority in Transylvania. So Hungary scores well on the political variables of interest yet would seem to be a burden strategically. Landlocked and noncontiguous with any NATO country, Hungary would be difficult to defend without violating the territory of other states, notably Austria and Slovakia. South of the Carpathian Mountains, it is not on

12. Lepgold 1998.
13. Schimmelfennig 1998/99. See also his analysis of EU expansion in Schimmelfennig 2001.
14. Schimmelfennig 1998/99, 211.
15. Ibid., 213–14.
16. NATO 1995.

a central axis of advance to or from Western Europe, unlike Poland. Furthermore, it is contiguous with Yugoslavia and hence in a historically unstable neighborhood. Yet because Hungary meets the political criteria, it was admitted in the first round.[17]

The boon of NATO membership, then, seems to have been used to reward those East European states that took certain political steps, such as entrenching democracy and civilian control over the military and resolving ethnic and border disputes with each other, rather than in pursuance of any strategic logic related to defense or deterrence. This seems to accord with Schimmelfennig's constructivist account of NATO enlargement rather than with any received rationalist account. NATO is attempting to foster democracy because it is composed of democratic states, and such states simply have a preference that other states be democratic too. NATO expands to include states that are "like us" because we want other states to be "like us." The community of norms is extended through socialization.

Note that this explanation of the membership criteria differs sharply from Rational Design conjecture M2, restrictive MEMBERSHIP increases with UNCERTAINTY OVER PREFERENCES. In the constructivist account, the restrictive membership criteria are a product of the desire to have others be like us. They are a test of how socialized the new potential members are. The stringency and nature of the admission criteria are therefore determined not by uncertainty or instrumental calculations about who is likely to cooperate, but by how the identity of the institution gets defined. Who we are determines who we admit.

Trust, Mistrust, and NATO Enlargement

There are alternative rationalist accounts that can explain the same pattern of behavior, however, as Schimmelfennig himself acknowledges, and there are many questions about NATO enlargement that the constructivist account leaves unanswered. Most importantly, the constructivist account seems to lack a compelling explanation of why NATO enlargement was controversial. If this were a simple case of an international institution extending its norms by socializing new members, why did large sections of the Western policy community, individuals who presumably subscribe to those norms, object so vociferously to it? The debate over NATO enlargement was a battleground of competing arguments, to be sure, but it is difficult to interpret it as a battleground of competing norms. No one was arguing for a different set of norms, or that socialization of new members is bad. In fact, the primary arguments against NATO enlargement, and many of the ones in favor, were of a strategic nature. Costs and benefits were weighed, and the impact of actions on beliefs, and beliefs on actions, were central. Indeed, I argue that the essence of the NATO enlargement debate was an argument about benefits and costs having to do

---

17. For the beneficial effects of NATO enlargement on Hungarian democracy and Hungarian–Romanian relations, see Kramer 1999, 429–30.

with trust, mistrust, and cooperation, and that these issues are eminently suitable to strategic analysis. NATO enlargement, in this view, is primarily designed to foster trust and cooperation amongst the East European states, and its primary drawback is the increased distrust and potential noncooperation it might foster between NATO and Russia.

If we are to take the rhetoric surrounding enlargement seriously, the most important goal for the existing NATO members is to "enhance stability," that is, to foster cooperation and prevent conflict between the East European states themselves. This explains the strong emphasis on resolving territorial disputes and ethnic frictions that might lead to war. The role of democracy is also instrumental in this context. It is clear that members of the Clinton administration, particularly Anthony Lake, were influenced by the democratic peace literature and explicitly adopted the goal of fostering democracy. The main assertion of this literature is that democracies do not fight each other or are much less likely to do so than other regime types.[18] A democracy, then, is unlikely to have conflicts with other democracies and will be able to resolve those that it does have peacefully. To foster democracy, therefore, is to foster peace. Thus an alternative explanation of NATO's insistence on democracy and the resolution of disputes as criteria for membership is a desire to reduce the likelihood of conflict in Eastern Europe.

Furthermore, this need not be a purely altruistic preference on NATO's part. Conflict in Eastern Europe is bad for NATO even in the absence of any other-regarding desire to increase the welfare of East Europeans. Conflict in the region could generate refugee flows into the West, trigger increased criminal activity and smuggling, and reduce the gains from trade and economic integration with the region, as well as generate opportunities for Russia to reassert its influence in the area, possibly generating pressures for a NATO response. Secretary of State Madeleine Albright argued that the Eastern European states, to demonstrate their worthiness of admission, had "strengthened their democratic institutions, improved respect for minority rights, made sure soldiers take orders from civilians, and resolved virtually every old border and ethnic dispute in the region. This is the kind of progress that can ensure that outside powers are never again dragged into conflict in this region."[19] Thus, acting purely on the basis of self interest, NATO could reasonably insist on democratization and confidence building in Eastern Europe as a criteria for NATO membership.[20] NATO's goal in expansion, then, as many NATO officials have publicly stated, is to prevent conflict in the East by fostering mutual trust and cooperation.[21]

---

18. See Brown 1996; and Chan 1997.
19. Albright 1998.
20. Schimmelfennig acknowledges this point. Schimmelfennig 1998/99, 230.
21. For an interesting argument that NATO enlargement has not actually accomplished these goals, in particular, has not fostered democracy, see Reiter 2001. Reiter argues that the countries admitted were solid democracies with civilian control of the military before NATO enlargement became a possibility, and hence that NATO enlargement was irrelevant in promoting cooperation in Eastern Europe. Even if one agrees with this point, which I do not fully, my analysis still can explain both the enlargement criteria

Building trust between alliance members is not typically thought to be a central task of alliances, though it has often been mentioned as a salutary side effect. The reintegration of Germany into Western Europe was facilitated by its participation in NATO, as well as in the European Community. Trust building is more often thought of in the context of "security communities." As Karl Deutsch and his colleagues put it over forty years ago, "A security-community . . . is one in which there is real assurance that members of the community will not fight each other physically, but will settle their disputes in some other way."[22] For war to be unthinkable, it must be that members of these communities have reassured each other of their intentions to the extent that they no longer fear that other members might want to attack them. Secretary Albright's statement that enlarging the alliance would expand "the area of Europe where wars do not happen" reflects this security community logic.

If the chief benefit of NATO enlargement can be seen as building trust and fostering cooperation amongst the East European states, the chief cost of NATO enlargement is surely the lessening of trust and decline in cooperation between NATO and Russia. Many prominent opponents of enlargement have focused on this issue. In a remarkable open letter dated 27 June 1997 from a group of foreign policy experts to President Clinton opposing NATO enlargement, the Russian reaction was the first issue of concern. Signed by a broad spectrum of opinion leaders from Richard Pipes and Paul Nitze to Senator Bill Bradley and Arms Control Association president Spurgeon Keeny, the letter warned that, "In Russia, NATO expansion, . . . will strengthen the non-democratic opposition, undercut those who favor reform and cooperation with the West, bring the Russians to question the entire post–Cold War settlement, and galvanize resistance in the Duma to the Start II and III treaties."[23] Other opponents echoed this warning. Raymond Garthoff argued, "To have driven Russia from support of Desert Storm to support for the Saddam Husseins of the future by denying it a responsible role in the security architecture of the new world order would be a heavy burden to assume for expanding NATO."[24] John Lewis Gaddis lamented the fact that the Clinton administration appeared to be following the example of the harsh Versailles settlement after World War I, rather than that of the Vienna settlement after the Napoleonic wars or the post–World War II settlement, and thereby was violating a key principle of grand strategy: be magnanimous to defeated adversaries.[25] Other analysts of enlargement have also focused on this theme.[26]

---

and the enlargement dilemma, which are a function of policymakers' perception that NATO enlargement would promote democratization and trust building while harming NATO–Russian relations.

22. Deutsch et al. 1957, 5. For a constructivist take on security communities, see Adler and Barnett 1998.

23. Available on the Web at ⟨http://www.cpss.org/nato/oplet.htmd.⟩

24. Garthoff 1997, 10.

25. Gaddis 1998, 145.

26. See Pierre and Trenin 1997; Asmus and Larrabee 1996; Brown 1995; and Mandelbaum 1995.

The idea that alliance formation can be provocative, or produce fear on the part of an excluded country, has also not been central to the alliance literature, but it has been explored. Glenn Snyder presents the most thorough analysis of the "security dilemma" aspects of alliance formation.[27] He argues that states that are basically security seekers will nonetheless feel a need to form alliances because they are not sure of the intentions of other states. Since possible adversaries may have aggressive intentions, it is necessary to build up one's own power against them, and acquiring allies is one way to do so. Forming alliances, however, and increasing one's level of commitment to one's allies, will be provocative, and increase the adversary's level of fear, causing the adversary to seek to strengthen its alliances in turn.[28] This generates a familiar "spiral" of increased fear and conflict, even though both sides have fundamentally defensive motivations.[29] It is this phenomenon that opponents of NATO enlargement see as the primary strategic cost to be paid as a result of admitting new allies.

The relationships among the criteria for membership, the rules governing expansion, and how provocative expansion is to the Russians are rarely discussed by proponents or opponents of enlargement. It is widely recognized that admitting certain specific countries will be especially provocative, particularly states that were once part of the Soviet Union, but the relationship between the general membership criteria and the beliefs of the outside power is underanalyzed. It would seem that unconditional expansion would be highly provocative, because an aggressive alliance might want to maximize the number of adherents, and hence encircle its potential victim.[30] Intuition also suggests that the more restrictive the criteria for membership, the less provocative the alliance would be to outsiders. The model I present later takes this logic further, however, and demonstrates that if the criteria are restrictive enough, conditional expansion may actually be reassuring, thus eliminating the dilemma of expansion altogether. Conditional expansion can reassure by demonstrating that the alliance is not interested in unconditional expansion. By not expanding to include any country that asks to join, NATO demonstrates that it is not attempting to encircle Russia with a ring of hostile allies. Not expanding at all would be even more reassuring, of course, but conditional expansion can still be at least somewhat reassuring.

This, then, is the dilemma of NATO enlargement. The chief benefit of enlargement is to extend the security community to new members, building trust and fostering cooperation. The chief downside is the increased distrust and weakening of cooperation between NATO and Russia. In this sense, NATO enlargement is all about trust. Trust, in turn, is a suitable subject for rationalist, strategic analysis. Beginning with the work of James Coleman, a rational choice literature on trust and

27. Snyder 1984.
28. Ibid., 477.
29. See Jervis 1976, 62; and Kydd 1997.
30. For a contrary argument that offensive alliances are smaller than defensive ones, see Schweller 1998, 61.

reassurance has taken root in sociology, as well as in economics, political science, and international relations.[31] What moves build trust, and what moves decrease it? How are the costs of trust breaking to be weighed against the benefits of trust building? These are questions that a strategic analysis can answer for us. Before getting to a specific model of NATO enlargement, however, I discuss the relationship between trust and uncertainty about preferences.

Trust and Uncertainty About Preferences

The idea that mistrust causes conflict is a basic element of the security dilemma, the spiral model, and in a sense, structural realism as a whole.[32] How should we understand trust and mistrust? I argue that trust is related to uncertainty about the underlying motivations or preferences of the other side, one of Koremenos, Lipson, and Snidal's key variables. Classical international relations theory makes a useful distinction between status quo and revisionist states.[33] Status quo states, or security seekers, are basically satisfied with the way things are and want to preserve the status quo. Revisionist states are not content with the status quo and want to modify it in some way or perhaps even overthrow it entirely. They would be interested in expansion even if all other states were too weak to threaten them and their security was assured. Status quo states might be interested in expansion as well, but only tactically, to fend off a perceived threat to their security. In game-theoretic terms, status quo states would cooperate if they thought the other side would too, whereas revisionist states would defect even if they thought the other would cooperate.

A central problem that states face is that others' motivations are not always apparent; there is uncertainty about preferences. Countries may claim to be status quo and yet harbor revisionist desires. Given uncertainty about the preferences of other states, even status quo states may feel the need to compete for power in the international arena by engaging in arms races, building spheres of influence, or even launching wars if preventive or preemptive windows of opportunity arise. If other states cannot be trusted, it may make sense to take advantage of temporary or wasting assets and subdue them while it is still possible, rather than waiting until the potential threat can no longer be defeated.[34]

Trust is therefore related to uncertainty about preferences. I define a state's level of trust for another as its estimate of how likely it is that the other is status quo oriented, rather than revisionist. To trust another state is to think it relatively likely that the state is status quo oriented, so that if it acts aggressively it is because the state fears some other state, not because it is intrinsically expansionist. To mistrust a state is to believe it relatively likely that the state is really revisionist, and that it

---

31. See Coleman 1990, 91; Güth and Kliemt 1994; Watson 1999; and Kydd 2000a.
32. See Jervis 1976 and 1978; and Glaser 1994/95 and 1997.
33. Schweller 1998, 15–38.
34. On preventive war, see Copeland 2000, 11–34; on preemptive war, see Van Evera 1999, 35–72.

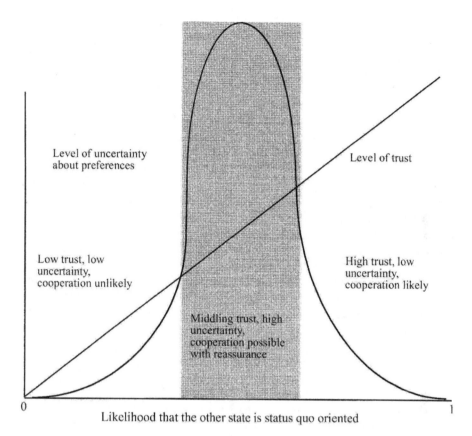

FIGURE 1. Trust and uncertainty about preferences

would be expansionist even if it thought its neighbors were status quo. With a state that one trusts, therefore, conflicts can be overcome through reassurance. If you can persuade them to trust you, to believe that you too are status quo oriented, then cooperation should be feasible since both sides would prefer to reciprocate co-operation. With a state that one mistrusts, however, no amount of reassurance can eliminate conflict, which is driven by the revisionist goals of the other state.

The relationship between trust and uncertainty about preferences is shown in Figure 1. The underlying variable is the likelihood that the other state is status quo oriented, or trustworthy. This probability ranges from zero to 1. Near zero, the state is relatively certain that the other is revisionist, not status quo oriented. Uncertainty and trust are both low, and cooperation is unlikely given the state's pessimistic beliefs. In the middle, the state is relatively unsure whether the other side is status quo oriented. Here uncertainty is maximized, and trust is at a middling level. In this zone of great uncertainty, whether cooperation takes place may hinge on costly signals of reassurance or other incentives. Reassuring gestures, such as those posed by stringent admissions criteria to an international institution, can push the level of trust over the critical threshold and make cooperation possible. At the right in the figure, the state is relatively convinced that the other state is a trustworthy security seeker. Trust is maximized here, and uncertainty about preferences has declined to minimal levels again. Here, cooperation is quite likely because trust is high and costly signals of reassurance are less important.

In this context NATO was asking the Central European states to do two things, to cooperate with each other in the present in the face of mistrust in order to reveal their status quo nature, and to lock in domestic institutional structures that would provide assurance that they would cooperate in the future, that is, remain status quo states. NATO asked the Central Europeans to resolve outstanding territorial and ethnic disputes, and Hungary's eagerness to do so was both directly cooperative and a reassuring signal about its present underlying motivations. Furthermore, NATO asked them to lock in domestic structures, in particular, democracy and civilian control over the military, which are associated with status quo states, and are thus reassuring for the future. While the model I present is a single-shot game and thus focuses on present cooperation, NATO's insistence on democracy and civilian control over the military as institutional constraints on future behavior is in much the same spirit.

Modeling NATO Enlargement

The model of NATO enlargement I offer here is based on previous game-theoretic work on trust and cooperation but is closely tailored to the NATO enlargement question.[35] Consider a game involving $n + 2$ players, west (W), east (E), and a set of n potential allies, numbered 1, 2, 3, ... n. As shown in Figure 2, west and east have a bilateral relationship, as well as relationships with each of the potential allies. The allies also have relationships with each other.

The game is divided into three stages. In the first stage west decides whether to offer a security guarantee to the potential allies. In the second stage the potential allies play a multilateral "trust game" with each other in which they may cooperate or defect. In the third stage east and west play a bilateral trust game. I first describe the structure of the game and then turn to the equilibria.

In the opening move of the game west can offer a security guarantee to the potential allies. I model this as a choice among three options. First, west could offer no security guarantees at all. The allies would then be left to fend for themselves, cooperating or not as they see fit. Second, west could offer conditional guarantees; that is, to encourage the allies to cooperate among themselves in the next stage, west can make membership in the "western bloc" contingent on cooperating with one's

---

35. Kydd 2000a,b.

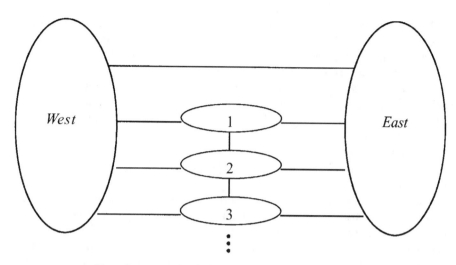

FIGURE 2. The players and relationships in the NATO enlargement game

neighbors in the subsequent multilateral trust game.[36] Third, west could offer unconditional guarantees to all the potential allies. In this case west offers a security guarantee regardless of the behavior of the potential allies. Receiving the security guarantee is worth g_i to country i.[37]

The second stage is a multilateral trust game between the potential allies. Each of the n players can be one of two types, "nice" or "mean." Nice types have Stag Hunt preferences, so they prefer to cooperate if they think the other players will. Nice types correspond to the concept of the status quo state. Using the traditional payoff notation in the analysis of the Prisoners' Dilemma, where T stands for temptation to defect while the other cooperates, R stands for reward for mutual cooperation, P stands for the punishment of mutual defection, and S for the sucker's payoff of unilateral cooperation, the payoff ordering for the nice type (player i) is $R_{iN} > T_{iN} > P_{iN} > S_{iN}$. Mean types have Prisoners' Dilemma preferences and thus prefer unilateral defection to mutual cooperation, corresponding to the revisionist state. Their payoff ordering is $T_{iM} > R_{iM} > P_{iM} > S_{iM}$.[38]

36. This raises a commitment problem. Given that NATO pays a cost (discussed later) to extend a security guarantee, it might be best for them to promise a security guarantee, and then renege on the promise after the allies have moved. I will assume that NATO faces reputational costs sufficient to render such a deceitful strategy unappealing.

37. In reality, of course, there is a much larger set of possible offers. Some states could be given guarantees even if they do not cooperate; others could be denied a guarantee even if they do. The three-part choice is the simplest framework in which we can examine how expansion could be threatening or reassuring, depending on whether it is conditional or unconditional.

38. For quasi-game-theoretic analyses of trust along these lines, see Bennet and Dando 1982; and Plous 1988. Glaser also suggests this strategy for modeling the security dilemma. Glaser 1997.

Nature chooses whether each player is nice or mean. The likelihood that player i is nice is denoted p_i. These probabilities are the game-theoretical representations of trust. A higher p_i corresponds to a higher level of trust or a lower level of fear. These exogenous levels of trust can come from past experience with another state, general experience with many states, or theoretical ideas about how international politics works. For instance, France was mistrustful of Germany in the aftermath of World War II because of the experience of invasion, whereas the United States may be more trusting of democracies out of a general experience that democracies keep their commitments more often than nondemocracies and because policymakers buy into the democratic peace theory. Each player knows its own type but not the type of the other players.

The players must choose to cooperate or defect in ignorance of what the other players have chosen, just as in a simple normal form game. When a player cooperates or defects, this act affects all other players. To allow for the fact that some countries are more important to a given country than others, however, I allow each country to weight the other countries individually. That is, country 1 can care very much if country 2 cooperates, but not so much if country 3 does. These weights are denoted w_{ij}, which represents how much country i cares about country j. For instance, countries would tend to weight countries close to them more highly than countries farther away, because the behavior of nearby countries has more of an impact than the behavior of more distant countries.

In the third stage of the game, west and east play a bilateral trust game of their own. For east, I assume that, as for the potential allies, there are simply two types, nice and mean, with a probability p_{EN} that east is nice and prefers to reciprocate cooperation, and consequent a probability of $p_{EM} = 1 - p_{EN}$ that east is mean and prefers to exploit cooperation.

For west, I posit four possible types, two nice types and two mean types. Instead of one nice type for west, there are two different versions of the nice type. Both have Stag Hunt preferences in the trust game and so would cooperate in it if they believed that east was likely enough to be nice. They are differentiated by the payoffs they receive from the behavior of the potential allies. The first nice type for west is "isolationist" (WISO). An isolationist west is not concerned with the behavior of the potential allies and finds that the costs of extending a security guarantee to potential allies, c_{WISOi}, outweighs the benefit to be derived from their cooperation, b_{WISOi}. The second nice type for west is "internationalist" (WINT). For the internationalist west, the benefit b_{WINTi} from each of the potential allies who cooperates in the multilateral trust game outweighs the cost of extending the security guarantee, c_{WINTi}. The internationalist west values the cooperation of the allies for its own sake and hence feels no need to expand the alliance if the potential allies will cooperate without a security guarantee. In spite of its willingness to acquire new allies, the internationalist west is not vindictive toward east and is not seeking to maximize power, and hence is willing to cooperate in the trust game with east, if east is. The prior probabilities are p_{WN} that west is nice, p_{WINT} that west is internationalist, p_{WISO} that west is isolationist, so that $p_{WN} = p_{WINT} + p_{WISO}$.

There are also two mean types for west, both of which have Prisoners' Dilemma payoffs and so will defect in the final trust game with east. First, west could have "limited aims" (WLIM). The limited aims west is interested in expanding the alliance and not interested in cooperating with east. However, the limited aims west is not trying to maximize the size of the alliance and harm east at any cost. The limited aims west is therefore picky about who should be admitted to the alliance and tends to favor allies who cooperate, as does the internationalist west. For the limited aims west, however, the motivation is simply to have a well-regulated anti-east alliance, not to foster cooperation per se. Thus the limited aims west will offer security guarantees to cooperative allies even if the guarantees are unnecessary to get the allies to cooperate, that is, even if they would have cooperated without them. Hence, the limited aims west derives a benefit b_{WLIMi} from acquiring each new ally, provided that that ally cooperates. Noncooperative allies provide no net benefit. This benefit from acquiring cooperative allies outweighs the cost of extending the guarantee, c_{WLIMi}. For the limited aims type the benefit is only realized if the potential ally is brought into the alliance, not just by virtue of the country's cooperation.

The second mean type is the "expansionist" west (WEXP). The expansionist west is interested in expanding the alliance as far as possible, to maximize the size of the anti-east coalition. The expansionist west is east's worst nightmare. I model this by positing that the expansionist west derives a payoff b_{WEXPi} from every potential ally to whom a security guarantee is offered, and this outweighs the costs, c_{WEXPi}, regardless of whether the ally cooperates. This net benefit outweighs any possible signaling effect; that is the expansionist west will prefer to extend unconditional guarantees even at the price of convincing east that west is mean. The expansionist west therefore has a dominant strategy to offer guarantees to all the potential allies, regardless of their type and likelihood of cooperation. The prior belief that west is mean is p_{WM}, the likelihood that west has limited aims is p_{WLIM}, and the likelihood that west is expansionist is p_{WEXP}, so that $p_{WM} = p_{WLIM} + p_{WEXP}$.

Play in the bilateral trust game between east and west is simultaneous, just like the multilateral trust game among the potential allies. The players must decide whether to cooperate or defect based on their payoffs and their beliefs about each other's type at that point in the game.

Equilibria in the Model

The model was created to analyze the dilemma between building trust and fostering cooperation among the members of a security community and breaking trust and damaging cooperation with an outside power. The two most basic questions to ask, then, are when does this dilemma arise, and how will the security community resolve it when it does. To answer these questions I now turn to the equilibria of the game.

TABLE 1. Types of equilibria in the model

Equilibrium name	Unconditional guarantees	Conditional guarantees	No guarantees
Semi-reassuring	WEXP		WLIM, WINT, WISO
Reassurance	WEXP	WLIM	WINT, WISO
Spiral	WEXP	WLIM, WINT	WISO

Note: WISO = west isolationist (nice), WINT = west internationalist (nice), WLIM = west limited aims (mean), WEXP = west expansionist (mean).

Equilibria in the game can be divided into three categories based on which type(s) of west extend conditional security guarantees, as shown in Table 1. In each of the equilibria, the expansionist west offers unconditional guarantees to all the potential allies, and the isolationist west offers no guarantees at all. In semi-reassuring equilibria, the internationalist west and the limited aims west offer no guarantees along with the isolationist west. In reassurance equilibria the internationalist west offers no guarantees, but the limited aims west offers conditional guarantees. Here the internationalist west reassures the east by not offering any guarantees. Finally, in the spiral equilibria, the internationalist west extends conditional guarantees, as does the limited aims west. This makes conditional expansion potentially provocative, as the nice internationalist west is behaving like the mean limited aims west. As we will see, however, this equilibrium is not always provocative; sometimes it can be reassuring as well.[39]

Mathematical details of the model are given in the appendix. Here I focus on a graphical representation (Figure 3) of the equilibria in the model. The vertical axis is the level of trust among the potential allies, or p_i. To keep the illustration two dimensional I focus on the symmetrical case in which $p_i = p_j$, so the level of trust among the potential allies can be considered as a single dimension. The horizontal axis is the level of trust between east and west, where again I consider the symmetrical case where $p_{WN} = p_{EN}$, so they can be represented as a single dimension. As foreshadowed in the introduction, the dilemma arises when the levels of trust are middling both between the potential new members and between the community and the outside power, hence in the center of Figure 3. This is the zone in which uncertainty about preferences is maximized.

At the top of the figure are the first and second reassurance equilibria, R1 and R2. Here the potential allies are so trusting of one another that they are willing to cooperate amongst themselves even without the added inducement of a security guarantee from a internationalist west. In this case the internationalist west can reap

39. I use the name spiral because this equilibrium is sometimes provocative. Perhaps "conditional spiral" would be a more accurate, if more cumbersome, name.

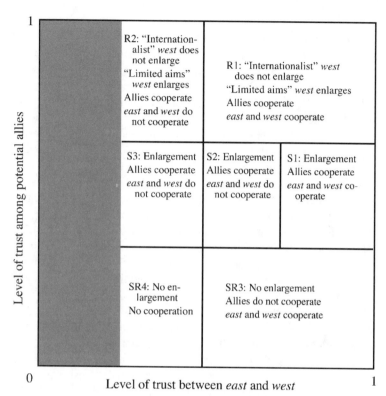

FIGURE 3. Equilibria in the model

the benefits of cooperation among the potential allies without paying the costs associated with the security guarantee and so has no incentive to extend the alliance to new members. Thus, the isolationist and the internationalist west both fail to expand the alliance, but the nice potential allies cooperate anyway. The limited aims west extends conditional guarantees, thereby revealing its type to the east and causing east to defect in the bilateral trust game between east and west. The limited aims west will be willing to do this provided the payoff from extending the alliance and the resulting mutual defection with east is greater than the payoff from refraining from expanding the alliance, imitating the nice types, and possibly exploiting a trusting nice east. The first and second reassurance equilibria are distinguished by the level of trust between east and west. In the first reassurance equilibrium, west's prior level of trust for east exceeds a critical threshold, so the nice east and west will be able to cooperate. In the second reassurance equilibrium, the level of trust is low and this causes a failure to cooperate. That is, even though a nice west does not expand the alliance and this acts as a reassuring signal to east, east has done nothing to reassure west, so west will fail to cooperate. While some might think that these equilibria are unrealistic because they posit high trust, there are plenty of cases where states have sufficient trust that they are able to cooperate in security affairs with each other without institutional incentives from third parties, the U.S.–Canada and U.S.–Great Britain relationships being perhaps the most salient examples.

At the bottom of Figure 3 are the third and fourth semi-reassuring equilibria, SR3 and SR4.[40] Here the potential allies are so suspicious of each other that not even the potential inducement of a security guarantee can persuade them to cooperate. Since a security guarantee would fail to persuade the nice allies to cooperate, the internationalist west does not bother to offer it and so behaves like the isolationist west by failing to expand the alliance. Here, however, the limited aims west also does not extend conditional guarantees, because the allies will not cooperate and the limited aims west wants cooperative allies as well. The only type offering guarantees is therefore the expansionist west, which offers unconditional guarantees. Thus some information is revealed if no guarantees are offered, and not offering guarantees serves as a signal that at least west is not the expansionist type. Some trust is built, but not as much as in the reassurance equilibrium, where not building serves as a perfectly reliable signal that west is nice. Cooperation is possible between east and west in the third semi-reassuring equilibrium where the likelihood that east is nice is high enough, and it is impossible in the fourth semi-reassuring equilibria where east and west are less trusting of each other.

In the reassurance and semi-reassuring equilibria, then, expansion produces no dilemmas. In the reassurance equilibria the internationalist west can refrain from offering guarantees because the allies will cooperate without them. In the semi-reassuring equilibria the internationalist west will refrain from offering guarantees because the allies will not cooperate even with the inducement of guarantees. In these regions uncertainty about preferences is low; the allies either trust each other or do not.

In the middle band of the figure are the spiral equilibria. Here trust is at a middling level among the allies, and uncertainty over preferences is maximized. The key feature of the spiral equilibria is that the internationalist west extends conditional guarantees to the allies and the limited aims west does the same, so the internationalist and the limited aims west behave identically. The isolationist west does not extend guarantees, and the expansionist west extends unconditional guarantees. This means that beliefs about west's type change after the first round. If west does not expand the alliance, it is identified as isolationist and hence nice for sure. If west extends unconditional guarantees, west is identified as expansionist and hence mean for sure. If west extends conditional guarantees, it is identified as either internationalist or limited aims, and there will be lingering uncertainty over whether west is nice or mean. The likelihood that west is nice will be equal to

---

40. The first and second are not possible for the parameter values illustrated in Figure 2. See the appendix for details.

$$P'_{WN} = \frac{P_{WINT}}{P_{WINT} + P_{WLIM}}$$

This posterior level of trust p'_{WN} may be greater than or less than the prior level of trust, p_{WN}. If it is less than the prior, conditional expansion will have been provocative, and trust will have been weakened. If the posterior belief is greater than the prior, interestingly, conditional expansion will have been reassuring, and trust will have been increased. The posterior will be smaller, and hence expansion will be provocative if

$$\frac{P_{WINT}}{P_{WN}} < \frac{P_{WLIM}}{P_{WM}}$$

and expansion will be reassuring otherwise.

It may seem paradoxical that conditional expansion of the alliance could be reassuring to east, so let us examine this condition more carefully. The key is that expansion is conditional on cooperation among the allies; that is, there are limits on expansion. Conditional expansion does two things. It proves that west is not the isolationist type (who would not have expanded at all), and that is provocative because the isolationist west is nice and would cooperate in the second round. That is, by expanding conditionally, west has shown that it is not east's ideal partner, someone who will not expand at all in order to reassure east. West has some interests that override its concern for east. However, conditional expansion also proves that west is not the extreme expansionist type (who would have expanded uncondition-ally), which is reassuring, because the expansionist type is mean and would defect in the second round. Establishing significant restrictions on who may join signals that west is not east's worst nightmare, the hostile power bent on encircling east with a ring of offensively capable military bases. Thus conditional expansion has both provocative and reassuring effects. Whether conditional expansion is provoc-ative or reassuring on balance depends on the relative weight of these two factors. As the preceding equation indicates, if the proportion of mean types that have limited aims is large (the right side of the equation), conditional expansion is likely to be provocative, because then the likelihood that west is expansionist will be small, so eliminating this possibility will not be very reassuring. Conversely, if the proportion of nice types that are internationalist is large (the left side of the equation), conditional expansion may be reassuring, because west is unlikely to be isolationist, and eliminating this possibility is not very provocative.

The more restrictive the criteria for entry, and hence the smaller the expansion, the more reassuring expansion is likely to be. The more restrictive the criteria, the harder it is to imagine the mean type choosing such criteria, that is, having limited aims that correspond to the allies selected. If NATO expansion criteria ended up selecting only the Czech Republic, among all the possible entrants, it would be difficult for Russia to interpret this as the act of an aggressive west, because it would be such a strange choice from an anti-Russian point of view. In this case the proportion of mean types that would have limited aims leading them to select only this ally would be small, and hence conditional expansion could be reassuring. However, if the criteria are fairly inclusive, so that almost anyone can join, it would be easy to interpret this as an act of a mean west that simply wants to expand the alliance to all but a few troublesome potential allies. If the rules for admission granted entry to all the former Warsaw Pact states that applied and all the former Soviet Republics but Tajikistan, such rules would be easily interpretable as a fig leaf for a mean west. Here the proportion of mean types who would like to expand to include this set of allies is potentially large, making expansion provocative. Thus highly conditional expansion may be reassuring, whereas the less restrictive the conditions on membership, the more likely expansion is to be provocative.

There are three varieties of spiral equilibrium, depending on what happens in the second-round trust game between east and west. In Figure 3 I illustrate the case in which conditional expansion is provocative. On the right side is the first spiral equilibrium, S1, where even though the internationalist west expands the alliance, the diminution in trust between east and west is not sufficient to make cooperation impossible between them in the trust game. This can occur when the posterior level of trust between east and west is high enough to begin with to compensate for the lessening in trust caused by expansion. Here, there is no downside to enlargement.

On the left side is the third spiral equilibrium, S3. This equilibrium holds when the level of trust falls below a certain threshold, such that east and west would not have cooperated even if west had refrained from enlarging. Here, west does not trust east, so it does not bother to refrain from enlarging because there would be no east–west cooperation anyway. Once again, there is an incentive to enlarge and no cost to be paid.

In the middle is the second spiral equilibrium, and, here, enlargement really does pose a dilemma. The prior level of trust between east and west is sufficient that cooperation, absent enlargement, would take place. Enlargement, however, lessens east's trust for west to an extent where cooperation is no longer possible. Enlargement comes at a cost; therefore, cooperation between the allies is secured by expansion, but expansion hinders cooperation between east and west.

If securing cooperation in the east–west relationship was more important than getting the allies to cooperate, a reassurance equilibrium would be possible in part or all of this central box. In such an equilibrium, the internationalist west forgoes expanding the alliance to reassure east. The potential allies therefore fail to cooperate, but east and west do, provided that they are nice. In this reassurance equilibrium (R3) the tradeoff of the second spiral equilibrium between cooperation among the allies and cooperation between east and west is resolved in the opposite way, in favor of establishing cooperation between east and west.

How the community resolves the dilemma in this central region will depend on the payoffs involved in the two relationships. The greater the importance of achieving cooperation among the new members, compared with maintaining cooperation with the outside power, the more likely the community is to expand. For this reason, analysts who opposed NATO expansion tended to stress the importance of the NATO–Russian relationship and the possible harm that would result if Russia stopped cooperating. They pointed to the still unratified START II treaty in the Russian Duma, the problems of loose fissile material and the potential for smuggling, and the other issues on which the West sought Russian cooperation. Proponents of NATO enlargement tended to minimize the possible extent of Russian noncooperation, arguing that they would at worst delay action on arms control treaties such as START II, which is of lesser importance in the post–Cold War world in any event.

Conclusion

States can use restrictive membership criteria as filters that enable potential members to signal their strong interest in cooperation and keep out problematic members who would be less cooperative. NATO enlargement is a case in point. The membership criteria NATO adopted—democratization, civilian control over the military, and the resolution of border and ethnic conflicts with neighbors—are a response to uncertainty over preferences and constitute signals that identify certain states as status quo oriented, and hence as good potential alliance members. However, NATO enlargement came at a price. Expansion deepened Russian suspicions of the west and strengthened nationalist sentiment. In combination with the NATO conflict with Serbia over Kosovo, NATO expansion helped worsen Western–Russian relations in the second half of the 1990s. This provocative effect of expansion, however, may have been mitigated by the restrictiveness of the criteria employed. That NATO did not expand to include all countries who desired membership signaled Russia that NATO was not an unlimited expansionist alliance, bent on minimizing Russian security regardless of the cost. Excluding several potential members helped mitigate the damage done by the inclusion of others.

Russian suspicions can be further assuaged by more reassurance from the West, but they will be greatly inflated if NATO continues its expansion into the territory of the former Soviet Union. Given the political and economic status of Belarus and Ukraine, it will be many years before they can meet NATO criteria for membership, even if they were to want it. The Baltic states are another story. These countries are making rapid strides, consolidating democratic political systems, free market economies, and resolving ethnic and territorial disputes with each other and with Russia. The West's principled stand against their incorporation into the Soviet Union by Stalin gives a historical and moral legitimacy to arguments that they should be defended against potential future Russian revanchism, even as their long history before World War I as part of Russia leaves Russians feeling that they are not really foreign.[41] In considering the next round of expansion NATO should take care not to dilute the membership requirements already set down. If anything, the criteria should be made more stringent rather than less, to maximize the potentially reassuring effect of restrictive membership criteria on those left outside.

Appendix

I consider Perfect Bayesian Equilibria of the model.[42] Off the equilibrium path, I assume that conditional guarantees convince east that west is mean with limited aims, while no guarantees convince east that west is nice and isolationist. I restrict attention to equilibria in which the nice types cooperate in the trust games if cooperation is sustainable given their beliefs and payoffs, and hence never coordinate on mutual defection when mutual cooperation is possible. I also assume that when a security guarantee does not improve the payoff, it is not offered; that is, the west breaks ties in favor of not offering the security guarantee. Finally, I assume that the limited aims type of west is at least minimally interested in expansion, that is, would find it worthwhile to expand if it had no adverse impact on the prospect of east–west cooperation.

Cooperation in the Multilateral Trust Game

The column vector containing the likelihoods that each of the potential allies is nice is denoted $p = (p_1, p_2, p_3 \ldots p_n)'$. I assume that the w_{ij} sum to 1 for each country and that $w_{ii} = 0$. The row vector, $w_i = (w_{i1}, w_{i2}, w_{i3} \ldots w_{in})$ contains the weights that player i assigns to the other players. If nice types cooperate and mean types defect, the expected payoff for the nice type of player i for cooperating can be derived as follows. If no other country cooperates, player i gets the sucker's payoff, S_{iN}. For each other country j, there is a p_j chance that they cooperate, yielding a benefit of $w_{ij}(R_{iN} - S_{iN})$, and a $1 - p_j$ chance that they will defect, yielding nothing. Thus the overall expected value of cooperating for player i is:

$$S_{iN} + w_{i1}p_1(R_{iN} - S_{iN}) + w_{i2}p_2(R_{iN} - S_{iN}) + w_{i3}p_3(R_{iN} - S_{iN}) + \ldots w_{in}p_n(R_{iN} - S_{iN}).$$

Using vector notation, this expression can be more simply expressed as

$$S_{iN} + w_ip(R_{iN} - S_{iN}).$$

If player i defects, the payoff is

$$P_{iN} + w_{i1}p_1(T_{iN} - P_{iN}) + w_{i2}p_2(T_{iN} - P_{iN}) + w_{i3}p_3(T_{iN} - P_{iN}) + \ldots w_{in}p_n(T_{iN} - P_{iN}),$$

41. For the debate on NATO and the Baltic states, see Asmus and Nurick 1996; Kamp 1998; and Blank 1998.
42. Morrow 1994b, 170.

which can be re-expressed as

$$P_N + w_i p(T_{iN} - P_{iN}).$$

The payoff for cooperation beats that for defection if

$$w_i p > p^{*i} \equiv \frac{1}{1 + \dfrac{R_{iN} - T_{iN}}{P_{iN} - S_{iN}}}.$$

If a guarantee has been offered, the expected payoff for the nice type of player i for cooperating is

$$g_i + S_{iN} + w_i p(R_{iN} - S_{iN}).$$

If player i defects, it does not get the security guarantee. The payoff is the same as before so that cooperation beats defection if

$$w_i p > p^{*ig} \equiv \frac{1 - g_i}{1 + \dfrac{R_{iN} - T_{iN}}{P_{iN} - S_{iN}}}.$$

Note that since $p^{*ig} < p^{*i}$, cooperation is possible for lower levels of trust if a security guarantee is offered than if it is not.

For simplicity, I assume that all of the nice types are willing to cooperate at the same level of risk, though their payoffs and weightings may vary, so that we can restrict attention to symmetric equilibria in which either all nice types are willing to cooperate or none of them are. This enables us to consider three zones of trust between the potential allies. In the low trust zone, $w_i p < p^{*ig}$ for all i, so that the nice allies would not be willing to cooperate even with a guarantee. In the medium trust zone, $p^{*ig} < w_i p < p^{*i}$ for all i, the potential allies would cooperate if and only if they got a security guarantee. In the high trust zone, $p^{*i} < w_i p$ for all i, all allies will cooperate even without a security guarantee.

Cooperation in the East–West Trust Game

Analogously to the previous case, one can show that cooperation is possible in the east–west trust game if

$$p_{EN} > p^{*W} \equiv \frac{1}{1 + \dfrac{R_{WN} - T_{WN}}{P_{WN} - S_{WN}}}$$

and

$$p'_{WN} > p^{*E} \equiv \cfrac{1}{1 + \cfrac{R_{EN} - T_{EN}}{P_{EN} - S_{EN}}},$$

where the prime denotes a posterior belief, after west's first move.

West's Decision on Enlargement

The expansionist west has a dominant strategy to offer unconditional guarantees, and this strategy is dominated for the other three types. Given three other types of west—internationalist, isolationist, and limited aims—and two remaining options—offer no guarantees or conditional guarantees—there are eight conceivable patterns of behavior for the first decision, three of which are possible in equilibrium, as indicated in Table 1. In the five patterns not shown, either the isolationist west is offering guarantees when it could switch to not offering guarantees and convince east that it is nice and thereby save on the potential costs of expansion with no adverse signaling effects, or the limited aims west is not offering guarantees when it could defect to offering conditional guarantees, which is preferred and would have no adverse signaling effects.

Semi-Reassuring Equilibria

In the semi-reassuring equilibria the expansionist west offers unconditional guarantees, and the other types offer none. Therefore, if east observes unconditional guarantees, it is convinced that west is expansionist, and therefore mean. If east observes no guarantees, its belief that west is nice shifts to

$$p'_{WN} = \frac{p_{WN}}{p_{WN} + p_{WLIM}}.$$

This is greater than the prior belief, but not equal to 1, hence the equilibrium is called semi-reassuring.

If west deviates to offering conditional guarantees, this convinces east that west is limited aims, therefore mean. The isolationist west is always happy with this equilibrium, since the isolationist west prefers not to extend guarantees for its own sake, and extending them will have adverse signaling effects.

The internationalist west is happy to refrain from offering guarantees in the low and high trust zones, where guarantees would have no impact on the behavior of the potential allies. In the medium trust zone, guarantees would cause the allies to cooperate but would produce noncooperation for sure with east. If $p_{EN} < p^{*W}$ or $p'_{WN} < p^{*E}$, cooperation with east is impossible anyway, so this does not act as a disincentive; consequently, the equilibrium is impossible. If $p_{EN} > p^{*W}$ and $p'_{WN} > p^{*E}$, this is a sacrifice, so the payoffs must be compared. If we gather the benefits and costs of extending security guarantees into row vectors $b_{WINT} = (b_{WINT1}, b_{WINT2}, b_{WINT3}, \ldots b_{WINTn})$ and $c_{WINT} = (c_{WINT1}, c_{WINT2}, c_{WINT3}, \ldots c_{WINTn})$, we can write the payoff for enlarging the alliance for the internationalist type as: $(b_{WINT} - c_{WINT})p + P_{WN}$. The payoff for not enlarging, which makes cooperation with east possible but not certain, is $p_{EN}R_{WN} + (1 - p_{EN})S_{WN}$. Failing to enlarge beats enlarging if

$$p_{EN} > p^{*WINT} \equiv \frac{(b_{WINT} - c_{WINT})p + P_{WN} - S_{WN}}{R_{WN} - S_{WN}}.$$

For the limited aims west, in the low trust zone this equilibrium works, since no allies will cooperate anyway. In the medium trust zone, allies will cooperate conditional on getting the guarantee, so the mean type will get $(b_{WLIM} - c_{WLIM})p + P_{WM}$ if it expands, and $p_{EN}T_{WM} + (1 - p_{EN})P_{WM}$ if it does not. So not expanding is best if

$$p_{EN} > p^{*WLIM} \equiv \frac{(b_{WLIM} - c_{WLIM})p}{T_{WM} - P_{WM}}.$$

In the high trust zone, for the limited aims type the calculation is identical because this type does not reap the benefits of cooperation without expansion, unlike the internationalist type. So the same constraint holds.

Summing up, the semi-reassuring equilibrium is possible in the low trust zone; in the middle trust zone if $p_{EN} > \max(p^{*W}, p^{*WINT}, p^{*WLIM})$, and $p'_{WN} > p^{*E}$; and in the high trust zone if $p_{EN} > \max(p^{*W}, p^{*WLIM})$, and $p'_{WN} > p^{*E}$. There are four versions of the semi-reassuring equilibrium. In the high trust zone is SR1 (see Figure 3), in which both the allies and east and west cooperate if no expansion takes place. In the medium trust zone is SR2, in which the allies fail to cooperate and east and west do if no expansion takes place. In the low trust zone are SR3, in which the allies do not cooperate and east and west do (without expansion), and SR4, in which neither the allies nor east and west cooperate. The strategies in the trust games and the boundary conditions of the equilibria are shown in Table 2.

Reassurance Equilibria

In the reassurance equilibria the limited aims west extends conditional guarantees, but the internationalist west does not. Extending guarantees therefore convinces east that west is mean for sure, $p'_{WN} = 0$, whereas not extending them persuades east that west is nice for sure, $p'_{WN} = 1$.

The isolationist west is again happy with this equilibrium under all conditions. Expanding would be costly and provocative.

The internationalist west is happy with this equilibrium in the low trust zone, where the allies will not respond to incentives anyway. In the high trust zone, the internationalist west is also happy; the allies will cooperate without guarantees. In the medium trust zone, expanding will cause the allies to cooperate and east and west to fail to cooperate. Not expanding makes it possible for east and west to cooperate. The conditions are therefore the same as in the semi-reassuring equilibrium, and the internationalist type will refrain from expanding if $p_{EN} > \max(p^{*W}, p^{*WINT})$. The condition on east's level of trust for west, p_{WN}, is not binding here, because not expanding will reassure east completely no matter its prior beliefs.

TABLE 2. Boundary conditions for equilibria in the model

Equilibrium	Trust game behavior of nice east and west	Trust game behavior of nice allies	Boundary condition on trust between allies	Boundary conditions on trust between east and west
SR1	Cooperate only if no guarantees	Cooperate	$p_i > p^{*i}$	$p_{EN} > \max(p^{*W}, p^{*WLIM})$ $p_{WN} > p^{*E}$
SR2	Cooperate only if no guarantees	Cooperate only with conditional guarantees	$p^{*i} > p_i > p^{*ig}$	$p_{EN} > \max(p^{*W}, p^{*WINT}, p^{*WLIM})$ $p_{WN} > p^{*E}$
SR3	Cooperate only if no guarantees	Defect	$p^{*ig} > p_i$	$p_{EN} > p^{*W}$ $p'_{EN} > p^{*E}$
SR4	Defect	Defect	$p^{*ig} > p_i$	$p_{EN} < p^{*W}$ or $p'_{WN} < p^{*E}$
R1	Cooperate only if no guarantees	Cooperate	$p_i > p^{*i}$	$p^{*WLIM} > p_{EN} > p^{*W}$
R2	Cooperate only if no guarantees	Cooperate	$p_i > p^{*i}$	$p_{EN} < \min(p^{*W}, p^{*WLIM})$
R3	Cooperate only if no guarantees	Cooperate only with conditional guarantees	$p^{*i} > p_i > p^{*ig}$	$\max(p^{*W}, p^{*WLIM}) > p_{EN} > \max(p^{*W}, p^{*WINT})$
S1	Cooperate only if no or conditional guarantees	Cooperate only with conditional guarantees	$p^{*i} > p_i > p^{*ig}$	$p_{WN} > p^{*E}$ $p_{EN} > p^{*W}$
S2	Cooperate only if no guarantees	Cooperate only with conditional guarantees	$p^{*i} > p_i > p^{*ig}$	$p_{WN} < p^{*E}$ $p^{*W} < p_{EN} < p^{*WC}$
S3	Cooperate only if no guarantees	Cooperate only with conditional guarantees	$p^{*i} > p_i > p^{*ig}$	$p_{WN} < p^{**E}$ $p_{EN} < p^{*W}$

The limited aims type expands in equilibrium; not expanding would convince east that west is nice. The equilibrium is therefore impossible in the low trust zone, because expanding is pointless and ties are broken in favor of not expanding. In the medium trust zone the calculation is the same as in the semi-reassuring equilibrium, but the sign is reversed, so that the mean type will expand if $p_{EN} < \max(p^{*WLIM}, p^{*W})$. The constraint on p_{WN} is not present, because not expanding is reassuring. The same is true in the high trust zone.

Summing up, the equilibrium is impossible in the low trust zone, possible in the medium trust zone if $\max(p^{*W}, p^{*WLIM}) > p_{EN} > \max(p^{*W}, p^{*WINT})$, and possible in the high trust zone if $p_{EN} < \max(p^{*W}, p^{*WLIM})$. Note that the equilibrium is possible in the middle trust zone only if $p^{*WLIM} > \max(p^{*W}, p^{*WINT})$. There are three versions of the reassurance equilibrium. In the high trust zone is R1, in which allies cooperate and east and west cooperate provided there is no enlargement, and R2, in which the allies cooperate, but east and west fail to cooperate because of west's low trust for east. In the medium trust zone is R3, in which allies cooperate only if west is mean and extends guarantees.

Spiral Equilibria

In a spiral equilibrium, not extending guarantees persuades east that west is isolationist and hence nice for sure, $p'_{WN} = 1$. Extending guarantees causes beliefs to be updated according to Bayes's rule, such that

$$p'_{WN} = \frac{p_{WINT}}{p_{WINT} + p_{WLIM}}.$$

The posterior belief p'_{WN} may be greater than or less than the prior, p_{WN}. The posterior will be smaller, and hence expansion will be provocative if

$$\frac{p_{WINT}}{p_{WLIM}} < \frac{p_{WN}}{p_{WM}},$$

and the posterior will be larger, and hence expansion will be reassuring, if the reverse holds.

In the low trust zone the internationalist west will deviate to not offering guarantees, because they would be pointless. In the high trust zone, the same holds. Therefore the equilibrium is only possible in the middle trust zone. The isolationist west is happy with the equilibrium always, as before.

The internationalist west must be willing to offer guarantees, in spite of the possibly adverse signaling consequences. For a high enough level of p_{WN}, east will still be willing to cooperate. This level can be found by equating p'_{WN} to p^{*E} and solving for the prior p_{WN}, which indicates that east will still be willing to cooperate if

$$p_{WN} > p^{**E} \equiv p^{*E} + (1 - p^{*E})p_{WISO} - p^{*E}p_{WEXP}.$$

Thus if $p_{WN} > p^{**E}$, the internationalist west will be willing to enlarge, because there will be no downside. For p_{WN} below this cutoff, the consequences of enlarging will be noncooperation between east and west. If $p_{EN} > p^{*W}$, cooperation would be possible without enlarging, so the internationalist west will enlarge if $p_{EN} < \max(p^{*W}, p^{*WINT})$. Otherwise, cooperation is not possible between east and west, so the internationalist west is happy to expand.

The limited aims west must be willing to offer guarantees. For p_{WN} above p^{**E}, there is no downside, so the mean west will be willing to do so. Below p^{**E}, the limited aims west will be willing to offer guarantees if $p_{EN} < \max(p^{*W}, p^{*WLIM})$.

Summing up, there are three versions of the spiral equilibrium. In S1, $p_{EN} > p^{*W}$, and $p_{WN} > p^{**E}$, so that there is no downside from enlarging and the mean and internationalist west enlarge but east and west cooperate anyway. In S2, $p_{WN} < p^{**E}$, and $p^{*W} < p_{EN} < p^{*WINT}$, and the internationalist and mean west expand, causing the allies to cooperate and east and west to fail to cooperate, but if west does not expand, east and west cooperate. Finally, in S3, $p_{EN} < p^{*W}$ so that east and west would not cooperate even if west refrained from expanding. (West would reassure east, but east would not reassure west, so cooperation would still be impossible.)

Numerical Example

The numerical example illustrated in Figure 3 has the following parameter values. For the payoffs, I use the typical 4, 3, 2, 1 values. For the potential allies, $R_{iN} = T_{iM} = 4$, $T_{iN} = R_{iM} = 3$, $P_{iN} = P_{iM} = 2$, $S_{iN} = S_{iM} = 1$. For east and west, $R_{EN} = T_{EM} = 4$, $T_{EN} = R_{EM} = 3$, $P_{EN} = P_{EM} = 2$, $S_{EN} = S_{EM} = 1$, and $R_{WN} = T_{WM} = 4$, $T_{WN} = R_{WM} = 3$, $P_{WN} = P_{WM} = 2$, $S_{WN} = S_{WM} = 1$.

I assume five potential allies, and that $w_{ij} = 0.25$. For the benefits from getting the allies to cooperate; for the internationalist west I assume $b_{WINTi} = 3$, $c_{WINTi} = 1$; for the isolationist west, $b_{WISOi} = 1$, $c_{WISOi} = 2$; and for the limited aims west, $b_{WLIMi} = 3$, $c_{WLIMi} = 1$. I let the benefit from having a security guarantee be $g_i = 0.5$. For the probabilities, I assume that for the allies, $p_i = p_j$, and for east and west that $p_{EN} = p_{WN}$ so that I can illustrate the equilibria in two dimensions. I also assume that the likelihood that west is isolationist is 1/3, ($p_{WISO} = 0.33$) so that p_{WN} varies between 1/3 (if $p_{WINT} = 0$) and 1, hence the gray region along the left axis of Figure 3 where $p_{WN} < 1/3$.

Plugging the numbers into the formulas given earlier, we get $p^{*i} = 0.5$, $p^{*ig} = 0.25$, $p^{*E} = 0.5$, and $p^{*W} = 0.5$. The boundary conditions for east and west are $p^{*WINT} = 10p/3 + 1/3$, $p^{*WLIM} = 5p$, and $p^{**E} = 2/3 - 1/2p_{WEXP}$.

The Optimal Design of International Trade Institutions: Uncertainty and Escape

B. Peter Rosendorff and Helen V. Milner

International institutions differ greatly in their forms; the number of states included, the decision-making mechanisms, the range of issues covered, the degree of centralized control, and the extent of flexibility within them all vary substantially from one institution to the next. What accounts for such variation? In this article, as part of the larger Rational Design project on the design of international institutions, we claim that such variation can be accounted for as part of the rational, self-interested behavior of states. We show that at least one important aspect of institutional design can be explained as a rational response of states to their environment.

Almost all international trade agreements include some form of "safeguard" clause, which allows countries to escape the obligations agreed to in the negotiations.[1] On the one hand, such escape clauses are likely to erode both the credibility and the trade liberalizing effect of international trade agreements. On the other hand, they increase the flexibility of the agreement by adding some discretion for national policymakers. The first question we address is the institutional design issue that escape clauses raise: when is such increased flexibility rationally optimal for states making international trade agreements? The answer to this question hinges on the costs of using escape clauses and retaining the overall agreement compared with not using them and abrogating the agreement.

Our second question concerns the effects of different institutional designs. If escape clauses allow states more flexibility in meeting their obligations, what impact does this have on their compliance with the agreement? What are the consequences

We thank the editors of the Rational Design project for their efforts: Barbara Koremenos, Charles Lipson, and Duncan Snidal. We are also grateful to two anonymous reviewers, and to James Morrow, Robert Pahre, Lisa Martin, Chris Canavan, and the editors of *IO,* David Lake and Peter Gourevitch, for many helpful comments and suggestions.
1. Hoekman and Kostecki 1995, 161.

International Organization 55, 4, Autumn 2001, pp. 829–857

of increased flexibility for institutional performance: is cooperation enhanced, and is it more durable?

An escape clause is any provision of an international agreement that allows a country to suspend the concessions it previously negotiated without violating or abrogating the terms of the agreement. Escape clauses are a prominent feature of many international agreements and are included in most trade agreements. Not all international agreements, however, have such clauses; for instance, some international arms control agreements, such as the Strategic Arms Limitations Treaty (SALT) agreements, do not contain such escape mechanisms. Most trade agreements do contain them, but their nature often differs across agreements and they are usually vigorously contested in negotiations. For example, in both the North American Free Trade Agreement (NAFTA) and the General Agreement on Tariffs and Trade (GATT) Uruguay Round negotiations, antidumping and countervailing duty laws were critical issues that impeded agreement among the countries. Since its inception in the 1940s GATT (and the subsequent World Trade Organization, WTO) has slowly built an arsenal of safeguard mechanisms to protect states from import pressures in the wake of extensive trade liberalizing agreements. These include an escape clause, countervailing duty penalties, antidumping statutes, and a national security exception. For each of these, GATT (now the WTO) specifies the conditions under which a government can grant relief to an industry from import competition, and industries then have the option of choosing which mechanism to file their complaints under. In each of the GATT negotiating rounds, the inclusion and/or modification of these different laws have been the subject of intense debate among the signatories.

Many have noted that these different clauses can be substitutes for one another. Bernard Hoekman and Michael Leidy and Wendy Hansen and Thomas Prusa suggest that countervailing duty and antidumping laws are really "a poor man's" escape clause.[2] Antidumping and countervailing duty complaints allege that exporting countries are playing unfairly and thus the harmed country avoids the payment of compensation that GATT requires on use of the escape clause. They are thus means for industries to limit import competition on the cheap: they enable a country to abrogate some portion of its treaty obligations under GATT and to pay a lower penalty than were they to use the escape clause. These and other measures, such as the infant industry and balance-of-payments exemptions in GATT, are all designed by governments to reduce domestic pressures to withdraw from the entire agreement when protectionist pressures grow at home. While these laws are generally seen as substitutes, they do differ substantially in the costs they impose on the countries using them. Usually antidumping and countervailing duty clauses are seen as less costly to use than traditional escape clauses. This type of variation is important, as we will explain later.

---

2. See Hoekman and Leidy 1989; and Hansen and Prusa 1995.

We make three central claims here. First, escape clauses are an efficient equilibrium under conditions of domestic uncertainty. When political leaders cannot foresee the extent of future domestic demands for more protection at home (and/or more open markets abroad), such clauses provide the flexibility that allows them to accept an international agreement liberalizing trade. A more general statement is that the greater the uncertainty that political leaders face about their ability to maintain domestic compliance with international agreements in the future, the more likely agreements are to contain escape clauses. In issue-areas where the impact of high uncertainty about domestic pressures to comply is less, governments are less likely to desire such safeguard measures.

We show that the use of an escape clause, a flexibility-enhancing device, in institutional design increases institutional effectiveness whenever there is domestic political uncertainty. We offer support therefore to Rational Design conjecture F1, FLEXIBILITY increases with UNCERTAINTY, as developed in the framing article by Barbara Koremenos, Charles Lipson, and Duncan Snidal.[3] This conjecture suggests that uncertainty about the state of the world rationally leads to the creation of institutional flexibility. Note that flexibility in this context refers to the ability to adapt and respond to unanticipated events within the context of a well-designed institutional system. The system itself is not subject to renewed bargaining. Alternative flexibility-enhancing devices are, of course, available: sunset provisions or anticipated renegotiations are often used. But we think that these mechanisms are even more costly and hence less used than the ones we examine.

Second, for escape clauses to be useful and efficient they must impose some kind of cost on their use. That is, countries that invoke an escape clause must pay some cost for doing so, or else they will invoke it all the time, thus vitiating the agreement. Paying this cost signals their intention to comply in the future. But the different costs of alternative escape clause measures will affect the frequency of their use. Less costly measures will be used more often. If governments understand this, they should rationally prefer the set of escape clauses that best matches the extent of protectionist pressure they expect to experience from domestic interests. Thus we anticipate that the architects of international agreements will design such agreements so that the costs of the escape clauses they most desire are balanced by the benefits of future cooperation. Variation in the nature of the escape clause mechanism, primarily its cost, is thus an important feature of different agreements. If states rationally design such agreements, we should expect such variation to be an important element of the bargaining process.

The exact size of the cost will depend on the gains from cooperation relative to the benefits of defection; they are a function of what might be called the "preference configuration." The costliness of the escape clause is crucial to the effectiveness of the escape clause regime, and the preferences of the domestic players in the negotiating countries will affect the optimal choice of this cost. We claim, therefore,

---

3. Koremenos, Lipson, and Snidal, this volume.

that domestic preferences and institutions matter in the design of optimal international institutions.

Third, we argue that including escape clauses makes initial agreements easier to reach. Their flexibility allows states to be reassured about the division of the long-term gains from the agreement. Indeed we claim that without escape clauses of some sort many trade agreements would never be politically viable for countries. This fits with Rational Design conjecture F2, FLEXIBILITY increases with DISTRIBUTION problems; that is, increased flexibility (necessary to deal with the uncertainty about future states of the world) lessens the problems of bargaining and distribution that may plague an initial agreement.

We use a formal model to examine why countries might desire escape clauses and how this type of institutional design might affect an institution's performance. We examine a two-stage game: an international bargaining game where an agreement over the design of the institution is adopted and then a repeated trade (sub)game where the countries set their trade policies, given the design of the institution.

Escape Clauses and Political Uncertainty

The key factor that renders escape clauses desirable is the presence of uncertainty. In each period the political pressure for protection at home (and/or for more open markets abroad) is subject to a shock. Some unanticipated change in the economy or political system produces a bigger or smaller value for the impact of domestic firms' demands for protection. We model this shock very generally; it is any exogenous and unanticipated change in the state of the world (such as price or supply changes, technological change, political change) that affects domestic firms' demand for, or ability to lobby for, protection of their markets.

Although we model uncertainty as a political shock, we recognize that the strength of the political support for protection (or for liberalization) is determined by many factors, for instance,

- unexpected price or supply shifts that intensify international competition may induce enhanced lobbying efforts by domestic firms;

- changes in production technology that reduce employment in a sector, and hence its political clout;

- changes in a country's political institutions or preferences: tastes might change in favor of enhanced protection, or campaign finance reforms might alter the political pressure that firms can apply;

- changes in domestic political cleavages or alignments that might make a previously pivotal sector less influential in domestic politics, implying that protection is politically less expedient.[4]

---

4. For analytical tractability, we assume in the model that the shocks in each country are independent. Price shocks—for example, an unexpected rise in the price of an input or the emergence of a

We assume that in the current period leaders in each country know their own domestic political situation but that both sets of leaders are equally uninformed about the degree of political pressure at home and abroad in all future periods. We show that uncertainty about the state of the world creates conditions favorable for the use of escape clauses. That each country has limited knowledge about the domestic politics of the others is central to our argument; furthermore, this uncertainty has a lasting impact because each country faces new shocks in each period that determine the amount of political pressure that domestic groups exert.[5]

The two stages of the model combine the two critical elements of cooperation theory: bargaining and enforcement. The trade game played by the countries is a modified version of a repeated Prisoners' Dilemma. In this second stage enforcement is critical; the temptation to cheat makes cooperation very difficult, especially in international politics where third-party enforcement is absent. Countries must be punished if they protect, but sometimes because of domestic shocks leaders will be forced to protect when they would otherwise want to maintain the agreement—or, forced to undertake "involuntary defection," as Robert Putnam calls it.[6] Such equilibria to the Prisoners' Dilemma are often supported by the requirement that each player automatically punish the other when cheating is observed, and continue to punish forever or for long periods of time. If their discount value is high enough and punishment is sure and strong enough, then they will resist the temptation to cheat. This set of results has often been used to argue that cooperation in international politics is possible, if not frequent.[7] But such punishment often implies abrogation of the entire agreement.

George Downs and David Rocke show that shorter punishment periods can also support cooperation.[8] They identify domestic political uncertainty as an explanation for "imperfect" treaties, where imperfection is measured relative to the "most cooperative" agreement possible. Using a repeated Prisoners' Dilemma game with trigger strategies, where defections are punished by the other player for a limited number of periods, they argue that domestic political uncertainty leads to agreements with shorter punishment periods and therefore less cooperation. But what if

---

third-country competitor—that affect the lobbying strength of firms at home may simultaneously affect the lobbying strength of firms abroad. Allowing for correlated shocks would not alter our central result; agreements with escape clauses allow countries the option to temporarily exit when political pressure is unexpectedly intense, and when this defection is tolerated by the trading partners in the interests of the system's stability.

5. Uncertainty here concerns the "future state of the world": the configuration of political pressure in future periods is not known with certainty. Uncertainty regarding the preferences of key domestic players is another possibility, one we consider elsewhere in an investigation of the effect of elections on the design of international agreements (Milner and Rosendorff 1997). Alternatively, the agreement itself is too complex (or time is too valuable) for the domestic policymakers to fully understand the consequences of its passage, and policymakers therefore rely on the information provided by lobbies and other interested third parties. Milner and Rosendorff 1996.

6. Putnam 1988.

7. See Axelrod 1984; and Oye 1986.

8. Downs and Rocke 1995.

countries every now and then face intense pressure to cheat yet do not want to spark retaliation and a breakdown in cooperation? Can an alternative institutional structure be devised to maintain a cooperative agreement, even in these periods of high political pressure to protect? In the presence of exogenous shocks, international institutions may be much better served by allowing countries to make temporary, ad hoc use of escape clauses that permit them to break the rules for a short period and pay a cost to do so. There is no retaliation. The defection is tolerated, exactly because the other side may wish to use the same instrument in the future.[9] Cooperation, as we demonstrate, is deeper and more likely, and international trade institutions are more durable, with escape clauses than without them. In the choice between rules and discretion, therefore, rules with costly discretion may be better than no discretion when the future holds unexpected, unpleasant surprises. Our first key result is that greater domestic uncertainty makes the inclusion of escape clauses more likely in international agreements.

Many trade agreements include such escape clauses; indeed, all GATT agreements have at least one type, if not several types, of such escape clauses. Moreover, these alternative escape mechanisms have different costs for their use. In general a country appealing to an escape clause is allowed, under the institution's rules, to protect the affected industry for the duration of that period, as long as it (in effect) voluntarily and publicly incurs some penalty. This voluntary penalty is consistent with the reciprocity norm of GATT, which requires a country that applies a temporary trade barrier to reciprocate by lowering some other barrier elsewhere so that its trading partners are unaffected by the action or to face equivalent trade barriers by its partners.

But this penalty may take any number of forms. For example, countries using GATT's escape clause must negotiate compensation with the affected exporter or face equivalent retaliation from the exporter. For other safeguard measures, the cost is often smaller and less explicit. Sometimes there is a presumption that a country invoking the escape clause will be forced to devise and implement a plan of structural adjustment for the affected industry; such plans have costs, both economic and political. Moreover, the costs of filing an escape clause, antidumping, or countervailing duty complaint are also part of the cost that the import-competing firms must face. For many of these the technical and legal requirements for producing evidence of injury are sufficiently high to merit consideration. In any case each safeguard mechanism entails some costs when it is used, although these costs do differ in important ways.

After invoking the safeguard, in the next period the country returns to the cooperative regime, having preserved its reputation as a cooperator. Moreover, no supranational enforcement agency must force the country to pay this penalty; the

---

9. Very little retaliation for treaty violations is actually observed. Under current WTO rules, any punishment can only come after a finding by the dispute settlement procedure at the WTO, and frequently the dispute is "settled" before punishments are applied. The pre-Uruguay Round rules in fact made findings of allowable retaliation quite rare. Rosendorff 1999.

country (and everyone else) realizes that paying the penalty will preserve its credibility in the future. The institution serves as a verification agency, much as the Law Merchants institution does;[10] it monitors whether defection occurs with a penalty.

Low Costs, Frequent Escape

The cost a state must pay for using the escape clause is of great importance. If the penalty is set at an appropriate level, a country may temporarily use the escape clause and then return to the cooperative path. If the cost is too high, countries will abandon the institution and defect when they experience a severe shock. If the cost is too low, there is repeated recourse to the escape clause, and the agreement enforces little actual cooperation over time. Escape clauses will thus be used more often when their costs of use are lower. This implies that policymakers should attempt to design efficient escape clauses; they should act so that the incentive to exercise relief is balanced with the gains from cooperation. Variations in the costs of different escape clause mechanisms will be an important feature of the rational design of international trade agreements.

The first stage in the model focuses on bargaining over the size of the escape clause penalty. When will countries be able to agree to such escape clauses? In particular, when will they be able to agree to impose a cost on themselves for using the escape clause, and when will this be credible? Furthermore, when will they pick a level of costs so that the optimal degree of cooperation is induced? To address this issue, we model a first stage before the trade barrier setting game is played. In this stage the countries bargain with each other over the penalty they are willing to pay for using an escape clause. One can think of this as bargaining over the nature of the trade agreement itself. Thus making an agreement means agreeing on a value for the penalties that all countries will (voluntarily) pay to use an escape clause. We show that the countries negotiate an optimal penalty, one that balances the need for as much cooperation as possible, while allowing some flexibility in times of domestic political pressure. Such a penalty must not be too high or it will eliminate any flexibility and make the system unstable; but it must also not be too low or it will render "cooperation" ineffective. In effect international institutions that are able to adopt an escape clause should do so in ways that generate more durable and stable cooperative regimes.

The escape clause itself is endogenous to the model: choosing a prohibitive cost for invoking the escape clause is equivalent to ruling it out of the institutional structure. Yet in equilibrium we show that the negotiating parties adopt an escape clause with moderate costs. While such bargaining can have distributional consequences, we study only the symmetric case here where the two countries are identical; nevertheless, our model combines both bargaining and enforcement problems.

10. Milgrom, North, and Weingast 1990.

Agreements Are Easier to Conclude

Our model also touches on a point made by James Fearon. He uses a model somewhat like ours, which combines a bargaining game in the first stage and a Prisoners' Dilemma game in the second. He points out that "as the shadow of the future lengthens, both states choose tougher and tougher bargaining strategies on average, implying longer and longer delay till cooperation begins."[11] That is, as the possibility of durable cooperation grows in the second-stage Prisoners' Dilemma, the possibility of stalemate in the first-stage bargaining game rises. Hence, making agreements easier to enforce may make them harder to initially conclude, since the distribution of gains set initially will be so important and fixed throughout the future.

Here, the inclusion of escape clauses may reduce this dynamic. That is, if in future periods players can deviate, pay a penalty, and return to cooperation, this escape clause may mean that their initial distributional bargaining is not so important. The pattern of distributive gains agreed upon today may be altered in the future through the use of the escape clause. Therefore, inclusion of an escape clause may have another benefit: it may make agreements easier to conclude initially! We provide some evidence that certain agreements would not have been politically feasible had they not included escape clauses. This is our third result.

The Model

Consider a world with two countries, home and foreign, that trade a single good. The good is produced by a single firm in each country, and hence there is reciprocal dumping or cross hauling. The profits of the home firm depend therefore on the trade barriers at home, t, which raise the domestic price and are good for profits, and the trade barriers abroad, t*, which reduce exports and induce a fall in the home firm's profits; hence, firm profits are a function of both, that is, $\Pi(t, t^*)$.

Government Objectives

A government's utility depends on the sum of consumer surplus, $CS(t)$, which falls with t, producer surplus or profits, $\Pi(t, t^*)$, which rise with t and fall with t*, and tariff revenues, $tM(t)$, which first rise and then fall with the level of the barriers. Let $\gamma > 0$ denote the weight that a government attaches to the firm's profits. The home government's (one period) utility function then is $W(t, t^*) = CS(t) + \gamma\Pi(t, t^*) + tM(t)$. Similarly, for the foreign government, $W^*(t, t^*) = CS^*(t^*) + g\Pi^*(t^*, t) + t^*M^*(t^*)$, where $g > 0$ is the weight of the foreign firm's profits in its government's utility function.

This objective function is "politically realistic" in Richard Baldwin's sense; that is, governments desire to maximize consumer surplus because it helps them recruit

11. Fearon 1998, 282.

votes, but they also value firm profits for the contributions and political support that firms can give them.[12] This utility function is also consistent with the objective function used in Gene M. Grossman and Elhanan Helpman's model of lobbying and campaign contributions.[13] Here, governments are concerned with their reelection and hence have political economy motivations.

In the following sections we use these utility functions to define the payoffs for each outcome that the governments can arrive at in a simple noncooperative trade barrier setting game. These payoffs resemble those of a standard Prisoners' Dilemma: mutual cooperation, which we call the Pareto optimal outcome; mutual defection, or the Nash equilibrium; unilateral defection; and the sucker's payoff. This defines what happens in the second-stage trade game.

Political Uncertainty

Policymakers seeking to maximize their political support choose to adopt trade policies that redistribute revenue among politically salient groups. Here policymakers are balancing the interests of consumers with those of the firms. In each period the political pressure exerted by firms is subject to a shock. Some unanticipated change in the economy or political system allows firms to exert a larger or smaller amount of political pressure. We have deliberately chosen to be vague about the specific nature of this shock—for example, whether it is political or economic. This gives our model greater explanatory breadth. Any exogenous and unexpected change that alters the impact of domestic firms on the demand for protection is relevant. In some periods, firms' political influence will take on a "low" value; in others, however, the pressure applied by the domestic industry is "abnormally" high. The same is true in the other country: its leaders have the same objective function and face the same forms of political pressure. Notice that the firms can be either import competitors or exporters. As defined here, a period of unusually "high" political pressure applied by the firms means a heightened demand by the firms for higher trade barriers at home and lower ones abroad.[14]

In any period, γ and g are stochastic and are independently and identically distributed with distribution Φ: this captures the notion that ex ante policymakers are not fully informed about the degree of political pressure to protect local industry that they might experience in any future period. At home, some unanticipated change in the economy or political system creates a larger or smaller value of γ. The same is true in the other country: its leaders have the same objective function and face the same forms of political pressure. For simplicity, we assume that in the

12. Baldwin 1987.
13. Grossman and Helpman 1994.
14. The reader may be tempted to draw a contrast with Milner 1988. There export interests organize in favor of lower domestic tariffs. That is an equilibrium outcome, however, not a statement about preferences. In that model, exporters simply prefer lower tariffs abroad, and adopt, for strategic reasons, political action domestically so that tariff concessions at home can be traded for concessions abroad. A similar dynamic is at work here: firms are willing to trade lower tariffs at home for lower tariffs abroad.

current period each country knows its own state of politics but not the other's, and that both are equally uninformed about the values of γ and g (at home and abroad) in all future periods. That each country has limited knowledge about the domestic politics of the other is central to our argument; furthermore, this uncertainty has a lasting impact because each country faces new shocks in each period that determine the amount of political pressure domestic groups exert. Uncertainty about the state of the world in the other country creates conditions favorable for the use of escape clauses.

While we model the political uncertainty as exogenous (and hence as uncertainty about the state of the world), national preferences are actually an aggregation of the preferences of the domestic groups. Individual preferences per se do not change, but national ones might as the intensity of firms' demands change. Each player thus is uncertain about how influential various domestic groups are likely to be in the future when policymakers choose their trade policies. In the future each government may be easily capturable by the protectionist lobby, or it may be able to stand firm in the face of protectionist pressure. Neither player knows beforehand which of these types the other is likely to be.

Without an Escape Clause: Prisoners' Dilemma Game

Under Political Optimum (Cooperation)

First, we find the pair of trade barriers that maximize the sum of the two governments' utility functions. If γ and g are known, we can define the cooperative solution:

$$(t^P(\gamma, g), t^{*P}(\gamma, g)) = \arg\max_{(t, t^*)} (W(t, t^*) + W^*(t, t^*)).$$

Denote the utility of each of the governments under the political optimum as

$$P(\gamma, g) = W(t^P, t^{*P}) \quad \text{and} \quad P^*(\gamma, g) = W^*(t^P, t^{*P}).$$

Under Nash Equilibrium

Under the Nash equilibrium (NE), each player chooses a level of domestic trade barriers as a best response to the behavior of the opponent. In any period in which γ and g are known we can solve for the Nash equilibrium in trade barriers for that period. Let

$$t(t^*) = \arg\max_t W(t, t^*) \quad \text{and} \quad t^*(t) = \arg\max_{t^*} W^*(t, t^*).$$

Solving these simultaneously leads to the Nash pair of trade barriers (t^N, t^{*N}). Denote home government's utility under the Nash equilibrium as

$$N(\gamma, g) = W(t^N(\gamma, g), t^{*N}(\gamma, g)).$$

Defection

Home's optimal defection (when foreign cooperates) is

$$t^D = \arg \max_t W(t, t^{*P}),$$

and its utility under the optimal defection is

$$D(\gamma, g) = W(t^D(\gamma, g), t^{*P}(\gamma, g)).$$

If instead foreign defects and home cooperates, home receives the sucker's payoff:

$$S(\gamma, g) = W(t^P(\gamma, g), t^{*D}(\gamma, g)).$$

Prisoners' Dilemma

So we have $D(\gamma, g) > P(\gamma, g) > N(\gamma, g) > S(\gamma, g)$, a Prisoners' Dilemma game as represented by the standard 2×2 normal form matrix:

	P*	D*	
P	$P(\gamma, g), P^*(\gamma, g)$	$S(\gamma, g), D^*(\gamma, g)$	(1)
D	$D(\gamma, g), S^*(\gamma, g)$	$N(\gamma, g), N^*(\gamma, g)$	

To simplify the notation, $D(\gamma, g) - P(\gamma, g) \equiv B(\gamma, g)$. Each player is susceptible to political pressure both to protect against foreign imports and to open export markets; in the future both are equally unsure how much pressure each will experience. Hence, home must make its best guess about the value of raising domestic trade barriers (defecting) in any period by taking expectations over g; we denote this best guess by

$$B(\gamma) = \int_g B(\gamma, g) d\Phi.$$

Similarly, both players are completely uninformed about the possible draws of γ and g in any future period. Hence, the values of $P(\gamma, g)$ and $N(\gamma, g)$ are unknown for future periods. Expectations can be formed however; denote

$$P = \int_\gamma \int_g P(\gamma, g)d\Phi d\Phi \quad \text{and} \quad N = \int_\gamma \int_g N(\gamma, g)d\Phi d\Phi.$$

The Prisoners' Dilemma in Matrix (1) is played in the presence of uncertainty; as in the standard Prisoners' Dilemma; however, a cooperative equilibrium in trigger strategies can be supported by a large enough discount rate.

LEMMA 1. A pair of grim trigger strategies (cooperate until a defection is observed, then punish forever) is an equilibrium to the game in Matrix (1) for all

$$\delta > \frac{\max_\gamma B(\gamma)}{P - N + \max_\gamma B(\gamma)}.$$

The (expected) incentive to defect in any period with draw γ is $B(\gamma)$. The largest value that $B(\gamma)$ can take is $\max_\gamma B(\gamma)$. If this maximal incentive to defect is less than the present discounted expected value of future punishments $[\delta/(1 - \delta)] \times (P - N)$, cooperation is possible.

Escape Clause Game

In any period of the Escape Clause game, a player can take the Pareto action, that is, play P as in the Prisoners' Dilemma above; or it can exercise an escape clause EC at cost k; or it can defect D as before. The stage game is now 3 by 3:

	P*	EC*	D*
P	$P(\gamma, g), P^*(\gamma, g)$	$S(\gamma, g), D^*(\gamma, g) - k$	$S(\gamma, g), D^*(\gamma, g)$
EC	$D(\gamma, g) - k, S^*(\gamma, g)$	$N(\gamma, g) - k, N^*(\gamma, g) - k$	$N(\gamma, g) - k, N^*(\gamma, g)$
D	$D(\gamma, g), S^*(\gamma, g)$	$N(\gamma, g), N^*(\gamma, g) - k$	$N(\gamma, g), N^*(\gamma, g)$

Define "cooperation" as the play in any period of P or EC. Define defection as the play of D in any period.

DEFINITION 1. An escape clause strategy (for home) is a strategy in which home plays D if D* has been played in any period in the past, otherwise home plays P if $B(\gamma) < k$, plays EC if $k \leq B(\gamma) \leq K$, and plays D if $B(\gamma), k > K$ for some K to be defined later.

The extent of the exogenous shock determines the gains to be had from defection in this period; these gains rise with the political pressure that the firms can bring to bear; that is, $B'(\gamma) > 0$. If these gains are small ($B(\gamma) < k$), the government sticks to its Pareto optimal strategy, play P. If the penalty is not too onerous ($k < K$), moderate gains from defection ($k \leq B(\gamma) \leq K$) cause the government to appeal to the escape clause, EC. If the gains from defection are very large and the escape clause penalty is large, that is, $B(\gamma)$, k > K, the government ceases to cooperate entirely. A useful way to summarize the government's strategy is to say that the government cooperates (by playing P or EC) when $\min(B(\gamma), k) \leq K$, and defects otherwise.

The critical value of K is determined as the cost that would make any player of this game exactly indifferent between exercising the escape clause and then returning to the cooperative regime, and defecting and exiting the system forever. It is intuitive, therefore, that if the costs of the escape clause and the gains from defection are large, the government will cease to cooperate entirely.

PROPOSITION 1. A pair of escape clause strategies is a Nash equilibrium. All the proofs are in the appendix. Notice that in the standard Prisoners' Dilemma game, Matrix (1), cooperation is sustained only for discount factors that are large enough; that is,

$$\delta > \frac{\max_\gamma B(\gamma)}{P - N + \max_\gamma B(\gamma)}.$$

However, in the escape clause equilibrium here cooperation can be sustained for any value of the discount factor as long as k $\leq$ K. Recall that at cost K, any player is indifferent between the escape clause and defection; if δ falls, future cooperation is valued less, and the critical K falls. Hence, the cost of exercising the escape clause must fall as well. So a low discount factor can still produce cooperation. Cooperation now is more flexible in that temporary defection is now possible—unlike in the standard Prisoners' Dilemma, where no defection of any kind was permissible.

One particularly appealing aspect of this equilibrium in the context of institutional design is that the penalty associated with the escape clause is self-enforcing. Any country that wishes to exercise the escape clause in an agreement must visibly penalize itself; no external enforcement agency is required. For a defector to avoid being punished, it must pay the penalty k in a visible way. The international institution is an information provider rather than an enforcer here: it is entrusted as an agent of the contracting states to check that each country that adopts an escape clause pays a penalty and to inform the others of this. Only when penalties are not paid do the states need to punish each other.

COROLLARY 1. There exists an agreement with an escape clause that Pareto dominates one without it in the presence of political uncertainty.

In any period in which the escape clause is exercised, there is no "true" cooperation: the escaping player is defecting, and the defection is being tolerated. Hence, the value of the game under an escape clause equilibrium will decrease as the use of the escape clause increases. If the escape clause is used infrequently or not at all, there is more "true" cooperation; however, domestic political uncertainty is likely to lead at some point to a complete breakdown of the regime, and then the punishment phase will be applied forever. This corollary establishes that either there is an escape clause with a level of cost that induces enough cooperation and no breakdown such that the value of the game in an escape clause equilibrium is larger than that of the same game without an escape clause, or the cost of escape is too high and the escape clause equilibrium is the same as the grim-trigger equilibrium of the standard Prisoners' Dilemma. Hence, there is an escape clause cost such that the escape clause equilibrium Pareto dominates (perhaps weakly) the grim-trigger equilibrium of the game without an escape clause.

Notice that the more salient the domestic political uncertainty, or the greater its likely impact on electoral returns, the more likely are political leaders to view an escape clause as an essential element of any agreement.

Uncertainty and Escape Clauses: Implications and Some Evidence

As already noted, most international trade agreements include at least one form of escape clause, and many include several. Our claim is that this prevalence of escape clauses is due to the high levels of domestic uncertainty that surround trade politics. We predict that domestic uncertainty affects the use of escape clauses. Greater domestic uncertainty, or situations where political leaders are more sensitive to unanticipated changes in political pressures, should be associated with more reliance on escape mechanisms. An interesting test of our model would be to identify those political institutions that magnify the effect of unanticipated shocks and see whether countries with these types of institutions are more likely to devise and use escape clauses in their trade relations. Another test would be to deduce which issue-areas are more subject to unanticipated domestic shocks and see if they are more likely to have escape clauses associated with them. Such an exercise, unfortunately, is beyond the scope of this article. However, we can suggest two facts about escape clauses that accord with our theory: certain countries that arguably are more sensitive to domestic pressures are the main proponents and users of escape mechanisms, and certain issue-areas seem more likely to have escape clauses than others due to their greater levels of uncertainty.

Escape clauses in trade policy exist both at the national and the international level. Interestingly, international usage has often copied domestic laws. It is notable that several countries dominate the international use of all forms of escape clauses and that all of these countries have tended to use escape clauses domestically first. The main countries using GATT (now WTO) antidumping, countervailing duty, and safeguard clauses are the same ones that earlier developed a battery of domestic laws to use these trade remedies. By and large, the United States, Canada, the European Union, and Australia are the main users of these clauses.[15] These are the same countries that initially built domestic trade laws around such escape mecha-

15. Trebilcock and Howse 1995.

nisms. The first instance of an antidumping law was Canada's 1904 dumping regime.[16] In 1947 the United States instituted the world's first safeguard clause.[17] And the United States and Canada were both the early designers of countervailing duty laws. This suggests that the need for escape clauses may be associated with democracies. It may well be that unanticipated shocks are far more damaging for political leaders in democracies than in nondemocracies. These shocks may be more likely to get them ejected from office as the negatively affected groups mobilize against the incumbents in election periods. If so, this would account for why these types of countries are more likely to have such national escape clause provisions and why they are also more likely to be proponents of these provisions at the international level.

In the realm of safeguard clauses, for example, it is the United States that has the oldest domestic laws and has been the most vocal proponent of them in international trade negotiations. U.S. trade law puts the escape clause into practice through Section 201 of the Trade Act of 1974. Following a petition—from the industry or from government (the president, the U.S. Trade Representative, or Congress, among others)—the U.S. International Trade Commission (ITC) conducts an investigation to evaluate whether imports have threatened to injure or been a substantial cause of injury to the domestic industry. After an affirmative finding by the ITC, the president may grant protection for up to five years, with the possibility of extending it for another three.[18] This practice has been followed closely in GATT, largely at the United States' insistence. Article XIX of GATT permits a member to escape from its obligations not to raise trade barriers when one of its industries is suffering an economic downturn and is experiencing "serious injury."

In the realm of antidumping and countervailing duties the same association is apparent. U.S. and Canadian laws have preceded international ones and set the pattern for them. Article VI of GATT, and the Second Antidumping Code of the Tokyo Round, which define practice in antidumping and countervailing duty law, allows member states to apply duties when imports are sold at "less than fair value," following U.S. practice. Ronald A. Cass and his colleagues describe the U.S. antidumping laws (and those of other countries) as "miniature escape clauses," in that the antidumping code extends protection to smaller cases on which agreement would be impossible ex ante.[19] Similarly, the U.S. countervailing duty code (which is consistent with GATT's Art. VI) allows member states to apply a countervailing duty when a subsidy is being provided to the foreign industry.[20] Other forms of the

16. Ibid., 172.
17. Ibid., 227.
18. Between 1975 and 1990, ninety-two cases under sec. 201 were initiated, of which thirteen industries received relief and seven more received trade adjustment assistance. High profile cases included color televisions in 1982, which received protection on $1,543 million of imports that year, and nonrubber footwear, $2,480 million in 1981. Hufbauer and Rosen 1986.
19. Cass et al. 1997, 24.
20. Between 1994 and 1999 alone, 77 antidumping petitions were filed in the United States. Stern 1997. Worldwide, the antidumping clause has been invoked over two thousand times since 1970.

escape clause appear throughout GATT. Balance-of-payments exceptions (Art. XVIII and XII), infant-industry protection (Art. XVIII), and tariff renegotiation (Art. XXVII) allow temporary escape from a member's obligations under the agreement.

Trade is, of course, an area where governments are likely to face strong domestic pressures for import protection from time to time. When imports surge or when economic conditions facing an industry turn downward, pressures for protection may suddenly appear. Unfortunately, governments may not be able to anticipate perfectly the magnitude of such pressures or their origin. Cass and his colleagues claim that these safeguard mechanisms allow "protectionist sentiment to hold sway" when political pressures are large.[21] Democratic leaders may be especially vulnerable to such unexpected changes, and hence may seek escape clause protection more than leaders in other systems. The greater impact of uncertainty in democratic systems may make their leaders particularly desirous of escape clause mechanisms in trade.

The need for escape clauses may also vary by issue-area. It is widely believed that trade is an area where governments face domestic uncertainty that has significant costs; such international economic exchanges are susceptible to swift changes due to price or supply shocks, technological change, and/or foreign government policy changes. The same is true in the macroeconomic area. Fixed exchange-rate systems may be especially vulnerable to unanticipated domestic pressures to devalue. High uncertainty over the timing and magnitude of these domestic pressures seems likely. Thus we see escape clause measures in many fixed exchange-rate agreements. In the Bretton Woods regime, for example, the simple rule was the requirement to maintain fixed exchange rates. But a country could devalue in the event of "fundamental disequilibrium," a vague phrase allowing escape from the simple rule since even economists were unable to agree on what balance-of-payments equilibrium meant. The regime did not dictate in advance the size of the devaluation. Instead, it required a member state to seek approval from the International Monetary Fund (at least for an exchange-rate realignment of more than 10 percent).

The European Payments Union, the postwar multilateral trade-deficit clearing system, gave signatories the right to suspend liberalization measures in the event of serious economic disturbance or if liberalization was too disruptive.[22] Similarly, Europe's Exchange Rate Mechanism required member states to maintain bilateral exchange rates within clearly demarcated target zones, but did allow for realignments of the parity. While the architects of the mechanism recognized the need for occasional parity realignments, they did not specify exactly when such realignments should take place. Instead, realignments were required to be negotiated among all

---

21. Cass et al. 1997, 24.
22. Oatley, this volume.

members.[23] In all three cases, escape clause mechanisms were included in the design of these institutions to deal with situations where policymakers face high levels of domestic uncertainty over the pressures that will arise for them to abrogate any international agreement they sign.

Notice that under all three regimes (Bretton Woods, European Payments Union, and Exchange Rate Mechanism), devaluation (the use of an escape clause) was not without cost. Devaluation was permitted only in concert with other measures designed to bring core macroeconomic aggregates back to within "acceptable" levels. Devaluation was therefore frequently associated with fiscal and monetary contraction and policy liberalization and reform, all of which come at a domestic political price.

In some noneconomic issues, uncertainty may be consequential enough so that temporary noncooperation may arise as an equilibrium in isolated cases. James D. Morrow, for instance, argues that prisoners of war treaties are often robust in the face of frequent battlefield violations of the rules of war in an environment where monitoring and acquiring accurate information are very costly.[24] Moreover, similar to our model, violations must be policed by the violators themselves, and punishment (in the case of gross violation) must be publicly implemented for cooperation to be sustained. But in other noneconomic areas, it seems that domestic uncertainty is less pervasive and consequential. In an area like arms control, the public and interest groups tend to be less organized and involved. The most important constituent of these agreements is often the military, which may take part in the negotiations and hence shape them directly. The impact of unexpected changes in this area may be less for political leaders than in areas like trade. Notably, arms control agreements have frequently not included escape clauses. The Antiballistic Missile Treaty, most of the SALT agreements, and the Intermediate-range Nuclear Forces treaties do not contain escape mechanisms; some of these allow countries to withdraw with certain notification provisions, and some have definite time limits, but none seem to contain clauses that allow temporary abrogation of the agreements. This suggests, if our claims are correct, that arms control is an area where domestic uncertainty is less important for leaders. Unexpected shocks that greatly increase pressures for leaders to cheat on the agreement (or pay substantial domestic costs), are less common in this area. Hence, one would not expect states to be as concerned about including escape clauses in these agreements as they are in trade and the monetary area. Where domestic uncertainty is less consequential for leaders, escape clauses will be less important and hence less used. We return to this question later.

The Optimal Penalty: Institutional Design

If the cost of exercising the escape clause is too high, the gains from temporary defection and preserving one's cooperative reputation are more than likely out-

23. Canavan and Rosendorff 1997.
24. Morrow, this volume.

weighed by the penalty associated with the use of the escape clause. In such circumstances, the cost of exercising the escape clause is too high, that is, $k > K$. Then, in any period where a large shock is experienced, the escape clause option is too expensive, and the system breaks down entirely. As a corollary to Proposition 1 above, the same equilibrium strategies in an environment where $k > K$ lead to an equilibrium path in which P is played until $B(\gamma) > k$, in which case home plays D and the system beaks down. Over time, if the escape clause is too costly, the system breaks down with probability 1 (as long as the discount rate is not too high).

But this raises a question of implementation: when will countries be able to agree to escape clauses that do not lead to the breakdown of all cooperation? In particular, when will they be able to agree to impose a cost on themselves for using the escape clause, and when will this be credible? Furthermore, will they pick the optimal level of costs so that the optimal degree of cooperation is induced? To address this issue we model a first stage before the trade barrier setting game is played. In this stage the countries bargain with each other over the penalty they are willing to pay for invoking an escape clause. One can think of this as bargaining over the nature of the trade agreement itself. Much of the bargaining in trade talks concerns escape clauses and exceptions to the agreement rather than the general amount of liberalization. Thus making an agreement means agreeing on a value for the penalties that all countries will (voluntarily) pay to use an escape clause.

Therefore, we add a pregame negotiation phase over the size of k. We consider the symmetric case where both countries are identical. Each wants to choose a penalty that maximizes the value of playing the game. But the value of the game is the same for both players (they are identical), so they agree merely to the level of k that maximizes the value of the game.

PROPOSITION 2. Let V_C and V_C^* be the present discounted expected value of the escape clause equilibrium for home and foreign, respectively. Then both countries agree on $k^* = \arg \max_k (V_C + V_C^*)$ when $k^* \leq K$; they agree on K otherwise.

Larger distributional questions arise when the assumption of symmetry is relaxed. If one country has a greater capacity to absorb exogenous shocks, or alternatively is immune to capture by political interests, this country would prefer a larger value of k; a country that is easily captured by special interests will instead prefer a smaller k. The outcome of this bargaining among asymmetric countries will have important consequences for the international institutions, but it is a subject that we leave for future consideration.

On the Design of Escape Clauses

We have established that escape clause equilibria exist, and that for the escape clause to be exercised in equilibrium, it cannot be too expensive to adopt. This also points to an important trade-off in the design of international institutions between rigidity and stability. As the system becomes too rigid—or as k rises—it becomes

TABLE 1. The trade-off between rigidity and stability

Size of penalty	Regime stability	Regime rigidity
$k \leq K$	High	Low
$k > K$	Low	High

increasingly unstable (Table 1). At low values of k, the system is stable. For any value of the shocks, either pure cooperation or the escape clause is exercised; there is never any exit from the system and hence the regime is very stable. But this comes at a cost: At low values of k, the escape clause is cheap to adopt, leading to many periods in which defection is being tolerated in exchange for the benefits of long-term stability.

Instead, if the cost of exercising the escape clause is too high, it is never used, and as soon as the shocks become severe, the system breaks down and exit occurs. The regime is now too rigid and becomes unstable. It becomes clear then that the traditional Prisoners' Dilemma game without an escape clause is equivalent to this game with a large k: cooperation will break down at some point.

COROLLARY 2. As the costs of using an escape clause rise, it will be used less frequently.

Costs and Use of Escape Clauses: Some Empirical Implications and Evidence

If we are right that governments rationally design escape clause mechanisms, we should see that variations in their cost lead to variations in their usage. Low-cost escape mechanisms should have much appeal; those with high costs should not. A good deal of evidence seems to suggest that this argument is valid. For instance, in U.S. trade law, the escape clause (Sec. 201) has been used far less often than have various other safeguard mechanisms. Wendy Hansen and Thomas Prusa show that the average number of escape clause cases filed has never gone above eleven a year, whereas for antidumping and countervailing duty cases the average reached a peak of ninety-two a year in the early 1980s.[25] Moreover, escape clause complaints have been decreasing steadily, with less than one a year filed in the early 1990s. In contrast, antidumping and countervailing duty cases have been growing over time. What accounts for this difference in usage?

We argue that it is the greater cost of invoking escape clauses that makes firms less likely to do so. Hanson and Prusa claim that the lower probability of success

25. Hansen and Prusa 1995, 299, tab. 1.

encourages firms to file antidumping and countervailing duty complaints instead. But our claim is that the lower probability of success results from the fact that escape clause actions when implemented cost the importing country more and thus make policymakers less likely to accept petitions for them. Thus firms see the mechanism as less successful and choose other means. The main reason they cost more is that exporters have a right to demand compensation for escape clause relief and, if it is not forthcoming, to retaliate. Compensation and retaliation create large domestic costs for governments, and thus they try to avoid such measures.

GATT also provides evidence that greater costs mean less use. Under GATT rules, exporters were entitled to compensation or retaliatory action if Article XIX, which involved the escape clause, was invoked. Moreover, the standards of proof for "serious injury" caused by imports needed to invoke the escape clause have been the highest of all. Among all the various safeguard means in GATT, Article XIX was among the least used. It was invoked only 150 times from 1950 to 1994. And its use has declined over time: 3.9 times a year from 1950 to 1984, and 3.2 times a year from 1985 to 1994. In contrast, the antidumping clause is much more frequently invoked: over two thousand times since 1970 alone.[26]

Moreover, scholars have noted that the costliness of escape clause actions has led to the proliferation of so-called voluntary export restraints. As Jeffrey Schott states,

> Most major trading countries, however, have been deterred from invoking Article XIX less by its requirements than by the availability of less onerous and more flexible channels of protection. These have included coercing trading partners to accept VERs [voluntary export restraints] and other so-called gray area measures, as well as frequent recourse to unilateral relief actions under Article VI (i.e., antidumping and countervailing duties).[27]

Voluntary export restraints are less costly to use than escape clauses because they do not assume compensation or allow retaliation from the affected exporter. But an importing country using them may incur costs. Unlike a tariff or quota, which provides rents for the importing country, a voluntary export restraint transfers those rents to the exporter. As Bernard M. Hoekman and Michael Kostecki maintain,

> Affected exporters tended to accept VERs because they were better than the alternative—often an AD [antidumping] duty—as they allowed them to capture part of the rent that was created. Instead of being confronted with a tariff, the revenue of which is captured by the levying government, a VER involves voluntary cut-backs by exporters in their supplies to a market. This reduction in supply will raise prices—assuming that others do not take up the slack. Exporters therefore get more per unit sold than they would under an equivalent tariff. . . . The key point to remember about VERs is that they imply some direct compensation of affected exporters and selectively target exporters. Thus

26. Hoekman and Kostecki 1995.
27. Schott 1994, 94.

they practically meet GATT-1947's compensation requirement, while allowing for circumvention of its nondiscrimination requirement.[28]

Hence, voluntary export restraints were preferred to escape clause actions because they were less expensive to employ, but even they imposed costs on the importing country.[29]

Interestingly, GATT recognized that the costliness of using the escape clause was hurting the system and pushing states to develop other means, such as voluntary export restraints, to deal with domestic pressures. Many GATT officials found other safeguard remedies—such as antidumping, voluntary export restraints, and countervailing duties—very undesirable. They preferred that countries use the escape clause mechanism. But they also realized that this process was too costly and thus underused.

In the Uruguay Round, GATT officials made several changes to reduce the costs of the escape clause relative to other safeguards. First, they banned the use of voluntary export restraints in the agreement on safeguards.[30] This in effect raised the costs of such measures. Second, they decided that it was necessary to reduce the costs of the escape clause option. So they proposed, and countries agreed, that one way to do this was to eliminate the right of retaliation. In the WTO, countries that use the escape clause no longer have to pay compensation and the injured exporters can no longer legally retaliate for the first three years of its use.[31] As Hoekman and Kostecki note, "by the time of the Uruguay round the major objective of 'target' countries was to constrain the use of AD and VERs and assert the dominance of Article XIX in safeguard cases . . . Two options were available: either to tighten the discipline on the use of AD, or to reduce the disincentives to use Article XIX. Both approaches were pursued."[32] Lowering the costs of using the escape clause was therefore seen as a key way to shift countries away from using alternative safeguards like antidumping and countervailing duties, and toward using more escape clause actions. This seems to provide some evidence that leaders do indeed rationally design international agreements.

In the international monetary arena, the costs of exercising relief have varied both across institutions and within institutions over time. Again, one could argue that these variations are the rational responses of political leaders to the problems associated in part with domestic uncertainty. The Bretton Woods system's vagueness about the conditions under which a devaluation could occur meant that it was frequently appealed to, and effective cooperation was limited. The European Payments Union and the Exchange Rate Mechanism both were more specific about

28. Hoekman and Kostecki 1995, 168–69.
29. Similarly, Rosendorff establishes that voluntary export restraints are preferred by policymakers to antidumping duties because they generate higher electoral returns at lower costs when policymakers experience political pressures for protection. Rosendorff 1996.
30. Schott 1994, 94.
31. See Preeg 1995, 100–101; and Schott 1994, 94–97.
32. Hoekman and Kostecki 1995, 169.

the terms of realignments; moreover, the Exchange Rate Mechanism became increasingly more restrictive about the conditions under which escape was possible as the system moved toward monetary union, and accordingly less tolerant of realignments. Consequently, the system became somewhat more rigid and less flexible, leading to more periods of instability and exit, as happened in Britain and Italy in 1992.[33]

Fearon's Dynamic

The escape clause adds flexibility to an agreement that might be difficult to sustain in the presence of uncertainty. Hence, bargainers are not stuck in a commitment to a distributional outcome for the infinite horizon, thereby making initial bargains easier to strike. This result lies in contrast to Fearon's concern that infinite horizon models with large discount factors make agreements difficult to strike.

COROLLARY 3. Agreements should be easier to achieve when escape clauses are included than otherwise.

As many analysts have noted about GATT, signing would have been impossible for many countries had it not included various safeguards. John Gerard Ruggie, for example, has argued that all of the international economic agreements, or regimes, negotiated after World War II had to embody the norms of "embedded liberalism," by which he meant that they had to combine multilateralism with the requirements of domestic stability.[34] Domestic safeguards that allowed countries to protect their economies were thus essential parts of this norm in both the trade and monetary areas. Without such safeguards, countries would never have signed the trade and monetary agreements.

Moreover, Hoekman and Kostecki claim that "political realities often dictate that there be a mechanism allowing for the temporary reimposition of protection in instances where competition from imports proves to be too fierce to allow the restructuring process to be socially sustainable. Indeed, a safeguard mechanism is likely to be a pre-condition for far-reaching liberalization to be politically feasible."[35] Or as Alan Sykes has shown, "when self-interested political officials must decide whether to make trade concessions under conditions of uncertainty about their political consequences, the knowledge that those concessions are in fact 'escapable' facilitates initial trade concessions."[36] Following Kenneth Dam,[37] Sykes maintains that

unanticipated changes in economic conditions may create circumstances in which the political rewards to an increase in protection (or the political costs of

---

33. Canavan and Rosendorff 1997.
34. Ruggie 1982.
35. Hoekman and Kostecki 1995, 191.
36. Sykes 1991, 259.
37. Dam 1970, 99.

an irrevocable commitment to reduce protection) are great. Consequently, in the absence of an escape clause, trade negotiators may decline to make certain reciprocal concessions for fear of adverse political consequences in the future. But, with an escape clause in place the negotiators will agree on a greater number of reciprocal concessions, knowing that those concessions can be avoided later if political conditions so dictate.[38]

Our point is that the inclusion of escape clauses should make reaching an initial agreement easier.

This argument shares much with the theory of efficient breach used in legal theory. This theory advances the idea that "there are circumstances where breach of contract is more efficient than performance and that the law ought to facilitate breach in such circumstances."[39] In order to do so, there must be mechanisms that can determine and compel payment of the appropriate levels of damages for such breach. Jeffrey L. Dunoff and Joel P. Trachtman also note that "entry into contract may be facilitated by the understanding of parties that breach may be permitted under certain circumstances."[40] They point out that the WTO's safeguard system and its notion of compensation or retaliation provides just such a mechanism for efficient breach.

An alternative flexibility-enhancing device is to build into any agreement the opportunity for regular renegotiation, as in GATT, or the International Coffee Agreement.[41] John E. Richards notes that the International Air Transport Association, an airfare-setting cartel, allowed suspension of current agreements for the one-year period in which renegotiation occurred.[42] In the same way that an escape clause adds the necessary flexibility and does not fix the distributional impact immutably, Barbara Koremenos suggests that allowing for renegotiation and finite duration reduces the distributional impact of the agreement, making bargaining over an initial agreement easier, without reducing the effect of the "shadow of the future" in enforcing the agreement.[43] The escape clause, like the opportunity for renegotiation, reduces the effects of Fearon's dynamic. We do think, however, as does Sykes, that renegotiation of an entire agreement is likely to be the most costly means by far and to have a lower probability of success than will the mere inclusion of escape clauses in the original agreement.[44]

There is a second reason escape clauses may diminish Fearon's dynamic. In our model the countries are in a position similar to John Rawl's "initial position," where one is behind the veil of ignorance and cannot tell exactly how one will benefit (or lose) in the future from agreements made now.[45] Because shocks occur in each

---

38. Sykes 1991, 279.
39. Dunoff and Trachtman 1999, 24.
40. Ibid., 26.
41. Koremenos, Lipson, and Snidal, this volume.
42. Richards, this volume.
43. Koremenos 1998.
44. Sykes 1991, 280.
45. Rawls 1971.

future period that cannot be predicted beforehand, the players do not know the future distribution of gains and losses from the initial agreement with certainty. Hence this is likely to mitigate how hard they bargain in the first place. For these two reasons in our model, Fearon's argument may not hold: the length of the shadow of the future may play no role in affecting the bitterness of bargaining over the initial agreement. Moreover, including escape clauses may make both enforcement and distributive bargaining easier!

Conclusion

International institutions vary substantially. Their design reflects the rational calculations of, as well as the strategic interaction among, countries creating them. These different designs also have implications for the functioning of these institutions. International institutions matter, but so do their forms.

We have shown that international institutions that include an escape clause can generate more durable and stable cooperative regimes. The escape clause itself is endogenous to the model: choosing a prohibitive cost for using the escape clause is equivalent to ruling it out of the institutional structure. Yet we have shown that in equilibrium the negotiating parties will adopt an escape clause with moderate costs when faced with domestic political uncertainty. Indeed, this particular institutional feature—the escape clause—is determined endogenously as an equilibrium outcome to the strategic game between the countries. Thus our model not only derives the rational form of an institution but also shows the impact of that institution once in place. We think future research should explore this result when more than two players are involved and/or when the countries are assumed to be different, such as Giovanni Maggi does.[46]

We make three claims here. One is that escape clauses are an efficient equilibrium under conditions of domestic political uncertainty. When political leaders cannot foresee the extent of future domestic demands for protection, such clauses provide the flexibility that allows them to accept an international agreement liberalizing trade. One testable proposition is that the greater the domestic uncertainty that political leaders face about their ability to maintain domestic compliance with international agreements, the more likely leaders are to negotiate agreements that contain escape clauses. In issue-areas where governments face less uncertainty about future domestic pressures to comply, they are less likely to design such safeguard measures. This may help account for the differences between international trade agreements, where escape clauses are prevalent, and arms control agreements, where they appear to be less salient. Another testable proposition would involve examining whether certain domestic political institutions that reduce domestic uncertainty reduce the incentives for leaders in these countries to pursue escape clauses. Our model's results thus support Rational Design conjecture F1, FLEXIBILITY

46. Maggi 1999.

increases with UNCERTAINTY ABOUT THE STATE OF THE WORLD. Future research to examine the empirical hypotheses we have outlined would lend credence to this conjecture.

Our second claim is that escape clauses are useful and efficient only when they impose some kind of cost for their use; that is, importing countries must pay for invoking them or else they will be invoked all the time, thus vitiating the agreement. Paying the cost signals an intention to comply with the agreement in the future. Hence, another testable proposition is that the different costs of different escape clause measures should affect their use. Less costly measures for the importer should be used more often. We assume that governments understand this dynamic. And we anticipate that the architects of international agreements will rationally design such agreements so that the types of escape clauses they most desire will be neither too cheap (encouraging frequent use) nor too expensive (discouraging their use altogether). Furthermore, since paying the penalty is self-enforcing, we expect that the institution's role will be less that of an enforcer making countries pay this penalty and more that of an information provider telling others that the penalty has been paid. Thus we expect that countries will pay penalties, while looking to international institutions for information on whether others have done the same. The role of international institutions here is to provide a particular kind of information about other states' behavior. Again, this is a testable proposition that might warrant future attention.

Our third claim is that escape clauses make initial agreements easier to reach. Fearon's dynamic breaks down; the flexibility provided by escape clauses ensures that the division of the long-term gains from the agreement is not immutable. This result of our model provides theoretical support for Rational Design conjecture F2, FLEXIBILITY increases with DISTRIBUTION problems. Our argument also shares much with the legal theory of efficient breach, where the inclusion of measures allowing parties to later breach a contract may make initial agreement on a contract more likely. Indeed, we claim that without escape clauses of some sort many international agreements would never be politically viable for political leaders to sign in the first place. And this explains why rational political leaders design flexibility into their international commitments when they are uncertain about the future.

Here we have investigated whether the inclusion of escape clauses in international agreements could be a rational response of political leaders to their domestic problems, especially to unanticipated domestic political pressures. These escape mechanisms help political leaders to maintain international cooperation without sacrificing their domestic political positions; they thus reduce the costly, contradictory pressures that can emanate from domestic and international politics, helping to make international cooperation more compatible with domestic political success. As we have argued elsewhere,[47] such solutions to the two-level game faced by political leaders are essential for successful international cooperation. Rationally designing

---

47. See Milner and Rosendorff 1996; and Milner 1997.

flexibility into international agreements thus is important for political leaders when faced with domestic uncertainty and international distributional problems. The likelihood of and the probability of success of international institutions thus depends on their internal design, as well as other factors.

Appendix

DEFINITION 2. Let $N(\gamma, g) - S(\gamma, g) \equiv A(\gamma, g)$.

DEFINITION 3. Denote

$$I(\gamma) = \int_g I(\gamma, g)d\Phi \quad \text{and} \quad I = \int_\gamma \int_g I(\gamma, g)d\Phi d\Phi$$

for any function $I = A, B, P, D, N, S$.

DEFINITION 4. Let $p = \Pr(P \mid \text{cooperation})$.

That is, p is the probability of playing P given that P or EC is to be played. Consider the current period in which nature has drawn (γ, g). Home knows γ but is unsure of g, and hence is unsure of the behavior of the foreign country. Since the countries are symmetric, we know that foreign plays P* with probability p and plays EC* with probability $1 - p$. If home plays P, then home earns in that period $pP(\gamma) + (1 - p)S(\gamma)$; whereas if home plays EC, home earns $p(D(\gamma) - k) + (1 - p)(N(\gamma) - k)$. Then P is played if $pP(\gamma) + (1 - p)S(\gamma) > pD(\gamma) + (1 - p)N(\gamma) - k$, that is, if $k > pB(\gamma) + (1 - p)A(\gamma)$. Hence, $p = \Pr(k > pB(\gamma) + (1 - p)A(\gamma))$.

LEMMA 2. For any k, the function $\Lambda(p; k) = \Pr(k > pB(\gamma) + (1 - p)A(\gamma))$ has a fixed point, $p = \Lambda(p; k)$.

Proof. For any k, Λ is a continuous function of p mapping from $[0, 1]$ into $[0, 1]$. Now $[0, 1]$ is a compact, convex set. Therefore, a fixed point exists by Brouwer's Fixed Point theorem.

Lemma 2 implies that there exists a distribution function Γ such that $p = \Gamma(k)$.

LEMMA 3. $\Gamma(0) = 0$ and $\lim_{k \to \infty} \Gamma(k) = 1$.

Proof. $\Gamma(0) = \Pr(0 > A(\gamma)) = 0$, since $A(\gamma) > 0$ for all γ; $\lim_{k \to \infty} \Gamma(k) = \lim_{k \to \infty} \Pr(k > pB(\gamma) + (1 - p)A(\gamma)) \to 1$, since $B(\gamma)$, $A(\gamma)$ are finite for all γ and $p \in [0, 1] \forall k$, since p is a distribution function.

PROOF OF PROPOSITION 1. A pair of escape clause strategies is a Nash equilibrium.

The expected current period return from defection at home is $D(\gamma)$, and hence the gains from defection are $D(\gamma) - \max(P(\gamma), D(\gamma) - k) = \min(B(\gamma), k)$. Consider the event that a deviation has been observed in some period. From then on, the one-shot Nash strategies are played, yielding the Nash payoff (in expectation, since the draws in the future periods are unknown, forever). That is, the aggregate Nash payoff (starting in the next period) is

$$V_D = \frac{\delta}{1 - \delta} N.$$

What is the forgone cooperative aggregate payoff? If cooperation occurred in the last period, in the next each player has the option of cooperating again or defecting. The value of the game in a cooperative phase is the earnings from the play in that period plus the continuation value, $V = p[p(P + \delta V) + (1 - p)(S + \delta V)] + (1 - p)p(D - k + \delta V) + (1 - p) \times (N - k + \delta V)]$.

Solving we have

$$V = \frac{1}{1 - \delta} (p^2 P + p(1 - p)(S + D) + (1 - p)^2 N - k(1 - p))$$

$$= \frac{1}{1 - \delta} (p^2(A - B) + p(-A + D - N) + N - k(1 - p)).$$

Hence,

$$V - V_D = \frac{1}{1 - \delta} (p^2(A - B) + p(D - N - A + k) + N(1 - \delta) - k).$$

Recall that $p = \Gamma(k)$. The no defect condition in any period is therefore

$$\min(B(\gamma), k) < \frac{1}{1 - \delta} ((\Gamma(k))^2(A - B) + \Gamma(k)(D - N - A + k) + N(1 - \delta) - k).$$

Let

$$Z(k) \equiv \frac{1}{1 - \delta} ((\Gamma(k))^2(A - B) + \Gamma(k)(D - N - A + k) + N(1 - \delta) - k),$$

and define K to be a fixed point of $Z(k)$, that is, $Z(K) = K$. Setting $z(k) = Z(k) - k$, we have

$$z(k) \equiv \frac{1}{1 - \delta} ((\Gamma(k))^2(A - B) + \Gamma(k)(D - N - A + k) + N(1 - \delta) - k(2 - \delta)).$$

Now $z(0) = N > 0$ and as $k \to \infty$, $\Gamma(k) \to 1$, and $z(k) \to -\infty < 0$ from Lemma 2. Then we have a nondegenerate fixed point by the intermediate value theorem. Then K is the upper bound on any penalty in order to invoke EC, and home plays P if $B(\gamma) < k < K$; plays EC if $k \leq B(\gamma) \leq K$; and plays D if both $B(\gamma)$, $k > K$. Hence, a pair of escape clause strategies is an equilibrium.

PROOF OF PROPOSITION 2. Let k* satisfy

$$k^* = \frac{1 - \Gamma(k^*)}{\Gamma'(k^*)} - 2\Gamma(k^*)(A - B) - (D - N - A),$$

then both countries agree on k* when $k^* \leq K$ and agree on K otherwise.

The value of the game to either player in which an escape clause equilibrium is played is

$$V(k) = \frac{1}{1 - \delta} ((\Gamma(k))^2(N - S - D + P) + \Gamma(k)(S + D - 2N + k) + N - k)$$

when $k < K$. What value of k maximizes this value? We solve $k^* = \arg\max_k V(k)$. The first order condition $V'(k^*) = 0$ yields

$$k^* = \frac{1 - \Gamma(k^*)}{\Gamma'(k^*)} - 2\Gamma(k^*)(N - S - D + P) - (S + D - 2N).$$

Checking the second order condition, note that $V''(k^*) < 0$ iff

$$\Gamma''(k^*) < (1 + (A - B)\Gamma'(k^*)) \frac{-2(\Gamma'(k^*))^2}{1 - \Gamma(k^*)} .$$

A sufficient condition for this to hold is that $\Gamma(\cdot)$ has an increasing hazard rate, and $A - B > 0$. Moreover, we know that at $k = K$, each player is indifferent between exercising the escape clause and defecting permanently. If $k^* > K$, then $V(k^*) < V(K)$, implying the optimal choice of penalty is K.

PROOF OF COROLLARY 1. An agreement with an escape clause Pareto dominates one without in the presence of political uncertainty.

This follows from the previous proposition. Any escape clause game with $k > K$ is equivalent to a game without an escape clause. This is because if $k > K$, the escape clause is never exercised, and at some point defection occurs (unless the discount rates are very high). However, countries optimally choose $k \leq K$; hence, an agreement with an escape clause dominates one without.

PROOF OF COROLLARY 2. As the costs of using an escape clause rise, it will be used less frequently.

In any escape equilibrium, the probability that the escape clause is used is $1 - p = 1 - \Gamma(k)$. As k rises, $1 - \Gamma(k)$ falls, reducing the frequency with which the escape clause is exercised.

PROOF OF COROLLARY 3. Agreements should be easier to achieve when escape clauses are included than otherwise.

With escape clauses, true cooperation occurs as long as k ≤ K; there is no restriction on the discount factor δ. That is, given any discount factor δ, there exists a penalty k ≤ K such that an escape clause equilibrium exists. In the standard Prisoners' Dilemma in the face of uncertainty, cooperation occurs whenever

$$\delta > \frac{\max_\gamma B(\gamma)}{P - N + \max_\gamma B(\gamma)}.$$

Hence, the set of discount factors under which the standard Prisoners' Dilemma under uncertainty can support a cooperative equilibrium is

$$\left[\frac{\max_\gamma B(\gamma)}{P - N + \max_\gamma B(\gamma)}, 1\right] \subset (0, 1],$$

the set of discount factors under which an escape clause equilibrium exists. Hence, if we were to draw a discount factor at random, we are more likely to be able to support an escape clause equilibrium than a cooperative equilibrium in a game without an escape clause.

Most-Favored-Nation Clauses and
Clustered Negotiations

Robert Pahre

Centralization, which plays a key role in many international regimes, takes two major forms. The first is centralized monitoring and enforcement. An international institution may be responsible for collecting information on compliance or for disseminating compliance information given to it. For example, the secretariat of the World Trade Organization (WTO) collects self-reported information on compliance and oversees the dispute resolution system. Centralized enforcement has attracted substantial attention in the theoretical literature, reflecting concerns about monitoring and enforcing cooperation under anarchy.[1]

The second form is centralized negotiation, where many countries bargain simultaneously within a regime. This has received some attention, largely as one of several features within the norm of multilateralism.[2] Important substantive examples include the General Agreement on Tariffs and Trade (GATT)/WTO, which has clustered negotiations into a few "rounds" with longer periods of no negotiations between them. This centralized bargaining, or "clustering," is the focus of this article.

Most scholars who study the international trade regime have treated clustering as an unexceptional consequence of GATT/WTO multilateralism. This view neglects the history of the international trade regime. Such clustering is not exclusively a characteristic of the postwar trade regime, since similar clustering occurred, for example, in 1891–93 and 1904–1906. Even in the postwar period, multilateral coordination did not become an important feature of the trading system until the 1960s.[3] This clustering became less important in the 1980s as the major trading

Earlier versions of this article were presented at the Rational Design conference in May 1998 and the 1998 Annual Meeting of the American Political Science Association. For comments on earlier drafts, I thank discussants George Downs, Robert Keohane, and Lisa Martin; the editors of this volume and *IO;* the anonymous reviewers; and the participants in the Rational Design conferences.

1. See Koremenos, Lipson, and Snidal, this volume.
2. Ruggie 1993.
3. See Curzon and Curzon 1976; Finlayson and Zacher 1983; and Pahre 1999, chap. 10.

International Organization 55, 4, Autumn 2001, pp. 859–890

nations negotiated bilaterally with one another on market opening, voluntary export restraints, and other issues.

Because clustering varies even within a single regime such as GATT, we should not view it as an inevitable consequence of that regime. Bilateral negotiations that are not clustered can have undesirable distributional effects. A most-favored-nation (MFN) clause may force a state to make concessions to one state after having already made politically costly concessions in its negotiations with another on the same issue. Clustering avoids this, making simultaneous concessions with many states possible. Consequently, clustering has distributional benefits for those who cluster.

To explain clustering I use a model of trade policy negotiations in which distribution and domestic politics interact with international regime norms. "Distribution" as defined by Barbara Koremenos, Charles Lipson, and Duncan Snidal in the framing article of the Rational Design project ("differences over which alternative cooperative agreement to implement") provides the fundamental reason for clustering. While distribution does not vary, because all trade negotiations face a distributional issue, clustering occurs only as a solution to a particular distributional problem.

Regime norms explain variation in clustering more directly. Clustering occurs when countries grant each other MFN status and negotiate with several countries over the same tariff lines. Additional variation comes from expansion of the trade treaty network to include more countries. Because this increase in number leads to greater clustering, it is consistent with Rational Design conjecture C3, CENTRALIZATION increases with NUMBER, though the causal mechanism differs somewhat.

Showing the empirical role of clustering requires looking at a period containing variation, not only in clustering but also in numbers and the MFN norm. For this reason I focus my empirical analysis on the nineteenth century, from 1815 to 1914.[4] Countries sometimes clustered their trade negotiations during this period and sometimes did not. Virtually all treaties were bilateral, so that clustering was not simply a logical consequence of the multilateral treaty form. States negotiated treaties both with and without MFN. The number of participants in the trade regime varied over time. This variation in both independent and dependent variables permits good tests of the hypotheses.

This choice of period has additional implications. While clustering is an important feature in the design of formal institutions, I study it by looking outside formal multilateral institutions. Every bilateral treaty within a cluster meets the Rational

4. The data in this are from the Trade Agreements Database, available at ⟨http://www.staff.uiuc.edu/~ pahre/tad.html⟩. This database currently contains all trade treaties signed from 1815 to 1913, except for Asian countries east of the Ottoman Empire and west of Japan (exclusive). For a treaty to be included it must make mutual reductions or bindings that directly affect bilateral trade; treaties concerning purely navigational matters or commerce alone (such as treaties granting reciprocal rights of establishment) are excluded, as are the unequal treaties signed by China and some other countries. The sources for the database are discussed on the website and include both official treaty series and secondary sources, such as diplomatic histories.

Design definition of an international institution: "explicit arrangements, negotiated among international actors, that prescribe, proscribe, and/or authorize behavior." Clustering itself may not always meet this definition. It can be either explicitly negotiated (as in the WTO) or an emergent property of a given system.[5] In the nineteenth century clustering was usually not explicit or negotiated, nor was it part of a formal international organization such as the WTO. However, Austria-Hungary and Germany did explicitly agree to cluster their negotiations with outsiders in the 1890s, a case thereby meeting the Rational Design definition exactly. Even when clustering does not meet the Rational Design definition of an institution, it meets the canonical definition of a regime, a norm "around which actor expectations converge in a given issue-area."[6] This means that my substantive focus overlaps considerably, but not perfectly, with the Rational Design definition of an institution.

My focus on the nineteenth century thus lets me investigate institutions and institutional design while also examining the historical origin of a particular design feature.[7] Looking at a less formal regime also has advantages for case selection and research design. Most studies of centralization select on the dependent variable, looking only at multilateral international organizations in which all negotiations are centralized. This is an inappropriate approach for testing anything but a necessary condition.[8] Second, looking at a feature only in the context of a formal institution represents a kind of selection bias because one cannot separate the underlying causal processes from the peculiarities of a given formal institution. If I were to examine centralized bargaining only in the GATT/WTO, for example, I could not separate the causal role of MFN from the specific features of the GATT/WTO, nor could I distinguish it from background variables such as hegemony, bipolarity, or the Cold War. For this reason, I approach the question of centralized negotiations in formal international organizations indirectly, by looking at centralized negotiations within a less formal regime. I return to the WTO and other formal international organizations in the final section of the article.

Clustering

Clustering is defined as a state's simultaneous negotiations with two or more countries on the same issue. Because the negotiations address the same issue, each bilateral negotiation will be implicitly or explicitly linked to the other negotiations. Like the definition of nominal multilateralism,[9] this definition requires only three states.

---

5. For the analysis of regime spread as an emergent property of the nineteenth-century trade treaty network, see Lazer 1999.

6. Krasner 1983, 1.

7. For a study of how the origins of trade institutions affect their present functioning, see McGillivray, McLean, Pahre, and Schonhardt-Bailey 2001.

8. Dion 1998; compare King, Keohane, and Verba 1994.

9. See Keohane 1990; and Ruggie 1993.

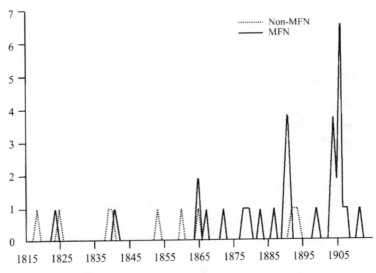

FIGURE 1. Prussian/German treaty signings by year

We often observe a substantively more important form of clustering, in which many states cluster at the same time and clusters overlap. I call such a cluster of clusters a "macro-cluster." A GATT round is an excellent example of a macro-cluster, where many states negotiate tariff reductions simultaneously. Sometimes a new loan facility at the International Monetary Fund (IMF), such as the External Fund Facility (1974) or the facility for sub-Saharan Africa (1985), produces a similar cluster of negotiations. The IMF also helps cluster negotiations among lender countries, debtor countries, private banks, and international organizations.[10]

While macro-clusters may sometimes be important, my definition of clustering requires only that a single state negotiate simultaneously with several others. To explain the phenomenon, I begin with the problem in a three-state setting.

Empirically, we can see clusters by looking at the treaties signed by a single state. Consider, for example, the non-Zollverein treaties that Prussia/Germany signed in each year from 1815 to 1913, graphed in Figure 1.[11] Before the 1890s, Prussian treaties were infrequent and scattered in time, with no more than one treaty reached in any year except 1865. The spikes in later years reflect a flurry of treaties in 1890–91 and 1904–1906, whereas tariff treaties remained uncommon between

10. Lipson 1986.
11. The figure distinguishes MFN treaties from non-MFN treaties for reasons I explain later. While it excludes Zollverein treaties between, say, Prussia and Bavaria, it does include Prussia's treaties with outside states that had territories within the German Confederation, such as Austria, Denmark (Holstein), Luxembourg/Netherlands, and for a time the United Kingdom (Hanover).

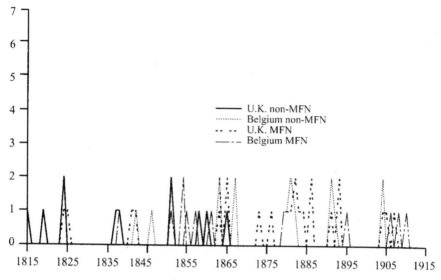

FIGURE 2. Belgian and U.K. treaty signings by year

these periods. The secondary literature identifies these two clusterings with Chancellors Leo von Caprivi and Bernard von Bülow, respectively.[12]

In contrast to Germany, Belgium and the United Kingdom did not cluster their treaties. Each country negotiated only one or two treaties a year over the course of the century (Figure 2). Both the treaties and the gaps between them appear to be randomly distributed, not clustered. With very few exceptions, such as Britain's simultaneous negotiations with France and Spain in the 1870s, the secondary literature confirms this picture.[13]

While such visual inspections help identify clustering, apparent clustering may reflect random processes by which a country occasionally negotiates several simultaneous agreements simply by chance. As I explain later, I rule out random processes by testing whether a country's annual treaty initiations are Poisson-distributed. My case study of the Caprivi cluster provides evidence that these clusters linked treaty negotiations both causally and intentionally.

Though a novel concept, clustering fits easily into conventional theories and the Rational Design framework. Clustering is a form of centralized decision making, defined by the Rational Design framers as "whether institutional tasks are performed by a single focal entity or not." The examples of centralization in the Rational Design framing article are international organizations, whereas the "focal entity" of

12. See Marsh 1999, chap. 8; Weitowitz 1978; and Werner 1989.
13. For Britain, see Marsh 1999. Belgium lacks a modern secondary literature (but Mahaim 1892), though one can piece together the details from Augier 1906; Marsh 1999; and others.

nineteenth-century clustering is one or more states that served as a focal point for negotiations. For example, the Anglo-French renegotiations of 1878–82, Caprivi's policy of tariff treaties in 1890–91, and von Bülow's negotiations of 1904–1906 each served as a focal point for a macro-cluster of treaties as several states carried on simultaneous clusters. The focal entity of each negotiation was, respectively, France, Germany, and Germany.

Of course, clustering is a decentralized form of centralized bargaining. It differs from the "unified and hierarchical control within a single organization or institution" that the Rational Design framework associates with centralized activities. It also differs from most of this volume's other articles, which focus on centralized monitoring or information gathering. This difference is most obvious in conjecture C4, CENTRALIZATION increases with the severity of the ENFORCEMENT problem. Like conjecture C4, conjecture C1, CENTRALIZATION increases with UNCERTAINTY ABOUT BEHAVIOR, and conjecture C2, CENTRALIZATION increases with UNCERTAINTY ABOUT THE STATE OF THE WORLD, also rest on the logic of monitoring and enforcement, because centralized information gathering might better ascertain whether others have defected intentionally or involuntarily. I show later that centralized bargaining works according to a different logic, one dominated by problems of distribution instead of enforcement and monitoring. Consequently, norms, distribution, and the number of actors provide more useful independent variables.

My approach most closely resembles the literature on linkage, especially multilateralism or "player linkage." Multilateral bargains link more than one bilateral bargain, either in a formal institution or simply through common conjectures that bargains are linked. Like the Rational Design hypotheses on centralization, rational-choice theories of linkage emphasize linked enforcement, in which cheating on one partner leads to punishment by others.[14] In contrast, clustering requires only linked bargaining, and states may enforce bargains independently. This resembles the prisoners of war regime, which exhibits both centralized bargaining and decentralized enforcement.[15]

As these examples show, this centralized bargaining process stems from individual states' decision making. States need not agree to centralize their trade bargaining, and indeed some states may be upset that others have clustered. Instead, this process reflects the choices of individual governments to launch negotiations with more than one country at the same time. In other words, clustering is a decentralized form of centralization. When several countries cluster at the same time, a macro-cluster emerges. This cluster and the states within it become a "focal entity" for decision making according to the Rational Design definition of centralization.

---

14. See Lohmann 1997; and Pahre 1994. While similar to player linkage, clustering concerns the number of actors and not the number of issues being negotiated (that is, scope). While such linkage may have interesting implications, this kind of linkage is not my focus here.

15. Morrow, this volume.

In short, my definition of clustering and the Rational Design definition of centralization overlap but do not coincide exactly, a point to bear in mind when applying the Rational Design framework to the clustering problem.

Explaining Clustering

Though clustering is a novel concept, three existing theories might explain it. First, transaction costs might induce states to cluster negotiations, just as they shape other problems of institutional design.[16] Bernard Hoekman argues that GATT rounds solve the problems of barter in political negotiations.[17] Political barter is inefficient because the market may not offer the goods a trader desires, a trader who has something to offer to one party may desire the goods of a third party in exchange, and it may be impossible to equate the marginal valuations of the goods on offer without a price mechanism. Clustered negotiations may solve these problems. A GATT/WTO round, for example, creates an agreed agenda that (1) ensures that every state finds something on offer, (2) links bilateral negotiations so that three or more parties can find feasible trades, and (3) links issues so that negotiators can equate the marginal valuations of goods across states. While conditional MFN status would also solve the barter problems, Hoekman argues that it would do so less efficiently than coordinated negotiations.[18]

Second, regime theories might explain clustering. Jock Finlayson and Mark Zacher argue that GATT clustering follows from regime norms of nondiscrimination, liberalization, and reciprocity.[19] Clustering occurs especially at the end of a negotiating round, when third-party beneficiaries of some bilaterally negotiated tariff reduction are pressured to make additional concessions to "pay" for these benefits. Others might see clustering as a decision rule that follows from the multilateral principles of the postwar order.[20]

Transaction-cost and regime theories may explain clustering, but neither explains variation between clustered and nonclustered regimes. Indeed, nonclustering would make sense only in terms of regime breakdown. For example, if the United States eschewed multilateral negotiations after the Tokyo Round in favor of bilateral voluntary export restraints with Japan and others, the conventional view would see this choice as a breakdown of the regime.[21] However, such breakdown is unlikely and unexplained if other parts of the regime remain intact. These theories also fail to explain cross-national variation whenever two states are both members of the regime but only one clusters its negotiations.

---

16. See Koremenos, Lipson, and Snidal this volume; and Lake 1996.

17. Hoekman 1993. This argument parallels transaction-cost explanations of multilateral negotiations and multilateralism. For example, see Keohane 1984, 90; and Oye 1986, 20. For a critique, see Pahre 1994.

18. Hoekman 1993, 44–45. Compare Bagwell and Staiger 1999.

19. Finlayson and Zacher 1983.

20. Ruggie 1993; especially Burley 1993; and Goldstein 1993.

21. See, among others, Aggarwal 1985.

Finally, linkage theory might explain intertemporal variation in clustering.[22] In particular, Susanne D. Lohmann's theory of linkage suggests that increasing interaction among major trading partners would lead to higher discount factors, making player linkage more likely. Yet, again, variation presents a problem. While linkage theory might explain the increasing use of clustering in the nineteenth century, it does not explain the cross-national variation we observe. Several major traders, including Belgium, the Netherlands, and the United Kingdom, certainly had high discount factors but did not cluster at any time. I argue that this variation depends critically on "distribution" and its interaction with the regime norm of MFN.

Distribution and MFN

Long informed by the Prisoners' Dilemma metaphor, theories of international cooperation have given primary attention to the monitoring and enforcement of bargains. Researchers have investigated how bilateral "hostages," international institutions, linkage, multilateralism, and relative gains make it easier or harder for states to cooperate.[23] Only recently have negotiation problems received wide attention, especially in the bargaining phase before two states reach an agreement.[24] The Rational Design framework, which focuses on both bargaining and enforcement, builds on these literatures.

Distributional problems are particularly salient in bargaining because negotiators disagree about how to divide the joint gains from agreement. One might view these problems as the concerns of unitary states, but the core of the strategic problem lies in domestic distributions: Politicians have an interest in satisfying both import-competers and exporters. Exporters desire lower foreign tariffs, which can be achieved only by negotiating away the domestic tariffs that import-competers favor. Politicians concerned about domestic political support would like to minimize the cost to import-competers necessary to obtain advantages for exporters. This connection to domestic political battles makes tariff treaties an interesting part of foreign policy.

Existing rules, or norms within international regimes, also affect the strategic situation in important ways. With MFN any concessions negotiated between two countries will be generalized to all other countries to which a state grants MFN status. As a result, a concession to one state today becomes a new, lower starting point for negotiations with another state tomorrow.

---

22. See Lohmann 1997; McGinnis 1986; Pahre 1994; Stein 1980; and Tollison and Willett 1979.
23. See Axelrod 1984; Keohane 1984; Martin 1992; Lohmann 1997; Oye 1986; Pahre 1994; Snidal 1991; and Yarbrough and Yarbrough 1986.
24. See Fearon 1998; Garrett 1992; Garrett and Tsebelis 1996; Krasner 1991; Oatley and Nabors 1998; and Snidal 1985.

The conventional view of the GATT/WTO argues that this feature of MFN encourages continual, gradual liberalization; for example, a state negotiates the steel tariff down with one country today and another country tomorrow. This assumes that states do not anticipate the consequences of the regimes they join.

Yet states do anticipate these consequences. In the 1860s Prussia wanted to negotiate a treaty with France before it negotiated with the United Kingdom. It feared that concessions to the United Kingdom would weaken its position relative to France because France would have already received Britain's concessions through MFN. Concessions to France, in contrast, would not harm any future negotiations with the United Kingdom.[25] Negotiating the French and British treaties simultaneously would also avoid giving away too much to the United Kingdom before turning to France.

The renewal and renegotiation of these treaties in the late 1870s supplies a further illustration. France had timed all its tariff treaties to expire in 1877, though they could be extended from year to year.[26] The government temporarily extended these treaties several times while negotiating with other European countries. Negotiations with Britain, France's chief trading partner, received priority. Commerce Minister Pierre Tirard, a free trader in the otherwise protectionist ministry of 1881, offered concessions on metals and machinery but not textiles, for he anticipated protectionist opposition to any British treaty. Because the British insisted on obtaining concessions on cotton textiles, they broke off talks in June 1881. They hoped that a Franco-Belgian treaty would yield Britain the tariffs they desired through MFN. This made the Belgian treaty a bellwether for the treaty system; "the conventional duties embodied in the Belgian treaty, if ratified, would single-handedly extend the liberal tariff system of the Second Empire."[27]

These examples show that states were certainly aware of the distributional consequences of MFN treaties. This awareness made them attentive to the sequence by which they negotiated treaties with other states. I address this problem formally in the next two sections, after which I turn to the evidence.

Tariff-making with and Without MFN

Understanding the strategic problem that states face requires an analysis of MFN because each nation can impose a separate tariff on the same good from each foreign country without MFN. This means that each country A will have a tariff t_{A1B} on good 1 from country B, a different tariff t_{A1C} on goods from country C, and so on. Tariff negotiations with country B over t_{A1B} need have no relation to t_{A1C}, nor would A's negotiations with C over t_{A1C} have any necessary implications for t_{A1B}. Each country could have in principle $m(n-1)$ tariff lines for m importable goods in a system of n countries.

25. See Davis 1997, chap. 7; and Henderson 1984.
26. Smith 1980, 182–95.
27. Ibid., 191. See also Marsh 1999, chap. 6–7.

MFN changes this situation.[28] Now for each good i, the tariff on imports from B and C will be identical, or $t_{AiB} = t_{AiC}$. As is well known, A's concessions to B now resemble a public good in that C may enjoy them without "paying" anything to receive them. By making these concessions public, MFN sharpens the distributional conflict in trade.

These tariffs affect the domestic political problem confronting a government. I illustrate this problem with a simple public choice model, one of a class of "politically realistic" trade policy models in which governments pay attention to both producer and consumer interests. I will not justify the functional form of the government's utility function here, though it can be derived from a model with electorally motivated tariff setting. The model simplifies existing two-country models of tariffs.[29]

Suppose that governments choose trade policy in response to demands from domestic economic actors. These pressures may come from exporting and import-competing interests or may include consumer demands for lower tariffs. Though these groups exist on both sides of the tariff issue, the fact that consumer interests are harder to organize than producer interests biases pressure in favor of a positive tariff. In response to these pressures, each government favors some nonzero domestic tariff on each good.

In contrast, there is no home lobby arguing for foreign protectionism. Home exporters obviously seek zero foreign tariffs, and home import-competers are indifferent to the foreign tariff, so the home government faces no distributional problems in seeking zero foreign tariffs. As a result, the home government's ideal foreign tariff is zero.

With these interests in mind, I now consider a simple model with three countries and only one imported good in each country. State A has the ideal point $\{t_A, 0, 0\}$, B has the ideal point $\{0, t_B, 0\}$, and C has the ideal point $\{0, 0, t_C\}$ with $t_A, t_B, t_C > 0$. For simplicity, I assume that utility is a negative function of the distance from the outcome of the game to this ideal point. As a result, indifference curves are spheres around each player's ideal point.[30] Rather than show all of these spheres, Figure 3 shows a slice of each, a circle through the $t_A t_B t_C$ plane.

Because each government selects only its own tariff, each chooses its ideal point. With A choosing t_A, B choosing t_B, and C choosing t_C, the noncooperative outcome N is the point $\{t_A, t_B, t_C\}$. Figure 3 shows this point N in three-dimensional space. There are joint gains to liberalization, so all three states prefer any point that lies inside the three indifference spheres to the reversion point N. Any of these points on the plane defined by these three ideal points (inside the dotted triangle in Figure 3)

28. I treat MFN as an exogenous regime rule. There are few modern explanations of MFN, but see Bagwell and Staiger 1999. The United States saw a vibrant debate on MFN culminating in the 1920s; for a good example, see Viner 1924.

29. See Grossman and Helpman 1995; Hillman, Long, and Moser 1995; Milner and Rosendorff 1997, app. B; Milner and Rosendorff, this volume; and Pahre 1998.

30. In a more elaborate model, the indifference curves would be elliptoids because home tariffs are more important than foreign tariffs to each government.

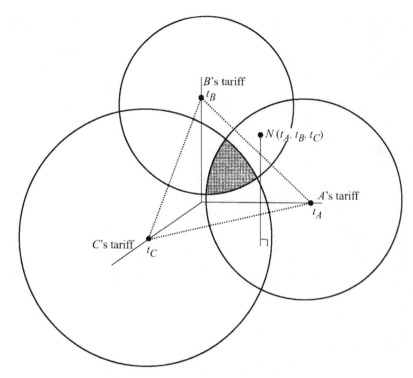

FIGURE 3. Tariff negotiations among three states

are Pareto-efficient, a triangular region known as the simplex. Inside the simplex, moving the policy toward t_A and t_B simultaneously can occur only by moving away from t_C, moving policy toward t_B and t_C simultaneously moves policy away from t_A, and moving policy toward t_A and t_C moves it away from t_B. There are many possible points of agreement on the $t_A t_B t_C$ plane that are also within the indifference curves (the shaded area in Figure 3).

This analysis implies that distributing the joint gains among these three states will present a salient problem in this strategic setting. How the states negotiate over this set of possible agreements will depend in part on the negotiating agenda they choose. In effect, different negotiating agendas decide how states move from N to an efficient point on the simplex that all prefer to N. I examine this problem in the next section.

Choosing the Agenda for Tariff Negotiations

When states can negotiate tariffs with many foreign countries, they have a choice between negotiating with one state at a time or with many simultaneously. To understand this procedural choice, I consider tariff negotiations under two different rules, "clustered" and "seriatim."

For ease of presentation, I assume that the outcome of any bargaining game is the Nash bargaining solution (NBS).[31] The NBS maximizes the product of the differences between each negotiator's payoff from the agreement and that negotiator's payoff from the reversion point or status quo. Whenever the game is symmetric, the NBS splits the difference between the two bargainers. Since the NBS is unaffected by monotonic transformations of the utility functions, any game that can be made symmetric through such a transformation will also have a split-the-difference outcome. This feature makes the NBS very useful for the presentation here, though the results of the analysis do not require it.

As discussed in the preceding section, each state's bliss point is a positive home tariff and zero foreign tariffs. Because the initial tariff levels do not matter for the subsequent analysis, I define the axes such that each state's ideal tariff equals 1, or $t_A^* = t_B^* = t_C^* = 1$. For simplicity of exposition, I continue to assume that utility functions use an unweighted distance, that is, that indifference functions are spherical. Negotiations among three states, A, B, and C, might occur under two possible agendas:

1. Seriatim. First, A and B negotiate over tariffs. Next, A and C negotiate over tariffs. (B and C may also negotiate, but the issues surrounding this choice are best raised in the case study presented later.)

2. Clustering. A, B, and C negotiate simultaneously over tariffs.

I assume that state A can choose between the two agendas regardless of B's and C's interests. This is simply a notational convenience: clearly, whichever state finds itself in the position to choose the agenda, for whatever historically contingent reasons, can be labeled A. This state might have a first-mover advantage attributable to greater power over its interlocutors or to some domestic political process, such as legislative granting of trade negotiation authority, that makes a particular state the first to make an offer. In the case study, Germany's market power, British aloofness from trade treaties, and the negotiating inflexibility of France's governing coalitions combined to make Germany the focal point of trade negotiations in the early 1890s.

Sequence has an important effect on the outcomes. If states cluster the negotiations, the three-player NBS is {1/2, 1/2, 1/2}. This solution simply splits the difference between each state's ideal point and the ideal point of its interlocutors in each dimension.

Negotiating seriatim poses a more subtle problem without a single, fully satisfactory analytical solution. To illustrate the issues I present three ways to think about the solution to the seriatim negotiation game. Though they vary in their assumptions about rational behavior, they yield qualitatively the same results; therefore, my qualitative claims are robust.

---

31. Nash 1950.

Consider first what would happen if the states approach each bargain myopically. This might occur if A and B do not accurately anticipate C's willingness to negotiate. The NBS at the AB node is {1/2, 1/2, 1}, splitting the difference between A and B. This agreement at the AB node changes the reversion point for the subsequent AC negotiations. Since the NBS depends on the reversion point, the AB negotiations change the NBS for A and C. As a result, the NBS at the AB node is {1/4, 1/2, 1/2}. If A myopically negotiates one agreement after the other, it makes greater concessions than it would if it clustered.[32]

Now suppose that A does not negotiate myopically but reasons through this problem with the aid of backwards induction. Though backwards induction is the normal way of solving an extensive-form game such as this, it yields an odd result. The NBS at the AC node is {1/2, 1, 1/2}, splitting the difference between A and C. However, this agreement at the AC node changes the reversion point for the AB negotiations, which occur first. As a result, the NBS at the AB node is {1/4, 1/2, 1/2}. This result strikes most people as strange because A gives B concessions right away out of the knowledge that C will get these concessions eventually. Odd as it is, however, it produces the same result as myopia. Because A prefers the higher home tariff, A will again prefer clustered over seriatim negotiations.

Both the myopic and backwards-induction solutions seem unsatisfactory to many people, who suggest a third approach to the game that I will call the "intuitive" approach.[33] One might expect A to withhold concessions from B, saving them for its negotiations with C. B would presumably also make smaller concessions to A, since it now gets less in return. Since we are intentionally considering some outcome other than the NBS, I must make an alternative assumption about the bargaining solution. I will assume that A offers some concession (k) and that B will make the exact same concession. We might suppose, for example, that A and B agree to k = 1/4, yielding agreement at {3/4, 3/4, 1}. Again, this agreement changes the reversion point for A and C, as in the myopic model.[34] After this agreement, A and C negotiate their NBS at {3/8, 3/4, 1/2}. In this "intuitive" approach, A still makes more concessions than the other states. This will happen as long as B insists on making concessions (k) equal to A in the range k∈(0, 1/2).[35] While A makes fewer concessions than in the first two seriatim solutions, it also obtains fewer concessions in return. Again, A does better under clustered negotiations, obtaining more concessions from B and giving up fewer itself.

---

32. It is ironic that A might rationally anticipate the outcome of its own myopic behavior. One way to square this circle is to suppose that a rational institutional designer anticipates that subordinate organizations will behave in a boundedly rational way; another is that today's government might anticipate myopia on the part of a successor government.

33. Both public presentation and anonymous review of this model have yielded this reaction.

34. Using backwards induction instead of myopia for this "intuitive" approach yields the same results: A withholds concessions from C at the AC node in order to make them at the AB node.

35. If B does not insist on parity, A could get away with making sufficiently few concessions to B that it might end up as well off as it does under clustering; however, I cannot see any reason why B might be nice to A in this way.

All these approaches to the seriatim game therefore yield qualitatively the same result: A makes more concessions under seriatim negotiations than it does under clustering. For this reason, A will prefer clustering to seriatim negotiations. Because labeling any state as A is simply a notational convenience, this means that every state will prefer clustering over negotiating seriatim.

Though all states prefer to cluster themselves, they also wish others to choose seriatim negotiations. In the above analysis, states B and C clearly prefer that A negotiate seriatim. Yet if they were given the chance (that is, to be in the position such that they would be the state labeled "A"), they would clearly choose to cluster themselves. Given this strategic setting, it seems reasonable to suppose that states find clustering an attractive focal point solution to the agenda-setting problem—any other solution produces asymmetric distributional consequences, and there is no reason to expect these asymmetrical effects in what is essentially a symmetric game. Symmetry results easily when everyone clusters.

Clustering is a reasonable focal point, and alternatives to clustering would be difficult to implement. If B and C wish to prevent A from clustering, they must form a coalition against A, agreeing not to negotiate simultaneously. Presumably, each would like to negotiate last, letting it enjoy A's concessions to the other before negotiating its own. The two will struggle with each other to obtain the last-mover position, and state A may successfully exploit these differences. We shall see such tactics in the case study.

Even if B and C were to form this coalition against A successfully, we would expect clustering to result. While agreeing not to negotiate simultaneously with A, they would presumably recognize that they had a common interest in negotiating simultaneously with outsiders D, E, and F. While the notational identity of the clustering states changes, the causal relationship is the same even here: MFN is a condition that produces clustering.

The conclusion that states will cluster when they negotiate MFN tariffs is affected by two background conditions, economic structure and the number of states in the trade network. Economic structure matters because A's preference for clustering depends on the fact that A negotiates the same tariff line with both B and C. If A imports good 1 from B and good 2 from C, there are two relevant tariffs in A, t_{A1B} and t_{A2C}. The reversion point is now $\{t_{A1B}{}^*, t_{A2C}{}^*, t_B{}^*, t_C{}^*\} = \{1, 1, 1, 1\}$. As in my analysis of MFN, t_{A1B} is of interest solely to B's exporters, whereas t_{A2C} is only of interest to C's exporters. With clustered negotiations, the three-player NBS is $\{1/2, 1/2, 1/2, 1/2\}$, which splits the difference among all tariff dimensions.

Now consider seriatim negotiations with backwards induction (the other approaches are similar). Here, the NBS at the AC node is $\{1, 1/2, 1, 1/2\}$, since A and C negotiate only over t_{A1C} and t_C. These tariffs are not part of the negotiations between A and B, who split the difference on the remaining tariffs. As a result, the NBS at the AB node is $\{1/2, 1/2, 1/2, 1/2\}$.

This means that when A negotiates different tariff lines with B than with C, the clustered and seriatim outcomes are identical. Anticipating negotiations between A and C does not change the reversion point between A and B for any of the variables over which A and B negotiate, and thus does not affect the outcome.[36] If A negotiates over a different tariff line with B than with C, A is indifferent between clustered and seriatim negotiations.[37] Whether this occurs is an empirical question of economic structure, not a subject of theory. There is no reason to expect clustering, especially if—as seems likely—the transaction costs of multilateralized clustering are greater than the transaction costs of bilateralism.[38]

The second background condition is the number of states in the trade treaty network. If there are many states, it is more likely that some dyads will negotiate over the same MFN tariff lines as some other dyads. Certainly this must occur if the number of states is greater than the number of negotiated goods. In these cases, the states meet the economic structure condition for clustering and we would expect clustering to occur. A case study can determine exactly when adding a particular state to the network means that several dyads will negotiate over the same MFN tariff. Where it is not feasible to collect this information for many states, we can assume a simple correlative relationship between the number of actors and the likelihood of clustering. This hypothesis parallels Rational Design conjecture C3, CENTRALIZATION increases with NUMBER.

The analysis here leaves open the question of why states use the MFN clause to begin with. I argue extensively elsewhere that MFN must be understood as a regime norm chosen for political reasons independent of the tariff bargaining problem.[39] An overview of the argument here is limited by space considerations.

Discriminatory bargains and the conditional and unconditional forms of the MFN clause were available to trade negotiators in the second half of the eighteenth century. Either form of MFN had political advantages for European countries supporting newly independent states in the Americas. For example, France had political reasons for wanting a conditional MFN clause included in the Franco-American commercial convention of 6 February 1778. To keep Britain isolated from the rest of Europe, France wanted to avoid the suggestion that it was fighting a war of aggrandizement, and it preferred to pose as protecting the colonies against British oppression.

36. To see that the concessions in the AC negotiations do not affect the NBS, consider that the outcome of the AC negotiations can be washed away with a monotonic transformation of A's and B's utility functions without affecting the AB negotiation problem. Because the NBS is resistant to monotonic transformations of the utility functions, this has no effect.

37. Conditional MFN, practiced mostly by the United States in the nineteenth century, has ambiguous status here. The ostensible American insistence on additional concessions in exchange for generalizing each MFN reduction often did not matter, since the United States had a single-column tariff. Even under the Dingley two-column tariff, all trading partners received the lower tariff within a few years. For discussions, see Fisk 1903; Lake 1988; O'Halloran 1994; and Viner 1924. Such examples mean in effect that conditional MFN is more an empirical question than a theoretical one.

38. Deardorff and Stern 1992. Multilateral bargains have higher transaction costs because they include irrelevant negotiations; A could participate in matters that affect only B and C.

39. Pahre 2001. Two modern explanations focus on MFN-cum-reciprocity as a renegotiation-proof bargaining rule or as a way to increase the sanction against defection. Viner's classic analysis would also fit well into any modern theory of political economy. See Bagwell and Staiger 1999; Pahre 1994; and Viner 1924.

Great Britain pursued a similar policy in the 1820s when negotiating with the newly independent countries of Latin America. Unwilling to offend Spain gratuitously, Britain negotiated MFN commercial treaties with Gran Colombia and México in the early 1820s, thereby renouncing any special privileges for itself. Latin America's own policies further encouraged nondiscrimination. When Mexico declared independence in 1821, it opened its ports to all nations on equal terms. In 1822, Gran Colombia offered commerce, free residence, and full reciprocity to all countries that would recognize it.[40] Following these examples, Latin American treaties generally included MFN clauses through the century.

These concerns were largely lacking in Europe. As a result, MFN did not become a part of regular British or French practice in Europe until the 1860s, but it was common in the Western Hemisphere much earlier. This political explanation accounts for variation between MFN and non-MFN treaties, a variation that the functionalism of modern bargaining theory cannot explain. Exogenous political concerns can also explain why a norm with some undesirable implications might nonetheless persist.

In summary, this exogenous MFN norm means that states will sometimes negotiate over the same tariff line with multiple states, since any concession to one nation will be granted to others as well. MFN exacerbates the distribution problem as defined by the Rational Design framework by linking each pair's negotiations to the negotiations between all other pairs. This particular distributional problem is a necessary condition for centralized bargaining. Two background conditions, economic structure and the number of actors, further explain variation between clustered and nonclustered negotiations.

Testing the Relationship Between Clustering and MFN

The preceding section argues that the regime norm of MFN, when combined with the distributional problem of tariffs, structures the distributional problem for a state. This distributional problem then shapes international decision-making rules such as clustering or seriatim negotiations. The analysis yields the following hypothesis:

HYPOTHESIS 1. MFN IS A NECESSARY CONDITION FOR CLUSTERING.

MFN is necessary because without it state A would always negotiate different tariff lines with states B and C. When A negotiates different tariff lines, it will negotiate seriatim because of the greater transaction costs of clustering.[41] At the same time, MFN is not sufficient because MFN could fail to lead to clustering if A

---

40. Williams 1972, 258–61.
41. Rephrased, this argument maintains that non-MFN is sufficient for nonclustering. A statement of this form is logically equivalent to the statement that MFN is necessary for clustering: $\langle \sim x \rightarrow \sim z \rangle \leftrightarrow \langle x \mid z \rangle$.

negotiated different tariffs with B than it negotiated with C. In this case lower tariffs from A's negotiations with B would not lead to a new starting position for negotiations with C, which would necessarily focus on different tariff lines. Naturally, if A negotiates the same tariff lines with B and C, these two variables (MFN and economic structure) are jointly sufficient for clustering.[42] While both MFN and economic structure are easily observed in a case study, a large-n test of this claim requires too much information about economic structure. However, it is straightforward to test the necessity portion of this claim in a large-n setting, namely, that MFN is a necessary condition for clustering.[43]

This test requires some way to capture clustering. One way to do this is by graphing a country's pattern of trade negotiations (as in Figures 1 and 2). Another approach would be to look at the distribution of treaty initiations over time. Seriatim negotiations should be Poisson distributed. This assumes that the observed number of treaties in a given year will depend on some underlying rate of treaty initiation whose realization as a count variable will vary from year to year. In contrast, clustered negotiations will not be Poisson distributed. More precisely, a test will allow me to reject the null hypothesis that these treaties are Poisson distributed at a high level of statistical significance.

To test this, I run a Poisson regression for each country's annual treaty initiations using only a constant and an error term.[44] The goodness-of-fit χ^2 tells us whether we can reject the null hypothesis that the data are Poisson distributed. Table 1 summarizes these tests, showing the confidence level at which we can reject the null hypothesis.[45] For example, the null hypothesis can be rejected at the $p < .01$ level that Austro-Hungarian MFN treaties are Poisson distributed. I can therefore feel confident asserting that Austro-Hungarian MFN treaties are not Poisson distributed.

---

42. I am making logical claims of the form that $\langle x \cap y \rangle \rightarrow z$ and $x \rceil$ z. MFN and economic structure are each an "insufficient but necessary part of an unnecessary but sufficient" (INUS) condition. For an influential philosophical explanation of why we would expect most causes to take this form, see Mackie 1965 and 1974; see also Kim 1971. For a probabilistic critique, see Trenholme 1975; and Friedman 1980. The INUS formulation concedes that we cannot know whether a given cause is truly necessary for a given effect without knowing all other imaginable theories that might explain that effect. This is clearly an impossible standard. Phrased differently, this formulation concedes that MFN is only a necessary condition for clustering within this theory. Since we do not have other theories of clustering, we can treat MFN as a necessary condition here.

43. Braumoeller and Goertz have recently proposed techniques for testing necessary conditions quantitatively; the dichotomous variables here allow for a simpler approach. Braumoeller and Goertz 2000.

44. Annual treaty initiations provide an adequate but not ideal measure. States cluster by negotiating simultaneously with many states, and by making sure that they reach agreement on particular tariff lines simultaneously. These agreements need not be reached in the same year, and unrelated issues sometimes drag out the final treaty. This annualized data series treats agreements reached in January and February as clustered, those reached in December and January as unclustered. These limitations can be overcome through sensitive use of the data, supplemented by qualitative evidence.

45. Because the null hypothesis of this test is that the data are Poisson distributed, the test might wrongly code some actual clustering as Poisson distributed. However, for almost all cases in Table 1 the confidence level for rejecting the Poisson null is either less than .10 or greater than .90 (these latter levels are not shown as such in the table). For these data, then, wrongly accepting the null is unlikely to be a problem. Only Serbia presents a serious question of inference in these data.

Hypothesis 1 states that MFN is a necessary condition for clustering. We should observe that all non-MFN treaty initiations are Poisson distributed. If this is a nontrivial necessary condition, we should also observe that some MFN treaties are not Poisson distributed.[46] Since the hypothesis does not state a sufficient condition, we need not expect that all MFN treaties will be non-Poisson distributed.

Table 1 shows the result of such a test for the countries of Europe, using treaty initiation data from the Trade Agreements Database. As expected, all non-MFN treaties are Poisson distributed. This is consistent with the necessary condition. MFN is substantively important and nontrivial because about half of the MFN observations exhibit clustering. It is noteworthy that the evidence in Table 1 would be inconsistent with a claim that MFN is a sufficient condition for clustering.[47] This makes the theory's successful prediction of a necessary condition all the more striking.

These Poisson data strongly confirm the hypothesis. The evidence also suggests that clustering plays an important role in the trade regime. Those countries that cluster are central to the nineteenth-century system. Austria, France, and Italy signed more treaties with more countries than anyone else. They are also central to the case study below. Denmark, Greece, and Montenegro were much more incidental to the regime.[48] In this way, the necessary condition explains the behavior we find in the most important players in the regime.

Number of Actors and Clustering

A state gains from clustering when it negotiates the same tariff line with more than one country. All else equal, adding more countries to the trade treaty regime makes it more likely that a state will negotiate the same tariff lines with several others. For example, adding southern countries to the regime meant that Germany would negotiate wine tariffs not only with Austria-Hungary and France but with Italy, Portugal, and Spain. Adding members therefore makes clustering more likely:

HYPOTHESIS 2. CENTRALIZATION (CLUSTERING) INCREASES WITH NUMBER.

Because this hypothesis follows from the distributional problems that states face under MFN, the causal mechanism differs from the mechanism behind Rational Design conjecture C3, CENTRALIZATION increases with NUMBER, which emphasizes enforcement and information-gathering purposes. This different focus may help

---

46. See Braumoeller and Goertz 2000. While this necessary condition would not be falsified even if none of the MFN treaties were non-Poisson distributed, such a condition would not be very interesting or useful.

47. Testing a correlative claim between MFN and clustering would raise more complicated issues, especially since both MFN and clustering are dichotomous variables.

48. The United Kingdom, though substantively important in international trade, was relatively unimportant to the treaty regime because it chose to rely on unilateral free trade accompanied by MFN treaties and only occasional bargaining over tariff lines after 1860. For details, see Marsh 1999.

TABLE 1. Distribution of annual treaty signings

	MFN treaties	Other treaties
Austria (-Hungary)	Not Poisson (48) p < .01	Poisson (23)
Bulgaria	Not Poisson (23) p < .01	N.A. (0)
France	Not Poisson (62) p < .01	Poisson (11)
Italy	Not Poisson (88) p < .01	Poisson (2)
Prussia/Germany	Not Poisson (37) p < .05	Poisson (12)
Romania	Not Poisson (16) p < .10	Poisson (2)
Serbia	Not Poisson (12) p = .33	Poisson (3)
Spain	Not Poisson (32) p < .05	N.A. (0)
Switzerland	Not Poisson (34) p = .16	N.A. (0)
Belgium	Poisson (22)	Poisson (7)
Denmark	Poisson (9)	Poisson (5)
Greece	Poisson (15)	N.A. (0)
Montenegro	Poisson (6)	N.A. (0)
Netherlands	Poisson (29)	Poisson (11)
Portugal	Poisson (14)	N.A. (0)
Sweden	Poisson (18)	N.A. (0)
Turkey	Poisson (5)	Poisson (6)
United Kingdom	Poisson (26)	Poisson (11)

Source: Treaty initiation data are from the Trade Agreements Database and are available by request from the author at ⟨http://www.staff.uiuc.edu⟩.

Note: Numbers in parentheses are the number of treaties signed in each category. The probabilities shown are the level at which I can reject the null hypothesis that the data are Poisson distributed. I can always reject this null at the .90 level or better for those cases labeled "Poisson."

explain how John E. Richards' analysis (this volume) of distributional problems in the air-traffic regime can yield the contrary hypothesis that increasing number, when combined with uncertainty, leads to decentralized monitoring and enforcement.

Testing Hypothesis 2 requires a measure of the number of actors. I will define a country's entry into the trade treaty network as the year in which it first signed a tariff treaty after 1815. This definition provides a simple operationalization of regime membership, where membership is a dichotomous variable and reflects a government's choice to enter the regime. Table 2 shows that states steadily joined the trade treaty regime throughout the century. This list generally provides a good

TABLE 2. Membership in the European trade treaty system

	First trade treaty, 1815–1913
Britain	1815
Portugal	1815
Sweden-Norway	1815
Prussia/Germany	1819
France	1826
Turkey	1838
Netherlands	1839
Belgium	1847
Russia	1847
Austria (-Hungary)	1848
Sardinia/Italy	1851
Greece	1853
Denmark	1864
Spain	1865
Romania	1875
Serbia	1879
Montenegro	1883
Bulgaria	1891

Source: Trade Agreements Database.
Note: Dates are the first year a country negotiated a trade treaty in Europe making reciprocal tariff concessions. Countries with a trade treaty in effect before 1815 are assigned a start date of 1815.

guide to each state's active participation in the regime, though it is misleading for a few countries.[49]

The reasons for joining the regime vary and lie outside the theory here. A few states entered the regime as a result of gaining either national independence or foreign policy autonomy. Romania is a good example.[50] However, most countries joined the system because of a domestic political choice to negotiate tariff reductions. Turkey's entry into the nineteenth-century regime coincided with the internal reform of Mahmud II's Tanzimat, whose goals were summarized a few years into the program in the Gülhane (Rose Garden) rescript of November 1839.[51] Austria did not sign tariff treaties until the beginning of constitutional government in 1848.[52] Denmark joined the treaty system only with the loss of Slesvig-Holsten in 1864, when the loss of German cities led to the political consolidation of rule by

49. The early date for Portugal reflects the Methuen Treaty with Britain (Portugal denounced the treaty in 1836) and not a general policy of trade treaties. Sweden-Norway was not very active despite signing an occasional treaty throughout the century, and Russia negotiated trade treaties only very rarely until the 1890s.
50. The countries of Latin America, not discussed here, provide many more such examples.
51. See Kasaba 1988, chap. 3; Pamuk 1987; and Shaw and Shaw 1977, 71–106.
52. Braunder and Lachmayer 1980, 112–33.

pro-export Danish aristocrats.[53] After having reached a domestic constitutional settlement in 1891,[54] the Bulgarian government readily joined the Caprivi cluster of 1891–92. In each of these cases domestic political change led to regime membership and contributed indirectly to clustering.

Paralleling this increase in regime membership, we see a steady increase in clustering throughout the century. France's cluster of MFN treaties in 1863–66, negotiated in the wake of the Cobden-Chevalier treaty of 1860, provides the first example. France's second cluster came in 1881–84, which renewed and extended the Napoleonic treaties after the new general tariff of 1881. This cluster included treaties with the Netherlands, Sweden-Norway, Portugal, and Spain, most of which had only recently become active trade treaty negotiators. This suggests that some clustering occurs through spread effects, as states join the regime to avoid intolerable exclusion from trade-diverting treaty regions.[55] These spread effects would be consistent with conjecture M3, MEMBERSHIP increases with DISTRIBUTION problems. States join the regime because of the severely distributional nature of trade negotiations, a feature that is exaggerated when states inside the network receive different terms than those outside it.

We may also count Hungarian autonomy in the Ausgleich of 1867 as raising the number of actors, since Hungary gained the right to impose its own tariffs—even on Austrian goods if it had so chosen. From 1867, therefore, Austria had to negotiate tariffs with Hungary every ten years as part of the Ausgleich. The first cluster of Austro-Hungarian treaties came in the same year. At the second renewal of the Ausgleich in 1887, Hungary tied the new common tariff to tariff reductions in any future German treaty.[56] This prompted Austria to pursue favorable treaties with its own natural markets in the Balkans. The Ausgleich renewal years coincided with Austrian tariff wars and treaty renegotiations with Austria-Hungary's Balkan trading partners: Romania in 1886 and Serbia in 1896 and 1906–10.

Therefore, through the decentralized decisions of many states, the number of actors increased, further centralizing the trade treaty regime. By 1904–1906, most of Europe's treaty negotiations pulsed to the rhythm of a single beat.

Distributional Effects of Clustering

If my claim is correct that clustering has important distributional consequences, states that cluster should make fewer concessions in trade treaties than those that do not cluster. Coding treaty provisions and comparing concessions is one way to test this claim, though measuring concessions is not easy. First, one could assess the actual tariff lines and how much they were reduced. The natural way to aggregate these concessions is to weight each tariff reduction by the value of imports entering

---

53. See Andersen 1958; and Jones 1970, 72–90.
54. See Black 1943; and Crampton 1997.
55. See Lazer 1999; and Pahre 2001.
56. von Bazant 1894, 28–29.

under that tariff line—though this import value is itself endogenous, a function of the tariff. This endogeneity complicates the task considerably. The concessions could be weighted by either their pre-concession or post-concession import value; these will consistently produce different results unless the import elasticities of all imported goods are exactly equal.

Another way to measure a trade concession is to observe the increased level of bilateral trade that results when a treaty is in effect. Under this approach the actual tariff change need not be observed; instead, the observed trade levels can be used to infer effective levels of protection. To simplify the weighting problem, I use a common metric (increased trade) to measure all concessions. With this more practical approach, my argument implies the following hypothesis:

HYPOTHESIS 3. THE EFFECTS OF A TRADE TREATY ON BILATERAL TRADE WILL BE SMALLER FOR A STATE THAT CLUSTERS THAN FOR A STATE THAT DOES NOT.

Testing this hypothesis requires finding a country for which bilateral trade data exist both before and after it began clustering. In addition, this country must have negotiated trade treaties before clustering, so that I can isolate the effects of individual trade treaties from clustered trade treaties. Finally, clustering should have no effect on bilateral trade with any country unless it has negotiated a treaty with that country.

Germany meets these requirements. Trade data begin in 1880, and Germany began clustering in 1890–91 (see Figure 1). Germany had treaties in effect with most European countries, but its first treaty with Belgium took effect only in 1882, and its sole reciprocal trade treaty with the Netherlands (1840–42) far predates unification and clustering.

I look at Germany's bilateral trade with three major trading partners that did not themselves cluster: Belgium, the Netherlands, and the United Kingdom. Figure 2, like Table 1, confirms that these were not clusterers. Excluding the major trading partners that did cluster, such as Austria-Hungary, France, and Italy, provides a cleaner test of the hypothesis since I need not worry about whether their own clustering years (that is, 1887–89 for Austria-Hungary) have an independent effect on bilateral trade.

The hypothesis predicts that clustering will reduce Germany's concessions in trade treaties. To measure concessions I use a dummy variable equal to 1 whenever Germany has a trade treaty in effect with a given country; a second dummy variable for 1890–1913 captures the clustering years. To provide a null estimate of bilateral trade, I use a modified gravity model. The basic gravity model predicts that bilateral trade equals the product of two countries' gross national products (GNP) divided by the square of the distance between them.[57] Because I fit a separate model for

---

57. For a review of these models and discussion of how they relate to economic theory, see Deardorff 1984.

TABLE 3. Clustering and trade concessions (dependent variable is bilateral trade value)

	Predict	United Kingdom	Belgium	Netherlands
German GNP	+	2.12 (0.40)	1.38 (0.44)	1.09 (0.51)
Foreign GNP	+	1.31 (0.51)	0.75 (0.21)	1.0 (0.40)
Treaty in effect	+	N.A.	0.13 (0.058)	N.A.
Clustering	—[a]	−0.084 (0.030)	−0.22 (0.064)	−0.044 (0.037)
Constant	N.A.	−0.010 (0.028)	0.023 (0.029)	−0.36 (0.040)
N		33	33	33
F		14.66	12.01	4.22
Adj. R^2		0.562	0.579	0.232
Durbin-Watson		2.63	1.47	1.69

Sources: Mitchell 1979; and Trade Agreements Database.
Note: Standard errors are in parentheses. All coefficients are statistically significant at the .01 level or better (one-tailed test) except for Dutch clustering and the constants; these are not significant at the .10 level. GNP and bilateral trade data are first differences of the logarithms.
[a] Because the Netherlands never had a treaty in effect with Germany, the clustering variable should not be significant for the Dutch regression.

bilateral trade with each foreign country, the denominator of this equation (distance squared) will appear in the constant of the regression. Taking the logarithms of both sides, I then regress logged bilateral trade against each country's logged GNP. Thus my null expectation for bilateral trade is simply that the logarithm of Germany's bilateral trade with each foreign country will equal the sum of the logarithms of the GNPs of Germany and that foreign country plus an error term.

Initial tests found significant serial correlation in the time series. To eliminate this I took the first differences of each variable. As a result, the equations that I report model annual change in the logged bilateral trade regressed against annual change in logged GNPs.

The results are reported in Table 3. The evidence strongly confirms the hypothesis, with all coefficients significant at better than the .01 level (one-tailed test). Moreover, clustering is not significant for Dutch-German trade, exactly as predicted. The models also seem to provide reasonable fits for the data, though the adjusted R^2 and F measures are not nearly as good for the Netherlands equation as for the others.

As discussed earlier, these results rest on an indirect measure of tariffs and tariff concessions, namely bilateral trade values. Because trade values can depend on many economic variables, such as transport costs, some variable outside the theory could lie behind the observations. It is therefore gratifying that the variables are all signed in the right direction, though the predicted signs vary. For example, the United Kingdom dummy for clustering is negative, as expected, whereas if the estimate had been greater than zero, it might simply be picking up increased trade as a result of improvements in transportation and communications. The positive estimate on the dummy for the Belgian treaty in effect without clustering is also exactly as expected. The theory also predicts statistical nonsignificance correctly in the case of Dutch clustering. An excluded variable, always a potential problem in simple models, would be unlikely to get this combination of results exactly right.

The data are consistent with the theoretical claim that clustering leads to higher tariffs than seriatim negotiations. This suggests that the spread of MFN in the second half of the nineteenth century produced higher tariffs than the nonclustered negotiations at mid-century. The historiography concurs, arguing that the treaties of the 1890s produced a period of greater protectionism.[58] While negotiated tariffs are presumably lower than nonnegotiated tariffs, this decision-making procedure had important consequences for the substance of the trade regime.

Qualitative evidence suggests much the same for earlier periods. France clustered its negotiations in the early 1880s by imposing a renegotiation deadline of 18 November 1881 on all its partners. This is closely associated with its efforts to increase its tariff without breaking away from the treaty network. In other words, France wanted its partners in cooperation to agree to a higher French tariff in the 1880s than they had negotiated in the 1860s or 1870s.[59]

A different mechanism by which clustering induced higher tariffs was the widespread practice of introducing tariffs in advance of a cluster of major renegotiations.[60] Many countries raised their tariffs in advance of the renewals and renegotiations in 1903–1905. Though I have not modeled the incentives for such tariff setting, the logic is fully consistent with the model.

The historiography provides additional evidence in support of Hypothesis 2. Historians typically describe 1890–1914 as a period of increased European protectionism, which eventually included even liberal Switzerland in 1906.[61] Some historians notice that this alleged protectionism was accompanied by an increase in trade treaty negotiations.[62] Some countries, notably France, used these treaties as part of an effort to revise tariffs upwards while retaining market access in a few sectors. Likewise, Germany and Sweden signed two significant treaties that guaranteed each country some protection while liberalizing only a few sectors such as iron ore, paving stones, and timber. I argue in the following section that these two trends go together, that clustering made these treaties less liberal than their often nonclustered predecessors.

58. See Lindberg 1983; Marsh 1999, chap. 8; and Matis 1973, 51.

59. Marsh 1999, 137.

60. Another trick that states used to combine protectionism with MFN treaties was greater tariff differentiation. Sweden used differentiation of iron export duties to good effect to force Germany to make major concessions. See Lindberg 1983; and Werner 1989, chap. 1.

61. Examples of the historiography include Coppa 1970 and 1971; Friedman 1978; Lindberg 1983; Howe 1997; Marsh 1999; Platt 1968; Rogowski 1989; Smith 1980; Weitowitz 1978; and Werner 1989.

62. Examples include Marsh 1999; and Weitowitz 1978.

Clustering and the "Comet Year" of 1892

While the Poisson tests uncovered a nonrandom distribution of treaties, no statistical test can show that states intended to cluster. Similarly, the quantitative evidence in the preceding section demonstrates only a correlation, not necessarily a causal link to the MFN clause. Showing intention requires more qualitative evidence, which I provide in this section.

My central claim is that MFN is necessary for clustered negotiations. Testing this hypothesis requires selecting on the dependent variable[63]—that is, finding a case of clustered negotiations and then looking to see if the MFN clause was necessary for it. The case should also reveal that decentralized negotiations between many states can be causally linked, that is, clustered. In a strategic model such as mine, showing causality further requires evidence that decision makers understood the dangers of seriatim negotiations under MFN. I also need to show that decision makers intended to cluster negotiations, recognizing that this would avoid the problems of MFN.

The case selection issue comes first. Several clusters present themselves, including France's clusters of 1863–66 and 1881–84, the Caprivi-Méline cluster of 1890–92, and the von Bülow cluster of 1904–1906. Minor powers also clustered their negotiations, but these generally coincided with major-power clusters and are derived from them. The most substantively interesting of these is the 1890–92 cluster because it stemmed from contemporaneous but causally distinct decisions in Austria-Hungary, France, and Germany. This case was also chosen because of the data-availability issues discussed in the preceding section, making both quantitative and qualitative analysis of the same cluster possible.

The French had arranged for their existing treaties to expire together in 1892, a date the German-speakers labeled the Kometenjahr (comet year). Domestic debates over the treaties and rising protectionism led France to adopt the Méline tariff of 1892, which established a supposedly nonnegotiable minimum tariff. In fact these duties could be negotiated downward, and were. France concluded treaties with sixteen countries from 1891 to 1893, though the concessions exchanged were much less significant than in earlier treaties.

While aware of French debates, German clustering occurred in a different context. Chancellor Caprivi sought a new foreign policy (Neue Kurs) distinct from Otto von Bismarck's. Trade treaties would mark his government's greater concern with economic issues. Treaty negotiations also posed an opportunity to attract labor support for the government, support that was especially attractive after the repeal of the Sozialistengesetz (anti-Socialist law) in 1890.

In contrast to France and Germany, Austria-Hungary did not have domestic political reasons for treaty negotiations in 1890–92. The Caprivi–Méline cluster thus occurred when the Dual Monarchy would not otherwise have negotiated treaties, for Austro-Hungarian negotiations typically occurred around the decennial renewal years of the 1867 Ausgleich (that is, 1877, 1887, 1897, and 1907). This

63. Dion 1998.

makes Austria-Hungary a useful control case, for its decision to cluster in 1890–92 must follow exclusively from MFN bargaining considerations and not merely domestic political calculations.

Having chosen this case, the next question is whether politicians worried about the distributional effects of MFN. It is not surprising that they did. The Austrian protectionist Joseph Neuwirth described MFN "as a gift to all states that neither can nor want to make mutual concessions, a clause through which every tariff reduction granted to one state immediately and ipso facto becomes applicable to all other states."[64] Supporters of MFN could not disagree with this assessment, though they naturally viewed nondiscrimination more favorably than did Neuwirth—even seeing it as an advantage. Because of the MFN clause, according to Foreign Minister Marschall, most of Germany's "concessions in cooperative treaty negotiations with Italy are obtained not only through concessions made directly to Italy but also with an eye on those concessions obtained indirectly through the Austro-Italian treaty."[65]

Wine tariffs, which played an important role in many of the negotiations, provide a good illustration of how these concerns manifested in practice. Britain well knew that the MFN wine duties that it had given to France also gave cheap Italian wines low-tariff access to the British market. Instead of being grateful, Italy's government could—and did—ask for still more reductions in these wine duties in exchange for lower tariffs on English exports. Spain had similar views. It was willing to trade reductions in its tariffs only for still more concessions on wines, particularly a structure of duties that treated heavier Iberian wines more favorably than the existing system based on alcohol content. The seriatim model captures this concern, whereby earlier concessions to one party become a new baseline for negotiations with third parties.

Germany, another wine importer, faced the same strategic problem. The Interior Ministry in Berlin opposed lowering any wine tariffs for Austria-Hungary because they would reduce the basis for future negotiations with Italy, Spain, and France.[66] As argued earlier, having MFN treaties and negotiations cover the same tariff lines are jointly sufficient for clustering. These conditions are met here, and wine did indeed provide important subject matter throughout the Caprivi cluster.

Problems around MFN also drove Austrian policy. In the early 1890s the imperial-and-royal government could not decide whether talks with Germany or the Balkan countries should be concluded first. Hungary wanted access to Germany and opposed opening markets to the Balkans, whereas Austria wanted cattle imports

---

64. "als eine Gratisprämie für alle Staaten, die Gegenkonzessionen nicht machen können oder wollen, eine Klausel, durch welche jede Zollverabsetzung, die irgend einem Staate für irgend eine Konzession gewährt wird, sofort und ipso facto auch allen anderen Staaten zugute kommt." Cited in von Bazant 1894, 34–35.

65. "daß bei kooperativen Handelsvertragsverhandlungen mit Italien . . . das Maß unserer Konzessionen, nicht nur durch die uns direkt angebotenen italienischen Konzessionen, sondern auch durch die Aussicht bestimmt wird, weitere Konzessionen indirekt durch den österreichisch-italienischen Vertrag zu erhalten." Cited in Weitowitz 1978, 144.

66. See Marsh 1999, chap. 5–6; and Weitowitz 1978, 58–59.

from Serbia and Romania but feared competition from Germany. Both sides feared that concluding any one treaty would make concluding later treaties more difficult.[67] MFN exacerbated the internal divisions over policy, for it would erode the concessions that each half of the monarchy would obtain in its preferred export market. For example, Germany could enjoy the Balkan market that Austria had opened, just as Serbia and Romania could obtain access to Germany on terms equivalent to Hungary's.

The solution to this internal dilemma lay in an informal agreement known as the "Montssche Proposition," a proposal by the German chargé in Vienna (Monts) that Germany and Austria-Hungary would not negotiate any treaties without coordinating with the other state. This meant that Hungary could consent to Balkan treaties since the negotiations would be linked to Hungary's own efforts to open Germany. Similarly, Austria could make concessions to Germany while working together on the Balkans, Italy, or Switzerland. Rolf Weitowitz argues that this arrangement "made it possible to appease the opposing interests of agrarians and industrialists in Austria-Hungary. This made it easier for the Vienna government to grant Germany industrial concessions, in the well-founded hope of obtaining tariff advantages in third markets."[68]

The agreement also put pressure on the Balkan countries. Their food exports could only gain access to Germany if their country also signed a trade treaty with Austria-Hungary. As a result, their treaties were negotiated and signed close to each other. Serbia signed its treaties with Austria-Hungary and Germany on the same day, 9 August 1892. Romania reached agreement with Germany on 23 October 1893 and with Austria-Hungary on 21 December 1893. The German connection made it unnecessary for Austria to postpone closing its negotiations with Germany until after having reached treaties with Serbia and Romania.

Concerns about MFN are also found in negotiations over industrial tariffs. The problems of MFN concessions were especially important for Belgium because of its small size and central location. It was always careful during the Austro-German-Belgian negotiations to see that France could not take advantage of the treaty tariffs. Anticipating an eventual MFN treaty with France, Belgium was also concerned to limit its concessions to Germany on the iron and textile tariffs that would be the focus of Franco-Belgian negotiations. The same concerns led Belgium to negotiate with France and Britain at essentially the same time, delaying the easier British talks until the outline of the French treaty was established.[69]

Clustering MFN treaties had other effects outside the narrower limits of the model. Because states knew that MFN treaties would shift the reversion point in

67. Weitowitz 1978, 55–56.
68. "denn sie ermöglichte, die widerstreitenden Interessen der Agrarier und Industriellen in Öster-reich-Ungarn zu beschwichtigen. Der Wiener Regierung wurde es hierdurch leichter gemacht, Deutschland industrielle Konzessionen zu gewähren, in der begründeten Hoffnung, Zollvorteile auf dritten Märkten zu erlange." Weitowitz 1978, 56.
69. See Marsh 1999, chap. 8; and Weitowitz 1978, 115–16.

negotiations with third parties, they had an incentive to keep the outcome of any negotiations secret. Once the first group of Austro-German treaties were made public in December 1891, there was a danger that third states would simply demand MFN treaties with Germany and Austria-Hungary to obtain the already given treaty tariffs. These partners addressed this problem by putting their tariff line concessions in a secret protocol. After reaching this secret agreement, these two then presented a common front in negotiations with Italy, Switzerland, and Belgium in the summer of 1891. By keeping these tariff lines secret, concessions that Germany and Austria-Hungary had already made to each other could be offered anew to these countries.[70]

Such secrecy was only one reason why other states did not want a government to cluster its negotiations with them. As the theory predicts, a country should oppose, on distributional grounds, being brought into a cluster. Austria-Hungary and Germany had various means to bring reluctant interlocutors along; the size of the German market, in particular, posed a potent source of power.[71] While Switzerland opposed simultaneous negotiations with Vienna and Berlin, it feared exclusion from the treaty network, especially if Italy were to sign a treaty whose benefits would be denied the Swiss. When this exclusion seemed a real possibility, Bern commenced common negotiations with Austria-Hungary and Germany in the fall of 1891.[72] The Belgian negotiator, Greindl, apparently did not even know about Austro-German coordination at first. After receiving common demands from the partners, he naively asked whether it might not be more advantageous for Belgium to receive separate lists of demands from Germany and Austria-Hungary. This objection was met by referring to the political friendship of the Dual Alliance countries and their wish for common negotiations.[73]

Because this alliance excuse was not available, Austro-German coordination against Italy provides evidence that distributional concerns were important. Out of respect for its partner in the Triple Alliance, the Dual Alliance had decided not to give Italy the same treatment as Switzerland, Belgium, and the Balkan countries. When given a choice in August 1891 between separate Austrian and German negotiations or a conference a trois, Italy naturally chose separate talks. The logic behind this choice follows directly from the earlier analysis. However, Italy's decision did not keep the German and Austrian commissioners from consulting each other in secret, a deception made easier by Italy's having agreed to conduct all these negotiations in Munich.[74]

When Prime Minister Rudinì discovered this deceit, he threatened to break off negotiations. Caprivi calmed him in telegrams explaining that common negotiations were necessary because of German domestic politics and the tightness of the Dual

70. Weitowitz 1978, 83–84, 154–55.
71. Lindberg makes exactly this argument for Sweden a decade later. Lindberg 1983.
72. Weitowitz 1978, 91, 104.
73. Ibid., 114–15.
74. Ibid., 136, 143.

Alliance; linking any Austro-Italian trade treaty to foreign policy would help ratification of the Italian treaty in Germany. Rudinì satisfied himself with a paraphrase of their secret treaty of October 1891—though Austria-Hungary and Germany did not give Italy a copy of the treaty itself. The Germans' account of these negotiations makes the connection to MFN clear: "What he [Rudinì] calls "pressure" and "threats" is just nothing but the indivisible connection between the various treaties, created by the idea of cooperation and MFN, which he has himself recognized by accepting our condition."[75] Again, this follows the logic of the theory.

Finally, the theory predicts that all this clustering would lead to treaties that make smaller concessions than nonclustered treaties. As we would expect, the concessions made in the Caprivi cluster were not particularly far reaching. Belgium's concessions can stand for many others. Germany received twenty-four tariff-line concessions in the Belgian treaty, mostly on industrial goods, and obtained eighteen additional tariff bindings. Belgium reduced only seven tariff line items, two of which responded to Austro-Hungarian demands. German agriculture was particularly disappointed in its hopes for greater access to the Belgian market. All these concessions were sufficiently small that an upward revision of the Belgian tariff in 1895 was consistent with the letter of these treaties. Such results add substantive meaning to the quantitative test in the preceding section, which found that Belgian-German clustering was associated with a smaller effect on German imports than earlier nonclustered treaties.

In summary, this case study confirms both the hypotheses and the underlying logic of the model. The qualitative evidence also fleshes out the quantitative findings of the preceding section, which covers the same states in the same period. This case also shows some of the steps that practical statesmen take in response to the strategic problems highlighted by the model. While these tactics are richer than those found in any model could be, they reflect the same strategic logic. The resulting policies of nondiscrimination, combined with threats of exclusion, careful attention to sequence and timing, and efforts at secrecy, play important roles in the negotiations of the early 1890s. As events show, states facing a clusterer have few choices available to them, making it easier for them to cluster when MFN provides the incentive.

Conclusions: Implications for the GATT/WTO Regime

The Rational Design framework represents a laudable move from the study of "cooperation" in the abstract to more concrete features of international cooperation and organizations such as centralization, membership, scope, and flexibility. I join

75. "Was er 'Pression' und 'Drohung' nennt, ist also nichts anderes als der durch die Kooperationsidee und die Meistbegünstigung geschaffene, untrennbare Zusammenhang der verschiedenen Verträge, den er selbst mit Annahme unserer Bedingung anerkannt hatte." Cited in Weitowitz 1978, 144.

this movement by arguing that regime norms and domestic politics can interact to produce centralized bargaining within an international regime or formal organization.

I have argued that MFN is a necessary condition for clustering, that clustering becomes more likely as the number of states in the trade network increases, and that states that cluster make fewer concessions than states that do not. The second of these claims is identical to Rational Design conjecture C3, CENTRALIZATION increases with NUMBER. My first major hypothesis, that MFN is necessary for clustering, is not formally a part of the Rational Design conjectures. However, it lends itself to a future Rational Design agenda, and would be consistent with a conjecture that centralization increases with distributional problems. Quite aside from MFN, my analysis also suggests an additional link between distribution and centralization based on a synthesis of two Rational Design conjectures. While I did not test it formally, my analysis of clustering supports conjecture M3, MEMBERSHIP increases with DISTRIBUTION problems. The distributional problems of MFN tariff bargaining encouraged new states to join the regime. For reasons also found in conjecture C3, this increased number of players produced more centralization (clustering).

Beyond its theoretical agenda, this article has some substantive implications. Its evidence helps reconcile two contending views of the nineteenth-century trade system. Many historians view the 1890s as a return to protectionism, evidenced by the Méline tariff and the supposed breakdown of the 1860s treaty system. In contrast, political scientists see continued openness under hegemony, led by Britain's refusal to engage in Tariff Reform. My analysis suggests a middle ground, continued openness undergirded by new treaties that did not reduce tariffs by as much as previous treaties had. Severe distributional conflicts within a cooperative regime limited the openness achieved.

Limited openness is also evident in other trade institutions characterized by clustering or other centralized bargaining. Because the GATT system clustered negotiations into rounds, it long seemed that this decision-making rule stemmed from regime norms such as reciprocity or multilateralism.[76] While I have not analyzed these norms directly, I have shown that reciprocity is not essential to explaining GATT clustering. Clustering certainly can follow from MFN clauses, economic structure, and the number of actors.

The distributional argument here suggests a rethinking of the negotiated tariff concessions of GATT. Although the GATT system successfully produced fifty years of liberalization, liberalization occurred slowly. Much of Western Europe achieved comparable liberalization in the 1860s alone.[77] A historical perspective raises the question of whether GATT somehow encouraged states to make small concessions or to liberalize only in a series of small steps.

---

76. For two otherwise different examples among many, see Curzon and Curzon 1976; and Ruggie 1993.
77. Marsh 1999.

Though this claim must remain speculative for now, the theory suggests that GATT's slow pace stemmed from clustering MFN negotiations. The first three rounds (Annecy, Torquay, and Geneva) made especially slow progress under conditions closest to those of the model. Gilbert Winham argues that MFN forced each state to attempt negotiations with all the relevant players simultaneously.[78] These negotiations made concessions more difficult since they would be generalized to third parties.

According to Winham, the Kennedy Round avoided these problems by moving to linear tariff reductions. This focused negotiations on exceptions to the basic cuts rather than on the basic offer. It therefore represents a novel agenda-setting rule, one that poses an alternative to clustering in its nineteenth-century form. Liberalization in the subsequent Dillon and Kennedy Rounds proceeded much faster than before. Future research could extend the theory of clustering to consider a linear tariff-cutting rule as well as the political effects of the GATT reciprocity norm.[79]

Though I drew examples from the nineteenth century, the analysis has testable implications for contemporary negotiations in trade and other issue areas. In the United States clustering seems to have broken down in the late 1970s and much of the 1980s. Bilateral negotiations over voluntary export restraints, structural imped-iments to trade, export subsidies in agriculture, intellectual property rights, and bilateral investment treaties dominated the policy agenda. These issues were not characterized by MFN treatment, so the theory predicts they were unclustered.

In contrast the theory predicts that quota negotiations in the textiles regime are likely to be clustered. In this case if the United States negotiates seriatim, it might concede a greater quota to Taiwan and then have to negotiate the same quota with Hong Kong.[80] Negotiating with Hong Kong and Taiwan simultaneously—that is, clustering—would give the United States a distributional advantage. The regime rules of the Multi-Fibre Arrangement and its predecessors do exactly this.[81]

Finally, contemporary regionalism should affect clustering. Preferential trading areas—such as the European Union, North American Free Trade Agreement, and MERCOSUR (Southern Common Market)—grant members better-than-MFN treat-ment. This effectively removes MFN status between members and outsiders, though each outsider still receives the same treatment as every other outsider. This discrimination between members and nonmembers pulls the rug out from under centralized bargaining. I would expect clustering to occur within these institutions, where all members are treated equally. Clustering would be less attractive between regions. Regionalization takes away an important motive for global negotiations, such as a proposed new round of the WTO.

78. Winham 1986, 62–63.
79. See Finlayson and Zacher 1983; and Bagwell and Staiger 1999.
80. Of course, quota negotiations would require a different kind of model than one focused on tariff setting.
81. Aggarwal 1985.

This argument does not address decision making between rounds, in particular, the workings of the dispute settlement mechanism.[82] These dispute procedures should be unaffected by regionalism, which subjects centralized bargaining and centralized enforcement to different pressures even within a single international organization.

These contemporary examples raise more questions than can be answered here. The theory and the historical evidence presented here show that clustering has important distributional effects in a trade regime; they also help to explain the slowness of GATT liberalization. Clustering, far from being a "technical" characteristic of a regime, is an important political strategy with significant distributional consequences.

82. See Rosendorff and Milner, this volume.

Situation Structure and Institutional Design: Reciprocity, Coercion, and Exchange

Ronald B. Mitchell and Patricia M. Keilbach

States create international institutions in attempts to resolve problems they cannot solve alone. Yet states vary in their desire to form and join such institutions and in their incentives to defect from those they do join. These obstacles to cooperation have produced considerable variation in the mechanisms institutions use to deter defection without deterring participation. Some rely on narrow issue-specific reciprocity, whereas others rely on broader linkages involving coercive sanctions or positive rewards. This diversity in institutional scope is neither meaningless variation nor simple experimentation. Instead, states tend to base institutions on issue-specific reciprocity when possible but incorporate positive or negative linkage to other issue-areas when the distribution and enforcement problems within an issue-area appear more severe.

In an interdependent world one state's behavior often imposes unintended costs on other states. Yet, though all such negative externalities create demands for their resolution, all externalities are not alike.[1] Some are symmetric, with all states being simultaneously victims and perpetrators. Others are asymmetric, with "downstream" states being victims of, or dissatisfied with, the externality and "upstream" states being perpetrators of it.[2] Dissatisfied states may accept both types of externalities,

We thank Frank Alcock, Jeffrey Berejikian, Thomas Bernauer, Liliana Botcheva-Andonova, Robert Darst, Walter P. Falcon, James Fearon, Robert O. Keohane, Barbara Koremenos, Charles Lipson, Lisa Martin, James Morrow, Rosamond Naylor, Thomas Oatley, Kenneth Oye, John Richards, Duncan Snidal, Alexander Thompson, Michael Zürn, and the other contributors to this volume for helpful comments on earlier drafts of this article. Insightful suggestions by David Lake, Peter Gourevitch, and two anonymous reviewers proved particularly helpful in refining the argument. Valuable research assistance was provided by Hannah Fairbank, Elyce Hues, Aaron Knott, and Jonah Spiegelman. Ronald Mitchell thanks the University of Oregon's Department of Political Science and Stanford University's Center for Environmental Science and Policy for research support that contributed to completion of this article. Patricia Keilbach thanks the University of Oregon's Department of Political Science for research support that contributed to completion of this article.

1. Milner 1997, 44.

2. See the discussion of the number of actors variable, NUMBER, in Koremenos, Lipson, and Snidal, this volume, 777–78.

International Organization 55, 4, Autumn 2001, pp. 891–917

or they may try to resolve them by force. But they often create international institutions to resolve them.[3]

In symmetric externalities the fact that all states prefer mutual cooperation to the status quo predisposes states toward narrow institutions that rely on issue-specific reciprocity. Although coercion or side payments could also be used to combat incentives to defect, such linkage is usually unnecessary. Asymmetric externalities, however, present more severe distribution and enforcement problems.[4] An institution limited to the single issue of an asymmetric externality would provide benefits only to victims and impose costs only on perpetrators. To create incentive-compatible institutions in the face of such distributional problems, states dissatisfied with the status quo must broaden institutional scope, using the linkage of incentives or coercion to convince perpetrators to join the institution (Rational Design conjecture S2, SCOPE increases with DISTRIBUTION problems).[5] Victims also realize that membership restrictions and the retaliatory noncompliance of reciprocity—which can support enforcement in symmetric settings (conjecture M1, restrictive MEMBERSHIP increases with ENFORCEMENT problems)—are either unavailable to them or ineffective at inducing upstream states to join and comply. Thus enforcement problems reinforce the tendency in asymmetric externalities to broaden institutional scope, as victims incorporate linkages to ensure perpetrators comply once they join (conjecture S3, SCOPE increases with ENFORCEMENT problems). Whether scope is broadened by coercion or exchange depends on the power of the downstream state. For weak downstream states, the exchange of side payments for cooperation is the only available means of engaging stronger perpetrators in resolving the problem. Downstream states that are stronger than the perpetrators may employ such positive linkage but also can use negative linkage to coerce perpetrators into mitigating an externality and can do so without the aid of an institution. The distribution of costs and benefits in asymmetric externalities makes actors reluctant to join an institution and encourages them to violate institutional rules if they do, suggesting that distribution problems are not always separable from, and indeed sometimes drive, enforcement problems.[6]

While our analysis strongly validates two of the three Rational Design conjectures regarding scope (conjecture S2, SCOPE increases with DISTRIBUTION problems; and conjecture S3, SCOPE increases with ENFORCEMENT problems), it directs attention to the design interactions mentioned in Barbara Koremenos, Charles Lipson, and Duncan Snidal's introduction to this volume, suggesting in particular that restricting membership and increasing institutional scope (conjecture M1, restrictive MEMBER-SHIP increases with ENFORCEMENT problems; and S3, SCOPE increases with ENFORCE-MENT problems) can serve as substitutes for enforcement, with the former more

---

3. Milner 1997, 8–9.
4. Asymmetries are discussed as part of the NUMBER variable in Koremenos, Lipson, and Snidal, this volume, 778.
5. Koremenos, Lipson, and Snidal, this volume.
6. On interactions among variables, see the comments by Koremenos, Lipson, and Snidal, this volume, 779–80.

likely in symmetric settings and the latter more likely in asymmetric ones.[7] Our analysis also sheds light on two other Rational Design conjectures. We provide some support for conjecture C4, CENTRALIZATION increases with ENFORCEMENT problems. Victims of an asymmetric externality realize that perpetrators have no incentives to cooperate unless compensated. Centralized and explicit coordination of compensation reassures each victim that (and how much) other victims will contribute and, by pooling resources, increases compensation to the perpetrators. We also refine the role of flexibility in institutional design. In many cases, increasing flexibility allows states to agree on some institutional form that provides benefits to all parties despite the remaining bargaining problems resulting from distributional problems or uncertainty. In asymmetric externalities, however, fostering institutional creation depends on limiting flexibility to reassure both sides that the carefully negotiated terms of agreement will not be subject to later renegotiation or reinterpretation. In such contexts both victims and perpetrators want to limit the flexibility of the other side to prevent it from separating the two distributional problems that, when linked, make the institution worthwhile.

Definitions and Clarifications

Although we recognize that states can regulate behavior through informal social practices, we follow Koremenos, Lipson, and Snidal's narrower definition of international institutions: explicit arrangements, such as treaties and conventions, that regulate behavior. We also use the term regime interchangeably with institution. We refer to states that initiate regime formation as either "dissatisfied" or "victim" states and to those whose behavior they seek to influence as "externality-generating" or "perpetrating" states to capture the fact that all the regimes we analyze attempt to mitigate externalities resulting from at least one state's behavior. These terms refer to a state's role in a problem rather than to inherent characteristics of a state. Indeed, symmetric situations are defined as circumstances in which states that generate an externality are also dissatisfied with the status quo. But these terms let us capture situations in which victims are distinct from perpetrators.

To simplify the situations states face, we use a model composed of two groups of states addressing a single issue. The increased clarity gained by this approach must be balanced against the decreased accuracy in depicting the problems states face and the ways states resolve them.[8] Focusing on a single issue constrains our ability to generalize, since states sometimes try to create institutions to address multiple, logically linked issues. In those cases the interplay of power, interests, and other factors that vary across issue-areas can produce complex dynamics not captured in the model. Yet frequently issues are not connected by "objective" necessity but by

7. Ibid., 796.
8. For a similar simplification of international economic interactions, see Oye 1992.

states finding it compelling or in their interests to link them. Indeed, it is precisely the endogeneity of institutional scope—that states choose to make (or not make) certain linkages rather than take linkages as givens—that interests us here. Even when states seek to create institutions to resolve problems within a single area of behavior,[9] as seems particularly common in environmental affairs,[10] they still face choices of institutional scope, choices we seek to explain through our model.

Limiting the model to two actors also has virtues and costs. In single-issue contexts, it seems possible and appropriate to categorize all states as falling into one of two groups: those who prefer to reduce the externality and those who do not. If no states prefer a reduction, then no "problem" exists and no institution will be created. When some prefer a reduction, costs and benefits will produce differences in the strength of preferences, and some may prefer to free-ride on others' contributions without contributing themselves. A two-actor or two-group view does not, however, remove collective-action problems even among those who dislike the externality, and we consciously examine how conflicts both between groups and within groups influence institutional design.

Finally, we seek to explain institutional design, not compliance or effectiveness. The incentives to defect from an institution's rules influence the rules states adopt, even as those rules, once adopted, influence the propensity to defect and hence compliance and effectiveness. We hope that by highlighting how incentives to defect influence institutional design, and not just compliance, we will encourage scholars concerned with effectiveness to control more explicitly for, rather than assume that, different regime designs were adopted in equivalent circumstances.[11] In short we argue that differences in design reflect differences in strategic structure.

Enforcement and Distribution Problems Across Situation Structure

States have incentives to establish international institutions whenever doing so offers improvements over the status quo. Often these incentives are the response of states seeking to mitigate some other state's externality.[12] Variation in these externalities affects regime design.[13] This point is commonly illustrated by noting that regimes addressing collaboration situations have carefully designed compliance

9. Limiting negotiations to a single issue helps states avoid the potentially debilitating complexity of linkages to other issues. See Sebenius 1983; and McGinnis 1986.

10. Thus states have created separate regimes for acid precipitation, climate change, and stratospheric ozone loss and for biodiversity, endangered species, deforestation, and desertification rather than broader ones covering atmospheric or wildlife issues, respectively. Many environmentalists criticize this tendency to compartmentalize as ineffective in resolving environmental problems that are fundamentally integrated. Esty 1994.

11. This insight has not been fully incorporated in the debate between the "managerial" and "enforcement" schools. See Chayes and Chayes 1995; and Downs, Rocke, and Barsoom 1996.

12. See Oye 1992, 17; and Milner 1997, 8–9.

13. Mitchell 1999.

mechanisms while those addressing coordination situations do not because the former pose more severe enforcement problems.[14] Yet the enforcement problems in collaboration situations are still not as severe as those in the asymmetric externalities addressed by many environmental regimes. Although international institutions addressing symmetric externalities exhibit some design variation, more fundamental differences exist between these and institutions designed to address asymmetric externalities.

Much international relations literature focuses on the symmetric and reciprocal externalities analogized as Prisoners' Dilemmas or Tragedies of the Commons. Consider states sharing a lake, each polluting it while also using it for drinking water.[15] These states are symmetric both in their capacities to cause the problem— each generates an externality that harms others—and in their preferences for alleviation of the problem—each feels victimized by the corresponding externalities of others. Each believes its benefits from others' halting those activities are greater than its costs of halting its own such activities. Cooperation nevertheless remains elusive because each state prefers unilateral defection even more than collective mitigation of the externality. Although the payoffs of mutual cooperation are rarely evenly distributed, we consider these situations "symmetric" in the sense that all believe they would benefit from mitigation of the externality, and all can either exacerbate or mitigate the problem by engaging or not engaging in the behavior generating the externality.

Consider states sharing a river, each polluting it but also using it for drinking water, with some situated upstream from the rest. These states are asymmetric in two respects. They are asymmetric in their capacities to cause the problem (upstream states generate externalities and downstream states do not) and in their preferences for solving the problem (downstream states prefer alleviation and upstream states do not). Although often assumed otherwise, states do create regimes to address such asymmetric externalities in which "some actors obtain their most preferred outcome while others are left aggrieved."[16] With symmetric externalities, actors differ in their preferences for alternative institutions, but all prefer some institution to none. With asymmetric externalities, perpetrating actors prefer no institution because, absent compensation, they would bear the institutional costs but receive no institutional benefits.[17] Such distributional asymmetries can arise from material conditions or from states having different values, with some preferring that all undertake externality-mitigating acts and others preferring the status quo.[18] States can have downstream-type preferences if they do not engage in the externality-generating behavior, mitigate the externalities of such behaviors for indepen-

---

14. See Stein 1983; Krasner 1991; and Martin 1992a.

15. Waltz uses a similar analogy. Waltz 1979, 196.

16. The quote is from Stein 1983, 120. On such externalities, see Coase 1960; Conybeare 1980; Oye 1992; and Bernauer and Ruloff 1999.

17. Koremenos, Lipson, and Snidal, this volume.

18. Asymmetric externalities have received scholarly attention only recently but do not appear particularly rare empirically. See Rittberger and Zürn 1990, 31–32; and Martin 1992a,b.

dent reasons, or engage in externality-generating behaviors that do not materially affect other states or have material effects to which other states are indifferent. Even when all states actually prefer mutual cooperation to the status quo, some may dissemble if, by doing so, they can extract concessions from other states.[19] Whether reflecting true or strategically manipulated preferences, asymmetric situations reflect the willingness of some states to act as if they were pure perpetrators and not victims, indifferent to whether others reduce some externality. Asymmetric situations create greater enforcement problems precisely because they involve unidirectional dependence rather than reciprocal interdependence.

Power has a role in symmetric settings (as we elaborate later), but it particularly influences institutional design in asymmetric settings. Although notoriously difficult to assess, the distribution of power among states nonetheless influences the likelihood and shape of the institutions states create. Downstream states, whether weak or strong, have incentives to try to induce an upstream polluter, or other externality generator, to desist. We define strong states as those that possess resources (such as military might or a strong trade relationship in a crucial good) that can be used to impose costs on others for undesirable behavior. Although weak states lack resources to coerce or compel by imposing costs, they may be able to persuade or induce behavioral changes by using other resources as rewards (such as technological or financial aid).[20] A state's power is thus relational and issue-specific, dependent on how committed it is to achieving its own goals and on how vulnerable and sensitive other countries are to the resources it controls.[21] Weak states cannot get other states to "do something against their will" but may be able to get them to be "willing to do something."[22] Weak states may simply suffer the harms imposed by upstream states. Indeed, if an externality imposes costs on several states but the costs of inducing the perpetrator to desist are greater than the benefits to any single state of getting it to do so, collective-action problems will almost ensure the externality continues. However, weak states sometimes find ways to overcome these problems or suffer harms sufficiently large that unilateral action becomes worthwhile. They may then seek to design institutions that look much different from those initiated by strong victims.

Institutional Design Options

Both symmetric and asymmetric situations give at least some states ongoing incentives to defect. To counter these incentives, states design institutional mech-

---

19. We are indebted to James Morrow for clarifying this point.
20. See Knorr 1975, 310–19; Baldwin 1979, 184; and Morgenthau 1993, 31.
21. Keohane and Nye 1989.
22. This distinction coincides with the "paradox of unrealized power," that whether a state can convert its control over resources into influence over outcomes depends on how it deploys those resources. Baldwin 1979.

anisms that often rely on altering the relative costs and benefits of cooperation and defection.[23] We view these institutions as varying in the scope of their "fundamental bargains," that is, in the behaviors externality-generating states agree to limit and the threats and/or promises other states make in response. These responses are designed to restructure the incentives for engaging in externality-generating behaviors so that externality-generating states deem it worthwhile to participate. We use the term bargain loosely since these institutions can involve coerced as well as voluntary participation. In the context of the Rational Design framework, we see institutional scope as the core trait that leads a state to join rather than remain outside an institution. Scope can be manipulated for many purposes, but we focus on how states limit or extend it to balance the twin goals of participation and compliance.

Unlike Andrew Kydd's analysis of NATO expansion in which "who to include" is endogenous to institutional design,[24] in the externalities we analyze membership is not a design choice reflecting enforcement problems (conjecture M1, restrictive MEMBERSHIP increases with ENFORCEMENT problems) but a parameter dictated by the number of actors (NUMBER) who must be included to resolve the problem.[25] Our argument suggests that the Rational Design conjectures on membership and scope (conjecture M1; and conjecture S3, SCOPE increases with ENFORCEMENT problems) are variants of an overarching conjecture: the more severe the enforcement problems, the more institutional design reflects efforts to target benefits at contributors and sanctions at noncontributors. Restricting membership is one way to prevent non-contributors from receiving institutional benefits (conjecture M1). Expanding scope is a substitute strategy—the benefits of positive linkage and the costs of negative linkage can be targeted and controlled in ways that the effects of issue-specific reciprocity often cannot (conjecture S3).

In manipulating scope to create an incentive-compatible institution, states choose among three ideal-type bargains: issue-specific reciprocity, coercion (negative linkage), and exchange (positive linkage).[26] Although states can combine two or more of these mechanisms, these ideal-types capture essential design differences. All three involve attempts by dissatisfied states (1) to get perpetrators to take some action they would not otherwise take, (2) to do so by adopting contingent behaviors that present perpetrators with only two possible outcomes, and (3) to structure those outcomes so that perpetrators' resultant preferences over alternatives match dissatisfied states' preferences.[27] Coercion and exchange differ from issue-specific reciprocity, however, in that they increase institutional scope.

States must also choose the degree of centralization appropriate for solving the collective-action and informational problems that arise with all three ideal-types.

23. In contrast to Oye, we seek to explain only cases in which the institution changes, rather than clarifies, the contingent response of the dissatisfied state, thus excluding his category of "explanation." Oye 1992.

24. Kydd, this volume.

25. Koremenos, Lipson, and Snidal, this volume, 777–78.

26. For other views on coercion, contracts, and extortion, see Oye 1992, 35; and Krasner 1999, 26.

27. See Hasenclever, Mayer, and Rittberger 1997, 106; Krasner 1991, 340f; and Amini 1997, 7.

Centralizing information can facilitate implementation of all three strategies by improving each state's knowledge about what other states are doing. Centralizing "enforcement," in the broad sense of responding to compliance and violation when they occur, can help states overcome collective-action problems that plague all three strategies. Centralization constitutes a not-always-successful attempt to help states coordinate retaliatory noncompliance in reciprocity, to coordinate sanctioning in coercion, and to pool resources in exchange.

Regimes adopting issue-specific reciprocity rely exclusively on intertemporal linkage within an issue-area, with dissatisfied states mitigating their externality if others also do so. The fundamental bargain involves a contingent offer quite narrow in scope: "if you do X, I'll do X, but if you don't do X, I won't do X," where X is some externality-reducing action.[28] Such reciprocity combines the promise of whatever benefits accrue to perpetrators from sustained mutual cooperation with the threat of reversion to the no-agreement status quo of mutual defection. Although states can estimate the benefits of mutual cooperation, reciprocity-based institutions rarely delineate these benefits explicitly. We use reciprocity to refer to the issue-specific contingent behaviors of Tit-for-Tat (as opposed to more diffuse reciprocity),[29] a strategy not always available and, when available, perhaps not effective or Pareto improving.[30] Equally important, in many multilateral settings, states discover that retaliatory noncompliance itself involves a collective-action problem among regime supporters, who can find it difficult to target the effects of such noncompliance so that only the original defector is punished, thereby undermining rather than reinforcing cooperation.[31]

Expanding institutional scope helps remedy these problems. Devising contingent responses other than mitigating their own externality allows dissatisfied states access to outcomes other than those dictated by the power distribution within the issue-area. Although issue linkage often involves combining complementary Prisoners' Dilemma conflicts, we use issue linkage in the very limited, tactical sense of a state using resources other than engaging in the externality or not.[32] Negative linkage involves dissatisfied states threatening some sanction (S) unless the perpetrator does X: "if you do X, I won't do S, but if you don't do X, I'll do S." Unlike reciprocity or exchange, the success of coercion requires that victims preclude perpetrators from continuing to receive the status quo payoff and instead choose

28. X can be either a positive or negative action, that is, A can be attempting to get B to commence a new activity or to halt or change an existing activity.
29. Although many regimes replace or reinforce issue-specific reciprocity with reciprocity based on positive and negative linkage to other issue-areas, the core of Axelrod's argument lay in demonstrating that Tit-for-Tat fosters cooperation without such linkage. Axelrod 1984.
30. Michael Zürn and Thomas Bernauer helped us clarify this point. Thus states can threaten to punish their political dissidents unless other states stop punishing theirs but do not do so because the nature of the situation makes it obviously ineffective.
31. See Axelrod and Keohane 1986; and Oye 1992, 17–33.
32. See McGinnis 1986; Sebenius 1983; and Haas 1980, 371–72.

between the costs of doing X or the costs of the sanctions.[33] Leaving the exact nature of the sanctions unstated can strengthen the threat's deterrent effect. Such sanctions can reduce the "targeting" problem of retaliatory noncompliance but may leave the collective-action obstacles of sanctioning unresolved.

States can also offer positive linkage. In such an "exchange" regime, dissatisfied states offer some side payment to perpetrators that prefer it to continuing current policies. The fundamental bargain involves an exchange promising some reward (R) if the perpetrator does X and the weak threat of remaining at the no-agreement status quo position otherwise: "if you do X, I'll do R, but if you don't do X, I won't do R." Exchange and reciprocity share a basic model of contingent behavior but differ in the rewards: they allow careful modulation of the benefits to the perpetrator, but the benefits are dictated by the payoffs of mutual cooperation when using issue-specific reciprocity. Unlike reciprocity and coercion, exchange usually requires specifying both the magnitude of the reward and the terms for granting it.

Using these theoretical distinctions to differentiate empirical cases requires careful consideration of the status quo and existing expectations. Consider two states (or groups of states), A and B, with a given level of trade. State A is not engaged in an influence attempt if it simply promotes increased trade with B without making this increase contingent on some policy of B's.[34] State A is engaged in issue-specific reciprocity if it makes its future level of trade contingent on B's level of trade. State A is engaged in negative linkage if it threatens to reduce levels of trade from those that B had previously expected would continue (or to block improvements in trade that B had previously expected would occur) and promises to maintain previously expected trade levels or improvements only if B improves its human rights policies. State A is engaged in positive linkage if it offers to increase trade with B beyond the level that B had previously expected only if B improves its human rights policies. Table 1 summarizes these distinctions.

How Situation Structure Influences Institutional Design

Situation structure strongly influences, without dictating, whether states create a narrow institution based on reciprocity or a broader one based on exchange or coercion. Asymmetric and symmetric externalities produce different incentives to defect. Differences in how institutional designs address these incentives to defect give rise, in turn, to different incentives for membership. Thus mechanisms adopted to restructure incentives to defect also restructure the incentives to join the institution. The bargaining or distributional problem (creating an agreement states will join) and the enforcement problem (inducing those that have joined to comply)

33. Krasner 1999, 26.
34. Baldwin 1971, 24.

TABLE 1. Distinguishing reciprocity, exchange, and coercion

	Alternatives offered by A (dissatisfied state) to B (externality-generating state) [and B's payoff]	
	If B does X	If B does not do X
Issue-specific reciprocity (no linkage)	A does X* [SQ − Cx + Bx]	A continues status quo behavior** [SQ]
Exchange (positive linkage)	A provides Reward [SQ − Cx + R]	A continues status quo behavior [SQ]
Coercion (negative linkage)	A continues status quo behavior [SQ − Cx]	A imposes Sanction [SQ − S]

* = mutual cooperation
** = mutual defection
SQ = Status quo payoff to B
Cx = B's costs of doing X
Bx = Benefits to B from A doing X
R = Value of A's reward to B
S = Cost of A's sanction to B

thus become linked, interacting in ways that reinforce each other, as suggested in the volume's introduction.[35]

Faced with a symmetric externality, states most dissatisfied with the status quo will tend to prefer reciprocity to coercion or exchange because it helps resolve the bargaining problem simply and the enforcement problem adequately. For most international negotiations, a wide range of outcomes are possible. Issue-specific reciprocity provides a strong and simple criteria for constraining bargaining to institutional rules that apply universally. Without creating a single focal point for discussion or eliminating bargaining conflict, imposing nominally equal requirements on all externality generators—for instance, a universal ban, equal reductions, or common technology requirements—significantly narrows the range of outcomes to be considered. Reciprocity rarely imposes equal burdens or provides equal benefits, but it avoids making those distributional differences explicit and salient aspects of the negotiation. In a symmetric setting the prospect of creating a Pareto-improving institution will lead those who could benefit from mutual cooperation to join the negotiations, hoping to define requirements that maximize their benefits while minimizing their burdens and risks. Their ability to use exit or voice will tend to produce agreements that make all better off, even if not making all equally better off.[36]

35. See Fearon 1998; and Morrow 1994c.
36. Hirschman 1970.

Of course, the shared preference for mutual cooperation that defines symmetric situations does not make it stable. States have ongoing incentives to violate. Direct reciprocity can support mutual cooperation if, as in trade agreements, the effects of violation are sufficiently concentrated that actors have incentives to carry out retaliatory noncompliance and can target the effects of such noncompliance onto the initial violator. But if large harms of violations fall on a diffuse set of actors, as often occurs in environmental affairs, retaliatory noncompliance will be unlikely. The individual costs of retaliating will exceed the individual benefits, creating collective-action problems, and even victims with incentives to retaliate will worry that their retaliation will undermine cooperation without succeeding at altering the initial violator's behavior. States can centralize the process of responding to violators in different ways in their effort to overcome these collective-action problems. They can promote information exchange, information dissemination, and alternative sanction mechanisms to increase the ability and incentives to retaliate and the ability to target initial violators, though these may not eliminate the collective-action problem. We view even regimes that authorize such sanctions as fundamentally reciprocal if sanctioning states engage in the behaviors they are seeking to induce in the targets and targets consider themselves as benefiting from those states' behaviors.[37]

States can, however, design truly coercive regimes in symmetric contexts. The Pareto-deficient outcomes of a Tragedy of the Commons do not require Pareto-efficient solutions. Malevolent hegemonic states can coerce weaker states to join regimes in which the weaker states provide collective goods while the hegemon free-rides.[38] They will do so if the benefits from the cooperation they can coerce (less the costs of coercing it) exceed those from the cooperation they could induce by their own cooperation (less the costs of that cooperation). Yet such coercion seems unlikely to be formalized since doing so requires coercing acceptance of inequitable institutional terms in the face of international norms that "stress social and economic equity as well as the equality of states [and make] opposition look more harshly self-interested and less defensible."[39] Institutions imposed by powerful states are unlikely to have highly centralized information and enforcement provisions: the powerful state can induce considerable compliance on its own, making the institution's enforcement problem less severe than when power is distributed more equally (Rational Design conjecture C4, CENTRALIZATION increases with ENFORCEMENT problems), and weaker states will resist efforts to get them to contribute to their own coercion.

Positive linkage is also possible but less likely as a response to symmetric externalities. Offering side payments would require identifying a distribution of benefits that all consider more equitable than reciprocal cooperation, but such

37. Axelrod and Keohane 1986.
38. See Snidal 1985; and Kindleberger 1981.
39. Keohane and Nye 1989, 36, 235–36. It remains unclear how often hegemonic states view imposed agreements as cheaper ways to coerce cooperation than traditional threats exercised outside of an international institution. Young 1989, 84–89.

alternatives will be difficult to identify. In Tragedies of the Commons, even participating in the negotiations reveals a preference for mutual cooperation over the status quo, making subsequent demands for compensation suspect. States may cheat on their obligations but will avoid public threats designed to extort compensation because doing so risks undermining the cooperation of others from which they benefit. At the same time, the biggest beneficiaries of cooperation can point to norms that "all who benefit should contribute" to resist demands for compensation. For these beneficiaries, such compensation is unattractive in itself and because it sets a precedent for future compensation, creating a reputation for "caving in" or getting "the short end of the stick." Thus, although institutionalizing reciprocity in symmetric contexts may be difficult, institutionalizing exchange or coercion is likely to be even more difficult.

These institutional choices appear quite different in cases of asymmetric externalities. In line with two of the Rational Design conjectures, both distributional and enforcement problems lead to institutions broader in scope than in symmetric situations (conjecture S2, SCOPE increases with DISTRIBUTION problems; and conjecture S3, SCOPE increases with ENFORCEMENT problems). Although institutions that provide absolute gains for all states but greater relative gains for some must address distributional difficulties (see Koremenos, Lipson, and Snidal's analysis of conjecture M3, MEMBERSHIP increases with DISTRIBUTION problems, in the introduction), those distributional problems become even more severe with asymmetric externalities. Reciprocity limited to the issue-area poses two distinct problems. First, perpetrators receive no benefits if dissatisfied states cooperate. This distribution, or bargaining, problem means perpetrators have no reason to join. Second, perpetrators are not harmed if dissatisfied states defect. This enforcement problem means perpetrators who nonetheless join have no reason to comply. Because reciprocity is not Pareto improving, dissatisfied states must expand institutional scope in ways that induce perpetrators to join while reassuring dissatisfied states that the perpetrators will comply. Whether that increased scope will entail coercion or reward depends on the relative power of the perpetrator.

When the victims of an asymmetric externality are stronger than the perpetrators, the former may simply threaten the latter to compel them to mitigate an externality at their own expense.[40] They may create international institutions to do so, but even states that have coercive resources at their disposal may have difficulty making credible threats because of the costs involved, the constraints of domestic political opinion, or the difficulties of getting other states to cooperate in imposing sanctions.[41] Nor are the benefits of formalizing coercive relations clear. Although the strong state still must expend resources to induce participation and compliance, formalization makes the coercion more explicit, allowing weaker states to use legal norms in appealing to other states when resisting such coercion. A formal agreement

---

40. See Young 1989, 84–89; Martin 1992a,b; and Rittberger and Zürn 1990.
41. Drezner 2000.

may enhance the stronger state's reputation for coercive strength, but reputation effects also make weak states more likely to resist.

Strong states may turn to rewards because making threats credible and potent can be difficult.[42] If strong states can choose between rewards and sanctions, weak states must choose between rewards and simply "suffering what they must."[43] Realizing that they lack the resources to coerce and that offering reciprocity will not alter perpetrators' incentives, weak states facing asymmetric externalities correctly see positive linkage as the only viable remedy.[44] For both weak and strong victims, the benefits of inducing the perpetrator's cooperation are evident in the damage from, or costs of mitigating, the externality. If this benefit to the victim exceeds the value the perpetrator places on continuing its current behavior, a Pareto-improving agreement is possible.

And institutionalizing an exchange offers advantages that do not exist with coercion. Formalizing the terms of exchange enhances the credibility of the exchange to both sides by clarifying what was promised and defining iterative bargains that reduce both sides' fear of being suckered.[45] Given that a perpetrator of an asymmetric externality will not willingly participate without side payments, centralizing those side payments through the institution pools resources and spreads the costs while helping each victim know how much all other victims will contribute. This information reduces the perpetrator's ability to extort additional compensation. In a form of weak centralization, making offers of rewards both collective and public engages reputational effects that help overcome the greater enforcement problems of asymmetric externalities (conjecture C4, CENTRALIZATION increases with ENFORCEMENT problems). Victims fear that perpetrators will "take the money and run"; perpetrators fear that victims will renege on compensation. Therefore, public, explicit, and formal obligations benefit each side by increasing normative and social pressures on the other to carry out its part of the bargain. Those offering rewards want clear terms of exchange to avoid moral-hazard problems that often plague offers of rewards, as evident in the postwar trade and payments cases described by Thomas Oatley.[46]

This discussion regarding formalizing compensation clarifies the role of flexibility in institutional design. When states agree that any of several possible institutions would be better than the status quo, institutional creation can still be held hostage by disagreements over which institution to create. In these cases flexibility can allow institutional creation to move forward without fully resolving distribution problems or uncertainty about the future state of the world (conjecture F1, FLEXIBILITY increases with UNCERTAINTY about the state of the world; and conjecture F2,

---

42. See Baldwin 1971; and Schelling 1960, 177.

43. Thucydides 1954.

44. See Hasenclever, Mayer, and Rittberger 1997, 106; Keohane and Nye 1989, 52–53, 122; and Krasner 1991, 340f.

45. This is evident, for example, in the agreement to induce North Korea to forgo its nuclear weapons ambitions. Dorn and Fulton 1997.

46. Oatley, this volume.

FLEXIBILITY increases with DISTRIBUTION problems). Allowing for redesign and reinterpretation ensures the agreement remains beneficial to all parties as circumstances
change. In contrast, the benefits of an exchange institution in resolving an asymmetric externality depend on, and are sensitive to, the agreement's exact terms.
Terms are carefully crafted to avoid the twin obsolescing bargains of behavioral
change without compensation and compensation without behavioral change. Each
side sees the institution as beneficial only if it is implemented as agreed. Here,
limiting flexibility and precluding renegotiation make institutional creation possible.
Thus examining asymmetric externalities affirms the Rational Design contention
that states manipulate flexibility to facilitate institutional creation but suggests that
this manipulation may involve either increasing it or decreasing it depending on the
nature of the problem being addressed.[47]

Finally, a caveat is in order. As Koremenos, Lipson, and Snidal note, rational
design does not require that policymakers immediately identify the situation
structure they face and propose reciprocity, coercion, or exchange accordingly.[48]
Informational and perceptual obstacles may prevent dissatisfied states from initially
recognizing the structure of the situation they face. States make mistakes, viewing
asymmetric problems as symmetric, projecting their own preferences onto others, or
hoping that simple reciprocity can produce their desired outcome. Even weak states
may try coercion first, because it may work and, if it does, will be less costly than
offering rewards. Thus reciprocity, coercion, or exchange may result not only from
a rational calculus by policymakers but also from a process in which the refusal of
other states to join reciprocal or coercive institutions clarifies preferences and hence
situation structure. Our argument requires only that dissatisfied states respond to
such insights by moving from reciprocity to coercion to exchange until perpetrating
states accept.[49] Such a trial-and-error process of design, though taking longer, is no
less rational or purposive.

Examining the Empirical Evidence

Three predictions on institutional scope stem from our argument. Although we
expect these to apply in many issue-areas, we examine them here only in the
environmental realm.

1. Issue-specific reciprocity should be the most common institutionalized response to symmetric externalities.

2. Coercion should be a more common institutionalized response to asymmetric externalities with strong victims than exchange, but exchange will still
   be possible.

---

47. See John Richards' example of airline regulation and Milner and Rosendorff's discussion of
escape clauses, in this volume.
48. Koremenos, Lipson, and Snidal, this volume, 766–67 and fn. 19.
49. We are indebted to Michael Zürn for this insight.

3. Exchange should be the only institutionalized response to asymmetric externalities with weak victims.

Although the third prediction is nonprobabilistic, a full evaluation of the other two would require contingency tables of situation structures and institutions for a large, representative sample of cases. In the absence of such a database,[50] we assess the initial plausibility of these predictions using five separate cases presented by three environmental institutions. Environmental problems complement the other issues analyzed in the Rational Design project and present many examples of both symmetric and asymmetric externalities.

We evaluate whaling, stratospheric ozone loss, and Rhine River chloride pollution because they allow us to observe how situation structure, and hence distribution and enforcement problems, influence the institutional bargains in five distinct cases. Ozone loss provides two cases distinguished by different situation structures among the states involved, with a symmetric externality among states concerned about the problem intertwined with an asymmetric externality between concerned and unconcerned states. International whaling provides two similar cases distinguished by time period: the initial symmetric externality among whaling states gained an asymmetric element as underlying state preferences changed and nonwhaling "victims," led by a strong United States, sought to induce whaling states to end commercial whaling. The Rhine River case presents a clear asymmetric externality with a weak victim.

Besides allowing our primary independent variables, distribution and enforcement problems, to vary, these cases share other important traits. Each involved the "low politics" of transboundary environmental problems, attracting less policy attention and concern than security and economic issues. All five fit the scope of our argument, involving cooperation on a single issue that actors could either support or oppose. Some parties in all the cases had ongoing incentives to defect. We could categorize each case by situation structure and fundamental bargain. Finally, despite these many similarities, the resultant institutions vary in the fundamental bargains they devised to deal with states' incentives to defect. These five cases allow us to evaluate Rational Design conjecture S2, SCOPE increases with DISTRIBUTION problems; conjecture S3, SCOPE increases with ENFORCEMENT problems; and conjecture C4, CENTRALIZATION increases with ENFORCEMENT problems.

International Whaling

After World War II, whaling states faced a quintessential Tragedy of the Commons.[51] Interest in recommencing whaling to bolster postwar supplies of food and oil prompted anxieties about repeating the overexploitation of whale stocks and

50. Mitchell 2001.
51. Peterson 1992, 158.

overcapitalization of the whaling fleet that had plagued the prewar period.[52] Whaling states were symmetrically situated—each state's overappropriation contributed to the externality of a declining whale stock, and each preferred that others reduce their overappropriation. In 1946 these states negotiated the International Convention for the Regulation of Whaling (ICRW) and created an International Whaling Commission (IWC) composed of one representative from each member state. The IWC became a "whaling club" in which all whaling states, but primarily the five major whaling states (Japan, Norway, the Netherlands, the Soviet Union, and the United Kingdom) sought to avert the declining whale populations, the increasing effort per whale killed, and the low profits of the prewar period.[53] Each state's economic incentives to support "rational management of a renewable common pool resource" were counterbalanced by predictable incentives for (and fears of) free riding as well as discount rates that often exceeded stock-replenishment rates.[54] Whaling states desired a healthy stock but preferred not to contribute to its production. For almost twenty years, major whaling states rejected any meaningful restraints within the IWC, and some smaller whaling states (Chile, North Korea, and Peru) refused to join. The smaller whaling states knew that refusing to join the regime would not prevent cooperation among major whaling states, cooperation from which they would benefit.

To the extent that the ICRW influenced state behavior at all, it did so almost exclusively through implicit, but nonetheless clear, issue-specific reciprocity. States accepted three-quarters-majority voting rules to set collective annual quotas on total whales killed and on some specific species. Governments agreed to promptly report catch statistics to the International Bureau of Whaling Statistics, which would close the whaling season on the date it estimated the quota would be reached.[55] Negotiated quotas and reported catches, even with misreporting, improved each state's ability to predict and respond to the behavior of others. States could "opt out" of any quota found objectionable (or that other states had opted out of), as well as invoke the standard withdrawal clause, facilitating the reciprocity of reversion to the status quo.[56] States used these mechanisms, often simply to escape from the agreement but at other times in reciprocal but decentralized Tit-for-Tat behavior, either to avoid being taken advantage of or to enforce the agreement.[57] The ICRW required governments to punish infractions committed by individuals, but did not specify sanctions for particular states' fleets exceeding the collective quota.[58] Reciprocity

52. Levy 1988, 5.
53. See Stoett 1997, 57; and Tonnessen and Johnsen 1982, 509.
54. See Stoett 1997, 57; Peterson 1992, 158, 160; and Levy 1988, 17.
55. See ICRW 1946, Art. IX; and Walsh 1999.
56. On escape clauses, see Milner and Rosendorff 2001.
57. Walsh 1999, 313. In 1959 Norway and the Netherlands withdrew altogether in protest of quotas they considered too restrictive. In subsequent cases opting out created the awkward but unsurprising situation of species-specific quotas that bound only states that did not hunt those species.
58. Even development of a system of independent inspectors to verify compliance failed to address the question of "after detection, what?" Ikle 1961.

was nonetheless clear in the implicit threat that no fleet could keep whaling after the International Bureau of Whaling Statistics closed the season without provoking continued whaling by other fleets, a strategy that appears to have prevented postseason whaling (although not misreporting of whaling during the season). Although several cases of egregious, particularly Soviet, violations have come to light, most states generally abided by regime quotas.[59]

During the 1970s, declining economic interests in whaling and increasing environmental animosity toward whaling transformed this symmetric externality among whaling states into an asymmetric externality between whaling states and antiwhaling states. Whaling was no longer solely the concern of those hunting them.[60] Although antiwhaling states did not contribute to the problem by hunting whales, they considered the whaling states' behaviors as threatening various whale species and conflicting with a growing moral sentiment against any killing of whales.[61] Taking advantage of a provision allowing universal membership, "non-whaling nations and conservation [nongovernmental organizations] attempted to persuade other non-whaling nations to join the IWC in an effort to obtain the three-quarters majority needed to establish a moratorium on [commercial] whaling."[62] Between 1978 and 1982, IWC membership grew from eight nonwhaling and eleven whaling states to twenty-seven nonwhaling and twelve whaling states. Nonwhaling states joined the regime precisely because they were not engaged in the activity and did not share the preferences of the whaling states, but considered their interests as harmed by whalers, even if whaling imposed no material impacts on them.[63] The new membership adopted a commercial moratorium in 1982, over the opposition of all but one whaling state. The major whaling states (Japan, Norway, and the Soviet Union) filed objections to it and threatened to leave the regime.[64]

The moratorium involved a new fundamental bargain. Had it been negotiated only among whaling states, it would have constituted a simple continuation of reciprocity. But the moratorium was adopted by nonwhaling states who viewed whalers as perpetrating a negative externality. Although nonwhaling states could have offered positive inducements to those who ceased whaling, they instead used coercion to address this asymmetric externality. Rather than relying on centralized enforcement, the United States, as a powerful dissatisfied state, became the "self-appointed 'policeman' of the IWC."[65] The United States made or carried out threats to reduce fishing rights or restrict fish imports both to induce member states to stay

59. Earlier Soviet violations seem quite distinct from more recent Japanese violations that have been smaller in magnitude and coupled with quite public denunciations of the IWC. See Yablokov 1994; Baker and Palumbi 1994; and Peterson 1992.

60. In terms of problem structure, a "conflict over means" had become a "conflict over values." Rittberger and Zürn 1990.

61. D'Amato and Chopra 1991.

62. Stedman 1990, 168.

63. See Levy 1988, 29; and Andresen 1989, 109, 116.

64. See Birnie 1985, 616; Sigvaldsson 1996, 330 citing Holt 1985, 192; and Stedman 1990, 168.

65. See Andresen 1989, 111; Wilkinson 1989; and Martin and Brennan 1989.

in the IWC and comply with the moratorium and to induce nonmember whaling states to join the IWC.[66] A U.S. threat of issue-specific reciprocity (that is, to recommence commercial whaling) would have lacked credibility because of its domestic unpopularity and would have been ineffective if carried out because its effects could not be targeted on whaling states who, in any event, increasingly considered some species as no longer threatened. In contrast, threats of economic sanctions that favored domestic fishing interests were both credible and targetable, soon leading major whaling states to discontinue their commercial whaling. Nongovernmental organizations also used direct action and publicity campaigns to sanction whaling, whether conducted within or outside the regime's rules.

Over time, whaling states have responded as one would expect of perpetrators of an asymmetric externality. They have switched from clandestine to public rejections of institutional norms, rejecting even the illusion of voluntary participation and regularly denouncing the IWC. Iceland has withdrawn, Norway has recommenced commercial whaling, and Japan and Russia have threatened to do both. Whaling states have granted numerous scientific permits over IWC objections and formed the North Atlantic Marine Mammal Commission as an alternative institution with membership restricted to commercial whaling interests.[67] This decreasing cooperation reflects, as our model predicts, the shift in underlying situation structure. Initially, symmetric interests among whaling states led them to accept and often, if reluctantly, to comply with a reciprocity-based regime. The emergence of strong antiwhaling sentiment created an asymmetric setting, but one with a strong "victim," the United States. The United States could have pressed for an exchange regime, but it chose coercion through economic sanctions, not only because this strategy appeared cheaper than offering rewards but also because of domestic resistance to paying states to cease a behavior that many viewed as morally wrong in the first place. Predictably, whaling states have resisted the institution's new form, increasingly participating and complying only under duress.[68]

Stratospheric Ozone Depletion

In the 1980s stratospheric ozone depletion resulting from chemicals released into the atmosphere by human activities presented states concerned about the problem (mainly industrialized states) with two interconnected strategic situations. Dissatisfied states faced a symmetric Tragedy of the Commons among themselves, since most industrialized states were both perpetrators and victims of ozone loss. They were perpetrators because their firms produced and their publics consumed most of the world's chlorofluorocarbons (CFCs) and other ozone-depleting substances. They

---

66. DeSombre 2000.
67. See Hoel 1993; and Caron 1995.
68. If the strategy is eventually judged ineffective, the United States, and even nongovernmental organizations, may yet decide that paying states not to whale is a more effective strategy, however morally repugnant.

were victims because growing awareness of the problem had mobilized their publics to demand protection of the ozone layer, for both material and symbolic reasons. Although reducing CFC use proved not particularly costly once cheap alternatives became available, the benefits of incurring those costs depended on the extent of similar action by others.[69] As in any environmental Tragedy of the Commons, the costs of cooperation were worth incurring and promised environmental benefits only so long as familiar obstacles to inducing cooperation by others could be overcome.

Concerned states faced an asymmetric externality, however, in relation to many developing states. Many developing states, with more pressing policy priorities, high discount rates, and weak domestic concern, considered the immediate benefits of using CFCs—to improve food refrigeration, for example—as outweighing any small future benefits of protecting the ozone layer.[70] Industrialized states feared that China, India, and other developing states would increase their use of ozone-depleting substances and hasten depletion of the ozone layer. Publics in industrialized states worried that their efforts to protect the ozone layer would make them "downstream" victims of developing states relatively unconcerned about damage to the ozone layer. Although the use of ozone-depleting substances by concerned states would constitute free riding, their use by many developing states would reflect a more deep-seated asymmetry of interests: "they were more concerned with accelerating industrial development than with saving the ozone layer, no matter what actions other states took."[71] Yet resolving the problem required their involvement.

As in the early whaling regime, issue-specific reciprocity was adequate for agreement among industrialized states. The 1987 Montreal Protocol to the 1985 Vienna Convention for the Protection of the Ozone Layer established deadlines for phasing out CFC use that applied to all industrialized states. The relatively mild distributional differences among industrialized states meant negotiators did not discuss positive incentives among industrialized states and expressed little concern about sanctions for violations, leaving their development to an executive body.[72] The issue-specific reciprocity of clear phase-out deadlines applicable to all industrialized states was sufficient to garner signatures by every Organization for Economic Cooperation and Development (OECD) state except Turkey by the end of 1989.

Developing states, however, were considered to be in a "special situation." The 1987 Montreal Protocol granted them ten years to meet phase-out deadlines and required industrialized states to "facilitate access to" aid and environmentally safe technology to foster their use of alternatives to CFCs. Yet this grace period and the vague offers of rewards, coupled with the threat that member states would halt all

---

69. Sell 1996, 100.
70. Ibid., 99–100.
71. Ibid., 102.
72. Three years later, that body adopted a weak "list of measures that might be taken" (including "issuing cautions" and suspending treaty rights and privileges) if industrialized states failed to meet deadlines for phasing out ozone-depleting substances or to fund the financial mechanism. UNEP 1991.

trade in ozone-depleting substances with nonmember states, failed to convince most developing states to sign on.[73] By June 1990, only three of the thirteen developing countries predicted to be the biggest CFC consumers—and only thirty-one of over one hundred developing countries—had signed the Montreal Protocol.[74] In the London Amendments of that month, industrialized states, recognizing this, established a Financial Mechanism involving centralized disbursement of pooled financial resources to cover developing states' compliance costs. The amendments carefully centralized and specified the exchange process. This reassured developing states by requiring that financial aid be "additional" and making their phase-out obligations explicitly contingent on receiving aid. It also reassured industrialized states by establishing specific criteria for developing states to receive aid and requiring the monitoring of performance.[75] Only this unambiguous codification of side payments convinced most developing states to join the regime.[76] Within three years fifty more developing countries, including all major prospective CFC users, had joined the regime. Sanctions played little role in this increase: the amendments added no sanctions, and countries known to be smuggling CFCs have yet to be sanctioned.[77]

States concerned about ozone depletion devised different fundamental bargains to deal with different problems. Facing a symmetric externality among themselves, concerned states promptly accepted noncontingent obligations that involved neither rewards nor sanctions, but the reciprocity of mutual CFC phase-outs. These same states faced an asymmetric externality in which less concerned developing states joined the institution only when offered explicit, well-codified side payments. Here, positive linkage was not driven by necessity but apparently was chosen by strong victims as less costly and more effective than using negative linkage to compel developing states to reduce their use of ozone-depleting substances.

Rhine River Chloride Pollution

Pollution of the Rhine River by chlorides involves a classic asymmetric externality that dramatically illustrates the distribution and enforcement problems they can pose.[78] Since the 1930s, French, German, and Swiss enterprises had dumped steadily increasing amounts of chlorides, among other chemicals, into the Rhine.[79] French and German enterprises contributed 90 percent of the chloride load, the

---

73. Sell 1996, 100. Restrictions on trade in ozone-depleting substances "would have no inhibiting effect on China and India because of their huge potential domestic markets." Benedick 1991, 100.

74. Benedick 1991, 151; and ratification list compiled by authors.

75. Montreal Protocol 1987/1990, Art. 5(5–7).

76. Weiss and Jacobson 1998.

77. Clapp 1997. Victor considers the threat of cutting off multilateral funds as a sanction, but it is one that would have been unavailable without initial adoption of the reward-based strategy. Victor 1998, 165–66.

78. The section that follows builds extensively on the excellent analyses of the Rhine River case by Bernauer 1995 and 1996.

79. See LeMarquand 1977, 125; and Mingst 1981, 164.

Swiss a small percentage, and the Dutch practically none.[80] France, Germany, and Switzerland are exclusively perpetrators since the nature of their water supplies "leaves them unaffected by chloride pollution."[81] The Dutch, in contrast, are exclusively victims, with high salt levels imposing significant costs on their water works and agricultural interests.

Within the larger regime based on the International Commission for the Protection of the Rhine Against Pollution (or Rhine Commission), the Dutch eventually succeeded in addressing this asymmetric externality through explicit side payments. As early as the 1930s, the Dutch had protested France's policy of allowing the Alsace Potassium Mine (MdPA; the single largest source, contributing almost 40 percent of the Rhine's chloride load) to discharge chlorides into the Rhine to avoid contaminating Alsatian groundwater. Although the Dutch government and individuals might have turned to international law to coerce a change in French policy, international legal norms did not lend much support to their position until the mid-1970s.[82] A 1963 Dutch proposal for issue-specific reciprocity with all states "freez[ing] the Rhine's chloride load at the 1954 level" was, not surprisingly, flatly rejected by France and Germany.[83] Dutch efforts only began to succeed in 1972 with a proposal that France reduce MdPA's chloride discharges by 60 kilograms per stere in exchange for the Dutch, Germans, and Swiss covering 34 percent, 30 percent, and 6 percent, respectively, of the costs.[84] These cost shares reflected an ad hoc balancing of each state's contribution to the pollution problem and the "intensity of their demand for chloride reductions."[85] Once cost estimates grew, however, France refused to implement the agreement.[86] Yet this ad hoc, historically contingent, and rejected proposal provided a surprisingly robust foundation for subsequent institutionalized cooperation.

Revisions to the 1972 proposal produced the 1976 Convention on the Protection of the Rhine Against Pollution by Chlorides. France agreed to reduce discharges by 60 kilograms per stere in three phases, with phase 1 requiring the French to reduce chloride discharges by 20 kilograms per stere by installing a system to inject salts underground.[87] The Dutch, Germans, and Swiss agreed to prevent any net increase in their own discharges. French cooperation was not a response to this reciprocity but to the application of the 1972 cost-sharing formula to the Fr 132 million costs of the injection system and to the costs of the deeper phase 2 and 3 reductions.[88] A 1991 Protocol applied this same cost-sharing formula to two additional projects.

80. See Kamminga 1978, 66; and LeMarquand 1977, 119.
81. Bernauer 1995, 372.
82. Bernauer 1996, 220–21.
83. Ibid., 209.
84. Although not specified in the convention and often misinterpreted as kilograms per second, the unit of measurement is kilograms per stere, with 1 stere equal to 1 cubic meter of water.
85. Bernauer 1996, 210.
86. LeMarquand 1977, 118.
87. Mingst 1981, 168.
88. Bernauer 1995, 377.

One involved eight years of carefully parsed Dutch, German, and Swiss contributions, totaling Fr 400 million, toward MdPA's costs of stockpiling salt on land during periods of high chloride concentrations in the river. Far more surprising, however, was an agreement by the three upstream states (France, Germany, and Switzerland) to contribute 32 million florins on the same cost-sharing basis for a Dutch project to reduce chlorides entering the IJsselmeer, a major source of water for Dutch waterworks.[89]

French acceptance of the 1976 convention illustrates how the situation structure shapes the fundamental bargain of an international institution. The distribution problem explains the absence of reciprocity. Dutch attempts to gain acceptance of a joint cap on discharges was, in the absence of positive linkage, not compelling to France, Germany, or Switzerland who, as upstream states, would not benefit from any changes in Dutch discharges, which were low in any event. The absence of any Dutch resources to coerce the more powerful upstream perpetrators, particularly France and Germany, explains the absence of sanctions. The Dutch surely would have preferred liability arrangements or adherence to a polluter pays principle, but they lacked legal or material means to force France or Germany to accept such arrangements.[90] The Dutch had to either accept the negative externality or identify positive linkages attractive to the French. They took advantage of the fact that the French mines were a single source that would soon be exhausted for economic reasons anyway.[91] By targeting MdPA reductions in particular, the Dutch minimized the costs of, and French resistance to, proposed reductions while simultaneously gaining German willingness to subsidize French reductions to avoid demands from the Dutch and from German domestic environmental groups for reductions in Germany.[92] The Swiss appear to have agreed more "in the name of basin-wide solidarity."[93] Although Swiss and German contributions mitigated the Dutch cost burden, the Dutch "had little choice except to contribute to the costs," and at a level that was slightly higher (34 instead of 30 percent) than that of the major polluters and much higher than its own contribution to the problem.[94] Here, a victim state compensated a state that was unambiguously capable but simply unwilling to halt its externality-generating behavior.

Events since 1976 illustrate how important positive linkage was to initial French participation, how positive linkage is not free of implementation problems, and how influential initial institutional bargains are to subsequent ones. Implementation of the 1976 agreement was anything but smooth. Although the Netherlands, Germany, and Switzerland paid their cost-shares in 1976, the French withdrew the agreement from parliamentary consideration in 1979, leading the Swiss to reclaim their

89. Bernauer 1996, 216.
90. See LeMarquand 1977, 119; and Bernauer 1996, 205.
91. Indeed, Bernauer argues that the agreement had only a small effect on French behavior. Bernauer 1996. As noted earlier, however, we are explaining regime design, not regime effectiveness.
92. Bernauer 1996, 209–10.
93. See LeMarquand 1977, 124; and Bernauer 1995, 372.
94. See LeMarquand 1977, 119; and Bernauer 1996, 221.

payment in 1981 and the Dutch to recall their ambassador to France.[95] The French finally ratified the agreement in 1985 and began implementing discharge reductions in 1987, but at a rate less than originally agreed (15 instead of 20 kilograms per stere). Nor were the reductions achieved by injecting chloride into the subsoil, as agreed, but by stockpiling it on land, leaving the prospect that the French subsequently would dispose of the chloride into the river.[96] That said, target levels for Rhine chloride concentrations have been achieved through discharge reductions that were due at least in part to agreements based on positive incentives, agreements that would not have been accepted by the French had they been based on sanctions or reciprocity.[97]

The Rhine River case highlights the power of formalized exchange. Initially, one might wonder whether this case involves simply an ad hoc arrangement rather than an institution.[98] Indeed, the underlying asymmetry does well at explaining Dutch side payments to France in 1976 but less well at explaining German and Swiss contributions, which require more context-contingent explanations. Institutional influence, however, is suggested in the design of the 1991 protocol. One anomaly is the application of the 1970s-era cost-sharing formula to the 1991 French project. Rather than renegotiate cost-shares to reflect current levels of pollution contribution and political concern, the states simply applied the institutionalized formula. This formula proved a particularly "sticky" focal point, as evident in Switzerland's being granted a Fr 12 million "credit" toward its share (for having closed a Swiss chloride-discharging enterprise) rather than recalculating cost shares. More surprising, and more indicative of the power of institutionalization, is the French, German, and Swiss agreement to contribute to the Dutch cleanup of the IJsselmeer, a project offering them neither environmental nor economic benefits. And this project also went through with no renegotiation of cost shares, cost shares that were based on a political and environmental reality almost twenty years old. Absent the Rhine Chloride Convention, it is difficult to explain why France and Germany contributed 30 percent each to a project in which the Netherlands was to stop polluting its own IJsselmeer. These outcomes seem explicable only in institutional terms and illustrate how institutional structures and forms, once created, can wield considerable influence over subsequent outcomes. Table 2 summarizes the evidence from the whaling, ozone-depletion, and Rhine River cases.

Comparing Cases and Alternative Hypotheses

These cases confirm that variation in situation structure, and corresponding variation in distribution and enforcement problems, influences institutional scope (conjecture

95. Bernauer 1995, 378.

96. Ibid., 378–79. See also the failure of efforts to induce Eastern European states to decommission unsafe nuclear reactors detailed in Connolly and List 1996.

97. Bernauer 1996, 225.

98. See Hasenclever, Mayer, and Rittberger 1997, 33, 42–43; and Keohane 1983, 153.

TABLE 2. Summary of cases

Case	Situation structure	Fundamental bargain
Whaling among whaling states	Symmetric externality	Issue-specific reciprocity (no linkage)
Whaling between whaling and nonwhaling states	Asymmetric externality, with strong victim	Coercion (negative linkage)
Ozone depletion among industrialized states	Symmetric externality	Issue-specific reciprocity (no linkage)
Ozone depletion between industrialized and developing states	Asymmetric externality, with strong victim	Exchange (positive linkage)
Rhine River chloride	Asymmetric externality, with weak victim	Exchange (positive linkage)

S2, scope increases with distribution problems; and conjecture S3, scope increases with enforcement problems). Although the timing of institutional formation surely depended on concern about the problem reaching certain levels, institutional shape depended more on underlying situation structure. Distribution problems among industrialized states concerned about ozone depletion and initially among whaling states were sufficiently mild that reciprocity was a readily negotiated and adequate solution. States joined institutions that had neither significant sanctions for noncompliance nor rewards for compliance. They joined simply because of the unequal and unspecified benefits each believed would arise from mutual cooperation and the desire to avoid decentralized retaliatory noncompliance and corresponding reversion to the status quo.[99] The more severe enforcement problems of asymmetric externalities produced greater centralization, evident in the Financial Mechanism of the Montreal Protocol and the cost-sharing formulas of the Rhine Convention (conjecture C4, centralization increases with enforcement problems).

Although reciprocity proves a nonstarter in asymmetric externalities, both the asymmetry and the futility of reciprocity may not be initially obvious. As Koremenos, Lipson, and Snidal observe in the volume's introduction, states use negotiations to collect information about others' preferences.[100] The reluctance of developing states to join a reciprocity-based regime to restrict CFC use showed that they did not share the industrialized states' concerns about stratospheric ozone loss. Industrialized states hoped, incorrectly, that banning trade in CFCs with nonmember states would coerce developing states to join. Likewise, the Dutch saw their reciprocity-based proposal that all Rhine River states reduce chloride discharges fall flat, and the failure of early lawsuits confirmed that they had few effective threats.

99. Hardin 1968.
100. Koremenos, Lipson, and Snidal, this volume, 782.

Such institutional false starts support the intuition that states extend institutional scope only when enforcement problems dictate that narrower institutions will be ineffective. The declining commitment of whaling states to the IWC despite coercive threats by the United States suggests that institutional survival may depend on states and/or nongovernmental organizations offering side payments to those still interested in whaling.

To confirm our analysis, consider alternative explanations for the variation we have documented. Certainly the observed differences in institutional design do not reflect variation in the incentives to defect. In all our cases at least some states had, and acted on, incentives to defect, through violating IWC rules and refusing to join the IWC, smuggling CFCs and missing phase-out deadlines, and failing to reduce chloride discharges on schedule.[101]

The choice of reciprocity, coercion, or exchange might reflect variation in dissatisfied states' costs of making them effective, rather than the difficulty of doing so.[102] The evidence refutes such an interpretation. Reciprocity was not considered and rejected as too expensive by victim states (the Dutch in the Rhine River case or the industrialized states in the ozone case) but rather was proposed by those states and rejected by perpetrator states (the upstream Rhine states and the developing states). Making offers of reciprocity more credible would have been easier and cheaper than devising sanctions or rewards, but doing so would not have made reciprocity more attractive to the perpetrators. In the ozone case, industrialized states had incentives to carry out their threats to end CFC trade with nonmember states since doing so would increase demand for the CFC alternatives they had to offer. They dropped this strategy because it failed to induce developing states to join the regime, and because offering rewards appeared a more effective means of achieving that end than finding more effective sanctioning tools.

Finally, the choice of positive linkage may reflect normative and domestic political constraints on the use of coercion. Policymakers, perhaps pressed by their publics, may reject coercion as inappropriate, even if effective, especially when dealing with developing states.[103] Such concerns may well have influenced the decision to frame side payments in the ozone agreement as targeting "lack of capacity" rather than "lack of will." Yet such a norms-based argument fails to conform to most of the evidence. First, negotiators did ban CFC trade with nonmembers, a ban that effectively applied only to developing states, since all OECD states planned to join. Second, norms were indeterminate. In the ozone case the norm against paying polluters contradicted the norm against sanctioning poorer states. In the Rhine River case, the norm that the polluter should pay was reinforced by the fact that France could clearly afford to stop polluting and merely lacked the will. The choice by states in both cases to pay polluters in the face of a counter-

---

101. See Yablokov 1994; Clapp 1997; Biermann 1997; Victor 1998; and Bernauer and Moser 1996.
102. We are indebted to an anonymous reviewer for clarifying these points.
103. On the distinction between a logic of appropriateness and a logic of consequences, see March and Olsen 1989; and Finnemore 1996.

vailing norm lends force to the argument that the situation structure made normatively more appropriate mechanisms unavailable or patently ineffective.

Conclusion

The choices states make in designing international institutions reflect rational efforts to create mechanisms compatible with the incentives in the strategic situations they face. Negative externalities create incentives for victims to induce perpetrators to change their behavior. But such externalities may be either symmetric or asymmetric. The latter pose more severe distributional and enforcement problems, which lead states to create institutions that involve linkages that broaden their scope, strongly confirming two of the Rational Design conjectures (conjecture S2, SCOPE increases with DISTRIBUTION problems; and conjecture S3, SCOPE increases with ENFORCEMENT problems). In symmetric, Tragedy of the Commons, externalities, all perpetrators are also victims, so those most dissatisfied can devise acceptable institutions through simple issue-specific reciprocity. Reciprocity is Pareto improving yet sufficiently attractive to induce participation without the complications of linkage. In contrast, in asymmetric externalities upstream states prefer the status quo to any agreement limited to the issue that concerns downstream states. Whenever issue-specific reciprocity is not Pareto improving, large distribution and enforcement problems arise that can only be addressed if dissatisfied states increase institutional scope through linkage. Linkage may involve those who would benefit by changes in behavior compensating those who must change their behavior. Indeed, weak victims that want an externality to stop must design institutions involving side payments to attract perpetrator participation. However, dissatisfied or victim states, if they are stronger than the perpetrators, may also choose the negative linkage of coercion, exacting "obedience" without institutions or imposing a regime.[104]

In the context of the Rational Design project, our findings demonstrate how the more severe distributional and enforcement problems of asymmetric situations lead states to expand institutional scope. Restricting membership will not induce participation by perpetrators in such situations (see conjecture M1, restrictive MEMBERSHIP increases with ENFORCEMENT problems), so states must use the substitute strategies of offering positive or negative linkage (conjecture S3, SCOPE increases with ENFORCEMENT problems). Situations with symmetric externalities tend to produce narrow, reciprocity-based institutions. Situations with asymmetric externalities and strong victims tend to produce broader coercion-based institutions, and those with weak victims tend to produce exchange-based institutions. Distribution and enforcement problems are tightly intertwined and mutually influential parts of international

104. Young 1979.

cooperation.[105] The argument provides some support for the conjecture that centralization increases with the severity of enforcement problems (conjecture C4, CENTRALIZATION increases with ENFORCEMENT problems), as evident in the careful attention paid to compensation schemes in the Rhine River and ozone-depletion cases. It also suggests, however, that the role of flexibility in institutional design is more complex than suggested by the Rational Design project's framers (conjecture F1, FLEXIBILITY increases with UNCERTAINTY about the state of the world; and conjecture F2, FLEXIBILITY increases with DISTRIBUTION problems). States will embrace flexibility if it allows them to reap near-term institutional benefits while reducing longer-term risks; they will eschew such flexibility and accept more binding, specific rules if, as in asymmetric externalities, each side's institutional benefits depend critically on the other side carrying out the exact terms of the agreed-upon exchange.

The argument reminds us that, along with symmetric Prisoners' Dilemmas and Tragedies of the Commons, asymmetric or unidirectional externalities are important features of the international landscape. These less symmetric contexts also create pressure for institutional formation. Variation in the symmetry and power of the underlying structure influences not only whether states will create institutions but also the mechanisms they design into those institutions they do create.[106] The issue-specific reciprocity common to symmetric externalities has received considerable study, as have coercive regimes imposed by strong states.[107] Exchange regimes have received far less attention. As Ronald Coase would have predicted,[108] states that lack the resources to force others to internalize a negative externality can, for a price, devise institutions that provide an alternative to simply accepting it. Finally, our argument sharpens the debate over whether sanctions are always (or never) the source of compliance with international regimes,[109] demonstrating that reciprocity, sanctions, and rewards tend to be adopted in circumstances that vary systematically, a source of variation that must be considered before the relative effectiveness of different strategies can be properly evaluated.

105. See Fearon 1998; and Morrow 1994c.
106. See Martin 1992b; and Rittberger and Zürn 1990.
107. On imposed regimes, see Young 1989; Martin 1992a; and Gruber 2000.
108. Coase 1960.
109. See Chayes and Chayes 1995; and Downs, Rocke, and Barsoom 1996.

Private Justice in a Global Economy:
From Litigation to Arbitration

Walter Mattli

The study of private settlement of cross-border trade and investment disputes through international commercial arbitration or other mechanisms has been much neglected by scholars of international political economy and international institutions. This oversight is attributable in part to the traditional focus of international relations on intergovernmental international organizations and the lack of attention to private international institutional arrangements.[1] A further reason for the oversight is that arbitration is resolutely private, making information exceedingly difficult to obtain. Two distinguished international arbitrators, Alan Redfern and Martin Hunter, recently observed that the study of the practice of international commercial arbitration is like peering into the dark. Few arbitral awards are published and even fewer procedural decisions of arbitral tribunals come to light.[2]

Despite this difficulty, private forums for international commercial dispute resolution, of which international arbitration is an increasingly popular type, deserve much closer attention by scholars of international relations. After virtually disap-

I am grateful to Ken Abbott, Beth Yarbrough, Barbara Koremenos, Charles Lipson, Ronald Mitchell, Antonio Ortiz, and Duncan Snidal for excellent comments on earlier drafts. I also thank Debbie Davenport, Miles Kahler, Robert Keohane, Lisa Martin, Jeffrey Stacey, and the participants of the Rational Design project, the Program on International Politics, Economics, and Security (PIPES) at the University of Chicago, and a seminar at Harvard University Business School for helpful suggestions. Special thanks to Dominique Hascher, General Counsel and Deputy Secretary General of the International Court of Arbitration of the International Chamber of Commerce in Paris, for inviting me to do an internship at the court in 1998, and to Anne-Marie Whitesell for welcoming me to her legal team at the court. I benefited greatly from discussions on international commercial arbitration with Adrian Winstanley of the London Court of International Arbitration, Eva Müller of the Arbitration Institute of the Stockholm Chamber of Commerce, as well as Gerald Aksen, Lucienne Carasso Bulow, Alessandra Casella, Yves Dezalay, Bryant Garth, Thomas Heller, Christian Joerges, William Park, Susan Rose-Ackerman, Martin Shapiro, Anne-Marie Slaughter, Hans Smit, Francis Snyder, Job Taylor, and Raymund Werle.

1. Two notable exceptions are Lipson 1985; and Cutler 1995.
2. Redfern and Hunter 1991, xv. Information mainly comes from tapping the experience of the principal arbitral institutions or by looking at individual cases that come before the courts, either as a result of enforcement proceedings or because an arbitral award is challenged by the losing party.

International Organization 55, 4, Autumn 2001, pp. 919–947

pearing during the age of nation-state ideology in the nineteenth century, international commercial arbitration has been staging a formidable comeback in the past twenty years. Today's scene calls to memory the flourishing era of arbitration practices and institutions associated with the international trade fairs of medieval Europe. The number of arbitration forums has grown from a dozen or so in the 1970s to more than one hundred in the 1990s, and the caseload of major arbitral institutions has more than doubled during the same period.[3] Lawyers and judges agree that "there is [now] clear evidence of something of a world movement . . . towards international arbitration."[4] The Economist recently called arbitration "the Big Idea set to dominate legal-reform agendas into the next century."[5]

Even though the focus of this study is on various arbitration options, it also reflects more broadly on the market of institutions for international commercial dispute resolution for private parties. It addresses the question of why different forums for dispute resolution are selected.

In the domestic context parties who seek a binding method of resolving disputes through third-party intervention have the choice between a national public court and private arbitration. In the international context such a choice does not exist because there are no international public courts that handle international commercial disputes involving only private parties.[6] Therefore, the choice for international private parties is between recourse to a national court (that is, litigation) and recourse to private international dispute resolution, namely international commercial arbitration or so-called alternative dispute resolution (ADR) techniques, such as conciliation and mediation.[7]

Arbitration is a binding, nonjudicial, and private means of settling disputes based on an explicit agreement by the parties involved in a transaction. Such an agreement is typically embodied in the terms of a contract between the parties. Alternatively, if the contract is silent about the dispute-resolution method, the parties can select the method when the dispute arises.[8] Arbitration entrusts the settlement of a question to one or more persons who derive their powers from the private agreement.[9] Unlike judges in public courts, who must follow fixed rules of procedure and apply the laws of the land, arbitrators can dispense with legal formalities and may apply whatever procedural rules and substantive law best fit a case.

---

3. Brown 1993.
4. Kerr, Lord Justice of England, preface to Craig, Park, and Paulsson, 1990, xii.
5. The Economist, 18–24 July 1992, 17, survey on the legal profession. See also Wetter 1995.
6. The only exception is the European Court of Justice, which may deal with certain disputes between private parties under European Community law. Redfern and Hunter 1991, 25; Burley and Mattli 1993; Mattli and Slaughter 1995 and 1998a,b.
7. The term jurisdiction clause in an international contract is generally used to describe a forum selection that designates a public court to hear a case, while an arbitration clause refers to private international dispute resolution.
8. Even if the parties have contractually agreed to use one method, they may switch to another if they feel that the latter is more appropriate for a given dispute.
9. Mustill and Boyd 1989, 38–50.

Arbitration becomes international when the parties to a dispute reside or conduct their main business in different countries. The term commercial in international commercial arbitration is broadly conceived and covers activities such as sale of goods, distribution agreements, commercial representation of agency, leasing, consulting, transportation, construction work, joint ventures, and other forms of industrial or business cooperation.[10]

International commercial arbitration can be conducted in two ways, as ad hoc arbitration or as institutional arbitration. Ad hoc arbitration does not rely on the supervision or formal administration of an arbitration center. Institutional arbitration, in contrast, is done under the aegis of an arbitral center, usually according to the institution's own rules of arbitration.[11] The most established of these institutions are the International Court of Arbitration (ICA) of the International Chamber of Commerce (ICC), the London Court of International Arbitration (LCIA), and the Arbitration Institute of the Stockholm Chamber of Commerce (SCC Institute).[12] Many more arbitral institutions have been set up in the past decade, notably in Asia, the Middle East, and North America.[13]

I argue that the various forums of dispute resolution can be understood as indirect products of rational selection where actors select those institutions that are most effective and appropriate for given disputes. In the United States, for example, the legal counsels of major corporations have spearheaded the recent trend away from sometimes cumbersome and lengthy court proceedings toward faster and less expensive methods, such as ADR. Similarly, the surge in popularity of arbitration as a means of international commercial dispute resolution can be attributed to features of arbitration that the international business community values for a growing number of disputes, notably in the areas of technology transfer, intellectual property, engineering, and construction. These features include flexibility, technical expertise, privacy, confidentiality, and speed. In short I describe a market of dispute-resolution methods where different "suppliers" offer different venues from which the firms on the demand side can select based on their design problems. This creates an accelerated evolutionary process of forum formation (that is, accelerated by rational

10. This definition is suggested in the United Nations Commission for International Trade Law (UNCITRAL) Model Law, Art. 1 (1), fn.

11. Institutional arbitration is also referred to in the literature as "administered" or "supervised" arbitration. On institutional arbitration, see Slate 1996; Hoellering 1994; Vigrass 1993; Graving 1989; and Lowenfeld 1993.

12. Another major institution is the American Arbitration Association. Its focus is primarily on domestic arbitration; for this reason, it is omitted from the discussion in this study. (Yearly, it handles about forty thousand domestic and two hundred international arbitration cases.)

13. Due to limited space, I focus primarily on international commercial arbitration and not the more specialized arbitration as offered, for example, by the Society of Maritime Arbitration (New York), the Grain and Feed Trade Association (London), and various stock and commodity exchanges. Nevertheless, I would argue that the framework used here does shed light on some key institutional features of commodity trade and maritime arbitration. See also Mentschikoff 1961; Harris, Summerskill, and Cockerill 1993; Summerskill 1993; Covo 1993; and Johnson 1991 and 1993.

anticipation of what will sell and what will work), and the result will be very much the same as a direct rational-design effort.[14]

The key institutional dimensions along which the various methods of international dispute resolution vary are (1) procedural and adaptive flexibility, and (2) centralization of procedural safeguards and information collection. For example, flexibility is typically much lower in public court proceedings than in institutional arbitration, ad hoc arbitration, or ADR; and centralization is present in institutional arbitration but not in ad hoc arbitration or ADR.

Drawing on the analytical framework developed by Barbara Koremenos, Charles Lipson, and Duncan Snidal, I elaborate on several of the Rational Design conjectures, linking the institutional features of dispute-resolution methods to the needs or demands of private parties.[15] These conjectures can be summarized as follows: Centralization of forums to which private international parties resort to resolve their disputes increases with uncertainty about the parties' preferences or behavior (conjecture C1, CENTRALIZATION increases with UNCERTAINTY ABOUT BEHAVIOR). Such uncertainty may be low, for example, if the parties are locked in a mutually beneficial, ongoing commercial relationship; in this case, the parties' institutional demands for resolving disputes will be markedly lower than those of firms with few interactions and little knowledge of each other.

However, full information and adequate knowledge are not always sufficient to ensure compliance; enforcement problems may remain severe if the payoff from unilateral defection is significantly greater than that from mutual cooperation at the dispute-resolution stage. In this case, strong centralized procedural safeguards will be necessary to foil defection. This argument is summarized in conjecture C4, CENTRALIZATION increases with ENFORCEMENT problems.

Centralization is also likely to increase with the parties' uncertainty about the state of the world (conjecture C2, CENTRALIZATION increases with UNCERTAINTY ABOUT THE STATE OF THE WORLD)—that is, with the parties' relative lack of information, for example, about the legal environment (the laws and integrity of judges) in which arbitration takes place and about the conditions for enforceability of arbitral awards. More generally, traders with little experience in international exchange or traders from very different cultural and linguistic regions may rely more heavily on centralized support and expertise for resolving their disputes than veteran traders operating in a relatively homogenous region.

Finally, uncertainty about the state of the world may also result from the susceptibility of an issue-area to new developments or unanticipated shocks that may leave parties in uncharted legal territory. In such situations institutional flexibility may be required to resolve disputes effectively. For example, firms operating at the forefront of new production and exchange methods are likely to

---

14. As illustrated later, the distinction between suppliers and demanders is useful analytically, but in practice it is often blurred because methods for resolving private disputes are provided mostly by private organizations run and funded by firms themselves.

15. Koremenos, Lipson, and Snidal, this volume.

prefer a flexible form of dispute resolution that allows them to tailor rules regarding procedure, evidence, and even the substance of the case to their evolving needs. This relationship is captured by conjecture F1, FLEXIBILITY increases with UNCERTAINTY ABOUT THE STATE OF THE WORLD.

The study is organized as follows. In the first section I briefly review and critique themes in the institutional literature in international relations and economics that are relevant to this study. In the second section I discuss the key institutional differences among the various methods of international commercial dispute resolution and introduce the principal international arbitral forums. After laying this groundwork I seek to explain within the Rational Design framework why private parties select the dispute-resolution forums they do. I conclude with a discussion of ways to broaden the study.

Private Dispute Resolution and the Institutional Literature

Political scientists and economists have developed two theoretical schools, regime theory and new institutional economics (NIE), respectively, that seek to explain institutional arrangements. Unfortunately, the two schools have based their theories in part on assumptions that move the theories' reach away from the types of institutional arrangements discussed in this study.

"International regimes" are defined broadly as sets of implicit or explicit principles, norms, rules, and decision-making procedures around which actors' expectations converge in a given area of international relations.[16] In a world of rapidly growing interdependence regimes are said to help states correct "market failures" stemming from asymmetric information, moral hazard, risk, and uncertainty.[17] Regime theorists have shed important light on the nature of interstate relations, but they have overlooked the importance of nonstate actors in international relations. In particular they have failed to examine the extent to which international market players themselves can remedy "market failures" by creating private institutional arrangements. This omission has deprived the theory of the comparative institutional perspective necessary to assess the desirability of intergovernmental regimes. Only a comparative institutional analysis that weighs the costs and benefits of both private and public institutional remedies of "market failures" can provide a framework to address questions of efficiency, effectiveness, and optimal institutional design.[18] I am not implying that regime theory is flawed but rather suggesting that the theory could be strengthened by extending its focus beyond state behavior. For example, there is nothing that keeps the ICC from being viewed as a regime for its members, as I show later.

16. Krasner 1983, 2.
17. Keohane 1984, 93.
18. A related point is made in Demsetz 1969.

NIE is a rapidly growing field that has developed from the pioneering work of Oliver Williamson. It offers a rigorous conceptual framework for comparative institutional analysis.[19] NIE seeks to explain varying types of industrial organization, from straightforward market exchange to vertically integrated exchange, based on differences in transaction costs. The principal dimensions within which transactions differ are asset specificity, uncertainty, and frequency. The first is the most important; it represents the degree to which durable investments are made to support particular transactions.

NIE postulates that transaction costs are economized by assigning transactions (which differ in their attributes) to governance structures (which differ in their adaptive capacities and associated costs) in a discriminating way. Governance structures are the organizational frameworks within which the integrity of a contractual relation is decided and maintained. In particular, the higher the asset specificity, the greater the institutional complexity needed to promote efficient exchange. Examples of governance structures are economic hostages, vertical integration, unitization, and multinationalism.[20]

Nevertheless, Williamson's framework is not without shortcomings. For example, none of Williamson's governance structures would be needed if courts could resolve disputes swiftly and inexpensively. But Williamson argues that court ordering or legal centralism is inefficient. "Most studies of exchange assume that efficacious rules of law regarding contract disputes are in place and are applied by the courts in an informed, sophisticated, and low-cost way. . . . The facts, however, disclose otherwise. Most disputes, including many that under current rules could be brought to a court, are resolved by avoidance, self-help, and the like. . . . [And] because the efficacy of court ordering is problematic, contract execution falls heavily on [governance structures]."[21] This proposition is problematic. First, courts are institutions, too. A comparative institutional analysis that sets aside a large universe of institutions on the grounds of their alleged inefficiency risks being internally inconsistent. Within Williamson's framework, it is incomprehensible why inefficient institutions come into being or survive. Second, even if it established analytically (by way of ad hoc assumptions) that public courts and public law are inefficient, there remains the question of why NIE does not consider their next best substitutes, namely private courts and private law.

In short, NIE provides a sophisticated analytical framework for studying varying forms of governance. However, by overlooking the importance particularly of private courts and law, NIE may be accused of truncating the full range of variation on the dependent variable (governance forms) and thus suffering from selection bias. Williamson recognized that "a place for law [should] properly [be] provided in

19. Williamson 1975 and 1985.

20. Yarbrough and Yarbrough have recently added to this list various forms of trade liberalization. Their analysis provides a good example of how NIE can enrich the study of international institutional arrangements. See Yarbrough and Yarbrough 1992.

21. Williamson 1985, 20, 32.

any comprehensive study of contract."[22] Beth Yarbrough and Robert Yarbrough have responded to this invitation and are presently extending Williamson's framework to incorporate law and public courts in a way that is consonant with the analysis offered in this study. Courts, they argue, are not generically inefficient; rather they are not very efficacious for certain types of transactions. One type is those transactions in which asset specificity makes the historical context of a relationship critical to resolving disputes. A second type is those in which the confrontational nature of court proceedings risks damaging future relations (hence courts' historical reluctance, until recently, to become involved in many family matters). In such cases, Yarbrough and Yarbrough predict noncourt means of dispute settlement.[23]

Institutional Features of International Commercial Dispute-resolution Methods

The range of methods for resolving international commercial disputes is wide. It includes litigation in public courts, several arbitration options, and so-called ADR techniques. In this section I highlight the institutional characteristics of the various methods.

Flexibility in Dispute Resolution

A key feature of arbitration is its high degree of procedural flexibility. Arbitration provides the parties with full control over the arbitral process. The parties may decide the number of arbitrators comprising the arbitral tribunal, the appointment procedure of the arbitrators, the place of arbitration, the powers of the tribunal, and the applicable law in the dispute. In contrast, a trial before a national court must be conducted in accordance with the rules of that court. Further, public court proceedings are typically open to the public, and court decisions are published and readily available. Arbitral proceedings, however, are held in private; details about the cases, including the arbitral awards, are confidential.[24] Privacy may help firms to hide a number of facts from competitors and the public in general, such as trade secrets and know-how not guaranteed by patents or financial difficulties and other problems. Nevertheless, the parties may choose to publicize arbitral decisions either to create precedents or to provide authoritative interpretations of standard contract terms.[25]

---

22. Ibid., 168.

23. Beth Yarbrough, pers. comm. with the author.

24. René David, a leading French expert of international arbitration, notes that "secrecy, which is one of the reasons why arbitration is resorted to by the parties, is easily extended . . . to everything concerning arbitration." See David 1985, 31.

25. Cost is a factor, unrelated to flexibility, that is frequently said to distinguish litigation from arbitration. Arbitration centers, for example, claim that litigation is much more expensive than arbitration. This need not necessarily be true, however. First, although litigants do not pay the salary of a judge,

Flexibility characterizes not only arbitral procedures but also the actual institutions of arbitration, such as the ICA, the LCIA, and the SCC Institute. These forums can respond much more quickly to demands for new dispute-resolution rules and services than public courts. The reason is evident: Private courts are demand driven. The very same market actors who request new rules also control these courts. As noted by Alessandra Casella, these forums are shaped from the "bottom," that is, by the firms that voluntarily finance and share the "club goods" they need.[26] Thus the demanders are also the suppliers; they possess full information on how new business practices or changing market conditions affect their dispute-resolution needs. They are capable of quickly responding to new needs by creating new services and by rewriting the charters of their courts. The frequent revisions of the rules of major arbitral institutions attest to the high degree of institutional flexibility of these forums.

Many of today's arbitration practices evoke medieval Europe's private courts and the Law Merchant, a body of private commercial rules and principles that were distinct from the ordinary law of the land. The merchant courts sat in fairs, markets, seaport towns, and most other large centers of commercial activity. Merchant courts chose as judges merchants who possessed intimate knowledge of particular commercial practices and techniques. W. Mitchell, a historian of the Law Merchant, writes, "The summary nature of its jurisdiction . . . characterized the Lex Mercatoria. Its justice was prompt . . . [and] the time within which disputes [had to] be finally settled was narrowly limited."[27] Sea merchants, for example, demanded that disputes be settled "from tide to tide according to the ancient law marine and ancient customs of the sea . . . without mixing the law civil with the law maritime."[28] Another reason for using guild courts was that "under severest penalties, [the guilds] forbade members to appeal, in cases where they alone were concerned, to any court save that of the guild."[29] Merchant courts relied on sanctions such as ostracism and boycott of all future trade to ensure that traders would be held to the resolution dictated by the arbiters.[30]

Besides arbitration and litigation, there are ADR techniques. The most widely known forms of these are conciliation and mediation. Like arbitration, conciliation and mediation offer the parties great procedural flexibility. The parties pick

---

parties involved in arbitration must pay the fees and expenses of the arbitrators. Second, litigants are not charged for using the public facilities of the courts of law, but the parties in arbitration pay the administrative fees and expenses of an arbitral institution and these can be substantial, particularly when they are assessed by reference to the amount in dispute. In short, arbitration may or may not be less expensive than litigation; much depends on the specifics of the case and the attitudes of the parties to a dispute. Consequently, in the analytical part of the study I do not consider cost as an institutional dimension.

26. Casella 1996; see also Dezalay and Garth 1996.
27. Mitchell 1904, 12–13.
28. Ibid., 20.
29. Ibid., 42.
30. Benson 1989. See also Milgrom, North, and Weingast 1990; Greif, Milgrom, and Weingast 1994; and Cutler 1995.

conciliators or arbitrators of their choice and design procedures that best fit their cases. Typically, a mediator seeks to reduce the distance between the parties' positions and make the parties understand each other's point of view, in order that they may achieve a compromise solution. A conciliator performs a different function. After consulting all sides and evaluating the evidence, the conciliator draws up the terms of a solution that is hopefully acceptable to all parties involved in the dispute. Conciliation and mediation differ in one important respect from arbitration: they do not result in a binding or enforceable award. A mediator cannot compel the parties to reach a settlement, and a conciliator has no power to impose a compromise solution on the parties.[31]

Centralization of Forums for Resolving Disputes

International commercial arbitration can be conducted in two ways, as institutional arbitration or ad hoc arbitration. Ad hoc arbitration differs from institutional arbitration in that it does not rely on the supervision or formal administration of an arbitration center. In this sense it is the least institutional form of arbitration. In ad hoc arbitration, the parties are "on their own"; they are not bound by time limits set by arbitral institutions, and their proceedings are not monitored by any central body. The parties can leave the issuance of arbitration procedures to their arbitrators or develop their own rules and design their own arbitral management either in the initial contract or after a dispute has arisen. Alternatively, the parties may simply adopt or adapt the rules of one of the major arbitration centers but, again, without entrusting the administration of the arbitration to such centers.[32] Another increasingly popular option is to use the arbitration rules of the UN Commission on International Trade Law of 1976 (UNCITRAL arbitration rules). Reference in the parties' contract to the UNCITRAL rules will immediately incorporate a full-blown set of procedures designed specially for ad hoc arbitration.[33]

Ad hoc arbitration to resolve international commercial disputes is similar to ADR in that neither the mediator nor the conciliator is monitored by any central institution. Like the mediator and conciliator, the arbitrator in an ad hoc case depends entirely on the good will of the parties for a smooth process of dispute resolution. Ad hoc arbitration and ADR contrast sharply with institutional arbitration as offered, for example, by the ICA, where the provision of procedural safeguards and information is highly centralized. They also differ from arbitration as conducted by the LCIA, and the SCC Institute. These three institutions are

31. For this reason, ADR is sometimes combined with an adjudicatory process as a fall-back solution. For example, a contract may provide for a specific time limit to start some form of mediation or negotiation after which arbitration becomes the only method available. Park 1997b.

32. In ad hoc arbitration, parties may rely nevertheless on an "appointing authority" (for example, a court, an arbitral institution, or the chairman of a trade association) to appoint arbitrators.

33. On ad hoc arbitration, see Aksen 1991; and Arkin 1987.

TABLE 1. Institutional dimensions of methods for resolving international commercial disputes

	Litigation (public courts)	Institutional arbitration (ICA, LCIA, SCC)	Ad hoc arbitration and ADR
Flexibility	Low (typically)	High	High
Centralization			
Centralized information gathering	N.A.	High to medium	None
Centralized monitoring and other safeguards	N.A.	High to medium	None

considered in order.[34] Table 1 summarizes the key institutional dimensions along which the various methods of international commercial dispute resolution vary.

Illustration of Institutional Arbitration: Three Private Forums

International Chamber of Commerce Arbitration.   The ICC is a business organization offering a wide range of services to firms engaged in international trade and investment, including commercial dispute resolution. Founded in 1919, it counts today as members over 7,000 enterprises and commercial organizations in 114 countries. Its organizational structure includes a general secretariat in Paris, employing some eighty-five persons and a secretary-general. The supreme organ is the council, which meets twice a year. Members of the council are appointed by the national committees of the ICC. Each committee may select one to three members according to its contribution to the ICC budget. The council's president is elected for a two-year term. The ICC has established several commissions and special committees to address major issues relating to international commerce, such as intellectual property, competition law, taxation, transportation, telecommunications, the environment, and bribery. Annual conferences are supplemented every three years by an ICC Congress, attended on average by some one thousand participants.[35]

A major organization within the ICC is the ICA, established in 1923.[36] The idea of such a court was conceived after World War I by businessmen wrestling with the practical difficulties of designing a dispute-resolution process acceptable to mer-

34. Most of the information about these forums comes from interviews I conducted during an internship at the ICA and visits to the LCIA and the SCC in March and April 1998.
35. Craig, Park, and Paulsson 1990, 25–27.
36. Before 15 June 1989, the court's name was Court of Arbitration of the International Chamber of Commerce.

chants of different national backgrounds.[37] It is composed of a chair, eight vice-chairs, and fifty-seven members selected by the ICC national committees and professional organizations. The members are professors, former judges, barristers, and lawyers with expertise in international commercial law and arbitration. They represent a wide range of legal traditions, including civil law, common law, and Islamic law. The ICA meets four times a month, once in plenary session and three times as comité restraint. The ICA is assisted by a secretariat located at ICC headquarters in Paris. The secretariat has a staff of thirty-eight people, including six teams of lawyers from various countries. It assumes responsibility for the day-to-day administration of ICA cases and keeps copies of all written communications and pleadings exchanged in the arbitration proceedings. It also provides assistance and information to parties, counsel, and arbitrators. The provision of centralized information is a particularly valuable service because in an international arbitration case many different national systems of law may need to be consulted, depending on where the arbitration takes place and what issues are involved. National arbitration laws may determine questions of the capacity of the parties to agree to arbitration, the validity of the arbitration agreement, the "arbitrability" of the subject matter of the dispute, and the recognition and enforcement of arbitral awards.[38]

ICC arbitration is characterized not only by a high degree of centralized information gathering but also by the extensive monitoring offered by the ICA. Arbitration proceeds in five steps:

1. The claimant submits a request for arbitration to the secretariat, and the secretariat transmits the request to the defendant, who must respond within thirty days.

2. The court appoints arbitrators and when the parties do not make their own selection chooses the place of arbitration.[39] In selecting the arbitrators, the court relies in part on recommendations from the ICC national committees. The court also fixes the arbitrators' fees and estimates the overall arbitration costs based on the amount in dispute. After receiving half of the advance on arbitration costs, the secretariat transmits the file to the arbitral tribunal. The fixing of fees by the court is intended to prevent the parties from being placed in the uncomfortable position of having to negotiate issues of remuneration with those who will be responsible for deciding their case or otherwise to avoid challenges to an arbitrator's independence.

37. Craig, Park, and Paulsson 1990, xxi. The ICA is supplemented by four other ICC bodies dealing with the settlement of international commercial disputes. They are the Commission on International Arbitration, which advises on the development of ICC Rules of Conciliation and Arbitration; the International Maritime Arbitration Organization; the International Center for Technical Expertise; and the Standing Committee on Regulation of Contractual Relations, which gives parties the possibility of referring to a neutral outsider to adjust contracts whose performance is threatened by fundamentally changed circumstances. See Craig, Park, and Paulsson 1990, 27–28.
38. Redfern and Hunter 1991, xvi. See also Gentinetta 1973.
39. ICC arbitral tribunals are composed of one or three arbitrators.

3. Within two months of receiving the file, the tribunal submits a document called the "Terms of Reference to the Court." This procedure for arriving at the terms can be compared to a prehearing conference, where the arbitrators get to know each other and become familiar with the specifics of the case. The document summarizes the parties' respective claims, states the applicable law and the place of arbitration, and specifies the procedural rules (for evidence, witness statements, and so on) The court checks the Terms of Reference for conformity with ICC rules.

4. As soon as the second half of the advance is paid, the arbitral tribunal proceeds with the case. Within six months (which the court may extend), the tribunal submits a draft award to the court.

5. The court scrutinizes the arbitral award. The court may draw the arbitrators' attention to points of substance or may suggest modifications to the form of the award.[40] Once the court is satisfied, it approves the award, and the secretariat notifies the parties.

The docket of the ICA reflects the growing popularity of ICC arbitration. The first three thousand requests for arbitration were filed between 1923 and 1977. The next three thousand were lodged between 1977 and 1987. In 1991 alone, 333 cases were filed; the yearly number of cases kept growing steadily, reaching 450 in 1997.[41] About 54 percent of the 5,666 parties involved in ICC arbitration are from Western Europe. The most frequently represented nationalities are, in order, France, United States, West Germany, Italy, United Kingdom, Switzerland, Yugoslavia, Netherlands, Belgium, Egypt, Spain, Austria, Rumania, Sweden, and Greece. A recent development is the upsurge of ICC arbitration involving parties from Eastern Europe, Latin America, and South East Asia (7.9, 11.5, and 9.5 percent, respectively, of all parties in 1996).[42]

The London Court of International Arbitration.   The LCIA, another long-established arbitration institution, was inaugurated in 1892 as the London Chamber of Arbitration on the initiative of the Corporation of the City of London and the London Chamber of Commerce and Industry. In 1903 the tribunal's name was changed to the London Court of Arbitration. A joint committee, comprising representatives from the Corporation of the City of London and the London Chamber of Commerce, was formed to administer the activities of the court. In 1975 the Institute of Arbitrators (later to become the Chartered Institute of Arbitrators) joined the other two administering bodies. In 1981 the name was changed to the London Court of International Arbitration to reflect the nature of its work, which

---

40. The ICA returns roughly 15–20 percent of the awards to the arbitrators for revision. See Dezalay and Garth 1996, 47–48; and Smit 1994, especially 68–72.

41. See Craig, Park, and Paulsson 1990; and The ICC International Court of Arbitration Bulletin, various issues.

42. The ICC International Court of Arbitration Bulletin, various issues.

was moving steadily from domestic to international arbitration. In 1986 the LCIA was incorporated as a limited company under the control of a board of directors. It is composed of a president, who is also the chairman of the board of directors, four vice-presidents, and about twenty other members, all of whom are international arbitrators from major trading countries. The number of members drawn from the United Kingdom is restricted to no more than one quarter of the total. The court is assisted by a small London-based secretariat of about five people.

The LCIA is somewhat less involved in arbitration proceedings than the ICA. Its main function is to select arbitrators or to confirm party-nominated arbitrators. Like the ICA, the LCIA has the right to reject party-nominated arbitrators if it judges that they are not independent or that they are otherwise unsuitable. The LCIA fixes the arbitrators' fees and ensures that the arbitrators comply with the procedural timetable and respect all other rules of LCIA arbitration. Unlike the ICA, the LCIA does not require arbitrators to draft terms of reference, nor does it scrutinize arbitral awards.

Despite recent efforts to further internationalize its services, notably through the creation of four so-called users councils for Europe, North America, Asia-Pacific, and Africa, the LCIA remains an institution with a British bent.[43] This is reflected, for example, in the fact that all LCIA presidents until 1993 were British, and that 60 percent of court-selected arbitrators and 65 percent of party-nominated arbitrators are nationals from the United Kingdom. The parties most frequently involved in cases being considered by the LCIA come from the United Kingdom, United States, Australia, Canada, India, and Hong Kong.

The Arbitration Institute of the Stockholm Chamber of Commerce.   A frequently named third major international arbitration institution is the SCC Institute, established in 1917 as an independent entity within the SCC. The SCC Institute is composed of a board of three members (and three deputies). The chairman of the board has to be a judge with expertise in commercial and industrial matters. Of the two other members, one has to be a practicing lawyer, the other "a person who enjoys the confidence of the business community."[44] The board is assisted by a small secretariat.

Similar to the LCIA, the SCC Institute's main role is to act as an authority to appoint arbitral tribunals. Challenges against arbitrators are handled directly by the board. The rules of the SCC Institute require that a tribunal deal with a case in an "impartial, practical, and speedy fashion," give all parties "sufficient opportunity to present [their cases]," and reach a decision "no later than one year after the case has been referred to the arbitral tribunal."[45]

---

43. "Users' councils" have been set up to keep the international business community apprised of the arbitration services offered by the LCIA and to identify the changing needs of business to be able to respond quickly to these needs. Membership in these councils is by invitation; members include lawyers, arbitrators, and multinational industrial, commercial, and trading organizations.

44. SCC 1988, para. 2.

45. Ibid., para. 16, 26.

The development of the SCC Institute into a major center of international commercial arbitration dates from the 1970s when the United States and the Soviet Union agreed that trade contracts between the two countries should contain a clause providing for arbitration according to the rules of the SCC Institute. The caseload of the institute grew to a yearly average of about thirty-five in the 1980s and one hundred in the 1990s. In 1997, eighty-two international cases and twenty-nine domestic cases were registered with the secretariat. The most frequently represented nationalities in recent years have been Russian, Ukrainian, and American.

Explaining Forum Selection and Institutional Variety

In this section I seek to explain why actors engaged in international trade and investment select different methods of international commercial dispute resolution. I argue that these methods respond to the varying institutional needs of different types of disputes and disputants. Such needs can be explained in terms of the uncertainty about the preferences or behavior of contractual partners, the severity of the enforcement problem, and the uncertainty about the state of the world. The empirical evidence discussed offers strong support for several Rational Design conjectures.

Uncertainty, Enforcement, and Centralization

Uncertainty about preferences and behavior varies with the relative intimacy of the relationship between parties involved in international exchange. Intimacy or closeness of a relationship, in turn, depends on the parties' homogeneity, their frequency of interaction, and their distance from each other. Robert Cooter and Janet Landa, for example, have documented how traders belonging to ethnically homogeneous commercial groups, such as the East Indians in East Africa, the Syrians in West Africa, and the Chinese in Southeast Asia, experience considerably lower levels of behavioral uncertainty when dealing with one another than when dealing with outsiders.[46] One reason is that such trading groups serve as repositories of trust, which reduces the probability of a breach of contract between insiders.

Disputes may occasionally erupt even among insiders, but they are likely to be resolved more cooperatively than conflicts among strangers.[47] Marc Galanter, a leading exponent of the law and society movement, has argued that "in order to understand the distribution of [domestic] litigation, we must go beyond the characteristics of individual parties to consider the relations between them. Are the parties strangers or intimates? Is their relationship episodic or enduring? Is it

46. See, for example, Cooter and Landa 1984; and Landa 1981. See also Greif 1992; and Curtin 1984.
47. For examples, see Auerbach 1983. See also Ellickson 1991.

single-stranded or multiplex?"[48] He finds that, generally, the more inclusive and enduring a relationship between a set of parties, the less likely disputes will be taken to official forums (public courts); instead, such parties will seek to resolve their differences in so-called embedded forums, that is, forums that are part of the social setting within which a dispute arose.[49] A classic illustration of embedded commercial interactions and dispute resolution is Stuart Macaulay's study of local business practices among firms in Wisconsin. Macaulay finds that uncertainty about contract performance is reduced by widely accepted local norms (for example, "commitments are to be honored in almost all situations—one does not welsh on a deal," and "one ought to produce a good product and stand behind it") and by close personal relationships across the boundaries of local business organizations. He notes that "salesmen often know purchasing agents well. The same two individuals occupying these roles may have dealt with each other . . . [for up to] 25 years. Each has something to give the other. . . . [T]op executives may [also] know each other. They may sit together on government or trade committees. They may know each other socially and even belong to the same country club."[50] Disputes in this business community are frequently settled without reference to the contract or potential or actual legal sanctions. "If something comes up, you get the other man on the telephone and deal with the problem. . . . One doesn't run to lawyers if [one] wants to stay in business."[51]

These examples shed light on the varying degrees of centralization of forums for resolving international commercial disputes, suggesting the following conjecture: Centralization of forums to which private international parties resort to resolve their disputes increases with the uncertainty about the parties' preferences or behavior. This conjecture is in line with Rational Design conjecture C1, CENTRALIZATION increases with UNCERTAINTY ABOUT BEHAVIOR.[52] Centralization implies a high degree of central provision of procedural safeguards and information. Such provision is characteristic of institutional arbitration; it is absent, however, in ad hoc arbitration or ADR (see Table 1).

Parties involved in an ongoing mutually beneficial relationship (possibly with dealings along many different fronts) are less likely to rely on highly institutionalized forms of dispute resolution than parties with no anticipated future relationship, that is, parties that are not repeat players or do not belong to some close-knit trading

---

48. Galanter 1993, 24.

49. See also Galanter 1981. For examples of embedded forums, see Doo 1973; Columbia Journal of Law and Social Problems 1970; Bernstein 1992; and Maitland 1936.

50. Macaulay 1963, 63.

51. Ibid., 61.

52. Note that I am interested in knowing not which dispute-resolution clause the parties write into a contract but which method they ultimately use. The contractual provision may differ from the actual method used. For example, parties that write an ICC arbitration clause into their contract may decide to use ad hoc arbitration when a dispute erupts. Similarly, parties may choose some form of arbitration rather than complying with a jurisdiction clause. Some contracts have no provision for resolving disputes; in these cases the parties will choose the appropriate forms when disputes erupt, provided the parties have an interest in settling their disputes. Coe 1997, 56, 161.

community. There are two reasons. First, parties in a continuing relationship can more easily control each other because the expected future gains can serve as hostage.[53] They are locked in a "win-win" situation; thus each other's behavior is quite predictable, for the parties have little to gain (but potentially much to lose) from using dilatory tactics or adopting other forms of noncooperation. They are anxious to maintain good relations and are therefore likely to be interested in reaching a quick and amicable settlement. Second, parties in a continuing relationship typically have good information about each other's past behavior, past problems, and past solutions. This knowledge may be usefully brought to bear in a new instance of conflict.

International arbitrators and lawyers whom I have interviewed have confirmed the importance of the nature of a business relationship in determining how a dispute is likely to be resolved. Typically, parties in long-term relationships have a strong preference for settling disputes through ADR or ad hoc arbitration. This finding is also supported in several writings. Bertie Vigrass, former registrar of the LCIA, summarizes the evidence as follows: "In the traditional fields of arbitration, such as maritime, construction, insurance, and commodity, it is usual for the majority of arbitrations to be 'ad hoc' in nature. This is probably because there is an on-going relationship between parties, their legal representatives, and arbitrators."[54] Four leading international arbitrators—Martin Hunter, Jan Paulsson, Nigel Rawding, and Alan Redfern—have similarly noted that "ADR provides an effective means of resolving disputes between parties who have an interest in maintaining an on-going business relationship. The parties approach the process in a spirit of negotiation and compromise, instead of adopting the adversarial positions associated with litigation."[55]

The extent of centralization of a dispute-resolution method, however, is not solely determined by the relative uncertainty about the parties' preferences or behavior. Enforcement problems may persist even in the presence of good information and knowledge about the parties if the payoff from unilateral defection is significantly greater than the payoff from mutual cooperation at the dispute-resolution stage. This implies that the more severe the enforcement problem, the greater the need for centralization (Rational Design conjecture C4, CENTRALIZATION increases with ENFORCEMENT problems).

Such enforcement problems are typical, for example, when contracts are about to expire. No long-term relationship will last forever. Construction, licensing, distributorship, joint venture, and other long-term contracts will eventually terminate, and relationships will come to an end. Logically, such changes will also affect the ways in which disputes that arise after a business relationship has ended will be resolved. Consider, for example, the case of a complex, long-term construction contract as

---

53. On the role of hostages in economic exchange, see Williamson 1983; and Kronman 1985.
54. Vigrass 1993, 469. See also Graving 1989, 368.
55. Hunter et al. 1993, 73. See also Perlman and Nelson 1983, 232; Coe 1997, 44–49; and Park 1997b.

described by James Myers, head of a major international construction group:[56] At the onset, the contractor, employer, and engineer are all anxious to maintain harmonious working relationships with one another. They realize that the ability of one party to perform over an extended period of time rests on the cooperation of the others. Disputes, when they arise, will be resolved swiftly, fairly, and in a friendly fashion. ADR and ad hoc arbitration are the preferred methods of resolving disputes in such settings. Parties may sometimes even refrain from presenting claims, lest the relationship be strained. Once the project is completed, however, the parties' attitudes are likely to change. A contractor who has no further business with the employer may now feel no compunction about demanding payment for additional costs accumulated during the course of the construction, and the employer will have no hesitation in dismissing such claims as baseless. Myers notes that "proceedings which occur after the completion of an [international construction] contract . . . are resolved in a distinctly adversarial atmosphere in which large sums of money are sought, with little or no 'commercial downside'—meaning that the commercial relationship has normally expired and the parties have nothing to lose by refusing to accommodate each other for the sake of continuous harmonious commercial relations."[57]

It is apparent from this example that good will, the prerequisite for successful use of ADR or ad hoc arbitration, can no longer be taken for granted after a contractual relationship has ended. In such a situation, ADR and ad hoc arbitration are doomed to failure, but institutional arbitration is in its element. Unsurprisingly, the vast majority of disputes submitted to institutional arbitration arise shortly before or after a commercial relationship has ended. The following example, a typical institutional arbitration case, explains why and illustrates how procedural safeguards and monitoring provided by arbitral institutions help to overcome the difficulties posed by defection strategies.[58]

In 1987 a large German company (the claimant) entered into an agreement with a firm in Colombia (the defendant) granting the Columbian firm the exclusive license to manufacture and distribute certain pharmaceutical and biological products in Colombia for four years. In 1991 the German company decided not to renew the license agreement, and one year later it initiated arbitration proceedings claiming that the defendant had breached certain of its surviving obligations, such as reporting inventory and sales of the licensed products and refusing to pay substantial sums. The Colombian firm refused to respond to these claims.

In this case the conflict erupted after one party decided to end a business relationship. For the Colombian firm, the termination of the contract seems to

---

56. Myers 1991. See also Schwartz 1995; Stipanowich 1996; and Vagts 1987.
57. Myers 1991, 316.
58. The example is based on an actual ICC arbitration case. The names of the parties have been omitted. The case captures many of the features typical of institutional arbitration, notably in licensing, distributorship, construction, and sale of goods. About 70 percent of ICC arbitration cases fall into these categories.

have triggered a change in its view about the necessity of acting cooperatively. Defection from "surviving obligations" may be seen as an attractive strategy because it brings immediate gains without imposing an obvious long-term cost. Such an uncooperative disposition typically also pervades the dispute-resolution process in this type of case. For example, the defendant could try to evade the contractual obligation to arbitrate the dispute, arguing that the matter falls under its national jurisdiction and can only be decided in a national court according to national law and procedural rules. This is precisely the strategy that the Colombian party took; it wanted the case to be tried in Colombian courts under Colombian law. If this fails, the defendant may seek to derail the arbitral proceedings by disagreeing on the choice of arbitrator(s), procedural rules, place and language of arbitration, and applicable law. It could also try to delay the proceedings by failing to appear on dates selected for hearings or by raising questions over procedural matters. If none of these dilatory tactics succeeds, the defendant still has the option of challenging the arbitral award before a national court, on the basis that the arbitral tribunal exceeded its jurisdiction or that there was a substantial miscarriage of justice in the course of the proceedings. Finally, the party may simply choose not to honor the arbitral award.

Ad hoc arbitration demands little more than simple coordination among the arbitrators, procedural rules, applicable law, and place of arbitration. The institutional demands on cases like the German-Colombian one are much more complex. Extensive monitoring and strong institutional safeguards are necessary to deprive potential bad faith and other forms of "defection" of their effects in such cases.

The ICA is an example of an organization well equipped to handle such "difficult" cases. Its rules and institutional apparatus effectively override obstacles that a noncooperative disposition by one of the parties may pose. For instance, if one of the parties refuses to participate in the arbitral proceedings, the ICA is entitled to appoint the arbitrator(s) and constitute a tribunal. The notice and summons procedure is performed by the ICC secretariat and is supervised by the court, assuring the arbitrators that the defaulting party had notice of the arbitration.[59] If one party fails to sign the Terms of Reference, the ICA may approve them and the proceedings continue. After the Terms of Reference are approved, the opportunity for a party to engage in dilatory tactics by presenting additional claims and counterclaims is minimized because such claims can only be heard on the agreement of all parties.[60]

The court closely monitors the arbitral proceedings, ensuring that time limits and due process principles are respected.[61] It replaces arbitrators who do not fulfill their functions or are behind in their work. At the end of the process, it scrutinizes the award in relation to jurisdiction and applicable law. This monitoring and checking

59. Aksen 1991, 12.
60. Ibid., 13.
61. Principles of due process include transparency of the arbitral process, the right of the parties to be called and heard, and equal treatment of the parties in the exchange of pleadings, in evidentiary matters, in resort to expertise proceedings, and in the holding of hearings.

increases the quality of the arbitral award and, in turn, reduces the chance that the losing party will challenge the award in a national court. As noted by an experienced international arbitrator, "most final awards rendered under ICC auspices are carried out voluntarily by the parties, because [of their high] quality. . . . A company that fails to carry out an [ICC award] is almost certain to lose subsequent[ly][62] and in addition runs the risk of jeopardizing its reputation in international circles."[63] Indeed, only about 6 percent of all ICC awards have been challenged by the losing party, and a minute 0.5 percent of awards rendered under the aegis of the ICC have been set aside by a national court.[64]

It is easy to see why ad hoc arbitration and ADR are ill-suited for situations represented by the German-Colombian case. If at any stage of the proceedings in ad hoc arbitration or ADR matters go unexpectedly awry and one of the parties starts acting in bad faith, there is no international supervisory institution to coerce compliance with procedural rules.[65] Furthermore, if the losing party in an ad hoc arbitration case challenges the award in a national court, the winning party will find it considerably more difficult to prove to the national court that due process rules were respected and the tribunal was impartial and objective. Not surprisingly, national courts are much more comfortable confirming commercial awards that result from a monitored arbitration process than those produced by ad hoc proceedings.[66]

Uncertainty about the state of the world and centralization. Uncertainty about the state of the world is a third variable that is useful in understanding the selection of different arbitration options. It refers to the extent to which actors involved in international exchange are knowledgeable about international commercial arbitration and possess information about the legal environment (the laws and the integrity of local judges) in which arbitration takes place and the conditions for enforceability of arbitral awards. Good information on the legal environment and enforceability is a prerequisite of successful resolution of commercial disputes. The conjecture here is straightforward: The greater the uncertainty about the present state of the world, the greater the need for centralized information on international commercial arbitration and domestic arbitration laws and practices (Rational Design conjecture C2, CENTRALIZATION increases with UNCERTAINTY ABOUT THE STATE OF THE WORLD). Such information may be particularly important in cases involving traders with little

<hr>

62. In other words, when the winning party applies to a national court for recognition and enforcement of the award.
63. Aksen 1991, 22. See also David 1985, 45; and Hunter et al. 1993, 10.
64. See Craig, Park, and Paulsson 1990, 32–33; and David 1985, 50.
65. The type of problem that can arise in ad hoc arbitration is illustrated in a recent case (Intercarbon Bermuda v. Caltex Trading and Transport), where one party refused to proceed with an arbitration pursuant to an arbitration clause that provided for no institution to set the arbitration in motion. The claimant was forced to spend seven years in litigation before obtaining a federal court order compelling arbitration. Park 1995, 70. See also Coulson 1993; Aksen 1991, 8–9; and Paulsson 1993, 438.
66. David 1985, 11.

experience in international exchange or traders from very different cultural and linguistic regions. Major arbitral institutions help to provide the necessary information and procedural guidelines to enable inexperienced parties to resolve their commercial disputes in an efficient and timely fashion.

"Legal environment" encompasses domestic legislation on arbitration and court interpretations of it. The law in the location where arbitration will occur is of great importance because it may determine questions of the capacity of the parties to agree to arbitration, the validity of the arbitration agreement, the "arbitrability" of the subject matter of the dispute, and the recognition and enforcement of arbitral awards. Thus parties seeking to maximize procedural certainty may benefit from relying on centralized information on domestic arbitration laws and practices; such information will help them choose an arbitral situs where annulment of awards is not likely to be facilitated by a bribe to a local judge, where the range of nonarbitral legal questions is narrow and well defined, where the integrity of the arbitration process is ensured and any judicial meddling with an arbitrator's substantive decision is minimized, and where arbitration decisions are enforceable—if necessary, through execution against the assets of the losing party by proceedings in national courts of any state in which these assets are located.

Some countries have clear arbitration legislation, but their courts may misapply the law, for example, by adopting overelastic interpretations of "violations of public policy" as grounds for setting aside awards. Other countries may have national laws containing mandatory provisions that override explicit contractual stipulations. Two examples serve to illustrate how arbitrary and fickle domestic legal decisions regarding international arbitration may be, thus underlining the importance of centralized information on developments in national arbitration laws and practices:[67]

The Indian Supreme Court held in May 1992 that if Indian law applied to an arbitration clause, an application to set aside an award could be heard in India, even if the place of arbitration were outside India, and the Indian courts could enjoin the enforcement of the award anywhere. In other words, an acceptance of Indian law in a contract with an Indian party would ultimately lead to the Indian courts irrespective of the choice of a neutral venue.

In Singapore, in a 1988 decision, the High Court affirmed restrictions on foreign arbitration parties imposed by local practice rules. This was followed by a new Singapore Legal Profession Act, which stipulates that foreign lawyers can only appear in arbitration proceedings when the law applicable to a dispute is not Singaporean law. When Singaporean law does apply, foreign lawyers may only appear jointly with lawyers who are Singaporean nationals.

The second issue of central importance is the enforceability of arbitral awards. An award rendered in a given country may not automatically be enforceable in other countries where the losing party's assets may lie. Thus, a key function of major

---

67. The examples are drawn from Hunter et al. 1993. See also Park 1997a.

arbitral institutions is to collect and continuously update information on the conditions of enforceability of awards in various parts of the world. For example, by 1997 over one hundred states had acceded to the 1958 New York Convention on the Recognition and Enforcement of Arbitral Awards.[68] The majority of these states adopted the so-called reciprocity reservation. That means that their courts will enforce an award under the New York Convention only if the award has been rendered within the territory of another state that has also adhered to the New York Convention.[69] A court in a signatory country may refuse recognition and enforcement of awards only on procedural grounds, including invalidity of the arbitral agreement, denial of an opportunity to be heard, arbitrator excess of jurisdiction, arbitral procedure contrary to the parties' agreement, and annulment of the award in the country where rendered.[70] However, the interpretation by national courts of these grounds for denying enforcement of arbitral awards may vary from country to country. Therefore, major arbitral institutions also keep information on the various national interpretations.

In sum, private firms and their lawyers may often lack sufficient information about the legal state of the world to avoid expensive delays and other negative surprises. This is particularly true if the parties are inexperienced in international trade and investment or if they deal with firms from distant regions.[71] Uncertainty about the legal environment and enforceability can be reduced, at least in part, by relying on information provided by major arbitral institutions, such as the ICA or the LCIA. Such forums have the institutional capacity to monitor and record changes in domestic arbitration laws and practices around the world, especially if their memberships have a broad geographic base.

An examination of the docket of the ICA offers supporting evidence for the conjecture that firms from different regions rely more heavily on centralized support and expertise for the resolution of their disputes than firms operating in relatively homogenous regions. Table 2 lists the origin of the parties in all ICA cases since 1974. Strikingly, Western Europeans have been involved in well over half of all cases. The key finding, however, emerges from Table 3. Despite the well-known fact that Europeans (and North Americans) trade much more intraregionally than with other regions, it appears that considerably more interregional commercial

---

68. See UN Doc E/Conf. 26/SR., 1–25. The standard work on this treaty is Berg 1981. Besides the New York Convention, there are at least two other international enforcement conventions, the 1975 Inter-American Arbitration Convention (also called the Panama Convention) and the 1961 European Convention on International Commercial Arbitration. In addition to these conventions, many bilateral commercial and investment treaties contain enforcement provisions. For a brief historical account of the development of the various enforcement conventions, see Redfern and Hunter 1991, 60–64; see also Sanders 1996, 41–42; and Jackson 1991.

69. Hunter et al. 1993, 19. Art. III of the New York Convention provides that convention states shall recognize foreign awards as "binding and enforce them in accordance with the rules of procedure of the territory where the award is relied upon," subject to no conditions more onerous than those imposed on domestic awards.

70. Park 1995, 55–56.

71. Aksen 1991, 14.

TABLE 2. Origin of parties in ICC arbitration cases (average per period)

Region	1974–85	1986–90	1991–95	1996–97
Western Europe	59.2%	56.9%	59.7%	49.5%
Central and Eastern Europe	3.8%	3.2%	6.1%	7.1%
Middle East	8%	5.2%	4.1%	3.2%
Africa	9.2%	8.9%	5.3%	5.7%
North America (United States and Canada)	13.3%	13.8%	11.8%	13.5%
Latin America and the Caribbean	3.4%	3.6%	4.8%	11.5%
Asia	3.1%	8.4%	8.2%	9.5%

Source: ICC International Court of Arbitration Bulletin, various issues; and author's notes taken during internship at ICC International Court of Arbitration, Paris, 1998.

disputes are submitted to the ICA than disputes arising among firms from the same region, that is, Europe, North America, or any other region listed in Table 2. On average, approximately three out of four disputes brought to the ICA involve parties from different regions. This statistic contrasts sharply with the finding about the geographic distribution of ad hoc cases. According to international arbitrators interviewed in Paris, Stockholm, and New York, ad hoc cases seem to be more common among parties from relatively homogenous regions and communities.[72] However, since no institution keeps track of ad hoc arbitration cases and full information therefore does not exist, the finding about ad hoc cases must be considered tentative.

Uncertainty about the state of the world and flexibility.   Uncertainty about the state of the world can also refer to the susceptibility of an issue-area to new developments or unanticipated shocks that may leave parties in uncharted legal territory. The conjecture, in this case, is as follows: The more uncertain the state of the world, the greater the desirability of a flexible method for resolving disputes (Rational Design conjecture F1, FLEXIBILITY increases with UNCERTAINTY ABOUT THE STATE OF THE WORLD), thus implying a preference of arbitration and ADR over litigation in public courts.[73]

   The flexibility offered in arbitration and ADR may be valued, for example, because it gives firms operating at the forefront of new production and exchange methods the possibility of appointing experts who have the necessary technical knowledge to evaluate complex, new situations and understand the facts; an ordinary judge cannot be expected to have this specialized knowledge. Complex

72. Based on interviews at the ICA (April 1998), the SCC Institute (April 1998), and law firms in New York (October 1998).

73. On institutional flexibility and its relationship to uncertainty, see also the studies in this volume by Oatley, Richards, and Rosendorff and Milner.

TABLE 3. Regional distribution of ICC arbitration cases (average per period based on available samples)

	1974–85 (37 cases)	1986–90 (36 cases)	1991–95 (19 cases)	1996–97 (140 cases)
Intraregional disputes	30%	11%	26%	32%
Interregional disputes	70%	89%	74%	68%

Source: Author's computation based on case collections in Jarvin and Derains 1990; Jarvin, Derains, and Arnaldez 1994; Arnaldez, Derains, and Hascher 1997; and author's notes taken during internship at ICC International Court of Arbitration, Paris, 1998.

technical issues may arise in cases dealing with transfer of technology, industrial property, trademarks, technical know-how, and financial products. Brian Neill, Justice of the Court of Appeals of England and Wales, observes that "cases arise from time to time which involve questions which lie at or near the frontiers of current scientific knowledge. Can they be tried satisfactorily in the ordinary courts? There must be doubt."[74]

Flexibility also permits the expert to disregard, to some extent, the technicalities of the law in favor of a solution that accords with new business practices. An arbitral tribunal, for example, may be given powers of so-called amiable composition or, as it is sometimes put, the right to decide ex aequo et bono (in equity and good conscience); that is, the tribunal may reach a decision without applying strict legal principles, provided the decision is fair. More generally, flexibility allows the parties to tailor the rules—regarding procedure, evidence, or even the substance of the case—to their specific needs.[75]

The advantages of flexibility in dispute resolution can be illustrated with the help of a major arbitration case that involved IBM and Fujitsu, two of the world's largest computer companies. The dispute erupted over intellectual property rights to operating system software. In the early 1970s Fujitsu decided to develop and market IBM-compatible operating system software for mainframe computers.[76] A decade later, IBM confronted Fujitsu with allegations that Fujitsu's operating system programs violated IBM's intellectual property rights. After lengthy negotiations, the two companies signed two agreements in 1983; one agreement granted Fujitsu immunity and waiver of IBM claims with respect to past and future distribution of Fujitsu's programs in exchange for payments from Fujitsu to IBM; the other agreement required each party to provide the other with information relevant to

74. Neill 1988, 235. For confirming evidence of the importance of this point, see recent survey results in Bühring-Uhle 1996, 136–37.

75. Redfern and Hunter 1991, 24; see also Jones 1958, 464; and Kerr 1987.

76. This account draws on Mnookin 1994.

compatibility. These agreements, however, quickly broke down, and in 1985 IBM filed a demand for arbitration accusing Fujitsu of copying its software in violation of copyright law and IBM's rights under the 1983 agreements. Fujitsu denied violating IBM's rights and accused IBM of failing to live up to its obligations under the agreements.

The case turned out to be highly complex because of enormous legal and factual uncertainties. IBM and Fujitsu were developing software in a world of rapidly changing technology. However, no clear understanding existed of what the law of copyright was and how it applied to computer software and the particular subject matter of the dispute. One of the arbitrators involved in the case, Robert Mnookin, noted that "this was not a dispute where there was a clear and agreed understanding of the underlying law and where it was only necessary to apply clear law to particular facts. . . . There were no [prior] . . . judicial decisions. No one knew the precise scope of copyright protection."[77] Legal uncertainties were compounded by factual uncertainties. Indeed, the disputed programs involved hundreds of thousands (in some cases millions) of lines of codes, rendering fact finding exceedingly difficult.

The arbitrators overcame some of these difficulties by themselves creating the law that would bind the two parties vis-à-vis each other. First, they probed the interests of the parties to identify areas of convergence.[78] They then proceeded to develop, in close consultation with the parties' technical representatives, detailed rules to define what would and would not be permitted in compatible software development. As a result of the arbitration effort, IBM and Fujitsu agreed to set aside the 1983 agreements and execute a new agreement in 1987 that provided a successful framework for resolving all issues in dispute.

In short, arbitration enabled the parties to take a flexible approach and tailor the rules to their particular problem and underlying interests. Rather than framing the strategies in terms of penalties or exoneration for past conduct, the parties took a forward-looking strategy and actively participated in the rule-making process that eventually established clear rights and obligations between them.

Far from being an isolated case, the IBM-Fujitsu dispute is representative of a rapidly growing body of international arbitration cases dealing with intellectual property rights. This growth has been fueled by the speedy reduction of trade barriers, the proliferation of digital means of communication, and the increase of commerce via the internet. Unsurprisingly, such disputes are the fastest growing

77. Robert Mnookin at Geneva Global Arbitration Forum (21 October 1993); see Mnookin, Méan, and Robine 1994, 141–42.
78. It became clear that Fujitsu's paramount interest was to develop IBM-compatible software, but it demanded access only to external interface information, not information about internal design of IBM programs. IBM in turn was interested in ensuring that Fujitsu did not copy internal design information and that it received adequate compensation for external interface information contained in IBM programs extracted by Fujitsu.

category of cases submitted to the ICA, increasing from 8.6 percent in 1982 to an average of almost 20 percent in the past four years.[79]

The institutional characteristics, such as flexibility, that render arbitration appealing in a growing number of areas, may not, however, be necessary or even desirable in other commercial contexts, and thus the requisite dispute-resolution methods will vary. Consider, for example, the case of international loan agreements between private parties. Big companies may take out large syndicated loans to finance trade, exploit natural resources, assist take-over bids, provide working capital, construct new plants, drill rigs, buy ships, and so on. When writing international loan agreements, the lending banks will take great care in covering all contingencies that may result in losses to the banks and in seeking the best possible protection against such events. The banks will also spell out as clearly as possible what sums of money are to be paid at any particular time, how they are to be paid, and by whom.[80]

Loan agreements also contain a governing-law or choice-of-law clause that sets forth the law that determines the validity of the contractual provisions that have been inserted in the loan agreement and the effect and scope of the contractual rights and obligations expressed in the agreement.[81] As Richard Slater explains, "A bank wants to be sure that if certain events of default, which it has taken the trouble to write into its loan agreement, occur, then it is entitled to accelerate the loan[82] without having to worry about whether the event is material, whether the borrower was to blame for its occurrence, whether it was fair, or whether it was in accordance with normal practice. A bank wants as little scope as possible for debate about the meaning of the provisions in its loan agreement."[83]

It is now easy to see why bankers shun arbitration clauses and, instead, insert in almost all international loan agreements jurisdiction clauses, selecting either New York courts or the London High Court as forums (depending on whether the contract is governed by New York or British substantive law).[84] Unlike in construction, engineering, and intellectual property cases, which tend to go to arbitration, the question in international loan cases is generally quite simple: has the debt fallen due and been left unpaid, and, if so, how much is it? In most cases, establishing this fact is simple. Thus disputes under a loan agreement will

79. Based on interviews at the ICA, Paris (April 1998). One area that several interviewees identified as likely to generate heavy arbitration activity is telecommunications, the fastest growing sector of most industrialized economies. Privatization of government-owned network operators, deregulation, and the introduction of cross-border competition are fundamentally changing the industry; and many telecommunication disputes are expected to involve intellectual property issues. Interviews at the Commission of the European Union, Brussels (March 1998), and the LCIA, London (April 1998).
80. Slater 1982, 177–78.
81. Gruson 1982, 17. The vast majority of loan agreements select British or New York law, in part because of these laws' strict approach to the concepts of breach of contract and sanctity of contract.
82. "To accelerate the loan" means to terminate a lending relationship and declare all amounts outstanding under the loan agreement immediately due and payable.
83. Slater 1982, 195–96.
84. Cates and Isern-Feliu 1983, 28–29, 34.

typically relate not to matters of fact but law.[85] However, legal uncertainties or intricacies are also rare in loan cases. Legal matters under loan agreements are well covered by case precedents and statutes; thus the courts in New York and the United Kingdom possess, in most cases, the requisite information to deal expeditiously with default cases.[86] For these reasons, litigation seems a more appropriate method than arbitration for the resolution of disputes arising from international loan agreements.

Conclusion

International commercial arbitration has emerged over the past two decades as the method of choice for settling a growing number of trade and investment disputes involving private parties. Its surge in popularity can be attributed in part to the institutional attributes of arbitration, which include flexibility, technical expertise, privacy, and confidentiality. These attributes match the needs of disputants in areas such as intellectual property, transfer of technology, engineering, and construction. Arbitration options, however, are not the only methods available to private parties. The market for dispute-resolution mechanisms also includes recourse to public courts and several alternative-dispute resolution techniques.

I have argued that firms on the demand side select methods for dispute resolution according to their design problems. In other words, the various methods respond to the varying institutional needs of different types of disputes and disputants, and these needs can be explained in terms of the severity of the enforcement problem, uncertainty about the preferences or behavior of contractual partners, and uncertainty about the state of the world. More specifically, the findings are that (1) centralization of forums to which private international parties resort to resolve their disputes increases with the severity of the enforcement problem (Rational Design conjecture C4, CENTRALIZATION increases with ENFORCEMENT PROBLEMS); (2) centralization also increases with uncertainty about the parties' preferences or behavior (conjecture C1, CENTRALIZATION increases with UNCERTAINTY ABOUT BEHAVIOR); (3) the need for centralized information on international commercial arbitration and domestic arbitration laws and practices grows with greater uncertainty about the legal environment in which arbitration takes place and the conditions for enforceability of arbitral awards (conjecture C2, CENTRALIZATION increases with UNCERTAINTY ABOUT THE STATE OF THE WORLD); and (4) the desirability of a flexible method for resolving disputes increases with the susceptibility of an issue-area to new developments or unanticipated shocks that may leave the parties in uncharted legal territory (conjecture F1, FLEXIBILITY increases with UNCERTAINTY ABOUT THE STATE OF THE WORLD).

85. Wood 1980, 71–73; see also Slater 1982, 197; and Cates and Isern-Feliu 1983, 28–36.
86. Ryan 1982, 89–132.

This study thus illustrates that Koremenos, Lipson, and Snidal's analytical framework not only sheds light on institutional arrangements among states[87] but can also account for varying forms of international governance established by private parties.

My analysis, however, has only scratched the surface of a complex but fascinating area of research for scholars of international relations and other social scientists. Several issues evoked in passing merit fuller analysis. One is the study of specialized arbitration, for example, as conducted in maritime affairs or as offered by various stock and commodity exchanges. Such arbitration is typically conducted within commercial groups with strong national roots. For example, the British Coffee Trade Federation numbers over one hundred firms as members, including the leading roasters, merchants, brokers, and wharfingers in the United Kingdom. Notwithstanding its national base, the federation is linked to a wide network of transnational commodity organizations such as the Committee of European Coffee Associations, the European Federation of Coffee Roasters Associations, and the Federation of Commodity Associations. This raises the question of how this "institutional embeddedness" is likely to shape the arbitral institutions and practices of national federations.

Another question that emerges from the study of arbitration is why states have traditionally been reluctant to resort to international arbitration. Indeed, while the number of arbitration cases involving private parties has grown exponentially, instances of interstate arbitration are few. For example, after a modest beginning, recourse to the Permanent Court of Arbitration at the Hague became infrequent in the extreme. Of the twenty-five cases considered by the court, twenty-two cases were disposed of by 1935; the other three were heard in 1940, 1956, and 1970, respectively.[88]

Another example are disputes submitted to the arbitration mechanism of the International Center for the Settlement of Investment Disputes (ICSID). ICSID was created in 1966 by the so-called Washington Convention as part of the World Bank organization. ICSID's authority is limited to investment disputes where one of the parties is the host state. By 1995, only thirty investment disputes had been brought to the ICSID for arbitration, resulting in what Stephen Toope calls a "highly limited case load";[89] and Aron Broches notes similarly that "advance acceptance of [ICSID's] jurisdiction has not resulted in a large number of cases."[90]

The specific reasons for the paucity of arbitration cases involving states are varied and complex. However, one theme runs throughout history, namely the deep concern of states with maintaining sovereignty and independence combined with a perception that national autonomy and international arbitration practices are not easily compatible. Consider the following examples: In 1903 France concluded an

87. Koremenos, Lipson, and Snidal, this volume.
88. Butler 1992, 44.
89. Toope 1990, 255.
90. Broches 1979, 374; see also Gray and Kingsbury 1992.

agreement with the United Kingdom that provided for the settlement by arbitration of certain disputes that may arise between the two countries. Reference would be made to the Permanent Court of Arbitration. Tellingly, however, the signatories added a clause to the agreement stating that only those differences would qualify for submission to arbitration "that . . . do not affect the vital interests, the independence, or the honor of the two contracting states."[91] Similar provisions were inserted in other arbitration treaties of the period. Needless to say, the malleability and subjective nature of these exceptions considerably weakened the legal obligation to arbitrate disputes.[92]

Some countries considered even such watered-down arbitration clauses as too intrusive. Latin American countries, for example, rejected arbitration and insisted on so-called Calvo clauses that required foreign parties to agree to adjudication within the host state of any dispute arising out of an investment contract.[93] More recently, oil-exporting nations have manifested similar hostility to arbitration, demanding that "disputes arising between a government and operator shall fall exclusively within the jurisdiction of competent national courts."[94]

States' concern with safeguarding sovereignty is also reflected in principles of international law. One example is the distinction made between immunity from jurisdiction, also called immunity from suit, and immunity from execution, which means immunity from measures sought against the property of a state for the enforcement of an arbitral award. A waiver of immunity from jurisdiction, which follows from entering into a valid agreement to arbitrate, does not automatically entail a waiver of immunity from execution. This principle is enshrined, for example, in the ICSID Convention, which stipulates that "nothing . . . [in the ICSID Convention] shall be construed as derogating from the law in force in any Contracting State relating to immunity of that State or any foreign State from execution."[95] Similarly, the draft Convention of State Immunity that the International Law Commission published in 1991, after thirteen years of work, states that "no measures of constraint such as attachment, arrest, and execution against property of a State may be taken in connection with a proceeding before the court of another state. . . . Immunity from execution may be viewed, therefore, as the last fortress, the last bastion of state immunity."[96] Today most states have accepted doctrines of restricted immunity and waiver of immunity with respect to jurisdiction; but they continue to apply absolute immunity when it comes to actual execution.

---

91. Art. 1 of the agreement is quoted in Carter and Trimble 1991, 332–33.
92. On sovereignty costs in the context of regional and international legalization, see Abbott and Snidal 2000; Mattli 1999; and Mattli 2000.
93. Shea 1955.
94. 1967 OPEC resolution quoted in Craig, Park, Paulsson 1990, 647.
95. Art. 55 of Washington Convention.
96. Art. 18 of the Draft Convention of State Immunity by the International Law Commission, and Commentary on Article 18 in the Report of the International Law Commission; quoted in Sanders 1996, 73.

In practice, the shocking result can be that a party, after having put every effort into an arbitration against a state and having obtained a judgment for enforcement in its favor, finds itself unable to collect the money to which it is entitled under the award.[97] One remedy, agreeing to a waiver of immunity from execution when entering into a contract, is rarely used.[98]

In sum, traditional aversion of states to compromising over issues of national control and autonomy, as well as practical problems in enforcement that stem from the age-old principle that with sovereignty comes immunity, may take us a long way toward explaining why arbitration cases involving states have been relatively few.

97. Carter and Trimble 1991, 366.
98. Sanders 1996, 81.

Multilateralizing Trade and Payments in Postwar Europe

Thomas H. Oatley

The liberalization of intra-European trade in the years immediately following World War II offered potentially large welfare gains to European societies. In this period European trade flowed through a network of two hundred bilateral agreements. In the two years after the war intra-European trade increased rapidly within this bilateral framework, but by 1947 the growth had halted.[1] Shifting from this bilateral system to a multilateral clearing union could have provided a first step toward trade expansion. In spite of the potential benefits multilateral clearing offered, however, it was not until September 1950 that European governments established an effective multilateral clearing union, the European Payments Union (EPU).

Once established, the EPU had a dramatic impact on intra-European trade. The clearing union freed trade credit and greatly reduced European governments' need to resort to discriminatory quantitative restrictions for balance-of-payments considerations. Trade liberalization within the framework of the Organization for European Economic Cooperation (OEEC) quickly followed. By 1954 80 percent of intra-European trade had been freed from quantitative restrictions, and governments had begun to consider meaningful tariff reductions as well.[2] Thus, inducing European governments to enter a multilateral clearing union in 1950 marked the critical first step toward nondiscriminatory trade in postwar Europe.

I use the Rational Design framework to explore how the institutional structure supporting the multilateral payments arrangements facilitated Europe's shift to

Earlier versions of this article were presented at the Program on International Politics, Economics, and Security at the University of Chicago, February 1998; the Rational Design conference, Chicago, May 1998; and the 1998 Annual Meeting of the American Political Science Association. For helpful comments, I thank Barbara Koremenos, Charles Lipson, Lisa Martin, Walter Mattli, Tim McKeown, Jim Morrow, Robert Pahre, John Richards, Duncan Snidal, Terry Sullivan, the Comparative Politics Discussion Group at the University of North Carolina at Chapel Hill, and the editors and anonymous reviewers of *IO*.

1. See Eichengreen 1993; and Diebold 1952.
2. Asbeek-Brusse 1997, 83.

International Organization 55, 4, Autumn 2001, pp. 949–969

multilateralism. This question has received little explicit attention in the existing literature. Standard accounts of the Marshall Plan, in which the EPU figures prominently, and the one detailed history of the EPU largely ignore the strategic and institutional aspects of Europe's shift to multilateralism.[3] Barry Eichengreen's work on the EPU is more explicitly institutionalist.[4] Eichengreen suggests that European governments chose the EPU over full convertibility because domestic political considerations—in particular, the need for business and labor agreement on wage moderation and investment levels—made them unwilling to accept the real income losses full convertibility would necessarily entail. What Eichengreen neglects, however, is the fact that the very concerns that made European governments reluctant to adopt full convertibility also made them reluctant to adopt more limited multilateral clearing arrangements like the EPU. Thus, existing work provides little insight into how distributive conflict, uncertainty, and enforcement problems blocked Europe's transition to multilateralism or into how specific elements of the EPU's institutional framework facilitated this transition.

In examining Europe's postwar shift to multilateralism I evaluate six conjectures drawn from the Rational Design project. The specific conjectures relate three dimensions of institutional design—flexibility, centralization, and control—to four of the project's independent variables: distributional problems, enforcement problems, uncertainty about the state of the world, and asymmetry of contributions. To evaluate the conjectures linking these variables, I first demonstrate that the independent variable did in fact frustrate European governments' transition to multilateralism. I then examine the degree to which the institutions that governments designed in response to these characteristics of the bargaining environment are consistent with the expectations of the Rational Design framework. The results are quite encouraging. Five of the six conjectures I examine receive very strong support. The sixth conjecture receives only moderate support, but this is more a result of idiosyncratic features of the Marshall Plan than of a weakness in the Rational Design framework.

The article proceeds as follows. I first describe the postwar bilateral trade system in western Europe and explain how multilateral clearing arrangements would work. In the second section I focus on distributional problems and uncertainty about the state of the world. I explain how distributive conflict and uncertainty about the state of the world made European governments reluctant to adopt multilateral arrangements; I then elaborate how the flexibility and centralization imparted to EPU institutions reduced the severity of these problems and thereby facilitated the transition. In the third section I focus on enforcement problems. I explain how the enforcement problem made U.S. officials reluctant to capitalize the payments union and how U.S. policymakers responded by designing centralized institutions that helped limit the kind of behavior they feared. In the final section I summarize the

---

3. See Hogan 1987; Kaplan and Schleiminger 1989; and Milward 1984.
4. Eichengreen 1993.

degree to which the case supports the Rational Design conjectures and offer some concluding comments.

Bilateralism and Multilateralism in Postwar European Trade

Bilateral agreements in postwar European trade were necessitated by the inconvertibility of European currencies and designed to ensure that imports from particular trading partners were paid for by exports to the same partner.[5] Each bilateral agreement established a list of commodities that the contracting governments agreed to import from each other in specified amounts. Many of these agreements also predetermined prices for these commodities. While bilateral agreements were oriented toward bilateral trade balance, most also contained short-term "swing" credit arrangements that allowed temporary departures from balanced bilateral trade. Bilateral deficits larger than the credit lines offered in the agreement often required settlement in 100 percent hard currency.

While the bilateral system allowed intra-European trade to reemerge in the immediate postwar period, by 1947 bilateralism had reached the limits of its usefulness. The assumption on which bilateral agreements were based, that bilateral trade would be balanced, proved incorrect. Intra-European trade was in disequilibrium. As Table 1 shows, Belgium, Italy, France, Sweden, and Switzerland ran net surpluses on their European trade, while the other countries ran net deficits.[6] These persistent imbalances exhausted available credit, and as a result "downward pressure was placed on the entire network of Europe's trade."[7] When the credit lines available in a bilateral agreement were exhausted, governments either used quotas to restrict their imports from specific countries or in extreme cases stopped trading with some partners altogether. France, for example, ceased importing entirely from Belgium in late 1947, as did Sweden in March 1948. The persistent imbalances and limited credit that characterized postwar bilateralism, therefore, constrained the expansion of trade. Moreover, heavy reliance on quotas to restrict trade when credit limits were reached introduced considerable distortions into European trade, as governments purchased goods from countries with which they had a bilateral surplus or that were willing to grant credit rather than making purchases from producers offering the lowest price.

A multilateral clearing union offered a solution to the problems posed by bilateralism. While the specific elements of clearing mechanisms can be complex,

5. For a description of this system see Patterson and Polk 1947; and Diebold 1952.
6. The British trade deficit in 1949 is, to some extent, misleading. This large deficit reflected the overvaluation of sterling. After the 1949 devaluation, the United Kingdom moved into surplus on its European trade. However, because of the problem of sterling balances, the British bargaining position shared more in common with the other European debtor governments than with the other European creditors.
7. Eichengreen 1993, 16–17.

TABLE 1. Net balances on European trade, 1949 (in thousands of $US)

Country	Net trade balance
Austria	−107,756
Belgium-Luxembourg	277,550
Denmark	39,851
France	49,350
Greece	−134,250
Italy	243,214
Netherlands	−120,037
Norway	−108,284
Portugal	−53,783
Sweden	113,783
Switzerland	93,817
Turkey	18,597
United Kingdom	−297,127
West Germany	−14,925

Source: The Operation of the Clearing Union, 20 February 1950, in File: Finance, P.; Finance and Trade Division, 1949–52; RG469.2.2, NACP.

the underlying principle is simple. Under a bilateral system each government has multiple bilateral balances; some of these bilateral balances will be in deficit, and others will be in surplus. Under a multilateral clearing arrangement the credits available in surplus bilateral accounts are used to settle the debts owed in the deficit bilateral accounts. A stylized example can illustrate. Suppose that Britain has a $6 million deficit with Italy, Italy has a $6 million deficit with Belgium, and Belgium has a $5 million surplus with Britain. Under a multilateral clearing system Italy could use its credit with Britain to settle its debt to Belgium.

Multilateral clearing offered two advantages to bilateralism. First, clearing would reduce total outstanding credit obligations. In the stylized example, multilateral clearing would reduce outstanding obligations from $17 million to $11 million.[8] The $6 million of cleared credit could then be used to finance additional trade. In the real world, it was estimated in 1948 that full multilateral clearing could cancel $278.9 million of an existing $762.1 million debt in the European trade system. Second, multilateral clearing would allow governments to focus on their net position against the OEEC as a whole rather than on individual bilateral positions. This in turn would allow governments to remove the discriminatory quantitative restrictions they had

8. Under the bilateral agreements, Britain owes Belgium $5 million, Italy owes Belgium $6 million, and Britain owes Italy $6 million, for a total debt of $17 million. Under multilateral clearing, Italy transfers its $6 million credit with Britain to Belgium, thereby paying its debt. The only remaining debt is Britain's $11 billion debt to Belgium (the $5 million of its own deficit and the $6 million arising from the Italian transfer).

relied on to balance bilateral trade, thereby reducing the distortions that character-ized European trade.

In spite of the apparent benefits to be realized from multilateral clearing, however, European governments were extremely reluctant to relinquish the system of bilateral agreements in favor of multilateral arrangements. The Council for European Economic Cooperation (CEEC) proposed multilateral clearing in 1947–48, but European governments showed little interest in the proposed multilateral scheme. The first clearing under this system, undertaken in 1948, eliminated only $1.7 million of the possible $278.9 million that could have been cleared, and total clearings throughout the agreement's lifetime amounted to only $51.6 million.[9] European governments' resistance to full multilateral clearing persisted throughout 1948 and 1949. U.S. officials consistently pressed Europe to move toward multi-lateral clearing arrangements, but met little success. As a consequence, multilateral clearing had little effect on European trade. Robert Triffin estimated that between 1947 and June 1950, the effective starting point of the EPU, multilateral arrange-ments "cleared only about 4 percent of the positions which would have been cleared under a system of full and automatic multilateral compensation such as was adopted later under the EPU agreements."[10]

Uncertainty, Distributive Conflict, and Europe's Shift to Multilateralism

European governments' reluctance to move toward multilateral clearing arrange-ments during the late 1940s was caused by the interaction between governments' uncertainty about how multilateral clearing would affect their hard-currency receipts and obligations and an underlying distributive conflict. Distributive conflict in an environment of hard-currency scarcity made European governments unwilling to cede even partial control over their external payments obligations to a centralized clearing union. Rational Design conjecture F2, FLEXIBILITY increases with DISTRIBU-TION problems, and conjecture C2, CENTRALIZATION increases with UNCERTAINTY ABOUT THE STATE OF THE WORLD, suggest that in such circumstances governments should seek to create centralized institutions to reduce uncertainty and flexible institutions to reduce the severity of the distributive conflict. The institutions created in 1950 strongly support both conjectures. A U.S. decision to capitalize the payments union relaxed Europe's hard-currency constraint and made possible a centralized clearing union based on a set of clearing rules that imparted considerable flexibility into creditor-debtor relations. This institutional framework enabled European govern-ments to adopt multilateral clearing arrangements.

9. Bean 1948, 408.
10. Triffin 1957, 149.

TABLE 2. Gold and dollar reserves, 1951 and 1938 (in millions of $US)

	1951		1938	
	Gold and dollar reserves	Months of imports covered	Gold and dollar reserves	Months of imports covered
Belgium	897	4.3	828	12.7
France	899	2.3	2,944	26.8
Italy	635	3.6	193	3.9
Netherlands	524	2.5	1,100	16.7
Switzerland	1,973	17.4	920	30.1
United Kingdom	2,335	2.6	3,313	8.8

Source: OEEC 1952, 60.

Uncertainty, Distributive Conflict, and Europe's Reluctance to Multilateralize

Uncertainty about the state of the world arose from European governments' inability to predict how multilateral clearing would affect their hard-currency payments and receipts. European governments held little hard currency in the immediate postwar period. The severity of the hard-currency constraint is shown in Table 2, which compares gold reserves in 1951 with prewar holdings. Before the war, European governments (excluding Switzerland) held, on average, reserves sufficient to cover almost fourteen months of imports. In contrast average reserves in 1951 (excluding those in Switzerland) were only about three months of imports.

The shortage of hard currency created problems for European governments. Postwar reconstruction depended on imports from the dollar area that had to be paid for with hard currency, while European exports to the dollar area were quite limited. European countries therefore ran deficits with the dollar area. The scarcity of hard currency coupled with the need to import from the dollar area to achieve reconstruction objectives made European governments extremely concerned about how intra-European trade would affect their hard-currency reserves. Bilateralism was adopted as the safest way to manage European trade in this environment. Bilateral agreements allowed governments to tightly control the amount of hard currency they expended through trade within Europe. By balancing trade on a bilateral basis, imports from a given trading partner could be paid for with exports to the same partner and no hard currency would need to change hands. Bilateral agreements also enabled European governments to shut off imports from a given country if the bilateral balance became unfavorable and threatened to impose hard-currency obligations. In other words, in an environment of hard-currency scarcity bilateral agreements allowed European governments to manage their external balance and conserve hard currency.

The problem with multilateral arrangements, given the scarcity and importance of hard currency, was that governments could not easily predict how multilateral clearing would affect their total hard-currency receipts and obligations. This is clear in creditor and debtor governments' reactions to a multilateral clearing arrangement proposed by the CEEC in 1947–48. The CEEC proposed that each government's bilateral credits and debits be pooled to produce a single net position against the entire CEEC. Debtors' total obligations to the system's creditors would be allocated across all creditor governments in proportion to each creditor's share of the system's total credit. Debtor governments would then settle in hard currency any debts above the credit lines established in the relevant bilateral agreement.

Uncertainty about how the proposed arrangement would affect hard-currency payments caused creditor and debtor governments to object to the proposal. Creditor governments objected to the proposed arrangement because the CEEC plan could reduce the amount of hard currency they earned from European trade. Pooling under the CEEC plan would distribute each creditor government's credits across all of the system's debtor governments. Belgium, for example, which under its bilateral arrangements might have a total hard-currency claim of 100 against Britain, France, and the Netherlands, might find that in the multilateral system it had a total hard-currency claim of 80 distributed across a large number of debtors.[11] By reducing the total claim and by distributing this claim across a larger number of debtor governments, Belgium might find that its intra-European trade surpluses were generating less hard currency under the multilateral arrangement than they would under bilateral agreements. Moreover, some of the governments against which Belgium gained claims as a result of pooling might not have the hard currency required to settle.

Debtor governments objected to the proposed system because it reduced their ability to control their gold obligations.[12] Under the bilateral system, debtor governments could avoid external demands for hard currency by shifting the source of their imports. If they reached the hard-currency payment point in one bilateral agreement, they could stop imports from that country and begin to import from a country with which they had a surplus or that was willing to offer credit. Under a multilateral system these techniques would no longer be effective. Because debts would be distributed across all of the system's creditor countries, shifting imports from one country to another would do little to economize on hard-currency obligations. Thus, debtor governments faced potentially larger gold demands under multilateral clearing than they would face under the bilateral system.

Creditor and debtor governments both preferred the certainty of existing bilateral arrangements to the uncertainty of the CEEC proposal. Instead of adopting the CEEC plan, European governments adopted a multilateral system that provided each government full control over its hard-currency receipts and obligations. The

11. This example comes from Bean 1948, 410.
12. See Hogan 1987, 119–21; and Diebold 1952.

First Agreement on Multilateral Monetary Compensation, as this system was called, distinguished between two categories of clearing. First category clearings were those that did not increase any bilateral balances. For example, if France owed Norway $3 million, Norway owed Britain $5 million, and Britain owed France $4 million, multilateral clearing would eliminate the French debt to Norway, reduce Norway's debt to the United Kingdom to $2 million, and Britain's debt to France to $1 million. Because these clearings did not increase any bilateral balances, they were to be conducted automatically among the system's full members. Second category compensations were those that did increase a bilateral balance. Because second category clearings would increase balances in certain bilateral trade accounts, they could occur only if all the parties involved—the primary debtor, the primary creditor, and the government whose currency was being transferred—agreed. In other words, rather than accept full automatic multilateral clearing, European governments created a multilateral clearing system in which they retained a veto over any clearings that would alter their hard-currency receipts or payments. But even with this veto, multilateral clearing proved too large a step. Only five governments joined the system as full members. Eight other governments joined as "occasional members" who reserved the right to veto even first category clearings. As a result, the First Agreement had a negligible effect on European payments arrangements, clearing only $56 million of the total debt in the system.[13]

An injection of hard currency into Europe could reduce European governments' resistance to multilateral clearing arrangements, and as we will see such an injection was an important part of the solution. A permanent shift to multilateralism, however, would require a solution to an underlying distributive conflict. This distributive conflict pitted European debtor governments against European creditor governments and revolved around one basic question: who would bear the costs arising from the existing imbalance in intra-European trade? Would creditor governments with current account surpluses have to reduce the size of their surpluses by importing more, or would debtor governments with current account deficits have to reduce the size of their deficits by importing less? This distributive conflict focused on two distinct, though intrinsically linked, sets of issues: financial arrangements and macroeconomic policy.

Distributive conflict over financial arrangements revolved around the role hard currency and credit facilities would play in any multilateral clearing system. Led by the Belgians, creditor governments saw that their surpluses in European trade could be a potential source of hard currency that could be used to cover their deficits with the dollar area. Creditor governments therefore sought to maximize the amount of hard currency used in settling debts with the clearing union and to minimize the degree to which these imbalances would be settled through credit. Led by the British, debtor governments saw that their deficits in European trade represented a potential claim on their hard-currency reserves, and this potential claim competed

13. Bean 1948, 408.

with their need to import goods from the dollar area. The more that debtor governments were required to use hard currency to settle intra-European deficits, the less hard currency they would have available to make necessary purchases from the dollar area. Debtor governments therefore sought to maximize the amount of credit available to finance trade with Europe and to minimize the amount of hard currency used to settle their European accounts. In short, creditor governments wanted to draw more hard currency from any clearing union that was created than debtor governments were willing to pay.

Distributive conflict over macroeconomic issues arose from different macroeconomic priorities. Debtor governments, the Scandinavians and British in particular, were putting the greatest emphasis on achieving full employment, whereas creditor governments, the Belgians and Italians in particular, were putting the greatest emphasis on domestic price stabilization. The combination of domestic demand stimulus in one set of countries and restrictive monetary policies in a second set of countries was one of the primary causes of the imbalance in European trade.[14] Liberal multilateral trade in Europe, therefore, would force either creditor or debtor governments to alter their macroeconomic policies.

The recognition that full multilateral trade would require macroeconomic adjustment predictably generated conflict. Creditor governments argued that the imbalance in European trade was due to the overly expansionary macroeconomic policies being pursued by governments in the deficit countries. Balanced European trade could be attained only if these governments concentrated on domestic stabilization. Governments in the debtor countries argued that their commitment to full employment and expansionary macroeconomic policies was defensible. The imbalance, they argued, was due to the zealous manner in which governments in the creditor countries pursued orthodox policies. For the debtors, the imbalance should be corrected by relaxing macroeconomic policies in creditor countries.

The distributive conflicts over gold and macroeconomic adjustment were intrinsically connected. In a fully automatic multilateral clearing union, hard settlement rules, that is, rules under which hard-currency payments played a large role and credit a small role, would produce creditor-favorable macroeconomic adjustment. As hard currency flowed from deficit countries in payment of their debts, deficit governments would exhaust their hard-currency reserves and be forced to adopt restrictive policies to balance their external account. Thus, under hard settlement rules debtor governments would bear the costs of multilateral arrangements by being forced to reduce their commitment to Keynesian strategies in favor of more orthodox policies. As Sir George Bolton, Governor of the Bank of England, told one

14. See Disadvantages of Pro-Debtor Proposals—Clearing Union—Full Employment, 24 January 1950; and Disadvantages of Pro-Creditor Proposals—Clearing Union, PS/AAP(50)14 AAP Policy Series, 24 January 1950; File: European Cooperation; Records of Special Assistant for Staff Planning Henry J. Tasca, 1949–51 (Tasca Papers 1949–52); Records of the Office of the United States Special Representative in Europe, Record Group 469.2.2 (RG469.2.2); National Archives at College Park, Md. (NACP).

U.S. policymaker, hard settlement rules would represent "a return to the old gold standard. [They] would cause extreme difficulties in the UK and the sterling area, a 4 percent decrease in European trade, and millions of unemployed in the UK."[15] A multilateral clearing union based on soft settlement rules, that is, rules in which hard-currency payments were minimized and credit facilities were maximized, would produce debtor-favorable macroeconomic adjustment. As credit expanded in surplus countries, domestic demand would increase, and domestic prices would rise. Expanded demand and rising prices would tend to reduce surpluses in the external account. Thus, under soft settlement rules creditor governments would bear the costs of multilateral arrangements by being forced to reduce their commitment to price stability in favor of more rapid credit creation.

In summary, uncertainty about the state of the world and distributional problems made European governments unwilling to abandon bilateralism in favor of multilateral clearing arrangements. Uncertainty about the state of the world, specifically about how multilateral clearing would affect their hard-currency receipts and payments, made governments cling to the certainty that bilateral agreements provided. And even with an increase in hard currency, European governments would need to solve two connected distributive conflicts arising from the existing imbalance in European trade: how much credit should be made available and who, the creditors or the debtors, should bear the costs of adjustment?

Flexibility, Centralization, and Europe's Shift to Multilateralism

The Rational Design project suggests three conjectures relevant to the problems that European governments faced. First, conjecture C2, CENTRALIZATION increases with UNCERTAINTY ABOUT THE STATE OF THE WORLD, suggests that European governments should have sought centralization as a solution to their uncertainty about the state of the world. Second, conjecture F2, FLEXIBILITY increases with DISTRIBUTION problems, suggests that European governments should have sought flexible institutions to solve their distributive conflict. Third, conjecture F1, FLEXIBILITY increases with UNCERTAINTY ABOUT THE STATE OF THE WORLD, suggests that European governments should have sought flexible institutions as a solution to their uncertainty about the state of the world. As these three conjectures suggest, the institutional framework that allowed European governments to make the transition to multilateral trade combined centralization and flexibility.

A U.S. decision to capitalize the clearing union (a decision examined in greater detail in the next section) yielded a highly centralized clearing union that substantially reduced creditor and debtor governments' uncertainty about how multilateral clearing would affect their hard-currency holdings. As discussed earlier creditor governments had objected to the multilateral system proposed by the CEEC in

---

15. Memorandum of Conversation, Hebbard and Bolton, 24 January 1950; File: Finebel-Fritalux; Tasca Papers 1949–52; RG469.2.2; NACP.

1947–48 in part because under this plan the credits that they had offered initially on the basis of the credit-worthiness of the individual borrower government would be transformed into claims against all debtor governments with little or no account taken of their individual credit-worthiness. Pooling in the CEEC proposal, therefore, could potentially transform ex ante hard-currency claims into worthless paper claims. Creditor governments were highly uncertain, in other words, about how decentralized pooling would affect the value of their credits.

The U.S. capitalization of the EPU allowed pooling to be highly centralized. Under the EPU, pooling generated claims against the clearing union rather than individual governments. Moreover, U.S. capitalization allowed the clearing union to hold sufficient hard currency to ensure payment of claims against it. Pooling under the EPU, therefore, protected the hard-currency value of credits in a way that the CEEC proposal had not.[16] Centralizing pooling and capitalizing the EPU therefore eliminated creditor governments' uncertainty about the ex post value of their credits. Once they were assured that any credit they advanced through a multilateral clearing union would not be transformed into claims against nonexistent hard-currency reserves of weak-currency governments, creditor governments became willing to extend credit on a multilateral basis.

Centralization also reduced debtor governments' resistance to multilateral clearing. By creating debts to a centralized clearing union rather than to individual governments, and by writing explicit rules (discussed later) about how much hard currency would be required to settle debts to the union, debtor governments became less uncertain about how multilateral clearing would affect the hard-currency obligations generated by a given set of bilateral balances. At the same time, creditor governments' willingness to extend multilateral credit through the EPU allowed debtor governments to balance their trade with OEEC members over a medium term.[17] Normal seasonal fluctuations in exports alongside a constant import stream, for example, could generate a large deficit in one month and a large surplus the next. Without credit mechanisms, governments facing deficits would be forced to choose between making hard-currency payments or tightening quantitative restrictions to limit imports to the level of exports. Given the scarcity of hard currency, European governments were likely to prefer the latter solution to the former. The clearing union's credit mechanisms relaxed this short-term constraint by allowing governments to borrow from the union against future export revenues to pay for current imports. The credit made possible by centralized pooling therefore made deficit governments more willing to expose their economies to the fluctuations inherent in liberal international trade than they would have been otherwise.

Of course, creditor governments were not willing to extend credit without limit, nor were debtor governments willing to enter into a clearing union irrespective of how much credit was made available. Thus, credit mechanisms were themselves the

---

16. Triffin 1957, 172–74.

17. Joel Bernstein to Henry Tasca, The Reconciliation of Intra-European Payments Objectives, 14 March 1950; File: Finance, P; Finance and Trade Division 1949–52; RG469.2.2, NACP.

object of considerable distributive conflict between creditors and debtors. The important point here, however, is that centralization reduced creditor and debtor governments' uncertainty about how multilateral clearing would affect their hard-currency receipts and obligations. The reduction of this uncertainty made governments more willing to enter into multilateral arrangements.

EPU institutions also provided substantial flexibility to creditor-debtor relations. The Rational Design framers conceptualize flexibility in two ways. First, institutions can allow governments to temporarily opt out of existing commitments by invoking escape clauses. Second, flexibility can be provided by substituting a series of short-term agreements for one permanent agreement. To these two types of flexibility, I add a third: flexibility as pliability. Pliable institutions are based on rules that have been designed to impart slack to what otherwise would be tightly binding constraints.

All three types of flexibility were evident in the design of the EPU. First, an escape clause was incorporated into the OEEC's broader trade liberalization program. In this regard it is important to recognize that the over-arching purpose of the multilateral payments system was to facilitate the liberalization of intra-European trade. To achieve this objective the OEEC Code of Liberalization was implemented in conjunction with the EPU.[18] The first step in the liberalization process was to eliminate quotas. While multilateral clearing would eliminate the need for discriminatory quotas—because gold obligations would arise from the deficit with the EPU as a whole rather than through bilateral debts—the possibility remained that a country developing a deficit with the union that it would be unwilling to settle with hard currency might find it necessary to resort to quotas to conserve hard currency. The OEEC trade liberalization program, therefore, allowed governments to suspend temporarily their liberalization programs and reimpose nondiscriminatory quantitative restrictions under a set of broadly defined events. This escape clause was embodied in Article III of the OEEC Code of Liberalization. This article gave governments the right to suspend or only partially implement the required liberalization measures if, "its economic and financial situation justifies such a course"; "any measures of liberalisation of trade . . . result in serious economic disturbance"; and "despite any recommendations made [by the OEEC Council] the deficit of a member country with the Union is increasing at a rate which it considers serious in view of the state of its reserves."[19] Thus, governments were allowed to opt out temporarily of the trade liberalization if this process proved too disruptive to a government's general economic objectives or to its narrower balance-of-payments objectives.[20] The flexibility that the escape clause provided

18. On trade liberalization, see Diebold 1952; and Asbeek-Brusse 1997.
19. OEEC Code of Liberalization, 1948.
20. While Article III did lay out the general conditions under which governments could opt out of the trade liberalization program, the article contained no explicit constraint on governments' ability to invoke these clauses. Determining whether opting out was necessary appears to have been left to the discretion of the government. Also not imposed were explicit penalties for invoking Article III or explicit

reduced the degree to which European governments' uncertainty about the state of the world—particularly their concerns that future shocks could create balance-of-payments problems—made them reluctant to embark on trade and payments liberalization.

Flexibility as pliability was imparted through the system's settlement rules. The U.S. decision to capitalize the EPU made it possible to write settlement rules that explicitly allowed creditor governments to withdraw gold from the union at a faster rate than debtor governments were required to pay gold in. The EPU's settlement mechanism worked in the following way. Each government's quota was broken into five tranches of equal size. In the first tranche settlement was entirely in credit and no hard currency changed hands. For all credits above the first tranche the clearing union's obligations to net creditors were settled in 50 percent hard currency and 50 percent credit. Debtors, however, faced a less steep escalation of gold payments. Twenty percent gold payment was required in the second tranche, 40 percent in the third tranche, 60 percent in the fourth tranche, 80 percent in the fifth tranche, and 100 percent once the quota was exhausted.[21] Consequently, in the second and third tranches debtors paid less gold into the clearing union than creditors withdrew. The impact of these settlement rules on intra-European gold flows can be best illustrated by comparing actual gold payments between creditors and debtors in the period October 1948 through March 1950 with the gold payments that would have occurred had the EPU's settlement rules been in operation during this period. According to calculations by the Economic Cooperation Administration, creditor governments would have received $535.5 million under EPU settlement rules compared with the $152 million they did receive. Debtors, in turn, would have paid less: a total of $106 million under EPU rules compared with actual payments of $152 million.[22] The gap between the EPU's hard-currency payments and receipts would be covered by the U.S. funds that capitalized the union.

This settlement mechanism had two effects on the distributive conflict. First, and most obvious, it broke the tight link between creditor hard-currency receipts and debtor hard-currency payments. As a result, the hard-currency consequences of multilateralism were acceptable to both groups. Second, loosening the link between hard-currency payments and receipts weakened the pressure for macroeconomic

---

requirements that the government doing so engage in some costly signal, as Rosendorff and Milner suggest one should see. Rosendorff and Milner, this volume. Rather than explicit penalties, an informal process does seem to have emerged, driven largely by the handling of the German crisis in 1950–51. See Kaplan and Schleiminger 1989, chap. 6.

21. Diebold 1952, 92–95.

22. See Gold Settlements Under EPU, April 1950; and Gold Payments Under EPU Compared with Actual Intra-European Gold Payments Since October 1948, 20 June 1950; both in File: Finance, P; Finance and Trade Division 1949–52; RG469.2.2; NACP. U.S. policymakers also reduced British concerns about sterling balances being cleared through the EPU by insuring British gold against this risk: "In the event that EPU operations should unexpectedly result in British dollar payment obligations beyond some agreed danger point, ECA would be prepared to consider the allotment of special dollar aid to the United Kingdom." Secretary of State to the British Secretary of State for Foreign Affairs, Aide Memoire, EPU, 11 May 1950. U.S. Department of State 1950, 3:655–56.

policy adjustments that multilateral trade would otherwise produce. Under these settlement rules, a balance-of-payments deficit of a given size would be less costly in terms of hard currency than under rules calling for 100 percent hard-currency payment. Deficit governments would therefore face a less-binding reserve constraint when pursuing expansionary macroeconomic policies.

Finally, the EPU was a short-term agreement that had legal standing for only two years. Of course, the short-term nature of the clearing union was due largely to the system's role as a stepping-stone to full currency convertibility. But it is precisely the longer-term goal of full currency convertibility that makes the EPU's evolutionary approach significant. With European governments unwilling to move directly from bilateralism to full convertibility, the EPU provided an evolutionary path toward this final objective. As originally designed, the system's settlement mechanism was to be gradually hardened over time. If any credit was to survive in the system, this was to take the form of strict swing credits that would be repayable in gold after twelve months.[23] Moreover, European governments were to be pressed during the two-year period of the first agreement's lifetime to move to general convertibility, that is, to 100 percent gold settlements for net deficits. Thus, over a medium-term period the flexibility provided in the short term was to be gradually eliminated from the system, thereby tightening the constraints European governments faced and pushing them gradually toward full convertibility.[24]

In summary, the institutions created to promote multilateral clearing in postwar Europe both centralized and imparted considerable flexibility to creditor-debtor relations. The combination of centralization and flexibility reduced uncertainty over the state of the world and distributional problems, thereby greatly reducing European governments' reluctance to abandon bilateralism in favor of multilateralism. Centralization was achieved by using a U.S. capitalization to create country positions against a gold-backed clearing union. Centralization reduced creditor and debtor uncertainty about how multilateral clearing would affect their hard-currency receipts and obligations. Flexibility was provided through temporary opt outs that allowed governments to conserve hard-currency reserves, by relaxing the constraints that multilateral trade and payments would otherwise impose on creditor-debtor relations, and by an evolutionary hardening of settlement terms. Flexibility reduced the severity of the problems caused by hard-currency scarcity, distributive conflict, and uncertainty about the state of the world, and made European governments willing to enter a multilateral clearing arrangement.

---

23. See Intra-European Credits in EPU, 8 May 1950, RG469.2.2, NACP; and National Advisory Council (NAC) Minutes, meeting no. 158, 29 June 1950; Minutes of Council Meetings 1945–70 (Minutes); Records of the NAC on International Monetary and Financial Problems and the NAC on International Monetary and Financial Policies, Record Group 56.12.1 (RG56.12.1); NACP.

24. In the event, these expectations proved optimistic. The EPU was renewed every two years until finally dismantled in 1959. Settlement mechanisms were not greatly hardened until the 1954 renewal, at which point all debts and all surpluses were settled in 50 percent gold and 50 percent credit. See Kaplan and Schleiminger 1989.

And while it is true that the central aspects of these institutions, the creation of the system's credit mechanism and the asymmetric settlement terms, were made possible by the United States' willingness to capitalize the clearing union, it is important to recognize how this U.S. contribution affected the outcome in Europe. U.S. assistance was not used as a simple side payment, that is, as cash payments to induce cooperation. Instead, the capitalization was used to create a centralized payments union and to write a set of rules that imparted flexibility to this system in a manner that allowed creditor and debtor governments to see clear benefits from participation. In other words, U.S. assistance made a difference through the institutional design that it made possible.

Enforcement Problems and the U.S. Capitalization of the EPU

The creation of the multilateral clearing union in 1950 suggests a puzzle I explore here. The U.S. decision to capitalize the EPU made it possible to create institutions that reduced uncertainty and softened distributive conflict between debtor and creditor governments and thereby allowed Europe to begin the transition to multilateralism. Yet not until two years after the Marshall Plan was adopted were U.S. policymakers willing to devote Marshall aid funds to a clearing union. It was not that U.S. officials were unaware of the problems blocking the adoption of multilateral clearing arrangements. As early as fall 1947, during the preliminary discussions over Marshall aid, European governments had made it clear to U.S. policymakers that distributive conflict and hard-currency scarcity would block their transition to multilateralism. Moreover, European governments requested at that time that a portion of U.S. aid be used to capitalize a clearing union. Without such a contribution, they told U.S. officials, the transition to multilateral arrangements would be delayed significantly.[25]

Why were U.S. policymakers reluctant to capitalize a clearing union between 1947 and 1950, and how did the institutions created in 1950 alleviate theses concerns? U.S. policymakers were reluctant to capitalize the clearing union because they faced an enforcement problem: they feared that using Marshall aid to finance European trade would lead to a multilateral system that could be sustained only through continued European discrimination against U.S. goods and continued injections of U.S. aid. The Rational Design framers offer two conjectures relevant to the U.S. role in Europe's transition to multilateralism. Conjecture C4, CENTRAL-IZATION increases with ENFORCEMENT problems, and conjecture V2, asymmetry of

---

25. See Memorandum of Conversation, Meeting of the Representatives of the U.S. Advisory Steering Committee with the CEEC Delegation, 3:30–6:00 p.m., 22 October, 1947; File: Memoranda of Conversation and Questions for Discussion; Lot 123; Formulation of the European Recovery Program; General Records of the Department of State, Record Group 59; NACP.

CONTROL increases with asymmetry of contributors (NUMBER), receive some degree of support here, though conjecture V2 receives weaker support than conjecture C4.

The Enforcement Problem: Moral Hazard and the Financing
of European Trade

In contemplating the use of Marshall Plan aid to finance intra-European trade U.S. policymakers faced a moral hazard problem. The nature of this problem was straightforward: using dollars to finance intra-European trade could alter European governments' behavior and make it more difficult to achieve the Marshall Plan's broader objective of returning Europe to full convertibility and nondiscriminatory trade.

Moral hazard arose in two distinct ways. First, financing intra-European trade with U.S. funds could give European governments an incentive to expand their consumption by the amount of the U.S. contribution. Thomas Schelling, who worked for the ECA in Paris at the time, noted that "if [recipients] were to believe that their own . . . shortfalls would be made up by U.S. expenditure, those deficits would be enlarged by the very evidence of American willingness to fill the gap."[26] This concern was explicitly discussed in the October 1947 Washington conversations between European and U.S. representatives. In these discussions Frank Southard (U.S. Department of the Treasury) asked the European CEEC delegates, "Suppose that one of the CEEC countries were to import from others some relatively less essential items . . . through reliance on settlement in dollars. Suppose further that you got a fair degree of freedom of trade. Would it, then, possibly be the case that the country would be piling up, or running the risk of piling up, a debit in the account, while the country which was supplying the relatively less-essential commodities would be, in a sense, earning dollars which have come in through the United States?"[27] Were this to come to pass, any shift to multilateralism could persist only for as long as the United States continued to inject hard currency into European trade. The reasoning behind this concern was straightforward. If U.S. funds allowed consumption to expand, imports would expand. These additional imports could be paid for in hard currency, however, only as long as dollars were injected into the system. Once dollar inflows stopped, imports would drain hard-currency reserves, causing governments to resort once again to trade restrictions to limit their imbalances and conserve hard currency. As one U.S. Treasury official commented, a European payments plan "can't work after U.S. dollars cease to be put in."[28]

26. Schelling 1955, 609.

27. See Memorandum of Conversation, Meeting of the Representatives of the U.S. Advisory Steering Committee with the CEEC Delegation, 3:30–6:00 p.m., 22 October 1947; File: Memoranda of Conversation and Questions for Discussion; Lot 123; RG59 Lot 123; NACP.

28. NAC Minutes, 14, 19, and 23 January 1950; File: Minutes, 21 August 1945–25 October 1968; Minutes; RG56.12.1; NACP.

Second, a U.S. hard-currency contribution might reduce European governments' incentives to become competitive in the dollar area.[29] The dollar gap was the primary problem that Marshall aid had been created to solve, and the solution to this problem lay in generating the productivity improvements necessary to allow European governments to export enough goods to the dollar area to earn the hard currency they needed to pay for their imports from the dollar area. If European governments were suddenly allowed to earn dollars by exporting to other European countries, they would have less incentive to make the economic adjustments necessary to become competitive against U.S. goods. At the extreme, allowing European governments to earn dollars by exporting to Europe might, according to one Treasury official, "make it impossible for the European countries to earn dollars from exports to the dollar area. . . . After the initial stages, [a European clearing union] would be used as a device to discriminate against American trade and would defeat the entire objective of the ECA program."[30]

Confronted with this moral hazard problem, U.S. policymakers initially opted to maintain tight control over all Marshall Plan resources used to finance intra-European trade. In the first two years of the Marshall Plan, the United States allocated only a small amount of aid to intra-European trade and maintained tight control of these resources through the offshore procurement program.[31] Under the offshore procurement system, each European dyad forecast its net bilateral trade balance for the forthcoming fiscal year, and the government expected to be in surplus offered a drawing right in local currency to the other government equal to the expected imbalance. The grantee then used these drawing rights to purchase goods from the grantor, who was then compensated with ECA dollar aid. As the State Department noted, financing intra-European trade through offshore procurement rather than through free dollars provided "greater control over any United States contribution to European multilateral clearing than would be the case if dollars were made directly available to settle these accounts."[32]

Limiting Moral Hazard: Centralized Institutions

The Rational Design framers suggest that U.S. policymakers should have responded to the problems they confronted in their decision to capitalize a European clearing union in two ways. First, conjecture C4, CENTRALIZATION increases with ENFORCEMENT problems, suggests that U.S. policymakers should have sought a highly centralized institution to mitigate the enforcement problem they faced. Second, conjecture V2, asymmetry of CONTROL increases with asymmetry of contributors (NUMBER), suggests

---

29. NAC Minutes, 14 January 1950; File: Minutes, 21 August 1945–25 October 1968; Minutes; RG56.12.1; NACP.

30. NAC Minutes, 19 January 1950; File: Minutes, 21 August 1945–25 October 1968; Minutes; RG56.12.1; NACP.

31. For State Department views on free dollars, see The Acting Secretary of State to the Embassy in France, 26 August 1947, in U.S. Department of State 1947, 3:386–87.

32. U.S. Department of State 1948, 50.

that given the asymmetric contribution made by the United States, U.S. policymakers should have sought greater control over EPU decision making.

U.S. policymakers did push for an institutional framework that combined a high degree of centralization with majority rule decision making in order to promote macroeconomic policy coordination among European governments.[33] The payment union's decision-making powers were vested in a managing board rather than in national governments. Thus European governments would not directly participate in the system's operation. The managing board was given the role of encouraging governments to adopt macroeconomic policies that minimized their trade imbalances with the union. Governments with large credits or debits against the EPU were required to justify their macroeconomic policies in front of the EPU's managing board, which could then recommend macroeconomic policy adjustments.[34] Decisions by the board about particular governments' macroeconomic policies were made by majority rule, thus preventing any single actor from blocking action.

The administrative apparatus worked in conjunction with the system's settlement schedule to minimize the moral hazard problem. As shown in the previous section, the EPU's settlement rules were "debtor friendly" in the lower tranches of the quotas because they required zero or small fractional gold payments in the settlement of debts to the union. Thus for relatively small amounts of short-term credit the system provided considerable flexibility. As a debtor government moved into its quota's higher tranches, however, the gold content of payments to the EPU increased. As the gold portion of repayments increased, debtor governments faced increasing pressure from gold outflows to adopt macroeconomic policy adjustments. Thus, while the system easily accommodated short-term deficits, more persistent deficits generated automatic pressure for tighter macroeconomic policies. As Triffin, one of the architects of the system, observed, "the rising schedule of gold payments, on the one hand, would place increasing pressures on persistent debtors to adopt readjustment politics." These pressures would be further reinforced by two factors. First, the administrative authority conferred on the managing board was designed to "foster and support national or mutual policies aiming at the correction of excessive surpluses or deficits."[35] In other words, the managing board would promote a process of macroeconomic policy coordination among European governments oriented toward sustainable trade positions. Second, the evolutionary nature of the EPU was to be used to gradually tighten the settlement terms as the system progressed. Thus, initially soft terms—a lot of credit relative to hard currency—would gradually evolve into sequentially harder terms until the clearing union was functionally equivalent to full convertibility. An explicit process of macroeconomic coordination around relatively conservative policies would place European govern-

33. See, for example, Proposal for the Establishment of a European Monetary Authority, PS/AAP(49)10 (draft), AAP Policy Series, 5 December 1949; File: European Cooperation; Tasca Papers 1949–52; RG469.2.2; NACP.
34. See Hogan 1987, 295–96; and Van der Beugel 1966, 203.
35. Triffin 1957, 170–71.

ments on the path to an early return to full convertibility and nondiscriminatory multilateral trade.[36]

European governments were reluctant to accept the degree of centralization the United States desired, resisting in particular a managing board empowered to make binding decisions through majority rule. Another Rational Design conjecture helps explain this behavior: conjecture V3, CONTROL increases with UNCERTAINTY ABOUT THE STATE OF THE WORLD. As Koremenos, Lipson, and Snidal observe in the volume's introduction, "because states are risk-averse with respect to distributional issues, they design institutions that protect them from unforeseen circumstances."[37] It was precisely this concern that motivated European bargaining positions during negotiations over the EPU's decision-making procedures. Given the underlying distributive conflict over the costs of adjustment and uncertainty about who would control a majority of the EPU's managing board, creditor and debtor governments both preferred the certainty of unanimity rule.[38] The most that debtor governments were willing to grant to the managing board was the authority to demand policy changes in connection with "special assistance" extended above the EPU's regular quotas. Creditor governments did see some advantage to decision-making procedures that would force debtor governments to adopt the policies necessary to service their debt. Yet creditor governments feared that a majority rule managing board could force them to adopt more expansionary policies. Uncertainty about who would control the majority on the managing board in conjunction with the underlying distributive conflict caused European governments to prefer the certainty provided by a veto to the uncertainty implied by majority rule.

While the Europeans were unsuccessful in blocking majority rule in the managing board, they were able to require that all board decisions would be adopted by the OEEC Joint Trade and Payments Committee and Executive Committee, where decisions were taken through unanimity rule. Thus European governments maintained veto power over board decisions through the wider OEEC.[39] In addition, the board was given limited authority. The original agreement did not give the board the right to "initiate proposals about economic and financial policies," nor did it give the board explicit authority to make proposals addressed to governments that generated substantial trade deficits.

U.S. policymakers did not gain greater influence over EPU operations than the European governments, an outcome that is inconsistent with conjecture V2, asymmetry of CONTROL increases with asymmetry of contributors (NUMBER). The lack of support for this conjecture in this case owes more to the idiosyncrasies of the OEEC

36. See, for example, OSR to Secretary of State, Relations EPU with International Monetary Fund, (draft) 23 January 1950; and Answer to Treasury Paper to NAC, 23 January 1950; File: Finance; Finance and Trade Division, 1949–52; RG469.2.2; NACP.

37. Koremenos, Lipson, and Snidal, this volume.

38. For creditor and debtor government positions, see Experts' Report on EPU—Suggested OSR Position; and The Reconciliation of Intra-European Payments Objectives, 14 March 1950; File: Finance; Finance and Trade Division, 1949–52; RG469.2.2; NACP. See also Diebold 1952.

39. See Van der Beugel 1966, 202; and Diebold 1952.

than to a problem with the conjecture's logic. The EPU was a part of the OEEC, and thus formal rights of participation were restricted to those governments that were members of this broader organization. The OEEC was created by European governments for the purpose of coordinating the administration of Marshall Plan assistance, and the United States was not an official member; therefore it could not acquire a larger share of the control over EPU decisions.

In summary, the institutions that facilitated Europe's move to multilateral payment arrangements combined centralization and control to reduce the severity of the underlying enforcement problems. U.S. policymakers were reluctant to use Marshall aid dollars to finance European trade because of an enforcement problem arising from moral hazard. Financing intra-European trade with U.S. dollars could create a European soft-currency area that could be sustained only through additional U.S. aid and continued European discrimination against U.S. goods. As the Rational Design conjectures suggest, U.S. policymakers responded to this enforcement problem by seeking institutions that combined centralized institutions and a relatively autonomous managing board empowered to make decisions with majority rule. Their ability to achieve this objective was limited, however, by European governments' responses to concerns arising from uncertainty about the state of the world. Uncertain who would control a majority of the managing board, creditor and debtor governments both preferred the certainty of unanimity rule.

Conclusion

Interaction between distributional problems, uncertainty about the state of the world, and enforcement problems complicated Europe's movement toward multilateralism in the immediate postwar period. Distributive conflict accentuated by uncertainty about the state of the world generated by hard-currency scarcity made European governments reluctant to adopt multilateral arrangements without substantial financial support from the United States. Concern about moral hazard made U.S. officials reluctant to provide the necessary support. European governments' shift to multilateral arrangements was greatly facilitated by the EPU's institutional framework. This institutional framework allowed U.S. policymakers to reduce the severity of the moral hazard problem, thereby making them willing to capitalize a clearing union. The U.S. capitalization relaxed Europe's liquidity constraint and made it possible to write a set of rules that imparted considerable flexibility to intra-European payments relations, thereby reducing European governments' concerns arising from distributive conflict.

In examining Europe's shift to multilateral payments arrangements, I have focused on six conjectures linking four characteristics of the bargaining environment to three dimensions of EPU institutions. I conclude with a brief discussion of the case's principal findings organized along the three institutional dimensions the case examined: flexibility, centralization, and control. The Rational Design project suggested that the degree of flexibility in the EPU should have been influenced by the severity of the underlying distributional problem (conjecture F2) and by uncertainty about the state of the world (conjecture F1). The case provided strong support for the conjectures as well as for their underlying rationales. Distributional problems and uncertainty about the state of the world did make European governments reluctant to engage in multilateral trade and payments cooperation, in spite of the large benefits such cooperation offered. Flexibility, provided by an escape clause, by the use of credit mechanisms and settlement rules to relax the constraints multilateral clearing would otherwise impose, and by the evolutionary nature of the EPU mitigated both of these obstacles to cooperation. Credit mechanisms, settlement rules, and the evolutionary nature of the agreement softened creditor and debtor distributive conflict and made common participation in multilateral clearing possible. The escape clause mitigated governments' concerns about how possible future shocks would affect balance-of-payments positions. As the conjectures suggest, therefore, flexibility reduced the severity of the distributional problem and uncertainty about the state of the world.

The Rational Design framework suggests that the degree of centralization in European multilateral clearing arrangements should have been shaped by the severity of the enforcement problem (conjecture C4) and by uncertainty about the state of the world (conjecture C2). These two conjectures were also supported. Once U.S. officials decided to capitalize the EPU, they addressed their enforcement problem by creating a highly centralized institutional structure that could constrain European governments' abilities to develop unsustainable trade positions. Centralization in the form of a gold-backed clearing union reduced creditor governments' uncertainty about the post-clearing value of their credits, thereby making them more willing to participate in multilateral arrangements.

Finally, the Rational Design framework suggests that the balance of decision-making power in the EPU, and the EPU's decision rules themselves, institutional components summarized in the variable CONTROL, should be influenced by asymmetry of contributions (conjecture V2), on the one hand, and by uncertainty about the state of the world (conjecture V3), on the other. The EPU provides mixed support for these conjectures. Conjecture V2 receives only weak support in this case, largely because U.S. policymakers could not participate directly in EPU decision making. U.S. policymakers did try to create a decision-making structure that limited European governments' direct control over EPU operations, but European governments' uncertainty about the state of the world had a much more transparent impact on CONTROL. Uncertain about whether a pro-creditor or a pro-debtor majority would dominate the EPU's managing board, creditor and debtor governments both insisted on maintaining the right to veto board decisions.

Overall, therefore, Europe's transition from a network of bilateral trade agreements to multilateral clearing provides strong support for the approach elaborated by the Rational Design framers. Five of the six conjectures investigated here, linking four of the project's independent variables to three of its institutional dimensions, are strongly supported by this case.

The Institutional Features of the Prisoners of War Treaties

James D. Morrow

During the twentieth century, a system for the treatment of prisoners of war (POWs) was legalized. This system improved the treatment of POWs in some cases, but in others it failed to induce states to abandon the abuse and murder of soldiers who had surrendered to them. My primary aim is to explain the form of the legal rules and the system they have induced to handle POWs. My secondary aim is to explain why the system succeeds in some cases but not in others.

International institutions vary widely in their forms. Among international institutions, international law has relatively less institutional structure. Compared with other international institutions surveyed in this volume, the laws of war do not require recurrent decisions to be made on proper policies as the International Air Transport Association did, nor do they judge the facts in individual cases as dispute-resolution panels do. Instead, POW treaties and other laws of war set standards and prescribe mechanisms for ratifying states to use when they are at war with one another. Enforcing the standards is left to the parties themselves. In the context of the Rational Design project my analysis provides an example of how normative values legalized into a treaty shape state behavior. It also addresses the central question of the project: why do these treaties take the form they do?

Informal understandings on the treatment of POWs are as old as war. In the twentieth century states formalized these understandings into negotiated institutional arrangements that prescribe appropriate treatment of POWs and provide ways for states to verify that their soldiers taken prisoner are being treated well. I argue that states created these arrangements as a rational response to four strategic problems POWs pose: monitoring under noise, individual as opposed to state violations, variation in preferred treatment of POWs, and raising a mass army. I

I thank the editors of this special issue of *IO*, the other participants in the Rational Design project, and the editors of *IO* for their comments on earlier drafts of this article. Comments by seminar participants at the Hoover Institution and University of California at Davis also improved the article.

International Organization 55, 4, Autumn 2001, pp. 971–991

address not just the legal principles underlying the treatment of POWs but also the system of monitoring and enforcement built on those principles.

The first three strategic problems correspond to the following independent variables of the Rational Design framework: UNCERTAINTY ABOUT BEHAVIOR, DISTRIBUTION and UNCERTAINTY ABOUT PREFERENCES, and ENFORCEMENT and UNCERTAINTY ABOUT BEHAVIOR, respectively. The fourth strategic problem concerns the relations between a state and its citizens and lies outside the scope of the Rational Design framework. I test several of the Rational Design conjectures to determine how they fit with membership, centralization, and flexibility in the POW system.

Briefly, I find that the POW system corresponds to a rational design that responds to the four strategic problems. The system incorporates a general standard of treatment applicable in every war. States then avoid the need to negotiate a specific standard when they go to war. The process of states ratifying the standard screens out some states that have no interest in following it. The standards produce general reciprocal responses that are irregular and may be disproportionate to apparent violations of the standard. When the system breaks down, it fails at both the individual and the state level. The power to monitor the agreement is devolved away from the warring parties.

The POW case broadly supports the Rational Design conjectures on membership, centralization, and enforcement. Specifically, the POW system corroborates the following conjectures:

M2: restrictive MEMBERSHIP increases with UNCERTAINTY ABOUT PREFERENCES
M3: MEMBERSHIP increases with DISTRIBUTION problems
C1: CENTRALIZATION increases with UNCERTAINTY ABOUT BEHAVIOR
C3: CENTRALIZATION increases with NUMBER
F1: FLEXIBILITY increases with UNCERTAINTY ABOUT THE STATE OF THE WORLD
F3: FLEXIBILITY decreases with NUMBER.

Because the POW system shows a greater level of complexity than the Rational Design framework predicts, it does not support conjectures M1, restrictive MEMBERSHIP increases with ENFORCEMENT problems; C4, CENTRALIZATION increases with ENFORCEMENT problems; and F2, FLEXIBILITY increases with DISTRIBUTION problems. For example, the POW system centralizes the determination of standards but decentralizes enforcement. The POW case suggests that the rational design of institutions depends on the strategic problems posed by an issue; consequently, the Rational Design conjectures should hold only when the case being examined contains the strategic problems the framework addresses.

In the next section I discuss some general issues about the laws of war as an international institution. I then present the four strategic problems and rational institutional responses to each. A description of the POW system in practice allows a comparison of the predicted forms of the institutions with their reality. I evaluate the Rational Design conjectures in the context of the POW system. I then examine some alternative arrangements for handling POWs and compare these to existing institutions.

How Can the Laws of War Work?

Political institutions must be self-enforcing to be sustained. In the language of game theory, institutions must form an equilibrium of a game, both in the sense that a particular institution induces equilibrium behavior and in the sense that the particular institution must be in equilibrium within the set of all possible institutions, including none.[1] Kenneth Shepsle calls these the questions of institutional equilibrium and equilibrium institutions.[2]

The POW treaties are one aspect of the laws of war, that is, prewar agreements about acceptable conduct during wartime. Such agreements operate as institutions by shaping the decisions of actors during wartime. They codify standards of treatment for POWs and rules for verifying that those standards are being upheld. The institutional equilibrium for the laws of war is the wartime behavior of states given the existing treaties. Such behavior includes not just treatment of POWs by states and individuals but also how actors develop and use the POW system. An agreed standard can shape what strategies states use to prevail in a war (I use strategy in its broadest sense, that is, all actions undertaken during war). A prewar agreement to abjure certain strategies can be upheld during war when reciprocity and audience costs make both sides unwilling to be the first to use a banned strategy.[3] The treaties of the laws of war are a public means for states to accept and understand their obligations during wartime. The agreement does not prevent the parties from acting in their own best interests; instead, it sways actors' decisions about which strategies they will use in their pursuit of victory.

If there are enforceable prewar agreements to restrict violence during wartime, there are likely to be many different ones. Having a precise standard matters to ensure that all know what treatment is unacceptable. Which standards to incorporate is the question in designing equilibrium institutions. A rational approach requires that existing institutions be Pareto optimal in the set of enforceable institutions; some party would be worse off if an institution were changed to another enforceable institution. Otherwise, no actor would object to a change of the institution, and the institution would not persist. Later, I will consider some alternative arrangements for handling POWs and compare them to existing institutions as a way to evaluate why the POW system persists.

The laws of war rely on reciprocity for enforcement. The threat of reciprocal response may deter violators. However, reciprocity can be implemented in many ways: which actions trigger a response, who should respond to an unacceptable action, and which responses are properly reciprocal rather than violations themselves? Reciprocity, therefore, requires shared understandings about appropriate treatment and responses that are institutional in nature. The shared understanding of how reciprocity will be employed on an issue shapes behavior on that issue

---

1. See Schotter 1981; and Calvert 1995.
2. Shepsle 1983.
3. Morrow 1997.

(institutional equilibrium), and that understanding can be changed if none oppose a change (equilibrium institutions). The laws of war can be thought of as the codification of the shared understanding at the heart of reciprocal enforcement of standards.

I now turn to the specifics of the POW issue. Actors create institutions to address problems they face, and an institution's character reflects those problems and how they are being addressed. I examine four strategic problems the POW issue presents to states and discuss states' rational responses to them.

Four Strategic Problems

The issue of how to handle POWs raises four strategic problems that shape the institutions addressing their treatment. In this section I describe each problem and discuss how the rational institutions literature addresses the institutional response to each. I detail the institutional forms we should expect on the POW issue and explain their underlying logic. In practice the four strategic problems are closely related; I discuss them individually so that I can apply results from analyses that consider these problems separately.

Monitoring Under Noise

Institutions built on reciprocity require actors to monitor one another's actions so that they can respond to violations of an agreement. Noise—uncertainty about behavior in the Rational Design framework—makes monitoring a significant issue for institutions because actors cannot observe what others have done. Actors must instead draw inferences about others' actions from outcomes. Because outcomes result in part from factors outside actors' control, drawing such inferences is not straightforward. A classic example from economics of uncertainty about behavior is cartel enforcement if the members of the cartel can only observe the market price.[4] They would like to know if any member of the cartel is cheating on the agreement by producing more than its agreed share. However, others' production cannot be observed directly. If one member overproduces, the market price should drop. Production alone, however, does not determine price; a drop in demand could also cause a drop in price. Should cartel members respond to a drop in price by raising their own production, the appropriate reciprocal response if a member has cheated on the agreement?

Alternatively, problems of uncertainty about behavior can sometimes be addressed by designating a neutral actor to collect and disseminate information.[5] The information provided by the neutral actor can alleviate some of the monitoring

---

4. Green and Porter 1984.
5. Milgrom, North, and Weingast 1990.

problems, provided that such a neutral actor can be found and the parties have incentives to comply with its requests for information. Rational Design conjecture C1, CENTRALIZATION increases with UNCERTAINTY ABOUT BEHAVIOR, is based on this argument.

Noise arises in the POW issue for two reasons. First and most important, a state cannot observe in detail whether another is complying with the standards of POW treatment because POWs are in the hands of the other side. Japan denied the Red Cross access to American and Commonwealth soldiers taken prisoner in the first few months of the war in the Pacific during World War II. Consequently, it took months, and in some cases years, before the Commonwealth nations and the United States knew how the Japanese were treating POWs.[6] Here a neutral actor to collect and disseminate information could have helped.

Second, much that occurs on a battlefield lies outside the view of commanders, so they rely on reports from lower-level personnel about their own soldiers' conduct on the battlefield. When soldiers commit atrocities, few are willing to report their personal involvement in such acts. Reports of summary killings of POWs commonly identify unspecified others as having carried out the act, and often such reports are indirect rather than eyewitness accounts. Within POW camps, camp commanders and guards have some autonomy in how they operate. Factors outside the control of a detaining power may prohibit them from providing full support for POWs. Because of the vagaries of war, a state may, in the course of military operations, inadvertently kill its own soldiers taken prisoner by the other side. During World War II, for example, U.S. submarines sank Japanese ships transporting Americans held prisoner to Japan.[7] A neutral actor is not likely to be helpful in addressing this source of noise because of the large amount of action to observe and the risks of combat to observers. Both of these problems create noise; POWs may not receive treatment up to the standards of the treaties even though the detaining power has tried to live up to its treaty obligations.

Uncertainty about behavior affects the problem of uncertainty about preferences. A government at war attempts to judge its opponent's preferences —that is, whether the opponent intends to honor its treaty obligations—by observing the opponent's behavior. Uncertainty about another's behavior can make it difficult to do this. Overreacting and underreacting to reports of violations are possible under noise, and any system must address this inferential problem and the appropriate response in the face of it.

The rational response to uncertainty about behavior requires moving from direct and immediate reciprocity to more general reciprocity involving "bright lines" of acceptable outcomes.[8] Tit-for-tat responses to noise can lead to feuds of reciprocal punishments triggered by outside influences rather than to a defection from the agreement. Instead, actors should ignore small violations of the agreement and only

---

6. Vance 1994, 185–88.
7. Bailey 1981, 53.
8. See Downs and Rocke 1990 and 1995.

respond to large violations of the accepted standard. A common standard for determining minor and acceptable levels of violations allows the actors both to predict one another's likely responses and to avoid reciprocal feuds triggered by small amounts of noise. Because reciprocal punishments are not always carried out in response to violations that appear minor, such punishments must be disproportionate in order to have the same deterrent effect as direct and immediate reciprocal actions. Therefore, uncertainty about behavior has two primary effects on reciprocal enforcement of an agreed standard: First, the sides adopt a common standard of acceptable behavior against which to judge significant defections, and second, punishments become irregular and disproportionate to violations.

Individual as Opposed to State Violations

An effective agreement on the treatment of POWs must operate not only at the state level but also at the individual level. The greatest risk of being killed as a POW occurs from the time the soldier attempts to surrender to the time the soldier enters a holding area behind enemy lines.[9] Soldiers of even the most-disciplined armies kill those attempting to surrender for a variety of reasons, including personal revenge, combat stress, and an immediate concern not to be bothered with the presence and care of prisoners.[10] The use of surrender as a ruse for surprise attack occurs at times. Factors that could be described as cultural can also make the act of surrender difficult.[11] For instance, German military law forbade soldiers to surrender until they had expended all their ammunition; American soldiers were often enraged by Germans who surrendered only after the Americans had closed in on their position under fire. Furthermore, German soldiers often killed any American prisoner who possessed German items under the assumption that the items had once belonged to a German soldier who that American had killed. Because of these practical difficulties and the risks of surrendering, an effective agreement on POWs must operate at the individual level as well as at the state level. The POW treaties do specify some important elements of conduct on the battlefield, such as the use of uniforms to identify soldiers and armies; nevertheless, much of the agreement in practice is ad hoc.

The consequences of failing to secure agreement at the individual level are stark. Atrocity breeds retaliation. Furthermore, state-level agreements play a large role on the battlefield. Rumors about how POWs are treated spread rapidly within armies and affect soldiers' willingness to surrender. When POWs are reportedly treated poorly by a state, the opposing side's soldiers are less likely to surrender, preferring to fight on even in unfavorable situations.[12] Such resistance makes the soldiers of the first state less likely to grant quarter to those who do attempt to surrender. This

---

9. Barker 1975, 27–35.
10. Holmes 1985, 381–87.
11. Linderman 1997, 107–14.
12. See Bartov 1985, 118; and Holmes 1985, 324.

was the case during World War II on both the eastern front, where Nazi Germany fought the Soviet Union, and in the Pacific, where Japan and the United States fought. On the eastern front state policy reinforced the tendency on the battlefield toward no quarter. In the Pacific, U.S. policy did not encourage acts of brutality, but the dynamics of the battlefield resulted in widespread brutality by U.S. GIs and Marines.[13]

The possibility of individual violations of a treaty standard creates an enforcement problem under uncertainty about behavior. The Rational Design framework focuses only on enforcement problems for actors directly involved in the institution; however, violations at the individual level pose an important enforcement problem in the POW system. If individual violations are not restrained, they can lead to widespread violations and a collapse of the system of enforcement at the individual level, as discussed earlier.

The institutional logic of controlling individual behavior parallels social institutions for controlling ethnic rivalry and conflict.[14] One way to control behavior between groups is to entrust each group's members to respond appropriately to violations by members of the other group. The fear of an overall breakdown, and the cost to all involved, deters bad behavior. Another approach is to give each group responsibility for punishing its own violators. When each group polices its own members, deterrence is stronger because a violator's own group may have better information about who did what as well as the ability to punish the violator personally. A system in which members from one group respond to violations by members of another is likely to break down when there is substantial noise because violations breed cross-group retaliation. Under some circumstances the threat of a complete breakdown may effectively restrain violence across armies. An example is the live-and-let-live principle found along some sections of the western front in World War I despite efforts by both sides' leaders to break down such agreements.[15] However, a system that decentralizes enforcement of individual violations controls more effectively the noise such violations produce and is less likely to break down into general cross-group violence.[16]

An institutional response to the two-level problem devolves responsibility for punishing individual violations on the militaries of the violators. A devolved system of enforcement will not prevent all individual violations, but it can prevent the spread of such violations. The punishment of individual violations by the violator's own national military is a sign of the institution's efficacy. When soldiers are not held accountable for their actions or when state policy encourages atrocities, general violations are more likely to occur on the battlefield. This centralization of monitoring and disciplining of individual violations follows the same logic as

13. See Dower 1986, 52–53, 61–71; and Linderman 1997, 143–84.
14. Fearon and Laitin 1996.
15. Ashworth 1980.
16. Fearon and Laitin 1996.

Rational Design conjecture C4, CENTRALIZATION increases with ENFORCEMENT problems, with centralization being the ability to punish violators.

Variations in Preferred Treatment of POWs

Devising a common standard for the treatment of POWs requires that states agree on many aspects of the handling of prisoners. However, states disagree about how prisoners should be treated. Each would like to see its own preferred standard enforced and may choose to violate an agreed standard. Other states are willing to live within an agreed standard even though they prefer some other standard. A state may choose not to sign an agreement because it disagrees with specific provisions in the draft agreement. The Soviet Union, for example, did not sign the 1929 Geneva agreement on POWs because it allowed captor nations to treat officers and soldiers differently. In short, the adoption of any standard creates a distributional problem;[17] furthermore, differences in preferences about treatment create uncertainty about other states' motivations and thus uncertainty about their future actions.

For insight into the variety of ways states view the issue of POWs, consider the strategic advantages warring states gain through their treatment of POWs. Bad treatment of POWs by one side encourages soldiers of the opposing side not to take prisoners themselves, making it harder for the first side's soldiers to surrender. Mistreatment does have consequences on the battlefield as rumors of the other side's treatment of POWs spread. Soldiers generally believe that reciprocity will hold; for example, after watching the German SS massacre nearly three hundred Russian POWs, one German soldier reacted, "It was already clear to us that it would have repercussions. That our prisoners [in Russian hands] would be treated in the same way."[18] States may decide to treat prisoners poorly to fortify their own soldiers' willingness to fight hard on the battlefield. In some cases POWs have been recruited into the army of the detaining power, though coercion is often present in such recruiting appeals, particularly when joining the enemy army is a way out of terrible treatment in POW camps.[19] POWs are commonly used as a labor force, though treaties ban their being forced to work in a state's war effort. Prisoners often welcome work, particularly agricultural, as a reprieve from a dreary existence in camps. The question is, what work and under what conditions? During World War II, Germany and Japan used some POWs as slave labor in mines and railroad construction. The death rate for prisoners forced to work in those efforts was extremely high. Soviet POWs used as mine labor in Germany were treated so badly that the Nazis had to improve their diet and accommodations and limit their work hours to get any valuable work out of them.[20] Captors can also extract useful military information from POWs, both on the battlefield (where the practice is more

---

17. See Krasner 1991; Morrow 1994c; and Fearon 1998.
18. Fritz 1995, 57.
19. Overy 1997, 128.
20. Barker 1975, 97–112.

common) and behind the lines. Upholding treatment standards is costly to the detaining power, so it is tempting for states to cheat.

There are also important ideological and moral differences in the treatment of POWs. Japan inculcated its soldiers with the doctrine that those who surrender are considered dead for all purposes by one's home country.[21] This doctrine fostered the exceptional willingness of Japanese soldiers to die in combat during World War II. It also led to a general contempt toward soldiers of other nations who surrendered to the Japanese. In contrast, democratic states generally provide good treatment of POWs as an expression of the value they place on the individual, despite the political debate it triggers about whether POWs are being treated too well under the circumstances. Finally, racial attitudes affect state policy toward POWs, a notable example being racist Nazi policies in Eastern Europe during World War II.

This wide range of strategic consequences from the treatment of POWs leads to a wide range of plausible positions states can take on the issue. Some provide a reasonable existence for POWs, and others seize the advantages that mistreating POWs offers. State leaders make judgments about how their states will treat POWs given their states' strategic situations and values. In terms of institutional design, a state's preferences reflect the considerations underlying these judgments.

These differences in state preferences create the dilemma of inferring future actions from unknown preferences. State leaders can try to infer others' preferences by observing their actions. Often, however, actors would like information on others' preferences, and are willing to transmit such information about their own preferences, before acting. One institutional response to this dilemma is to create systems that allow states to signal their preferences to one another or force them to screen themselves in or out of a group. Often, such signals or screens are costly so that actors with differing preferences will have an incentive to separate themselves.[22] Such costs could arise within the process itself though the consequences of separation, turning costless actions, "cheap talk," into effective signals.[23] Outside parties can then better judge the preferences, and likely future actions, of a state.[24]

Signaling or screening costs in international politics are commonly attributed to audience costs.[25] The signal may set up dynamics by itself that lead to other actors' imposing costs on the state leader who sent the signal. Such audiences could be external or internal. Other states might use violations of treaty obligations to judge the reliability of future promises; interested domestic parties could choose to remove

21. Japanese training manuals contained the warning, "Those becoming prisoners of war will suffer the death penalty"; see Barker 1975, 122.

22. Morrow 1999.

23. See Farrell 1987; and Morrow 1994c.

24. None of this discussion should be read as implying that signaling or screening is perfect. My contention is not that preferences are completely revealed by signals or screens, but merely that actors can refine their knowledge of others' preferences after observing a signal. Nor am I suggesting that all actors then act as the type they have signaled.

25. Fearon 1994.

leaders who fail to uphold state obligations.[26] Such audience costs could be sufficient to make treaty obligations binding in some cases. A treaty would screen out some states that are unwilling to live up to the obligations of the treaty, and it would inform other states that ratifying states were more likely to carry out their obligations under the treaty.

The adoption of a single standard of conduct through a treaty creates a screen to help separate those states who are willing to live with the agreed standard from those who are not. Furthermore, a uniform standard solves the distributional problem that setting a standard poses. Once a standard is set, the question moves from which standard is appropriate to which states will comply with this standard? A uniform treaty therefore addresses problems of both distribution and uncertainty about preferences inherent in the question of variation of preferred treatment of POWs.

These arguments reflect the logic behind Rational Design conjecture C3, CENTRALIZATION increases with NUMBER; and conjecture M2, restrictive MEMBERSHIP increases with UNCERTAINTY ABOUT PREFERENCES. A single standard of conduct centralizes the judgment of who accepts a standard. Restricting membership in the system to those who ratify the treaties reduces uncertainty about states' preferences regarding POWs.

Raising a Mass Army

Modern warfare is fought by mass armies, mobilized from a nation's citizenry. Conscription raises mass armies, and most armies since the Napoleonic Wars have relied on some form of it, particularly during wartime. Understandably, many able-bodied citizens are reluctant to face the risks of combat. Draft evasion and desertion are serious threats to raising a mass army and sustaining it in combat. The well-known logic of public goods applies here; all citizens enjoy the benefit of a victorious army, whereas those killed or maimed in combat and their families bear the cost.

Nevertheless, large numbers of citizens are willing to fight for their country when drafted, and others volunteer (though the likelihood of being drafted drives some enlistments in wartime). Margaret Levi calls this behavior "contingent consent."[27] Citizens are more willing to serve, and less likely to resist conscription, when they perceive that the state treats them fairly. Such fairness is judged by the treatment of potential inductees, war aims, and citizens' overall view of the legitimacy of their government. A state's enforcement actions against those who try to evade the system help to create a sense that the system treats all fairly. Quasi-voluntary compliance therefore combines citizens' cooperation with the state's enforcement actions. All types of political systems rely on a combination of citizen compliance and state coercion to fill out their mass armies, although democracies rely on coercion less than other systems do.

---

26. Bueno de Mesquita et al. 1999.
27. Levi 1997.

The implicit bargain between a state and its citizens extends to the treatment of citizens once inducted into the military. Standards for the handing of POWs should reflect the need of states to uphold their end of that implicit bargain. Institutionalizing those standards at the international level increases the credibility of a state's promise to protect its citizens serving under arms to the greatest extent possible in the vagaries of war.

Clearly, these four strategic problems are interrelated. Uncertainty about behavior plays a key role both in the character of reciprocal responses and in the handling of individual versus state violations. Some of the uncertainty about others' preferences stems from differences in states' commitments to their own citizens who serve in the military, and these differences make a screening system useful.

Pulling together the characteristics that would form a rational international institution on the POW issue, we find that there should be a common standard that states agree on in advance of conflict. This standard serves as a bright line to determine what constitutes a violation and also as commitment by member states to treat POWs well. Ratifying the standard before war begins serves as a screen that separates those willing to uphold the standard from those unwilling to live up to it. One standard also solves the distributional problem posed by states holding different preferences for POW treatment. Enforcement mechanisms for the standard must address the noise problem at both the state and the individual level. Retaliation for violations is likely to be irregular and disproportionate to the violations. Evidence of failing to uphold the standard should appear both between states and on the battlefield. During wartime, individual violators will be tried and punished only by their own militaries. Of course, many individual violations will go unpunished, if not unreported.

The POW System

The Geneva Conventions are the centerpiece of the institutions that deal with POW issues.[28] The rules codified in the treaties are applicable to all wars between members of the treaty. The treaties create a common standard that is subject only to limited and specified revision by individual pairs of warring states. For example, warring states may agree to exchange prisoners during wartime, but they are not obliged to work out an exchange agreement. The treaties cover nearly every facet of treatment of prisoners from the time of capture to repatriation at the end of the war. Diet, discipline, the right to escape, the type of work prisoners can perform, and who qualifies as a POW are among the topics covered in the 1949 Geneva Convention. Each successive convention has included more detail.

---

28. For text of the 1907 Hague Convention and the 1949 Geneva Conventions on the treatment of POWs, see Reisman and Antoniou 1994.

After each world war, the relevant treaties were renegotiated to account for experiences with them during the war. Negotiations occurred at multilateral international conferences open to representatives of all states, though not surprisingly the major powers dominated the negotiations. The Red Cross served as an important nonstate actor during the negotiations. National ratification signals acceptance of the renegotiated standards, and records of ratification are now centralized in the UN.

Treaty enforcement is decentralized. The warring parties alone may counter behavior that violates the treaties. Although member states at war are entitled to prosecute and punish those from the other side who violate the treaties, they rarely do so, owing in part to concern with retaliation against their own soldiers held captive. Even trials for prisoners' committing criminal acts during captivity are treated cautiously; for instance, there were several cases where Nazi POWs in the United States killed other German POWs for committing acts considered disloyal to the Nazi regime. The United States prosecuted the killers but did not carry out their death sentences until after the war was over.[29]

Reciprocity is the unstated but recognized tool of enforcement. When treaty rules are generally observed in a conflict, protests often suffice to remedy individual cases of mistreatment. Sometimes parties use very direct reciprocal sanctions. After the Dieppe Raid in 1942, a number of Germans taken prisoner by Canadian soldiers during the raid and then freed were found to have had their hands tied, a violation of the rules. In response German soldiers bound the hands of Commonwealth soldiers they held prisoner, leading to countersanctions by the British against Germans they held prisoner.[30]

In conflicts where major violations of the rules occur at the state level, reciprocity generally is the norm. Both sides typically mistreat prisoners in these wars, with the notable exception being treatment of Japanese POWs by U.S. and Commonwealth forces during World War II. Breakdowns of the agreement of treatment of POWs often also leads to direct retaliation by soldiers on both sides on the battlefield; surrendering becomes a much riskier proposition than in other types of wars (not that the act of surrendering is ever free of the risk of being killed by one's captors).

Because POWs are held behind enemy lines, the treaties provide for independent monitoring of camp conditions. The "protecting powers," neutral states that function as diplomatic liaisons for one warring state within the territory of the other, are the primary monitors of the agreement. Representatives from each protecting power are responsible for compiling lists of soldiers taken prisoner, conveying mail to and from POWs, and monitoring conditions in camps, including discipline of POWs, and must be given free rein by states holding POWs to do these tasks. Once war begins, each protecting power establishes a POW bureau, which serves as a clearinghouse for information on prisoners. The Red Cross also does many of these tasks, particularly when one side or the other finds it difficult to appoint a protecting

29. Krammer 1979, 169–73.
30. Garrett 1981, 159–60.

power. Its unique role as a humane agency that ministers to POWs, particularly those wounded in combat, places the Red Cross in the appropriate position to serve as a monitor. In either case, the collection of information is taken away from the national agents of either warring party.

Member states are also charged with educating their own soldiers about their rights as POWs and their responsibilities toward those from the other side who surrender. Member states must enforce the rules among their own soldiers and punish those who violate the treaties' provisions. Punishment occurs on the rare occasions when it can be established that a soldier violated clearly communicated military policy on the treatment of POWs. Member states are entitled to prosecute violators from other states as war criminals; the trials must be open to monitors from the protecting power, and the accused must be treated as a POW until convicted, but such trials are rare.

Membership in the treaties is open to all states that sign and ratify them. As is typical in international laws, ratifying states can object to parts of the treaty by filing a reservation at the time they ratify. States can make clarifying statements about how they interpret aspects of the treaty, and member states may also object to ratification by nonmember states seeking membership.

Joint membership by warring parties has been a strong signal that both parties will generally honor their obligations under the treaties. The notable exception to this generalization is the Iraq-Iran War, where both sides broadly violated the agreements despite their being members.[31] In cases where treaty standards have been broadly ignored, at least one warring side was not a party to the treaty, such as the Soviet Union and Japan in World War II and North Korea and China during the Korean War.[32] One measure of adherence to treaty standards is POW death rates because substandard treatment usually results in prisoner deaths. Table 1 shows death rates for the major combatants by front in World War II. The death rates on the eastern front and in the Pacific theater were substantially higher than in Western Europe. The difference in death rates between Soviet prisoners held by Germany and American and Commonwealth prisoners held by Germany is quite stunning and corroborates accounts of differences in treatment.[33] In some wars between a ratifying state and a nonratifying state, the ratifying state generally upheld its obligations under the treaty in the face of violations by the nonratifying state. During World War II, for example, Japan did not abide by the standards, whereas the United States upheld its treaty obligations for the small number of Japanese taken prisoner.

Escalation of retaliatory actions on the battlefield, such as summary killings of soldiers attempting to surrender, indicates the breakdown of an agreement. Reports of such killings are relatively common in wars where agreements have been violated, as occurred on the eastern front and in the Pacific theater during World

31. Best 1994, 361–62.

32. See Garrett 1981, 204–18; and Best 1994, 352–55. For lists of ratifying states and the date and status of their ratification as of their date of publication, see Reisman and Antoniou 1994.

33. For further detail on treatment of POWs during World War II, see Mackenzie 1994.

TABLE 1. Death rates of POWs in captivity

	Death rate[a]
Dyads involving Japan or the Soviet Union	
Soviet soldiers held by Germany	around 60%
German soldiers held by Soviet Union	15–33%
Japanese soldiers held by Soviet Union	10%
U.S. and Commonwealth soldiers held by Japan	27%
Japanese soldiers held by United States	relatively low, mainly suicides
Dyads not involving Japan or the Soviet Union	
German soldiers held by the United States and Commonwealth countries	<1%
U.S. and Commonwealth soldiers held by Germany	4%

Sources: Bailey 1981, 12–13; Barker 1975, 154; Bartov 1985, 153–54; Nimmo 1988, 116–17; Overy 1997, 297; Streit 1993, 271–72; and Vance 1994, 194

[a] Percentage of prisoners who died in custody.

War II.[34] All warring states engage in some violations of POW treaties; it is not unusual for soldiers, even in the most disciplined armies, to shoot soldiers from the other side attempting to surrender.[35] The critical factor is whether the violations are driven by a state's policy or its failure to control its own soldiers. Nazi Germany, the Soviet Union, and Japan all had army policies that encouraged their soldiers to kill soldiers from the opposition who attempted to surrender and to punish their own soldiers who had surrendered. Germany ordered its troops to execute any Soviet commissar captured during Operation Barbarossa.[36] In August 1941 Stalin issued Order 270, which declared that Soviet soldiers who surrendered were "traitors to the motherland" and that they were subject to execution when they returned and their wives to imprisonment.[37] Japanese military training emphasized that soldiers who surrendered would be considered never to have existed in the eyes of their families and the nation.[38]

Testing the Hypotheses

Does the POW system match the expectations derived from models of institutional responses to the four strategic problems? As expected, the system creates a common standard with little room for ad hoc adjustment for individual cases. Punishment of

34. For the eastern front, see Bartov 1991, 84–89. For the war in the Pacific, see Dower 1986, 62–71.
35. Holmes 1985, 381–87.
36. Barker 1975, 21.
37. Overy 1997, 80–81, 300–304.
38. Linderman 1997, 150–51.

apparent violations at both the state and individual level is irregular, and many violations go unpunished. The responsibility for punishing individual violators predominantly falls on the state of those violators. The ratification process screens out some states who do not intend to abide by the agreed standards during wartime. When state policy violates the standard or when individual violations either go unpunished or are encouraged, the agreement breaks down on the battlefield. Surrendering in such settings is unusually hazardous. Finally, the power to monitor compliance with the agreements is devolved from the warring parties to independent agents.

There are two areas where the POW system may not match the expectations of the models. First, determining what constitutes a "disproportionate" response is difficult, especially when soldiers committing atrocities are from states unwilling to uphold the standards. Were atrocities committed by U.S. Marines in the Pacific theater a "disproportionate" response to the Bataan Death March? Second, states may prosecute individual violators of the standard through war crimes tribunals, as occurred after World War II. Such tribunals are legally permissible under the Geneva Conventions, but they rarely occur during wartime, and the system does not rely on postwar trials. The tribunals held after World War II were ad hoc, and they were not recognized as part of the system before or after they occurred. The International Criminal Court seeks to codify such postwar trials and integrate them into the laws of war generally, but whether such a system will work or even be adopted is not yet clear.

Does the POW system match the conjectures of the Rational Design project? Clearly, a single case can neither prove nor disprove these conjectures, and conjectures, by nature, are open to modification as further evidence and argument emerge. I use this case to shed some light on three of the Rational Design dependent variables—MEMBERSHIP, CENTRALIZATION, and FLEXIBILITY.

Membership

An institution's membership, according to the Rational Design framework, should be determined by the severity of the enforcement and distributional problems and by the level and type of uncertainty. The membership rules of the POW system are not restrictive; states seeking membership need only ratify the treaties. Treaty ratification appears to screen out some states that do not intend to follow the standards, so the actual membership is not universal. One can imagine more restrictive membership rules tied to stronger enforcement of the system, as is the case in the recent Chemical Weapons Convention, where member states are prohibited from trading in restricted chemicals, both toxic and precursors, with nonmembers. This restriction provides a positive incentive to sign the treaty, which allows much stricter international inspections than earlier treaties.

The POW case shows mixed support for the Rational Design conjectures on membership, primarily because the logic underlying the POW system differs from the logic underlying the Rational Design framework. There is an enforcement problem regarding POWs when the warring states have ratified the treaties. In this situation the framework expects that membership should be restrictive to exclude possible defectors and free riders (conjecture M1, restrictive MEMBERSHIP increases with ENFORCEMENT problems). But because membership restrictions in the POW system are weak, free riding is not an issue; more crucial is identifying both a common standard and which states will agree to uphold it. Membership in the POW treaties does reduce uncertainty by screening out some states that are not willing to abide by the treaties' standards, supporting conjecture M2, restrictive MEMBERSHIP increases with UNCERTAINTY ABOUT PREFERENCES. The POW system weakly supports conjecture M3, MEMBERSHIP increases with DISTRIBUTION problems. Opting in is a signal that a state will abide by the system's rules, and this solves the distributional problem of agreeing on a particular standard. However, the logic of membership in the POW system is different from the logic behind conjecture M3, where inclusive membership allows for tradeoffs to solve distributional problems. In the POW system the distributional problem is solved by admitting only states who signal their willingness to abide by the standards of the treaty.

Centralization

The mix of centralization and decentralization in the POW system both supports and contradicts the Rational Design conjectures on centralization. Treaty negotiation and ratification are centralized, and enforcement is decentralized. Information collection is both, but making neutral parties responsible for collecting information is more important to the system than whether the task is centralized. In the absence of any evidence but words, states setting general standards face the problem of uncertainty about how other nations intend to treat POWs; enforcement involves just the problem of inferring intentions from actions amidst noise. In other words, the uncertainty involved in centralized treaty negotiation and ratification is more profound than the uncertainty involved in centralized enforcement.

Rational Design conjecture C1, CENTRALIZATION increases with UNCERTAINTY ABOUT BEHAVIOR, would explain why the mechanisms for negotiating and ratifying treaties in the POW systems are more centralized than those for enforcing them. Uncertainty about preferences, and hence future behavior, leads to a centralized system of setting and ratifying standards to address that uncertainty. Enforcement is decentralized in the POW system because, unlike the logic of conjecture C1, individual parties, rather than all states, enforce the agreement. The large number of actors involved in treaty negotiations leads to a centralized system for setting the standards of conduct, whereas the dyadic nature of war leads to a decentralized system of enforcement and monitoring, in accord with conjecture C3, CENTRALIZATION increases with NUMBER. This case does not support conjecture C4, CENTRALIZATION increases with ENFORCE-MENT problems. In the POW system the responsibility for enforcing treaties lies with individual member states rather than being centralized. The problems of uncertainty, instead of problems of distribution and enforcement, drive centralization in the POW issue.

Flexibility

Although the standards are generally inflexible, flexibility in the POW system arises in two ways. First, states can renegotiate the treaties to refine the standards, as occurred after both world wars. Second, noise on the battlefield and behind the lines creates some flexibility in the system by allowing sides to ignore small violations of the treaties. The standards are inflexible during wartime, but how and when the parties enforce those standards is up to individual states.

This case supports conjecture F1, FLEXIBILITY increases with UNCERTAINTY ABOUT THE STATE OF THE WORLD. In the POW system uncertainty about the state of the world is low, and the treaties' standards are inflexible. Indeed, lack of specificity in the earlier treaties can be thought of as undesirable flexibility in the sense that vague legal provisions provide excuses for some states' actions that others see as violations. The POW case does not support conjecture F2, FLEXIBILITY increases with DISTRIBUTION problems. The adoption of a standard creates a distributional problem among member states. Conjecture F2 suggests that the standards should be flexible between individual member states at war to accommodate different ideas of appropriate treatment, but the standards in the POW system are inflexible in order to sort out which states are willing to abide by them. Finally, unlike the large number of states involved in negotiating the standards, in a given situation typically only two states are involved in enforcing them. Flexibility therefore does decrease with the number of actors involved, in accord with conjecture F3, FLEXIBILITY decreases with NUMBER.

Where the Rational Design framework fails to fit the POW system, the strategic logic of the conjectures differs from that underlying the POW system. For example, conjecture M1, restrictive MEMBERSHIP increases with ENFORCEMENT problems, follows from a public goods logic where membership is used to prevent free riding. However, the logic of membership in the POW system centers on screening out those states unwilling to accept the standard. The strategic problem the POW system addresses, screening, differs from the strategic problem assumed in conjecture M1, free riding. In other words, the institutions an issue gives rise to depend on the strategic problems the issue poses. The Rational Design conjectures follow from certain strategic problems, so we should not be surprised that those conjectures do not hold when the assumed strategic problems are not present in the issue-area.

Alternative Institutional Arrangements for POWs

To draw out the institutional logic of the POW system, I consider some alternative institutional arrangements for handling POWs. I examine how other systems might shape state and individual responses to the strategic problems POWs present. I seek to clarify how the POW system deals with its strategic problems and to explain why the alternatives have not replaced the current system.

The first alternative is no framework whatsoever. Although there would be ideas about the proper treatment of POWs, states would not formalize them in a legal treaty or system. Instead, warring parties would devise ad hoc agreements on the treatment of POWs geared to a specific war. Because states differ in their views of appropriate treatment, the lack of an institution has the advantage that it would let warring states tailor agreements to their specific preferences rather than having to uphold a multilateral agreement negotiated to incorporate the views of all signatories. This added flexibility carries serious drawbacks, however. First, negotiating an ad hoc agreement during wartime is likely to be difficult because the specific agreement can affect the outcome of the war. For instance, a state that wishes to exploit POWs as slave labor can gain an advantage over an opponent who refuses to use POWs for this purpose. Indeed, such differences in intentions underlie the notable failures of the POW system. Second, an ad hoc agreement is likely to be a "lowest common denominator" between the warring parties. To reach an agreement the party with the higher standard will have to accept a standard lower than it wishes. In a general treaty all signatories operate in ignorance of the wars they will fight in the future, so the distributive conflict among states is reduced. If many different standards could be enforced in wartime, states may be willing to agree to the most rigorous standards beforehand. Third, ad hoc agreements forfeit the screening effects of ratification. Finally, it will be difficult to train troops in their rights and responsibilities under an ad hoc system. The two-level problem should be worse under ad hoc agreements for the lack of such training.

Some parts of the POW system, such as prisoner exchanges, are open to ad hoc agreements between warring parties. The Hague Conventions in effect during World War I were vague, and consequently, the standards for treating POWs were subject to wartime negotiations between warring parties. Those standards varied as the warring nations negotiated different ad hoc agreements. Furthermore, the general standards of treatment were lower in World War I than they were in World War II; POWs were fed less and worse food during World War I, even under agreements between Great Britain and Germany, and they were often forced to work in their captors' war effort, such as railroad construction.

The second alternative institution for POWs is a strongly centralized agency that would adjudicate and punish violators, similar to the proposed International Criminal Court. One could even imagine a system where all POWs would be detained in a neutral country and supervised by an international agency. A centralized system faces the problem of collecting information on violations and arresting violators, at both the state and individual levels. A state's defeat and occupation would enable the agency to collect evidence about violations, where it exists, and to detain violators, provided that the victors provide the agency with free rein.[39] However, few wars end in the occupation of the defeated state. At the individual level,

---

39. Would Stalin have allowed an agency over which he had little control to prosecute and punish Nazi war criminals after World War II?

evidence of violations is hard to collect even by the violator's army; it is hard to imagine that an international agency could do better than a military interested in controlling individual violations. A supernational agency charged with enforcing agreements on POWs may also remove the obligation of militaries to police their own soldiers, particularly those states seeking to bend the agreed standard. In both cases, conditions on the battlefield could worsen because of the shift in monitoring and responsibility. The signaling property of ratification would be lost in a centralized system where the international agency had authority over all violations, even those by a nonratifying state. Alternatively, if the centralized agency only addressed violations by signatory states and their soldiers, reciprocity against nonmembers would be undermined.

Less dramatic variations on the institutions are possible. Responsibility to provide for POWs could be placed on prisoners' home states rather than on the captor state. After all, a state has a greater interest in the welfare of its soldiers than its wartime opponent does. There is some precedence for such a system. The Hague Convention in effect during World War I asserted that POWs had to be fed as well as civilians would be fed. When the British blockade reduced Germany's food supply near the end of the war, the rations the Germans provided to POWs dropped to as low as a half-pound of bread a day. Many British, French, and American POWs survived because their home countries provided regular packages of food and clothing through the Red Cross.[40] Under such a system, the captor state could confiscate the packages, especially if the state were also blocking monitoring agencies from camps, as Japan did during World War II. Monitoring could be carried out by agents of the belligerents. That possibility raises the problem for the captor nation of providing free movement within its country to such agents during wartime. Understandably, neutral agents are preferable.

This discussion of alternate institutions should not be taken as a statement that the existing institutions in the POW system are the "best" possible. The system exists, continues, and succeeds because it provides a workable solution to the strategic problems posed by POWs. If one of these alternatives were clearly better for all, we would expect the system to move toward it. Some advocates of an International Criminal Court contend that it would be superior to the current system. The controversy of such a court indicates that not all relevant actors agree with its advocates.

Alternative Explanations for State Treatment of POWs

Culture is another common explanation for the treatment of POWs. Undoubtedly, cultural attitudes about the role and duty of soldiers affect which standards are judged appropriate. Japanese abuse of POWs during World War II stemmed in part

---

40. Dennett 1919.

from cultural traditions that emphasize individual loyalty and sacrifice to the group. Racist attitudes toward Slavic peoples in Nazi ideology played a large role in German abuse of Soviet POWs during World War II. As noted earlier, American attitudes about fairness in combat and German attitudes about surrender complicated the act of surrender on the battlefield between the two armies, even when both sides generally met the standards of the 1929 Geneva Convention. Culture does play some role in the treatment of POWs.

On closer examination, however, culture does not completely explain treatment of POWs. Japanese policy changed dramatically from World War I to World War II. During the Russo-Japanese War and World War I, Japan scrupulously fulfilled its obligations to Russian and German POWs under the treaties of the time. In both cases the Japanese government used good treatment of POWs to gain sympathy among the Western powers. Furthermore, Japanese soldiers who had been captured were not generally court-martialed on their return to Japan, though some were subject to scorn when they returned to their villages. By World War II, Japanese policy had switched to neglect of prisoners at best and outright abuse of them at worst, and through training and social pressure it discouraged its own troops from surrendering. Japanese cultural attitudes about the shame of surrender appear to have persisted throughout the war.[41]

There were also limits to how far Nazi ideology could shape Germany's treatment of POWs. Nazi Germany treated poorly POWs captured from the Polish Army in 1939. Polish soldiers and pilots who made their way to the West (including POWs captured by the Soviet Union who were later released to fight with the Western Allies) were formed into Polish units that fought with the French armies in 1940 and the Western Allies from 1943 on. The Nazis treated Polish soldiers captured from these units the same as they treated French and British POWs. They were placed in the same camps, received the same Red Cross aid packages, and could be elected to positions of leadership inside the camps. The British government explicitly warned the Nazis to consider Free Polish soldiers in the British army as Commonwealth soldiers. The Nazi government did so and kept Free Polish POWs separate from other Poles taken prisoner in 1939 even though the Red Cross pressured Germany to amalgamate its Polish POWs. In short, the possibility of reciprocal punishment overrode Nazi racist ideology in determining the treatment of Free Polish POWs.[42]

Culture does affect ideas about how POWs should be treated; nevertheless, the institutional standards of the treaties shape actual treatment. Explanations for actions taken in pursuit of state interests must also account for how institutions direct the consequences of those actions. In the case of POWs, the treaties define standards of treatment that lessen the problem of judging when a reciprocal response is appropriate. States can then anticipate likely responses to their treatment of POWs and adjust their policies. Some states choose to violate such standards even at the

---

41. Hata 1996.
42. ICRC 1948, 2:116–57, and 3:9–48, 251–55.

risk of retaliation, and cultural values play a role in that choice. Realists make a similar mistake when they argue that institutions are epiphenomenal in international politics, that outcomes are purely driven by interests and power.[43] Institutions influence a state's judgment of how it should use its power to pursue its interests; different institutions could produce different patterns of behavior.

Conclusion

The POW system addresses four strategic problems in the issue-area: monitoring under noise, variation in preferred treatment of POWs, individual as opposed to state violations, and raising a mass army. The system relies on a universal standard that applies to all wars between ratifying states. The Red Cross and Protecting Power serve as neutral monitors of the standards. Treaty ratification helps states to identify which states may not live up to the standards. Enforcement is generally reciprocal, although the consequences of violations are often seen on the battlefield rather than at the state level. When agreements break down at the state level, they also fail on the battlefield. The existence of a standard helps ratifying states to recruit soldiers.

The case of the POW system suggests that international law and norms more generally can operate as institutions in international politics. The standards persist and shape state actions, but they do not determine them. Because states can enforce many standards during wartime, the agreements help states to fix state behavior by prescribing which behaviors are unacceptable and what the consequences of unacceptable behavior may be. I am not suggesting that other factors such as state preferences are irrelevant to the treatment of POWs. Rather, the institution interacts with state preferences to produce behavior.

The Rational Design framework needs to attend more carefully to variations in the strategic dynamics of different issues. The framers contend that observed institutions fit the demands of the issues they address; otherwise, the relevant actors would replace the institutions with alternatives that better address those issues. Strategic problems like provision of public goods are well known, but not all problems are appropriately thought of as public goods. Carefully considering the problems an issue poses is necessary to determine what institutions we should expect in that area.

43. For example, Mearshemer 1994/1995.

Institutions for Flying: How States Built a Market in International Aviation Services

John E. Richards

In the aftermath of World War II, states created a complex set of bilateral and multilateral institutions to govern international aviation markets.[1] National governments concluded bilateral agreements to regulate airport entry and capacity and delegated to the airlines, through the International Air Transport Association (IATA),[2] the authority to set fares and terms of service in international markets.[3] Combined, the bilateral agreements and IATA produced national monopolies connected by strictly regulated international markets in which airlines supplied identical services at identically high prices. A mixture of public and private institutions thus produced a de facto cartel in international aviation services.

The cartel, or Bermuda regime, was not simply a set of institutions that facilitated profitable rent seeking, however. Indeed, despite consistent grumbling over the spoils of the cartel, the Bermuda institutions successfully facilitated the dramatic growth of international aviation markets in the postwar period. By the late 1970s, when U.S. policy began to erode the role of the Bermuda institutions in international markets, international aviation, once a small, specialized industry, had become one

Earlier versions of this article were presented at the University of Chicago, PIPES, February 1998, and at the Rational Design Conference, May 1998. I thank David Lake, Peter Gourevitch, Barbara Walter, Barbara Koremenos, Duncan Snidal, Kenneth Abbott, Beth Yarbrough, Charles Lipson, and Alexander Thompson for helpful comments. I thank Peter Cowhey for many useful conversations on related topics.

1. I examine scheduled aviation markets, not charter operations. Charter carriers largely did military contract work in the immediate aftermath of World War II and were therefore not considered in postwar institution building. Only later, in the 1960s, did charter operations become a significant part of international aviation markets.

2. Although the IATA was founded in 1919 as a trade association for European airlines, this early version of the organization is distinct from the post–World War II organization.

3. The bilateral agreements also retained authority over some aspects of service in international markets, such as the use of national ground-handling and catering services; the IATA was given authority over the most prominent features of in-flight services, including entertainment and food service.

International Organization 55, 4, Autumn 2001, pp. 993–1017

of the central pieces of the global economy.[4] But the existence and subsequent dramatic growth of the market, which we now take for granted, was not at all self-evident in 1945. In particular, concerns about state sovereignty over airspace made states leery of allowing foreign airlines to enter national airspace, and the distributional impact of international aviation markets, especially the difficulty inefficient national airlines would have competing with more efficient U.S. carriers, made states reluctant to allow international markets to develop on their own. Domestic politics thus dictated that laissez faire regulations were not an option. However, there were no well-established institutions to govern the emerging market nor were there preexisting arrangements on which institution builders could draw. In short, for international aviation markets to grow, states needed to agree on some set of institutions to establish marketplace rules to facilitate growth yet at the same time mitigate security and distributional concerns.

States could have created any number of regulatory institutions, ranging from a multinational airline owned and operated by the UN to a completely free market. Yet they chose to create a cartel by constructing a complex mix of public and private, bilateral and multilateral institutions. The inefficiencies the cartel introduced thus eroded at least some of the gains coordination generated—an outcome inconsistent with dominant theories of international institutions.

The Bermuda institutions raise a number of interesting empirical puzzles: Why did states create an inefficient set of institutions? Why did they create these institutions rather than others? How did the institutions function? Why did governments retain direct control over some aspects of the marketplace and delegate other aspects to the airlines? Why the mix of bilateral and multilateral, public and private institutions?

I show that the Bermuda institutions represent an equilibrium solution to the strategic dilemmas states faced in their efforts to coordinate interstate exchange in international aviation markets. As Barbara Koremenos, Charles Lipson, and Duncan Snidal observe in the introduction to this volume, states and other international actors design institutions with particular features to solve the specific problems they face.[5] The primary challenge facing national governments in aviation markets was to create some set of institutions that would establish property rights and thereby facilitate marketplace development. However, state concerns about airspace sovereignty and the distributional effects of international institutions meant that only a subset of possible institutions was acceptable to key negotiating states. Importantly, the lack of preexisting institutions meant that the distributional effects of institutions could not be separated from the creation of institutions in the first place. Resolving the distributional problems inherent in creating international institutions was thus inseparable from the creation of institutions to establish property rights and enable market-

---

4. For the politics behind U.S. efforts to dismantle the Bermuda institutions, see Kasper 1988; and Richards 1999.

5. Koremenos, Lipson, and Snidal this volume, 762.

place growth. Put differently, creating institutions to dictate property rights, and facilitate marketplace development, had to produce distributional outcomes acceptable to key states. Severe uncertainty about actors' behavior and about future states of the world, as well as the large number of actors relevant to joint welfare in some aspects of aviation markets, further complicated efforts to create institutional arrangements to regulate aviation markets.

This case supports several Rational Design conjectures. In particular, the extensive flexibility of the Bermuda agreements and the presence of institutional rules giving states veto power over all outcomes support conjectures V3, CONTROL increases with UNCERTAINTY ABOUT THE STATE OF THE WORLD; F1, FLEXIBILITY increases with UNCERTAINTY ABOUT THE STATE OF THE WORLD; and F2, FLEXIBILITY increases with DISTRIBUTION problems. The problems involved in distributing gains from cooperation and in monitoring any agreement created extensive uncertainty that led states to create institutions that gave all members veto power and thereby enabled them to protect themselves against unwanted outcomes. States retained direct control over most aspects of the market, particularly those components with severe uncertainty (such as traffic flows and pricing). Furthermore, they created flexible institutions that allowed them to escape negative distributional outcomes and limit commitments in the face of uncertainty.

The Bermuda institutions' scope, inclusive membership, mixture of centralization and delegation to individual actors, and strong mechanisms of control do not precisely fit a number of the Rational Design conjectures. My analysis suggests not so much that these conjectures are misguided but rather that some settings are more complex than the conjectures allow. In other words, the conjectures may require a more nuanced understanding of how the variables interact, or the basic framework may need to be extended.

The Bermuda institutions were not linked to other issue-areas despite severe distributional implications, so they do not confirm conjecture S2, SCOPE increases with DISTRIBUTION problems. Yet they did have extensive scope within aviation markets—for example, they regulated all aspects of the marketplace that could potentially upset coordination.

The Bermuda institutions suggest that the variable membership may interact with other aspects of institutional design. Institution builders sought to include all countries of the international aviation community in order to stem the potential for cheating. This would seem to cut against conjecture V1, CONTROL decreases with NUMBER; however, the role of the bilateral agreements, which reduced the number of actors to two, confirms the conjecture. Furthermore, intense distributional concerns in postwar aviation markets led to inclusive membership, confirming conjecture M3, MEMBERSHIP increases with DISTRIBUTION problems. In other words, because any given bilateral agreement could potentially upset the allocation of gains and affect the enforcement of other bilateral agreements (such as those making it cheaper to fly from A to B to C rather than directly from A to C), inclusive membership was crucial to maintaining incentive compatibility among bilateral agreements. At a minimum, the Bermuda institu-

236 International Organization

tions are evidence that the conjectures about membership are likely to interact with other conjectures, in particular those dealing with scope, as well as with other variables, such as control.[6]

The Bermuda institutions display a marked mixture of centralization, through annual IATA fare conferences, and delegation to actors, through monitoring fares and other aspects of the bilateral agreements. In many ways the Bermuda institutions are orthogonal to the conjectures on centralization simply because the goal of centralization—to ensure that outcomes were acceptable to key actors—was obtained through unanimity voting rules. Thus the choice of centralization or delegation was simply a function of logistics and efficiency because control did all of the heavy lifting in ensuring that outcomes were acceptable to all parties.

Finally, Bermuda control mechanisms contradict conjecture V1, CONTROL decreases with NUMBER. According to the Rational Design framework, individual members must give up control as numbers increase to capture the benefits from coordination. In aviation, however, institutional arrangements explicitly granted every member state veto power over the most important marketplace element: fares. Why might this be the case? In short, severe distributional considerations—in this case the fact that the lack of veto power could lead to the bankruptcy of individual national airlines—may lead states to place more value on control than on the gains from coordination. Put differently, if the potential costs of noncooperative outcomes outweigh the benefits of additional coordination made possible by moving away from unanimity voting, states may create institutions that provide individual actors veto power. Understanding the domestic roots of decision making about these trade-offs will increase our understanding of how and why states construct international institutions.

Bargaining over Postwar Arrangements

Advances in aircraft technology during World War II set the stage for the emergence of international aviation markets. But the growth and development of these markets was problematic given states' strong concerns about airspace sovereignty and the distributional implications of different sets of marketplace rules. Explicit state agreement on marketplace rules was thus required for market development. But agreement was not preordained, and states' concerns over sovereignty and distributional problems had the potential to severely limit market growth. The United Kingdom's efforts to create an intra-empire cartel, for example, suggests that postwar negotiations could have resulted in closed regional arrangements rather than

---

6. One way to view the different institutional instruments available to states—scope, membership, and voting rules—is to consider how governments use fiscal and monetary policy as interchangeable tools to grow their economies (and win reelection); that is, different instruments are substitutes for each other depending on actors' goals and their ability to secure different institutional outcomes in pursuit of these goals. I return to this issue in the conclusion.

an open global market. Indeed, the economic literature on networks suggests that a large network member could set fees for interconnecting in ways that would advantage it at the expense of overall efficiency.[7] Thus the United Kingdom could have realized large economic gains by limiting network interconnections (favoring empire over non-empire passengers, for example) even if this hampered overall marketplace development. The proliferation of closed telecommunications and data networks in the 1970s and 1980s, including early proprietary online services such as Prodigy and CompuServe, are examples of how traffic could have flowed across borders in this scenario.[8]

Fearful of such regional or restrictive marketplace outcomes, U.S. efforts to create open international aviation markets began even before the war ended.[9] In 1943 Churchill and Roosevelt discussed postwar aviation arrangements, and informal discussions between the United States, Britain, and the Dominions began to take place. These early discussions ultimately led to the Chicago Convention in November 1944, where representatives from more than fifty states gathered to discuss the structure of postwar aviation markets.[10] The discussion quickly broke down into a debate over the degree to which the industry should be internationalized and the competitiveness of international markets.[11] New Zealand, Australia, Canada, and Great Britain called for some form of internationalization and extensive limits on competition. The United States advocated national ownership and competitive markets. Faced with divergent plans for the structure of international markets, the convention broke down into a struggle between the U.S. and Commonwealth proposals.

The United Kingdom argued that micromanagement was necessary to ensure the viability of national carriers and pressed for the creation of an international institution that would control capacity, fares, and landing rights. The British envisioned that the proposed institution would dictate the number of flights each airline could make, allocate the percentage of traffic carried by individual airlines, and set strict limits on entry.[12] British negotiating positions were clearly designed to safeguard Britain's national carriers from more efficient U.S. airlines, as well as allow the United Kingdom to administer the British empire and maintain some control over the Dominions. When U.S. negotiators balked at the U.K. proposal, Britain attempted to create its own multilateral institutions by negotiating a series of

7. See Baxter 1983; Carlton and Klamer 1983; and Salop 1991.

8. For an overview of electronic data networks, see Guerin-Calvert and Wildman 1991. On Internet interconnection arrangements and the problems posed by closed networks, see Bailey 1997; and Srinagesh 1997.

9. International aviation markets were seen as an important piece of postwar reconstruction. The head of the U.S. delegation at Chicago, A. A. Berle, asserted that "aviation will have a greater influence on American foreign interests and American foreign policy than any other non-political consideration." Berle and Jacobs 1973, 481. For a similar conclusion, see van Zandt 1944.

10. For detailed discussions of the Chicago Convention and U.S.-U.K. bargaining at Bermuda, see Dierikx 1992; and Haanappel 1980.

11. See Jönsson 1987, 98; and Sochor 1991, 3–16.

12. Berle and Jacobs 1973, 498–509.

agreements with the Dominions to create a strictly regulated market within the British empire. Although the long range of today's jets makes landing rights less important, the limited range of aircraft and the large number of landings controlled by the British empire after World War II made Britain's attempt to construct a "market-within-a-market" with its colonies a viable strategy.

While the United Kingdom preferred strictly regulated international markets, the United States preferred national control of airlines and competitive markets. The distributional logic behind the U.S. position was quite clear: with its airlines left unscathed by the war and controlling 72 percent of world air traffic, the United States wanted competitive markets so that U.S. airlines could take advantage of their clear marketplace superiority.[13] Although U.S. domestic airlines were less keen on competitive international markets than Pan Am was, they both preferred private ownership and more competitive international markets than the U.K. proposal permitted.[14]

The United States and the United Kingdom ultimately failed to reach an agreement at the Chicago Convention on commercial aviation rights, but convention participants did successfully agree on some elements of international aviation markets that were important for market development, such as safety and technical matters. The convention created the International Civil Aviation Organization (ICAO) and adopted the International Air Services Transit Agreement (IASTA), which established basic safety and technical standards and guaranteed first and second freedoms (the right to transit the airspace of other signatories and to make technical, non-traffic, stops, respectively).[15]

Commercial rights proved most difficult, of course, because of the distributional effects of marketplace rules. In short, both the United States and United Kingdom (and all other states) stood to gain by the creation of international institutions to establish property rights in international aviation markets, but they disagreed over who should receive the benefits generated by coordination. Agreeing on property rights to facilitate marketplace growth thus depended on writing rules that produced distributional outcomes acceptable to key market participants. Ultimately, the United States and the United Kingdom turned to bilateral negotiations and the airline industry itself to organize the international aviation marketplace. These negotiations led to the 1946 Bermuda I bilateral agreement, which subsequently became the model for all the other bilateral agreements.

Bermuda Institutions

The central institution of postwar aviation markets was the bilateral agreements modeled on Bermuda I.[16] These agreements dictated the regulations governing

---

13. Dempsey 1987, 10. See also Milner 1997, 158–78.
14. See Milner 1997, 158–78; and Sampson 1984, 77–82.
15. See Dierikx 1992; and Kasper 1988, 47–50.
16. Although all bilateral agreements were roughly similar, there were important differences among them in regard to the amount of competition and potential for government intervention in the

entry, capacity, and some aspects of ancillary services. Negotiated on the principle of strict reciprocity (each state granted permission to foreign airlines to fly routes of a given economic value in exchange for permission to fly routes of equal economic value), the agreements set strict limits on entry and capacity and included explicit rules on the nature of services, including plane size, passenger capacity, and arrival times. Many agreements predetermined the capacity of each carrier in the marketplace (predetermination agreements), and in practice even agreements with less regimented capacity clauses strictly limited any one carrier's ability to offer more capacity than the foreign carrier offered. Almost all agreements delegated pricing to IATA,[17] although rates were still subject to each side's approval (double-approval pricing). The bilateral agreements dictated all other aspects of the marketplace, including specifying routes and airports. The agreements usually included private side-agreements between airlines that generally stipulated capacity restrictions and the terms of revenue sharing (pooling).[18] Many agreements required foreign carriers to use the maintenance, service, and sales staffs of the domestic carriers. Finally, almost all bilateral agreements allowed only a single national carrier to enter any given international route (single-designation).

The agreements were buttressed by IATA fare conferences. IATA rules dictated that traffic conferences concern themselves with "all international air traffic matters involving passengers, cargo, and mail . . . particularly the following: . . . (b) fares, rates, and charges for passengers and cargo."[19] For the purposes of price-setting, IATA was divided into three geographical areas, with each area having its own fare-setting conference at the annual IATA conferences; however, any agreement in any area required the agreement of all voting airlines before a fare schedule became effective. Strict unanimity thus governed IATA fare-setting conferences. It is also worth noting that only airlines were allowed at fare conferences (consumers or other interested parties could not participate).[20] The IATA conferences set rules for all aspects of aviation services, notably food service and in-flight entertainment; this

---

marketplace. The ability of carriers to pool revenues was one area of difference; others included whether or not capacity was predetermined, the minimum/maximum traffic one bilateral partner could carry, the circumstances under which governments could intervene to set fares, and the potential for new entry into any given city-pair. Because of these differences, they were not simply a set of bilateral agreements that could be easily multilateralized.

17. The IATA did not "capture" fare-setting authority. Rather, the Bermuda bilateral agreements contained explicit language granting the IATA authority to set fares. In the United States, IATA authority depended on the Justice Department's granting anti-trust immunity, which was renewed annually until 1955, when it was granted indefinitely. For a discussion of airline motivations regarding the IATA, see Sochor 1991, 13.

18. The United States was the exception here since anti-trust laws precluded U.S. carriers from concluding side-agreements with their foreign counterparts. The Civil Aeronautics Board (CAB) did, however, occasionally grant permission for U.S. carriers to collude with foreign airlines.

19. On IATA traffic conferences, see Lowenfeld 1981, 455–76. I draw heavily on this source for the discussion of IATA rules, except where otherwise noted.

20. On the secrecy surrounding the IATA and the fare conferences, see Haanappel 1978, 35–37, 57–63.

practice ensured that all airlines would provide standardized services at identical prices and could not accrue advantages by providing additional services.

Despite the fact that carriers provided identical services at identical prices and pooled revenue on most routes, there were always incentives to cheat, notably by selling large numbers of tickets to consolidators (bucket shops) or by violating agreements on in-flight services. TWA's early introduction of in-flight entertainment in the 1960s, for example, prompted a series of international disputes that ultimately forced TWA to delay the introduction of the new technology. Given constant incentives for cheating, the IATA maintained a compliance department to ensure airline adherence to IATA agreements.

Bermuda Institutions as Dependent Variables

To clarify how the Bermuda institutions fit within the Rational Design framework, I provide the following summary.

Membership.   All countries were required to conclude bilateral agreements with those countries they wished to provide air service to, and almost all concluded agreements modeled on Bermuda I. Although they could have done otherwise, as the Asian countries did in the late 1970s, this rarely occurred. Membership in the IATA was open to all airlines that wished to join, and airlines from states with agreements modeled on Bermuda I inevitably joined the IATA.[21]

Issue scope.   Fares and in-flight services were covered by IATA rules, and entry, capacity, and ancillary markets were governed by bilateral agreements. Overall, the Bermuda institutions were extensive in scope given the potential for nonfare competition (food and in-flight entertainment, for example) to erode the incentives for continued coordination.

Centralization.   Centralization was limited, though some activities were centralized in the IATA. Marketplace participants (airlines) performed most of the information collection, since they had incentives to make sure that other market participants did not cheat. The IATA collected information on fares and in-flight services and sanctioned cheaters; governments collected information on cheating in ancillary markets, such as ground handling services and computer reservation

21. All major international airlines were members of the IATA until the late 1960s, when many Asian carriers, including Thai Airways International, Malaysian Airline System, Cathay Pacific Airways, and Singapore Airlines, chose not to join the IATA. The role of these non-IATA carriers in the breakdown of the Bermuda regime suggests that universal membership was important for the success of the IATA in curbing incentives to break the cartel. See Dresner and Tretheway 1988, 8–9.

systems. In general, governments and the IATA relied on "fire alarms" rather than "police patrols" for information.[22]

Control.   States maintained tight control over all aspects of aviation markets. Unanimity voting rules governed annual IATA fare conferences.[23] And bilateral agreements, by definition, were also governed by unanimity rules, since no other states participated.[24]

Flexibility.   Extensive flexibility ensured that all marketplace outcomes were acceptable to all marketplace participants. In the event of serious economic disruptions or changes in the circumstances of market participants, the agreements authorized the IATA to hold emergency meetings. The agreements also contained provisions for terminating existing agreements (traditionally a one-year period to renegotiate) and rules for replacing them. Until the early 1990s, the one-year renegotiation period was sufficient; the state withdrawing from the old bilateral agreement almost always obtained a new one closer to its preferences.[25]

Explaining Bermuda Institutions

Why did states create the Bermuda institutions? Consistent with the equilibrium approach suggested by the Rational Design framework, I argue that features of the bargaining environment and marketplace characteristics led states to create institutions that had three primary effects: (1) clear property rights that enabled marketplace growth, (2) distributional outcomes consistent with the preferences of key actors, and (3) marketplace rules that were both durable and compatible with incentives. That is to say, states constructed the Bermuda institutions and the accompanying decision rules to establish property rights of a particular type to ensure that one-time coordination would be durable. I next examine important features of the bargaining environment facing states in aviation markets.

22. For the original distinction between fire alarms and police patrols as methods for political principles to monitor their agents, see McCubbins and Schwartz 1984. See also Lupia and McCubbins 1994.
23. Remember that the IATA fares conferences had to be approved by national governments (and that most airlines were state owned), so in effect states maintained veto power over fares as well as over entry and capacity.
24. There were clear rules for ending bilateral agreements, including time horizons and default rules once the agreements expired, which meant that states had a de facto veto over air services arrangements.
25. In the early 1990s, U.S. pressure for more competitive bilateral agreements led some states to renounce their Bermuda I agreements as a way to stifle U.S. initiatives. The U.S.-France market was perhaps the largest and most well known of those renounced. Of course, service still continued in the bilateral marketplace, but it was governed only by a set of regulations defined in the terms of the initial bilateral agreement (rather than through ad hoc bilateral bargaining).

Distribution Problems

All emerging markets present states with a coordination problem: without some accepted set of rules governing economic exchange—in particular, stable and well-defined property rights—market development will be slow or nonexistent. Douglass North, Paul Milgrom, and Avner Greif, and others, for example, have convincingly demonstrated the role institutions played in the early stages of modern trade.[26] Interstate economic exchange raises a similar set of issues: states must first agree on a set of property rights to govern interstate exchange.[27] Technological innovations that potentially open up new markets often make trade possible and thereby create the potential for gains from coordination. The Internet is the most obvious example today: e-commerce is now possible, and states and private actors are scrambling to define the property rights necessary to encourage on-line transactions to actually take place.[28]

After World War II, international aviation presented states with a similar situation: new technology—long-range passenger aircraft—enabled the creation of an entirely new market. But setting rules and creating property rights in this market were required for the market to develop. For example, to establish consumer confidence in the safety of international air travel, the industry needed safety requirements. And to encourage private firms to enter the marketplace and provide services, the industry needed well-defined and stable property rights. Absent interstate agreement on marketplace rules and regulations, market development would have been much slower and more problematic, and international air travel might have been precluded altogether. George Akerlof's market for lemons is one example where the lack of proper institutional solutions to contracting problems made marketplace exchanges impossible; international aviation markets could easily have been another.[29]

States had large incentives to coordinate on some set of marketplace rules in international aviation markets, and all states agreed on the need for coordination. Thus the debate centered not so much on the need to establish property rights but on what the marketplace rules would look like. States focused primarily on two issues: (1) sovereignty over airspace, and (2) distributional effects on marketplace participants, especially national airlines. Concerns over sovereignty, never really contested, were resolved early on, with all states agreeing to the principle of state control over national airspace.[30] The impact of different marketplace rules on

26. See Spruyt 1994; North and Weingast 1989; Greif, Milgrom, and Weingast 1994; and Milgrom, North, and Weingast 1990.

27. For a discussion of the emergence of the state, see Spruyt 1994.

28. On the ability to regulate the Internet and efforts of both public and private actors to establish property rights, see Lessig 1999.

29. Akerlof 1970.

30. The principle of state sovereignty over airspace was part of the 1919 Paris Peace Conference, where states saw the military potential rather than the commercial potential of international aviation. Post–World War II institution builders drew on this prior set of agreements regarding state sovereignty over airspace.

airlines was more problematic, however, largely because most airlines were less efficient than U.S. carriers and thus preferred strictly regulated markets to protect them from U.S. carriers. Distributional problems—such as foreign airlines' needing to have a strictly regulated market in order to survive—meant that only a subset of possible outcomes was acceptable to domestic interests in key negotiating states. As in Thomas Oatley's analysis of postwar European trade and payments arrangements, distributional problems thus removed certain marketplace outcomes and institutional arrangements from consideration.[31] Facilitating marketplace growth and addressing the attendant distributional effects were thus the two inseparable pieces of the Bermuda bargain. In short, any set of institutions had to ensure the survival of inefficient state-owned carriers.

Solving the dilemma was quite simple: The Bermuda institutions granted the IATA the power to set fares, and unanimity voting rules gave individual airlines the power to veto them. Put differently, the need to create rules that protected national carriers from the more competitive U.S. airlines resulted in the creation of a cartel that propped up prices.

Enforcement Problems

As with most cartels, the cartel in international aviation services created by the Bermuda institutions provided large incentives for individual airlines to cheat. The problem was straightforward: there were large gains to be had by cheating because the agreement inflated prices above market value and thus gave market participants incentives to offer lower fares and thereby capture a larger share of air traffic—all while enjoying the benefits of artificially high fares. This was obvious to everyone, and the Bermuda agreements thus required institutional arrangements to ensure that these incentives did not undermine marketplace coordination. There were also huge incentives for airlines to compete using nonfare services to capture additional customers. This sort of competition, a well-known side effect of price regulation, took a number of forms in aviation, such as lavish in-flight services, fast baggage handling, and large seats. Given the potential for these services to undermine the intent of the Bermuda institutions—to enable even the least efficient airline to remain solvent—the scope of the Bermuda institutions had to be broad enough to regulate all aspects of the market.

Number of Actors

Aviation markets presented national governments with an unusual problem: some aspects of aviation markets affected a large number of actors, and some affected only two. Specifically, fares on any given route could potentially affect many states, whereas entry and capacity on a given bilateral route affected only two states. Fares

---

31. See Oatley, this volume.

established on a bilateral basis in a single bilateral market could lead to inefficient route patterns and thus affect large numbers of states. For example, cheap fares on U.S.–Ireland routes could attract large numbers of passengers bound for final destinations elsewhere in the United Kingdom if fare differences were large enough. Entry and capacity issues, however, affected only two states. Increasing capacity on U.S.–Ireland routes did not encourage more people to go to Ireland rather than to visit relatives elsewhere in the United Kingdom;[32] in short, as long as fares were relatively equal from one route to the next, traffic diversion resulting from increased capacity was limited. In summary, entry and capacity in any given market involved two actors, whereas fares in any given bilateral market affected larger numbers of actors.

Uncertainty About Actors' Behavior and the State of the World

Three features of aviation markets—decentralized distribution channels (such as travel agencies), government ownership of most airlines, and problems in defining and measuring market access to essential facilities and ancillary services (such as distribution channels, ground handling, and airport services)—created extensive uncertainty about actors' behavior and about the state of the world. Consequently, monitoring, and subsequent sanctioning, of cheaters was extremely costly or outright impossible. This uncertainty created two problems for contracting in international aviation markets: transparency and commitment.

Transparency is essential for cooperation, either between firms or between states, simply because actors must be able to observe whether others are abiding by an agreement. If actions are not observable, then contracts cannot be designed around verifiable terms of behavior, and it is difficult, if not impossible, to rely on an independent arbitrator to enforce contracts. Knowing that enforcement will be impossible ex post, of course, precludes agreement ex ante. Transparency is always problematic in international markets (hence Robert Keohane's argument that information provision is the central purpose of international institutions[33]), but it is particularly problematic in aviation markets. Decentralized distribution channels meant that monitoring was very difficult and extremely costly. Moreover, government ownership of airlines, and the resultant lack of separation between state regulators and regulated firms, meant that it was impossible to define and subsequently monitor adherence to any agreement. The debate within the European Union (EU) over the terms of state subsidies to EU airlines and the competitive implications and meaning of these subsidies is only one example of the more general

---

32. This was particularly true in the postwar years, when most travel was for business or government purposes, rather than for leisure, which meant demand for final destinations was relatively inelastic. In addition, capacity was restricted, so there was usually excess demand in any given bilateral market.
33. Keohane 1984.

problem. Is France cheating when it props up Air France by subsidizing new aircraft purchases?[34]

Lack of information and thus uncertainty about actors' behavior were particularly problematic for pricing and market-access issues (entry issues were not as problematic, since monitoring the number and size of planes was fairly easy). Monitoring ticket prices was nearly impossible. Although individual passengers could be interviewed, the large number of passengers and the decentralized nature of distribution made this infeasible. Although the IATA did minimize differences in fares by establishing a simple fare structure, the success of bucket-shops and other forms of illegal discounting suggests that monitoring was imperfect at best. This situation meant that any pricing arrangements had to create the proper incentives for individual airlines to forgo cheating ex ante, because monitoring and sanctioning ex post would be highly ineffective.[35]

Market-access issues revolved around ensuring that foreign carriers could compete against national airlines for domestic-originating passengers on a fair and equal basis. Market access for trade in goods was successfully achieved by agreements to substantially reduce tariffs at successive General Agreement on Tariffs and Trade (GATT) rounds. Bear in mind, however, that tariffs, an at-the-border phenomenon, are easily monitored. Aviation markets were much less amenable to monitoring than traditional goods because of government ownership of airlines and the close relationship between national carriers and ancillary markets (ground handling, airport services, travel agents). Government ownership was problematic because it made separating legitimate regulatory actions from protectionist moves impossible. Did a generous treasury that allowed a carrier to purchase new aircraft represent unfair advantage?[36] Transparency in ancillary markets raised similar issues. Did slow cargo handling at Heathrow for U.S. airlines mean the United Kingdom was cheating? Barriers to entry in distribution channels (that is, the difficulty in contracting with foreign travel agents who worked closely with national carriers and depended on national carriers for most of their revenues) raised similarly difficult transparency and monitoring issues.[37]

Government ownership of airlines and uncertainty about future states of the world also made it difficult for governments to make credible commitments in interna-

34. Air France: $3.3bn State Aid Approved; and Europe: BA Angered at Air France Outcome, both in The Financial Times, 23 July 1998.

35. This is not to suggest that monitoring and sanctioning were irrelevant but that they were not as effective in aviation as in many other markets. Indeed, as discussed later the IATA compliance department monitored and sanctioned airlines. But the total failure of the IATA compliance machinery to slow rampant cheating once airlines had large incentives to cheat (in the early 1970s) suggests that making cheating less profitable was more important than any monitoring and sanctioning IATA did.

36. Although contractual rules could have been written for all these contingencies, this would have proven too costly or outright impossible in practice.

37. National carriers traditionally controlled travel agents through incentive schemes that provided large bonuses if travel agents sold a large number of tickets on a particular airline. Of course, this discouraged travel agents from booking tickets on airlines that had a smaller share of the market, which by definition meant foreign carriers.

tional aviation markets. Almost all states (except the United States) created government-owned national flag carriers to serve both domestic and international
markets. With aviation markets largely considered natural monopolies, state-
sanctioned monopolies were seen as the best way to ensure market growth (of
course, state-owned carriers and their unions were also the object of domestic
electoral dynamics). The problem was that states with national flag carriers could
not credibly commit to any international regulatory arrangements that might create
competitive difficulties for these carriers. With large electoral interests supporting
national carriers at home, it was a political loser to allow competition in the
international marketplace to undermine national carriers, especially since most
domestic markets were small and national carriers earned a large percentage of their
total revenues in international markets. Moreover, these revenues subsidized domestic fares, so there were very good domestic political reasons to avoid substantial
competition in international markets. Would governments actually deliver on
promises for competitive markets when doing so would result in massive losses,
perhaps even bankruptcy, for state-owned carriers? Would governments not face
domestic political pressure to renege on international agreements under these
circumstances? Uncertainty about future states of the world thus undermined the
ability of governments to credibly commit to marketplace outcomes that might
possibly damage the balance sheet of government-owned flag carriers. Knowing
these commitment problems ex ante made it impossible for states to agree on
international institutions that might undermine the economic health of national
carriers.

Drivers of Institutional Choice: Independent Variables

To summarize the preceding discussion and clarify how the Bermuda institutions fit
within the Rational Design framework I consider how the independent variables
drove the creation of the Bermuda institutions.

Distribution problems. The potential distributional consequences of regulating
aviation services—in particular, the adverse effects on government-owned national
airlines—were key drivers of institutional choice. Concerned about distribution,
states created an international cartel, and in turn states had to face all the problems
inherent in cartel maintenance, notably dividing the spoils and ensuring the cartel's
continued functioning.

Enforcement problems. The problem of enforcement in cartels was especially
troublesome in aviation because unanimity rules governed the IATA fare
conferences. In practice this meant that fares were set high enough to support
even the most inefficient carrier. Efficient airlines thus had very large incentives
to cheat. Enforcement was also problematic regarding a range of nonfare
services (notably in-flight food and entertainment, seat size, and baggage

handling) precisely because the lack of fare competition led airlines to seek other forms of differentiation.

Number of actors.   Fares on any given route were relevant for a large number of actors, whereas entry and capacity were largely bilateral concerns. Accordingly, fares were governed by multilateral arrangements, and entry and capacity were governed by bilateral agreements.

Uncertainty.   Three features of the postwar aviation market made it extremely costly or outright impossible to monitor and sanction cheaters: (1) decentralized distribution channels, (2) government ownership of airlines, and (3) problems in defining and measuring market access to essential facilities and ancillary services. This endemic uncertainty in the market created transparency and commitment problems that made contracting particularly difficult. Rather than try to curb cheating through enforcement, states created institutions—revenue sharing, unanimity rules in the IATA, and strict limits on capacity—to minimize the gains from cheating.

Bermuda Institutions as Equilibrium

As should be clear by now, the central challenge facing institution builders in aviation markets was to create institutions that defined property rights in ways that produced distributional outcomes acceptable to key actors. States agreed to create a cartel, which in turn created incentives to cheat on the agreement, which in turn raised the potential for the cartel to unravel. To address this situation states had to create institutions to neutralize the incentives for cheating. Institution builders faced four sets of incentive problems.[38] First, they had to put in place monitoring and sanctioning mechanisms to dampen incentives for defection and increase the utility of ongoing cooperation. Second, they had to devise some mechanism for allocating the gains generated by marketplace coordination. Third, they had to ensure access to key aspects of aviation markets and curb the ability of national carriers to use protected ancillary markets for competitive advantage. Finally, they had to prevent new firms from entering the market and upsetting these allocation arrangements.

The Incentive Effects of Bilateral Agreements

The bilateral agreements contained important institutional features that helped make cheating less desirable. First, they established rules governing entry and service provision in international aviation markets and thereby established stable and

---

38. For a discussion of incentive problems facing cartels, see McMillan 1991.

transparent property rights in these markets. They facilitated marketplace development by dictating the rules and procedures under which airlines could enter or exit from particular routes, the rules for contracting in ancillary markets, and the mechanisms for enforcement and dispute resolution. The agreements had four important effects: (1) they reduced uncertainty about actors' behavior, (2) they allocated the gains from coordination, (3) they prevented entry from upsetting allocative arrangements, and (4) they were flexible enough to enable states to contract in uncertain environments.

The agreements reduced uncertainty about actors' behavior by tightly controlling all aspects of the marketplace and limiting the gains from cheating. Strict reciprocity meant that states swapped route rights of equal economic value, and provisions for revenue sharing (pooling) and capacity further limited the gains from cheating. Pooling rules, for example, required airlines on a particular route to equally split all revenues, and capacity rules (known as predetermination) limited the amount of traffic that either airline in the bilateral agreement could carry. That the agreements also maintained strict control over entry in order to minimize the number of airlines and the size of the revenue pool and traffic shares helped to dampen incentives for cheating. By reducing the gains from cheating and increasing the value of ongoing cooperation, the agreements, in effect, relied on the structure of the regulated marketplace to reduce uncertainty about actors' behavior. Hence, they created a well-known incentive structure in which all players knew that all other players had limited incentives to cheat. With ongoing rents very high, and the gains from cheating strictly limited, why bother to cheat and risk losing the fruits of a successful cartel? Marketplace discipline of a perverse sort thus reduced uncertainty and made cooperation possible.

The key role of the Bermuda institutions, to reduce uncertainty about actors' behavior, suggests that two of the Rational Design conjectures may be interchangeable under certain circumstances—C2, CENTRALIZATION increases with UNCERTAINTY ABOUT THE STATE OF THE WORLD; and V3, CONTROL increases with UNCERTAINTY ABOUT THE STATE OF THE WORLD. As I have already noted, endemic uncertainty about actors' behavior (created by the three features of aviation markets) meant that states had to reduce the gains from cheating rather than monitor and sanction market participants. This was the case simply because the costs of monitoring and sanctioning were prohibitive. The challenge for the Bermuda institutions was therefore not to provide information but to reduce the expected range of actors' behaviors in international aviation markets and thus to enable coordination. The Bermuda institutions had to increase the gains from ongoing coordination, reduce the benefits of cheating, and thereby enable actors to believe with a high degree of certainty that other actors would cooperate. In contrast to the standard explanation for how international institutions facilitate interstate cooperation (such as by providing information), the Bermuda institutions simply reduced the need for information about actors' behavior by strictly limiting the range of permissible behaviors. These extensive arrangements to reduce uncertainty not only enforced an equal division of the spoils from coordination but also helped to keep the cartel in equilibrium. This case therefore suggests that information-poor environments may preclude states from constructing centralized institutions to deal with uncertainty and instead force states to rely on other mechanisms—control, perhaps—to enable coordination even in the face of uncertainty.

The second incentive effect of the bilateral agreements was their role in allocating the gains from coordination. Setting prices multilaterally did not divide the rents among different market participants; it merely determined the size of the pie. That is, IATA fare setting determined prices but did not determine how airlines allocated the rents from the cartel. It was the bilateral agreements, through revenue pooling and rules governing entry and capacity, that allocated the gains from coordination. This is consistent with Rational Design conjectures V3, CONTROL increases with UNCERTAINTY ABOUT THE STATE OF THE WORLD; F1, FLEXIBILITY increases with UNCERTAINTY ABOUT THE STATE OF THE WORLD; and F2, FLEXIBILITY increases with DISTRIBUTION problems.

In addition to providing some confirming evidence for these three conjectures, states' use of bilateral agreements to divide the spoils of the cartel raises an interesting question: Why were bilateral agreements better for allocating rents than multilateral arrangements? In other words, why did the IATA not collect and distribute revenues? In short, states relied on bilateral arrangements because restrictive multilateral institutions are difficult to maintain in the absence of clear, easy to monitor rules for allocating the rents produced by marketplace regulation. Witness, for example, the ongoing struggles within the Organization of Petroleum Exporting Countries (OPEC) and its general failure to influence oil production. Multilateral arrangements are particularly problematic when the potential exists for different traffic routings, which in effect give large generators of traffic market power to capture more of the gains from the cartel. The United States, for example, could have routed traffic through different European states and forced individual European states to "bid" for the traffic. This option was limited, however, by the additional costs involved in long-distance routings and by passenger impatience with long flights; it was also limited by the short range of aircraft in the early years of air travel. The potential for large states to use market power is only exacerbated by the problems involved in agreeing on a rule for distribution and in monitoring adherence to the agreement.[39]

In restrictive markets bilateral agreements may work better than multilateral arrangements largely because there is a natural and simple way to divide the spoils and because monitoring the allocation of benefits is easier. Pooling airline revenues bilaterally, for example, was simply a matter of splitting the revenues from any given city-pair route between the two national flag carriers.[40] This allocation rule

---

39. This is one reason most telecommunications alliances fail: monitoring traffic routing is difficult, and there is often no simple rule for allocating costs and profits. Aviation alliances are easier to monitor, so they have been more successful.

40. Revenue pooling was easiest with a limited number of city-pairs and large traffic flows (that is, passengers) to justify the time and expense of accounting and allocation. Since scheduled airline traffic

also decreases the incentives for cheating since any given actor can capture only 50 percent of the rents in any given market. More complicated multilateral schemes that share these incentive-compatible features are difficult to create and even harder to maintain.[41] These observations are consistent with conjecture V3, CONTROL increases with UNCERTAINTY ABOUT THE STATE OF THE WORLD.

The third effect of the bilateral agreements was their role in limiting entry and thus making ongoing coordination possible. As in all cartel arrangements, new entrants in international aviation had incentives to enter the market, undercut prices, and thereby destabilize marketplace coordination. By limiting the number of airlines that could offer services on any given route, the agreements ensured that the demands of continuous bargaining over the allocation of rents from the cartel did not upset marketplace coordination. For almost all of the intergovernmental bilateral agreements, single designation was the norm, and even those agreements with multiple designation still strictly limited the number of airlines on any given route.[42] Meanwhile, even if multiple designation was provided for, new entrants still had to obtain permission from their national governments to enter the market. National governments, in turn, were reluctant to allow large numbers of entrants because of the negative impact of new carriers on national flag carriers. Indeed, the agreements usually contained language that new entry was only allowed if it did not adversely effect the economic position of incumbent carriers. So strict property rights over particular bilateral routes were important in lengthening the time horizon of marketplace participants. The history of the breakdown of the Bermuda arrangements, in particular the entrance of non-IATA carriers into international markets in Asia and the emergence of widespread cheating and fare discounting in these markets, suggests that the role of the agreements in deterring entry contributed significantly to the stability of the Bermuda arrangements.[43]

The fourth effect of the agreements was the institutional flexibility they fostered. As the Rational Design framework suggests, states will avoid creating inflexible institutions in the midst of uncertainty or when there are strong distributional concerns (conjectures F1 and F2). Coupled with IATA provisions on renegotiating fare levels (discussed later), the Bermuda institutions support both of these conjectures. Specifically, either state in a bilateral agreement could request renegotiation to make short- and long-term adjustments to marketplace rules. Extreme flexibility

---

was largely composed of large flows between European capitals, it therefore made sense that revenue pooling dominated European markets. Note that charter traffic, not discussed here, was governed by a different set of regulatory rules.

41. The telecommunications regime also used bilateral rent sharing within a multilateral arrangement. See Cowhey 1990. Recent efforts by the U.S. Federal Communications Commission to erode the traditional cartel in telecommunications have focused on ending bilateral revenue sharing, one of the benefits to major carriers of maintaining the cartel. In short, bilateral revenue and service pooling created incentives for large carriers not to cheat on existing arrangements. See Cowhey and Richards 2000.

42. Dempsey 1978, 393–449.

43. International carriers not members of IATA include Thai Airways International, Malaysian Airline System, Cathay Pacific Airways, and Singapore Airlines. Dresner and Tretheway 1988, 8–9.

was explicitly designed into the agreements, of course, to enable state-owned carriers to remain in the black regardless of marketplace conditions.

The Incentive Effects of the IATA

Like the bilateral agreements, IATA fare conferences were set up to minimize the benefits of cheating or at least make it more difficult. To begin with, unanimity allowed any airline to veto proposed fares, so every airline should theoretically have been satisfied with fares (and hence have no incentive to cheat). But, of course, there were always some gains to be had from defection, in particular from the use of bucket shops and other forms of illegal discounting that provided revenues not subject to revenue-sharing arrangements.[44] The IATA thus made fare arrangements relatively simple (especially in contrast to the wide variety of fares available today) and consequently as easy as possible for the airlines and the IATA to monitor and sanction cheating. Although the system was far from perfect, more complicated fare structures would have made monitoring even more problematic.

IATA unanimity rules provide support for Rational Design conjecture V3. IATA fare conferences and the attendant rules were extremely flexible, thereby confirming conjectures F1 and F2; the conferences were in fact explicitly designed to ensure that all actors were satisfied with the distribution of rents produced by the cartel. As discussed earlier, if economic conditions changed, emergency IATA meetings could be held to adjust fares, and the bilateral agreements contained provisions for terminating them and rules governing what would replace them. Therefore, short-term defection from agreed-upon fares was a costly action, and there were other avenues for getting an airline back into the black.[45] As B. Peter Rosendorff and Helen Milner observe in their analysis of trade agreements, flexible provisions for intra-agreement adjustments to the economic circumstances of individual partici-pants support ongoing cooperation.[46] Indeed, flexibility, combined with unanimity rules, was explicitly incorporated to keep all market participants satisfied with the distribution of rents and thereby to keep the cartel up and running.

The ongoing nature of IATA conferences and the benefits of membership in the IATA also gave states incentives for continued cooperation and marketplace coordination. Although unanimity meant that any airline could block an entire set of agreed-upon fares, in practice much horse trading took place, and some airlines were more satisfied than others in any given year. In a one-shot game, this might have caused obvious problems. But because the set of actors participating in the annual conferences was stable from year to year, deals could be made both across routes and across years. If states failed to reach agreement at IATA fare-setting confer-ences, some other mechanism of fare setting would have been instituted; this

---

44. Because selling tickets to consolidators at discount prices was illegal, these revenues were not included in revenue-sharing arrangements.
45. See note 25.
46. See Rosendorff and Milner, this volume.

possibility only enhanced the value of cooperation because of the uncertainty it created about future benefits if the IATA were to cease to set international air fares. Although the exact type of fare-setting mechanism varied, the default procedures included greater involvement by national governments, more competition, and less carrier autonomy. For flights to and from the United States, for example, an open-fare mechanism would have been put into place, and airlines would have been free to set fares at any level (subject, of course, to government approval).[47] Overall, the threat of less desirable default mechanisms increased the attractiveness of the IATA and the incentives for agreeing and abiding by its fares.[48] Meanwhile, the IATA coordinated many airline activities and greatly reduced the transaction costs of doing business in international markets.[49] Defection on a particular fare thus threatened to undermine a long-term supply of benefits to airlines, and betting on the IATA provided a better deal over the long term than one-time defection and subsequent uncertainty.

The IATA fare conferences were designed to increase the benefits of cooperation (and decrease the benefits of one-time defection), and the IATA encouraged airlines to report cheating and maintained a compliance department to investigate and punish noncompliance. Airlines could either report cheating to their national governments, which could use government-to-government channels to signal dis-satisfaction with marketplace behavior, or could report a breach of IATA agreements directly to the IATA director general. The IATA therefore relied largely on the airlines themselves for information about noncooperative behavior (such as use of larger planes and bucket shops), and the airlines had obvious incentives for providing this information. But the airlines also employed IATA compliance inspectors to fly around the world and check fares (remember that IATA was a private association of airlines who set their own rules).[50] Once an IATA inspector or member reported a violation, the compliance apparatus would commence. In relatively short order, the IATA director general would contact the accused airline and an investigation would begin. If the investigating commission substantiated the allegation, it was authorized to impose one or more of the following penalties: (1) notify all conference members of the commission's findings, (2) reprimand the violator, (3) levy a fine of up to US $25,000 for each violation,[51] and (4) expel the violator from the IATA.[52] Although expulsion and subsequent termination of IATA benefits was relatively unlikely, the compliance procedures nonetheless significantly

47. The CAB could not directly set fares in international markets until 1972, when it was given greater authority over the fares of carriers on international routes.

48. See IATA Faces Increasing Pressures, Aviation Week and Space Technology, 7 November 1977, 27–28.

49. For a good discussion of these coordination functions, see Zacher 1996, chap. 4.

50. For a somewhat sensationalized version of how IATA inspectors worked, see Sampson 1984, 17–18.

51. Fines were due within sixty days, and the sizes of the fines were related to the breach and the disruptive effects on the traffic of interested parties.

52. Lowenfeld 1981, 471–72.

raised the cost of one-time defection on fares. The IATA also relied on national governments, through their domestic anti-trust laws and regulations, to force national carriers to abide by IATA agreements and reinforce IATA's compliance department. Indeed, many airlines were unable to cheat on IATA fares mainly because of the scrutiny they faced from their national governments.[53]

One final aspect of IATA is worth noting. As discussed earlier, using bilateral institutions to allocate the rents produced by the cartel made sense because it was easier to construct a decision rule that was simple, easy to monitor, and incentive-compatible. But bilateralism does not make sense when a single bilateral agreement might upset neighboring markets and thereby create overall market inefficiencies. Although this problem had little effect on entry and capacity,[54] contradictory fare arrangements in a single bilateral could have upset the entire regime. In particular, given that the fares of other states could have affected a large number of states (since passengers could choose to take roundabout, less expensive routes), contradictory fare levels could easily have resulted in inefficient route patterns and increased incentives for cheating. States therefore used the IATA to coordinate fares and thus prevent individual bilateral agreements from upsetting the regime. Fares were set, for example, such that flying from A to B and then on to C would not be cheaper than flying directly from A to C. In other words, multilateral fare setting precluded individual bilateral agreements from encouraging traffic diversion and inefficient route patterns. In the Bermuda case, enforcement problems led to centralization but also interacted with distributional concerns to produce a very specific set of institutions designed to address actors' concerns in both dimensions. Importantly, enforcement problems and distributional concerns reinforced each other and greatly complicated actors' incentives around building the necessary institutions. As former president of IATA Knut Hammarskjold put it in 1970, "IATA's fare-setting conferences act as a fluid mortar between the bilaterals, allowing continuous minor adjustments to all elements in the entry, pricing, and capacity equations."[55] This fluidity was an explicit design element that addressed both the enforcement and distributional concerns actors confronted in international aviation markets.

53. Taneja 1980, 91.

54. The potential for differences in entry and capacity in a single bilateral agreement to upset other bilateral agreements was limited for two key reasons. First, capacity was restricted, so demand almost always outstripped capacity, which meant in practice that there was excess demand for services in any given agreement. Second, most traffic (business and government travelers) in the early postwar years was very sensitive to time and distance, so alternative routes, regardless of the price, were unacceptable. Therefore, an increase in the number of seats in U.S.-U.K. markets, for example, had little impact on demand for seats in U.S.-French markets (as long as price was held constant across the markets, as it was by the IATA).

55. As quoted in Dresner and Tretheway 1988, 6–7.

Conclusion

The economic gains from coordination in international aviation markets after World War II were large and self-evident: without some arrangements for foreign airlines to fly over sovereign airspace and land at national airports, no international air travel was possible. States designed institutions to resolve coordination problems in international aviation markets—that is, to establish rules governing entry, fares, and the allocation of landing and other rights. Moreover, standardized ticketing, interairline payments, insurance requirements, safety rules, health regulations, and many other details of aviation markets increased consumer confidence in international travel and thereby increased demand for aviation services.[56] Although security and standardization issues could have been addressed case by case through bilateral agreements, the result would have been high transaction costs and perhaps even perverse incentives for route structures (since contradictory bilateral agreements could easily have led to inefficient route patterns). Governments resolved this problem by delegating authority over international fares to the IATA, which facilitated multilateral fare-setting; this prevented individual bilateral agreements from encouraging traffic diversion and inefficient route structures. Multilateral coordination of some aspects of international aviation markets therefore reduced the transaction costs of coordinating a large number of bilateral markets, reduced the potential for any single bilateral agreement to upset the regime, and enabled international markets to develop.[57]

The Bermuda institutions provide evidence in support of several Rational Design conjectures. In particular, they support conjecture V3, CONTROL increases with UNCERTAINTY ABOUT THE STATE OF THE WORLD, in this case uncertainty about the distributional allocation of the gains from coordination. In aviation, the difficult of monitoring created endemic uncertainty about both actor behavior and future states of the world, and thereby created actor concerns over the distribution of gains from creating the market in the first place. Uncertainty about the distribution of gains made possible by creating a market in international aviation services led states to create institutions that gave veto power to all members and thereby protected them against unwanted distributional outcomes. The fact that states retained direct control over most aspects of aviation markets, especially those with distributional implications, strongly confirms conjecture V3. The extensive flexibility of the Bermuda agreements also confirms conjectures F1, FLEXIBILITY increases with UNCERTAINTY ABOUT THE STATE OF THE WORLD; and F2, FLEXIBILITY increases with DISTRIBUTION problems. In short,

---

56. For an excellent discussion of the standardization functions performed by the Bermuda institutions, see Zacher 1996, 94–109.

57. A multilateral apparatus governing fares had large advantages because inconsistent bilateral agreements on fares could have led to perverse route structures and inefficient growth of international markets.

the distributional implications of international aviation markets, coupled with the endemic uncertainty produced by particular features of the markets, led states to create very flexible institutions that protected them from negative distributional outcomes and limited their commitments in the face of uncertainty.

The Bermuda institutions display design characteristics—particularly scope, inclusive membership, and strong control mechanisms—that weakly confirm, contradict, and/or suggest extensions to a number of the Rational Design conjectures. My analysis suggests not so much that the Rational Design conjectures are misguided, but that applying them in complex settings may require a more nuanced understanding of how the variables interact or an extension of the basic framework.

The Bermuda institutions were not linked to other issue-areas despite severe distributional implications, suggesting that conjecture S2, SCOPE increases with DISTRIBUTION problems, may be too limited. This conjecture stresses links to other issue-areas, but scope may be relevant within an issue area. In particular, the Bermuda institutions regulated all aspects of the marketplace that could potentially upset coordination. The scope of the Bermuda institutions was thus extensive precisely because the large incentives to cheat necessitated the regulation of all aspects of competition, yet the institutions made no attempts to link aviation to other issue-areas. Scope within issue-areas may be a natural extension of the Rational Design framework. Or it may have other implications altogether. Further thinking about scope would help to clarify conjecture S2 and its applicability.

Membership in the case of the Bermuda institutions suggests that this variable may interact with other aspects of institutional design. Moreover, an institution may encompass multiple institutions with distinct memberships and goals (consider the UN Security Council and the General Assembly, for example). To stem the potential for cheating, the Bermuda institutions explicitly sought inclusive membership. When many Asian airlines, for example, joined the international aviation community in the late 1960s but did not join the IATA the entire fare-setting apparatus was severely threatened. Yet the bilateral agreements were crucial to the cartel's functioning and remained in place far longer than the IATA did. The Bermuda institutions thus suggest that conjecture M1, restrictive MEMBERSHIP increases with ENFORCEMENT problems, may interact with other conjectures—notably conjectures M3, MEMBERSHIP increases with DISTRIBUTION problems, and V3, CONTROL increases with UNCERTAINTY ABOUT THE STATE OF THE WORLD—in ways beyond the current scope of the Rational Design project.

Finally, the control mechanisms of the Bermuda institutions suggest that conjectures C3, CENTRALIZATION increases with NUMBER, and V3, CONTROL increases with UNCERTAINTY ABOUT THE STATE OF THE WORLD, may have more complexity than the framework captures. According to the framework, to capture the benefits from coordination individual members must give up control as numbers increase. Likewise, organizations with large numbers must have centralized control in order to avoid actors losing all control. In aviation, however, institutional arrangements allowed every potential member to participate and granted every member veto power over the most important element of the marketplace: fares. Why was this the case? Two answers are possible. First, in some situations all actors must participate for the market to develop and function. Second, severe distributional problems can cause actors to place more value on control than on the gains from coordination. Therefore, extending the Rational Design framework to include the domestic roots of decision making about these trade-offs (costs versus benefits of coordination) would broaden our understanding of how and why states construct international institutions.

Taken together, the Bermuda arrangements involving scope, membership, and control suggest that many of the Rational Design independent variables may interact with one another (and with other situational dynamics) in more complex ways than the framework allows. For example, the fact that states did not create centralized institutions in response to the endemic uncertainty in aviation markets cuts against conjectures C1, CENTRALIZATION increases with UNCERTAINTY ABOUT BEHAVIOR, and C2, CENTRALIZATION increases with UNCERTAINTY ABOUT THE STATE OF THE WORLD. States relied instead on strong control mechanisms (unanimity rules) to ensure that all outcomes were acceptable to all parties; that is, control substituted for centralization.[58] Uncertainty about the environment did lead states to create institutional arrangements, but in this case the choice to use decentralized arrangements were driven largely by differences in the costs of centralized and decentralized information gathering. In short, centralization is only one way to obtain information about actor behavior. A more nuanced understanding of the underlying drivers of actor behavior (such as profit maximization, electoral success, and market efficiency) may enable more focused conjectures. My analysis suggests that actor incentives—in this case to severely limit the potential distributional downside for national carriers—led states to insist on control in ways inadequately explained by the Rational Design conjectures.

No system of governance is ever perfect, and despite careful crafting and maintenance we should not expect international institutions to last forever. In aviation, changes in the structure of demand for international air travel (the growth of leisure travelers) and changes in technology (the introduction of the jumbo jet) set the stage for the collapse of the Bermuda institutions in the late 1970s. Combined, these changes undermined the distributional logic of the Bermuda cartel and thus dramatically altered the strategic setting states faced. Specifically, changes in the domestic political economy of aviation in important states enabled the development of competitive international markets that did not require the Bermuda institutions. Governments were more willing to privatize their airlines and allow greater competition on many routes, which reduced the need for monitoring and consequently the need for extensive institutional arrangements. Governments have be-

58. Moreover, it could be argued flexibility substituted for centralization in response to uncertainty about the state of the world.

come less concerned with equalizing the gains from coordination than with decreasing the deadweight losses imposed by the cartel. But many of the difficult contractual problems remain, notably credibility issues stemming from domestic politics and uncertainty over legal jurisdiction and the need to obtain market access to key facilities, such as airport gates and slots.[59] No new set of institutions has emerged to govern international aviation markets, and airlines have largely created their own private governance mechanisms, such as global airline alliances, to deal with the economic incentives driving global consolidation. Remnants of the Bermuda institutions continue to regulate large pieces of international aviation markets, and the airlines themselves seek to devise private solutions more consistent with the economics of global networks.

59. Cowhey and Richards 2000.

Driving with the Rearview Mirror: On the Rational Science of Institutional Design

Alexander Wendt

How can social scientists best contribute to the design of international institutions? Presumably our value lies in producing knowledge about design that those designing institutions need but do not have. But what kind of knowledge is that? What should a science of institutional design be "about?"

As a discipline international relations (IR) has barely begun to think about institutional design. Anarchy makes the international system among the least hospitable of all social systems to institutional solutions to problems, encouraging actors to rely on power and interest instead. Designing institutions hardly makes sense, and could even be counterproductive, under such conditions. Thus, IR has plausibly focused most of its energy so far on the question of whether institutions mattered at all. Yet designing institutions has been a big part of what foreign policymakers actually do, especially since the end of World War I. The League of Nations, UN, European Union, World Trade Organization, North American Free Trade Agreement, Association of South-East Asian Nations, Nuclear Nonproliferation Treaty, and hundreds of other international organizations and regimes have been created. Skeptics may be right that all this activity is unimportant or a mistake, but policymakers apparently disagree. And that in turn has left IR with less to say to them than it might have. By bracketing whether institutions matter and turning to the problem of institutional design, therefore, this volume takes an important step toward a more policy-relevant discourse about international politics.

The articles in this volume deserve to be assessed on their own terms, within the particular rationalist framework laid out in Barbara Koremenos, Charles Lipson, and Duncan Snidal's introduction. That framework highlights collective-action problems and incomplete information as impediments to institutional design. It is important to note that this is only one possible rationalist model. One could imagine

For their helpful comments on a draft of this article, I am grateful to two anonymous reviewers, the *IO* editors, Michael Barnett, Deborah Boucoyannis, Martha Finnemore, Peter Katzenstein, and especially Jennifer Mitzen.

International Organization 55, 4, Autumn 2001, pp. 1019–1049

other rationalist models—for example, based on rent-seeking states or political leaders trying to maximize their chances of staying in office—that might lead to different conclusions.[1] However, offering an internal critique of the Rational Design project from any rationalist perspective is not something I am particularly qualified or inclined to do, nor was it the charge given to me when I was generously invited to contribute. From the start the editors deliberately set aside a number of "non-rationalist" arguments in order to see how far they could push their approach to the problem. The purpose of soliciting this comment was to get an outside perspective.

Actually, I am not that qualified or inclined to make a fully external critique either. Although some epistemological issues will come up, I share the volume's commitment to social science, and while I doubt that rationalism can tell us everything, I certainly think it can tell us a lot.[2] Additional insights about institutional design might emerge by rejecting social science or rationalism altogether, but I shall not do so here. However, in the space between a purely internal and purely external critique I hope to raise some fairly fundamental questions about the approach. Given space constraints, I do so by focusing mainly on the volume's introduction, which lays out the theoretical structure of the volume, and use the empirical articles to illustrate my points.

I shall raise two main concerns, one more external than the other. The first is the volume's neglect of alternatives to its explanation of institutional designs. At base, the theory of rational design is that states and other actors choose international institutions to further their own interests.[3] This amounts to a functionalist claim: actors choose institutions because they expect them to have a positive function.[4] Alternatives to this hypothesis come in at least two forms, both associated with "sociological" or "constructivist" approaches to institutions.[5]

On the one hand, alternatives could be rival explanations, where the relationship to the theory of rational design is zero-sum; variance explained by one is variance not explained by the other. At first glance it might seem hard to identify plausible rivals. One is tempted to say, Of course actors design institutions to further their interests—what else would they do? But in fact there are some interesting rivals, both to the proposition that institutions are rationally chosen and to the proposition that they are designed. I discuss each in turn and argue that neglect of these alternatives makes it more difficult to assess the volume's conclusions. Imre Lakatos argues that the theory-laden character of observation means we can never test theories directly against the world, only against other theories in light of the world.[6]

---

1. I thank an anonymous reviewer and the IO editors for emphasizing this point to me. For ease of exposition, however, when I say "rational-design theory," I shall mean the particular theory offered in this volume.
2. See Wendt 1999; and Fearon and Wendt forthcoming.
3. Koremenos, Lipson, and Snidal, this volume, 762.
4. On functionalism in design theory and its alternatives, see especially Pierson 2000b.
5. For good introductions to this extensive literature, see Powell and DiMaggio 1991; Hall and Taylor 1996; and March and Olsen 1998.
6. Lakatos 1970, 115 and passim.

Since the volume's research design does not set up such a "three-cornered fight," the most we can say is that rational-design theory is consistent with and provides some insight into the evidence, not that it definitively explains the evidence or even that it has survived falsification.

On the other hand, "alternatives" could refer to explanations that do not contradict rational-design theory but embed it within broader social or historical contexts that construct its elements (preferences, beliefs, and so on). Whereas the question with rival explanations is one of variance explained, the issue here is one of "causal depth."[7] Even if states choose rationally, this may be less interesting than the underlying structures that make certain choices rational in the first place. It is on such structures that sociological and constructivist approaches to institutions typically focus. This does not mean such approaches are right and thereby always provide the "deeper" explanation of institutional choice, since another rationalist theory might be able to explain the parameters that this volume takes as given (which reinforces the point that the Rational Design project is only one of several possible rationalist approaches). Notwithstanding provocative exceptions,[8] however, most rationalist scholarship in IR does take structural contexts and agents as given in order to focus on the logic of choice and interaction. By identifying potential sociological and constructivist explanations of deeper causes, therefore, I hope at least to challenge rationalists to offer rival explanations for things they often have taken for granted.

Although I will make some suggestions, in the end I do not know whether alternative explanations of either the rival or deeper type are compelling in the empirical cases addressed in this volume. However, before we can answer that question we first need to know what the alternatives are. This entails mapping what I will call the theoretical "contrast space" around rational-design theory, along both the horizontal and vertical dimensions. Only a start can be made here, but in the first two-thirds of this article I use existing sociological and constructivist scholarship on institutions to begin a survey of the terrain.

Despite its focus on alternative explanations, this first critique remains internal in the sense that it assumes, with the Rational Design project, that the question we are trying to answer about institutional design is an explanatory one: Why do institutions have the features they do? However, part of what makes the problem of institutional design interesting, in my view, is that it raises further questions which go beyond that explanatory concern. In particular, the term design readily calls up the policy-relevant question, What kind of institutions should we design? The volume's editors themselves use that question to help motivate their project, though they then switch gears to ask why states design the institutions they do.[9] This makes sense, since "should" is a normative problem at best only partially amenable to positive social science. So in raising it I do not mean to suggest it should have been

---

7. Wilson 1994.
8. For example, North and Thomas 1973.
9. Koremenos, Lipson, and Snidal, this volume.

addressed here; no study can do everything, and the explanatory question is big and important in its own right. Yet, given that this volume focuses on a theoretic issue with important policy implications, it seems useful in this essay to reflect on how the gap between positive and normative could be narrowed further.

Bridging this gap depends, I shall argue, on recognizing the epistemological differences between the kinds of knowledge sought in the scientific and policy domains, which stem from different attitudes toward time. Positive social scientists are after "explanatory" knowledge, knowledge about why things happen. This is necessarily backward-looking, since we can only explain what has already occurred, although there is the hope that with good explanations we can predict the future. Policymakers, and institutional designers, in contrast, need "making" or "practical" knowledge, knowledge about what to do. This is necessarily forward-looking, since it is about how we should act in the future. As Henry Jackman puts it, "we live forwards but understand backwards."[10] The former cannot be reduced to the latter. Knowing why we acted in the past can teach us valuable lessons, but unless the social universe is deterministic, the past is only contingently related to the future. Whether actors preserve an existing institution like state sovereignty or design a new one like the EU is up to them. The voluntarism inherent in this question is something that positive social science is not well-equipped to handle.

Practical knowledge may nevertheless interact in interesting ways with explanatory knowledge. To show this, in the last third of this article I briefly discuss two domains of inquiry about institutional design not addressed in this volume. The first is institutional effectiveness. The Rational Design project relies on a subjective definition of rationality, which means that even if states choose designs 100 percent rationally, they may not be effective. If design failures happen often enough, this might raise a normative question about whether subjective rationality should be the criterion for making design decisions. Functionalism ultimately has to be judged by whether the Titanic hits the iceberg, not by whether those on the bridge were rational. The second domain is the specifically normative one. What values should we pursue in institutions? In one sense this is the first question institutional designers face, and the most deeply political. It is not one that the contributors to this volume themselves need have asked, but its answers, too, may feed back on their positive concerns: if the effects of institutions are immoral, it may be better to do the "appropriate" thing than to do the rational one.

Positive and normative inquiries are, of course, in many ways distinct, but a science of institutional design that deals only with the former will be incomplete and useful primarily for "driving with the rearview mirror." The larger question I want to raise here, therefore, is an epistemological one—what should count as "knowledge" about institutional design? In social science we often assume that knowledge is only about explaining the past. Institutional design is an issue where the nature of the problem—making things in the future—may require a

10. Jackman 1999.

broader view of knowledge that brings positive and normative theory into conversation with each other.

Alternatives to Rational Design

Given the question, What explains variation in institutional design? it is clear that rational-design theory provides some leverage. But how much leverage? It is difficult to say until we make lateral comparisons to its rivals and vertical comparisons to deeper explanations. Ultimately, this must be an empirical affair, but the first step is to map the contrast space. Thus, assuming that the phrase "rational design" is not redundant, I break the volume's hypothesis down into two parts, that institutions are chosen rationally and that they are designed.

Alternatives to "Rational"

What makes the choice of an institutional design "rational"? Rationality can be defined in various ways.[11] In rational-choice theory it refers to instrumental or "logic of consequences" thinking:[12] Actors are rational when they choose strategies that they believe will have the optimal consequences given their interests. The expected costs and benefits of different choices are compared, and the one with the highest net value is chosen. This is a subjective definition of rationality in that a rational choice is not what will actually maximize an actor's pay-offs (we might call this an "objective" view of rationality), but what the actor thinks will do so. And neither does it problematize how actors define their interests. Even a self-destructive or immoral person can be rational in this sense.

If for a single actor rational action is what subjectively maximizes its interests, then when there are multiple actors, as in international politics, a rationally chosen institution will be one that solves their collective-action problem, not one that necessarily solves a problem in the external world. The design of the prisoners of war (POW) regime analyzed by James Morrow, for example, is a rational choice because it enables states to cooperate, even though thousands of violations (in effect, murders) occur.[13] In this respect the Rational Design project's framing of the design issue is indebted to 1980s regime theory, which defined its task as explaining how states could cooperate under anarchy. Collective-action problems, in short, are subjective at the group level, in that they are constituted by a shared perception of some facts in the world as (1) being a "problem" (versus not), (2) requiring "collective action" (versus not), and (3) having certain features that constitute what kind of collective-action problem it is (coordination, cooperation, security, economic, and so on). These understandings are only partly determined by objective

11. See especially Hargreaves-Heap 1989.
12. Jackman 1999.
13. Morrow, this volume.

facts in the world—the "structure of the situation" in Ronald Mitchell and Patricia Keilbach's terms.[14] They are also constructed by a communicative process of interpreting what that world means and how and why designers should care about it.[15] As such, there is ample room for institutional designers to ignore issues that others might see as problems (global justice?), or to define problems in mistaken ways ("fighting the last war").

This process of problem construction takes place prior to the questions in which this volume is interested and structures how institutional design proceeds. Given a definition of the design problem, the rational action is to maximize the expected value of institutional choices. This subjectivism gives the Rational Design framework a curiously "post-modern" feel, since the rationality of institutional choices is always internal to the discourses by which collective-action problems are constituted. That the Bermuda aviation regime studied by John Richards was a rational choice, for example, presupposes that states were committed to preserving national carriers. While that desire makes sense from the standpoint of the symbolic concerns emphasized by sociological institutionalists, it is less clear how it comports with the material economic interests rationalists tend to emphasize.[16] In the end, however, this volume anchors itself to the objective world by an at least implicit assumption of "rational expectations"[17]—that the expected consequences of design choices will generally correspond to the actual ones. This ensures that decision-makers' calculations are not completely divorced from reality. Without this assumption, the justification for defining rationality in subjective terms would be weaker.

What are the alternatives to the hypothesis that states choose subjectively rational institutions? One, of course, is that states knowingly choose institutions that will defeat their purposes, but that does not seem very plausible. We have to look elsewhere for interesting alternatives. I discuss two.

The logic of appropriateness.   One alternative is that states choose institutional designs according to the "logic of appropriateness":[18] Instead of weighing costs and benefits, they choose on the basis of what is normatively appropriate. This explanation is usually treated as a rival to the logic of consequences, although as we shall see their relationship is not unambiguous, so it might alternatively be seen in terms of causal depth. In international politics there are many examples of decision making on appropriateness grounds. An example I have used before is what stops the United States from conquering the Bahamas, instrumental factors or a belief that this would be wrong?[19] One can construct

14. Mitchell and Keilbach, this volume.
15. Kratochwil 1989.
16. See Richards, this volume; Meyer et al. 1997; and Boli and Thomas 1999. For a good overview of sociological institutionalism in IR, see Finnemore 1996.
17. Understood here in the objectivist sense of rational-expectations theory in economics, not in the subjectivist sense of rationality discussed earlier.
18. March and Olsen 1998.
19. Wendt 1999, 289–90.

an "as if," cost-benefit story to explain nonconquest, but I doubt this is the operative mechanism; it is more likely that U.S. policymakers see this as illegitimate. A more difficult and thus interesting example is provided by Nina Tannenwald's study of the "nuclear taboo," which suggests that even when instrumental factors weighed in favor of using nuclear weapons, as in the Vietnam War, U.S. decision makers refrained on normative grounds.[20] The way such a logic ultimately works is through the internalization of norms. As actors become socialized to norms, they make them part of their identity, and that identity in turn creates a collective interest in norms as ends in themselves.[21] The result is internalized self-restraint: actors follow norms not because it is in their self-interest, but because it is the right thing to do in their society. Society would not be as stable as it is if people always applied a logic of consequences to their actions, and so internalized norms may explain much of the rule-following we see in international life.

The Bahamas and nuclear taboo examples highlight the fact that the logic of appropriateness has usually been used in IR to explain compliance with regimes.[22] This is not irrelevant to the question of regime design. Morrow, for example, bases part of his analysis on the assumption that the reason most soldiers observe the POW regime is because of a rational fear of sanctions rather than because they think killing prisoners is murder. However, design is a different question from compliance, to which it is less obvious that logics of appropriateness are directly relevant.

Nevertheless, there are at least three ways in which normative logics might be rivals to rational explanations of institutional design. One is by supplying desiderata for institutions that make little sense on consequentialist grounds. A norm of universal membership, for example, operates in many international regimes. Why do landlocked states have a say in the Law of the Sea, or Luxembourg a vote in the EU? It is not obvious that the answers lie in the enforcement and distributional considerations emphasized by the Rational Design framework. Or consider the norm that Great Powers have special prerogatives. Without reference to this idea, it is hard to explain the inclusion of Russia in the Group of Eight, or to make sense of debates about the future of the UN Security Council. The norm that the control of international institutions should be democratic is also gaining strength. The Rational Design framework proposes that designs for institutional control reflect degrees of uncertainty and asymmetries of contribution, yet in debates about how to fix the "democratic deficit" in the EU and other international organizations such cost-benefit considerations seem less salient than questions of legitimacy and principle.[23] Arguably, this is because decision makers themselves see democratic accountability as an intrinsic good. Then there are solidarity norms stemming from collective identities, which to their credit Mitchell and Keilbach suggest may be necessary to

20. Tannenwald 1999.
21. Wendt 1999.
22. The Meyer School being an important exception.
23. See, for example, Pogge 1997; and Dryzek 1999.

266 International Organization

explain German and Swiss contributions to the Rhine River regime.[24] One wonders about the possible future role of norms of justice in international politics. And so on. These possibilities do not mean that rational factors are not also operative in regime design, but they do suggest the story may be more complicated than a pure consequentialism would allow.

A second, converse, way in which logics of appropriateness may constitute rival hypotheses is by taking design options that might be instrumentally attractive off the table as "normative prohibitions."[25] Peter Rosendorff and Helen Milner point to plausible rational reasons why trade regimes will include "escape clauses." Yet in other regimes such clauses are absent—there is no exemption for murder in the human rights regime, for example—which seems hard to explain on such grounds, since the norms are equally difficult to enforce.[26] This example also suggests that the relative tolerance of the POW regime for violations may be due to more than just enforcement problems, but reflects a "boys will be boys" belief that a certain level of murder on the battlefield is legitimate. Similarly, Mitchell and Keilbach note that in negotiations over the whaling regime the United States relied on coercion in part because of a reluctance to pay bribes to stop what was seen as an immoral activity.[27] Moving beyond the cases in this volume, in turn, one might expect a purely rational regime for dealing with "failed states" to include a trusteeship option, but because of its association with colonialism, this is unacceptable to the international community. Finally, norms about what kinds of coercion may be used in different contexts may also factor into regime design. Military intervention to collect sovereign debts was legitimate in the nineteenth century,[28] but it is hard to imagine this being done today. As a result, in designing the debt and many other regimes, the military dominance of the United States and its allies confers less bargaining leverage than it perhaps used to; normative prohibitions have made military power less fungible. A true test of rational-design theory would include all instrumentally relevant options, not just those that are normatively acceptable.

Finally, logics of appropriateness can affect the modalities used to design institutions, which as a result may be historically specific. For example, the ongoing conferences in the aviation regime discussed by Richards and the "clustered negotiations" on trade studied by Robert Pahre[29] presuppose a belief that issue-specific conferences could be kept insulated from military competition, but this belief is a relatively recent notion, dating to the Concert of Europe.[30] One wonders whether the recent growth of international private arbitration analyzed by Walter Mattli might be another instance of norm-governed cognitive innovation.[31] Mattli's

24. Mitchell and Keilbach, this volume, 914.
25. Nadelmann 1990.
26. Rosendorff and Milner, this volume.
27. Mitchell and Keilbach, this volume, 910.
28. Krasner 1999.
29. Pahre, this volume.
30. Mitzen 2001.
31. Mattli, this volume.

demand-induced explanation seems sensible, but also insufficient to explain the outcome. Private arbitration only took off in the late twentieth century—would it not have been equally rational in the nineteenth? To account for this difference a rationalist might appeal to rising transaction costs due to increasing density of interactions. However, such costs are hard to measure, often apparent only in retrospect, and, importantly here, may depend on the availability of ideas or language to express them.[32] Thus it is possible that the failure of nineteenth-century corporations to be rational had as much to do with normative changes in "appropriate" business practice as it did with cost-benefit calculations. Finally, there is the most general question of how states came to see "institutions" as solutions to collective-action problems in the first place. States have always had such problems, yet for most of the past five thousand years they never thought to create institutions to address them. Why not? Was it irrational, or was it that the very idea of using institutions to solve international problems was unknown or considered inappropriate? Following Hedley Bull, we might point to the norms of international society as a prerequisite, such that it is only with the attainment of a certain level of collective identity that the rational design of institutions becomes possible.[33]

In at least three ways, then, logics of appropriateness may help structure international institutions. These possibilities do not mean that consequentialism is wholly absent, as the case studies in this volume make clear. But insofar as our objective is to assess variance explained, the logic of appropriateness suggests that rival factors may be important as well.

One might argue in response that normative explanations are not really rivals to the rational account because they concern how design problems are framed in the first place, rather than a competing logic of institutional choice. Given that states want to conserve their soldiers' lives, that for racist or ideological reasons the destruction of certain enemies takes precedence over that objective, and that a high level of violations is acceptable, then the Geneva Convention is the rational regime choice for POWs. Or, given a norm that democratic states should stick together militarily, but also that arguably the most rational design of all—including Russia in NATO—is not considered an option, then the dilemmas of NATO expansion discussed so cogently by Andrew Kydd come into play.[34] Such a nonrival rendering of the contrast space positions the two logics in complementary terms as an analytical "two-step:"[35] a first step of defining the game, in which norms might be salient; then a second of solving the game, in which consequentialism rules. This has the virtue of isolating the causes emphasized by rational-design theory, and it also has precedent in IR scholar-

32. Buckley and Chapman 1997.
33. See Bull 1977; and Wendt 1999.
34. Kydd, this volume.
35. Legro 1996.

ship, where the value added of constructivism is often seen as using norms to explain identities and interests.[36]

However, the two-step frame also creates problems for rationalists. First, it leaves rational-design theory stuck in seemingly shallower explanatory waters than its constructivist counterpart. To be sure, since given ends can always be reinterpreted as means to higher ends, it may be possible to build a more ocean-going rational theory that explains the preferences and beliefs constituting design games as themselves rational choices in deeper games.[37] How much explanatory power such a theory would have remains to be seen, however, since to date there has been little rationalist work endogenizing identities and interests. Second, by turning potential rivals into complements, the two-step frame makes it harder to see what would falsify the rational explanation. Indeed, apart from Kydd, who discusses a constructivist hypothesis in some detail, and scattered remarks in a few other articles, for all its commitment to positivist social science it is not clear in this volume what would even count as a nonrational explanation of regime design and thus as evidence against the theory. Some of the empirical articles in fact find that the Rational Design hypotheses are not always supported, a sure sign that the contributors have approached their task honestly rather than just to prove the theory right. Yet, because rival explanations have not been engaged, it is difficult to know whether the problem lies with the rational approach as such or with the particular way in which that approach was specified in this volume. The latter possibility suggests that with suitable modifications a rationalist story could be told about any institutional design. Perhaps that means the rationalist story is true, but it also threatens to make it nonfalsifiable. In view of these considerations it may be better to frame the contrast space for future studies of institutional design in terms of rival explanations rather than a hierarchical two-step.

To do that we would need to decide what counts as relevant evidence either way. In particular, is it enough that design choices be consistent with an hypothesis, or do we need to know how states were actually thinking and motivated? If what we are doing is a plausibility probe, consistency is a good start. Moreover, the inferential value of such consistency is maximized by this volume's research design, which emphasizes cross-case comparison. These comparisons may even be sufficient to conclude in favor of rational-design theory in situations where logics of consequences and appropriateness make opposite predictions about outcomes. But the problem is that in many situations the two logics will make the same predictions, so behavioral evidence alone will not be dispositive. The fact that Great Powers today rarely use violence to advance their preferred institutional designs, for example, is consistent with there being significant costs to such an action in the modern international system, and with it being seen as wrong. Which is the real explanation? To answer this question we need to get inside the heads and discourse of decision

36. For more on the ambiguous relationship between these traditions, see March and Olsen 1998, 952–54; and Fearon and Wendt forthcoming.
37. Clark 1998.

makers and see what is motivating their behavior.[38] The empirical articles do a good job constructing plausible "as if" consequentialist accounts, but (with some exceptions) provide less evidence that actors really are thinking in such terms. Since it may often be equally possible to construct plausible "as if" normative accounts, for definitive conclusions about the explanatory power of rational-design theory we will need more direct evidence of self-interested motivation and instrumental calculation.

Finally, let us assume that rational-design theory is right that the features of modern international institutions are chosen through a logic of consequences. What are the implications? To answer this question we need to go further down the causal chain and ask more questions. Has this logic always been dominant, or were institutions like the Holy Roman Empire designed on a different basis? And if different, what explains how the logic of consequences became the "appropriate" logic today for institutional design? The question is important because this logic might not always be normatively desirable. The Rational Design framework hypothesizes, for example, that in the face of asymmetric contributions the rational design is to give dominant states more control over the institution, as in the International Monetary Fund or UN Security Council. This might be necessary to get such states to cooperate, but is it right? When consequentialism leads to undemocratic or otherwise unjust institutional designs, perhaps it should be resisted and states persuaded to adopt a logic of appropriateness instead. Indeed, one could defend such resistance even on consequentialist grounds, if normatively inappropriate designs lead to illegitimate and thus ineffective institutions. The term rational has such positive connotations in modern society that it is easy to forget that there are other bases for making decisions. As such, it seems important to remember that if instrumentalism dominates today, this should be seen as a social construction rather than as given by nature.

On uncertainty. In addition to instrumental thinking, rationality as understood in this volume relies on a particular, and contested, way of handling uncertainty. As the editors point out, a focus on uncertainty is one of the Rational Design project's significant departures from earlier rationalist (and nonrationalist) scholarship on international institutions.[39] Since uncertainty is intrinsic to social life, and especially to institutional design—which tries to structure an otherwise open future—addressing it can make IR more realistic and policy-relevant. However, the Rational Design framework seems to treat the nature of uncertainty as unproblematic and ends up with a conceptualization that effectively reduces it to risk. This assertion may seem wrong, since the editors say they are adopting the "standard terminology in using the term uncertainty instead of risk,"[40] but the premise of this terminology is that the two are equivalent. That there is an important distinction between risk and uncer-

---

38. For an interesting discussion relevant to this problem, see Pettit 1995.
39. Also see Koremenos 2001.
40. Koremenos, Lipson, and Snidal, this volume, 779.

tainty has been known at least since Frank Knight's classic 1921 work[41] and the distinction is used in some rationalist scholarship today, even elsewhere by Snidal himself.[42] But in most orthodox economics and formal theory the two are conflated, and it is to this literature that this volume seems most indebted. In contrast, heterodox Austrian and post-Keynesian economists vigorously uphold Knight's distinction and indeed base much of their critique of mainstream economics on its failure to do so.[43] In the volume's empirical articles the implications drawn from "uncertainty" for rational design generally seem plausible, so it is not clear that in those cases the heterodox view would support rival conclusions. As such, the discussion that follows is more speculative than in the previous section. However, I want to suggest that in some issue-areas, especially those where logics of appropriateness are strong, a heterodox conceptualization of uncertainty may in fact have different implications for rational behavior.

"Risk" describes a situation in which some parameters of the decision problem, such as other actors' preferences or beliefs, are not known for certain, but— importantly—all the possibilities are known and can be assigned probabilities that add up to 1. The utility of different courses of action is then weighted by these probabilities, leading to the formalism of expected-utility theory. A key implication of risk is that even though actors cannot be certain about the outcomes of their choices, they can at least see well-defined (if still probabilistic) relationships between ends and means, so that they can calculate precisely the chances of achieving their goals with different strategies.[44] Choose A, and there is a given chance that pay-off X will occur; choose B, another chance; and so on. This is significant because it means there is always a clear and principled answer to the question, What is the rational thing to do?

What is also interesting about the concept of risk, however, is that it is equivalent to the modern concept of "incomplete information," which is how mainstream economists usually define uncertainty (hence the editors' adoption of the "standard terminology" substituting one for the other). The origins of this definition are not clear to me, although it may have to do with an attachment to a subjectivist or "degree of belief" view of probability, which allows virtually any situation to be assigned a probability,[45] and to the fact that it makes decision problems tractable by the expected utility calculus. But whatever the cause, the effect is to collapse uncertainty into risk.

This collapse is challenged by Austrian and post-Keynesian economists, who draw a sharp distinction between uncertainty and risk. In their conceptualization, risk remains as above, whereas uncertainty exists when an actor does not know all

41. Knight 1921.
42. For example, Abbott and Snidal 2000, 442.
43. The literature here is extensive. See, for example, Davidson 1991; Vercelli 1995; and Dequech 1997.
44. Beckert 1996, 819.
45. For a good discussion of alternative conceptualizations of probability and the problems of the subjectivist view in particular, see Weatherford 1982.

the possibilities in a situation, cannot assign probabilities to them,[46] or those probabilities do not sum to unity. To distinguish it from the standard view, uncertainty in this heterodox tradition is often qualified with adjectives like "strong," "hard," "genuine," or "structural." It matters for rational action because where there is genuine uncertainty, the clear (if probabilistic) relationship between ends and means breaks down, so that optimal behavior may not be distinguishable from sub-optimal. If optimality is no longer calculable, then what is instrumentally rational is no longer well defined.

This suggests a rival hypothesis about how rational actors should behave. On the orthodox view, actors facing incomplete information should continually adjust their beliefs and strategies in response to changing estimates of the situation. The importance of such updating is reflected in the volume's conjectures about the effects of uncertainty on rational design, namely that institutions should maximize flexibility and individual control. In contrast, Ronald Heiner argues on heterodox grounds that actors facing genuine uncertainty may be better off not trying to optimize, because they are not competent to grasp the true problem and so are prone to make mistakes and have regrets.[47] On his view, in other words, in situations of genuine uncertainty expected-utility theory may actually be a poor guide to "rational" behavior. Instead, actors should do just the opposite of what that theory recommends: follow simple, rigid rules and avoid continually updating expected values. Heiner argues further that most people in the real world understand this, since their behavior is much more stable than would be expected if they were constantly optimizing. Under conditions of genuine uncertainty, it is our willingness to depart from the optimizing standard that is the "origin of predictable behavior."[48] In the context of institutional design, therefore, the rational action may be to minimize flexibility and control rather than to maximize them.

As I indicated earlier, the inferences drawn in the empirical articles about how "uncertainty" should play out concretely seem generally persuasive, and so it is not clear that the heterodox view would lead to different conclusions. Yet some interesting questions remain. In particular, one wonders whether the apparent empirical strength of the volume's treatment of uncertainty is related to the fact that five of its eight articles concern the economic issue-area.[49] One might expect this domain to have relatively weak logics of appropriateness, and so actors will have little incentive to bind themselves to inflexible rules over which they lack individual control. (Even here, states' commitment to the norm of sovereignty may play a role, since freedom of action and national control might be less important under a different norm, like subsidiarity; but be that as it may). However, in issue-areas where logics of appropriateness are stronger, like

---

46. Which may presuppose a nonsubjectivist view of probability.
47. Heiner 1983.
48. Ibid.
49. Of the remainder, one (Mitchell and Keilbach) does not address uncertainty much at all, and another (Kydd) does so in a somewhat idiosyncratic way due to the problem being addressed.

human rights or perhaps the environment, the heterodox view may be a better guide to "rational" design. In the face of (genuine) uncertainty in these domains states may prefer to define rigid criteria of acceptable behavior rather than maintain the conditions for optimizing their individual interests. On this continuum the security issue-area may occupy an interesting middle ground: in some respects a domain of pure rational self-interest where the volume's conjectures should apply, in others one of deep if limited norms, like those embodied in Just War theory and prohibitions on the use of chemical and biological weapons, which seem harder to square with a desire to maintain flexibility and control.[50] In short, the possibility that the meaning of rational behavior under (genuine) uncertainty varies by issue-area seems worth pursuing. And to the extent that this variation is a function of norms, it may make sense to adopt a broader, more sociological view of the origins of institutions under uncertainty, from which the volume's more orthodox treatment would then emerge as a special case.[51]

The Rational Design project has done an important service moving uncertainty to the center of thinking about institutional design, but it takes for granted a conceptualization that may be problematic. Unlike the logic of appropriateness, here the challenge is on the volume's home turf, to the very meaning of rationality. Again, no research project can do everything, and the orthodox treatment of uncertainty here is a valuable first cut. However, addressing the heterodox view would ultimately be valuable as well. First, by distinguishing more sharply between risk and uncertainty it raises the question of how many institutional design problems are characterized merely by "incomplete information" versus deeper, structural uncertainty, which this volume does not consider. And second, if genuine uncertainty turns out often to be present, then how should "rational" institutional design be defined? By relating means to ends according to an ever-changing subjective probability calculus, or by trusting instead in rigid norms, cognitive heuristics, or even Keynes' "animal spirits"?[52] Given the potentially different normative implications, such questions need to be answered if the turn to uncertainty is to be fully realized.

Alternatives to "Design"

In the preceding section I mapped some of the contrast space implied by "rationality" as a determinant of institutional variation. Although there will be some overlap, doing the same for "design" will put the volume in different relief.

To what does the concept of "design" refer? Curiously, little attention is devoted to this question in this volume, or to why this term is being invoked rather than the traditional one of "choice," which served rationalist IR scholarship on institutions in

---

50. On the chemical weapons case, see Price 1995.
51. See Beckert 1996; and Lawson 1993.
52. On animal spirits, see Dow and Dow 1985; and Marchionatti 1999.

the past. The volume's introduction makes clear that earlier scholarship focused on the conditions under which institutions would matter at all, whereas the Rational Design framework takes as given that institutions matter and seeks to explain their features. "Design" does seem more applicable to this concern than the earlier one. But is a new term really necessary? After all, this volume is asking the same kind of question as before (a causal explanatory one), explaining the same kind of object (choices), and using the same theory (rational choice). As such, it seems it could just as easily have billed itself as a study of the rational choice of international institutions. What we are dealing with here, in other words, is an extension of existing rationalist theorizing about institutions, not a wholly new research program. This is not a criticism but an effort to put the project in perspective. As I argue later, a virtue of the term design is that it suggests a broader research agenda than this volume presents. Rational-design theory would be a valuable part of that larger agenda, but only a part.

Thinking about rational design as essentially equivalent to rational choice is also useful for mapping contrasts to the design hypothesis. Intuitively the idea that designs are choices has three implications: (1) designers exist prior to designs, (2) designs are intended, and (3) designers have some freedom of action. Each points to alternative explanations, some rivals to rational-design theory and some with greater causal depth. I take these up in turn.

No designer?   Are institutional designers causes or effects of their designs? On one level the answer must clearly be causes. Institutions do not come out of the blue but are designed by people. However, on another level we can also see the reverse logic at work, with designers being constructed by designs. To that extent, perhaps more is going on in institutional design than the rationalist lens captures.[53] Designers could be constructions of designs in two ways, causally and constitutively.

First, institutional designs today may play a causal feedback role in constructing the actors who make designs tomorrow. This could occur on three levels. As Koremenos, Lipson, and Snidal briefly note, one level would be institutional designs that expand the set of members who make up the subsequent designing actor. In their example of the EU, enlargement choices made in the past affected who is making enlargement choices today, and this will affect who makes choices in the future.[54] A second kind of feedback on actors occurs when institutions affect designers' identities and interests. NATO is a good example: Even if its original design reflected the self-interests of its members, over time they arguably have come to identify with the institution and thus see themselves as a collective identity, valuing NATO as an end in itself rather than just as a means to an end.[55] One wonders whether Morrow's POW regime has had a similar effect, helping to create

53. For further discussion of this idea, see Wendt 1999, chap. 7.
54. Koremenos, Lipson, and Snidal, this volume, 778.
55. See Risse-Kappen 1996; and Williams and Neumann 2000.

a "we" of "civilized" states who even in war feel bound by norms, or whether Thomas Oatley's multilateral trade regime helped create a nascent collective economic identity that made future multilateralism easier to negotiate.[56] And third, institutional designs may affect actors by changing their beliefs about the environment. As Mitchell and Keilbach suggest, through institutional designs actors can acquire more information about uncertain contexts, enabling them to correct misperceptions through a trial-and-error learning process.[57] In each of these feedback effects we are dealing with a traditional causal process, in which X preexists and relates in some mechanical way to Y, but the causal arrows are reversed from those in this volume. Such feedback effects may not be intended at the moment of initial design, but the longer our time horizon, the more likely they will occur. Over time, designs cause designers as much as designers cause designs.

The rationalist approach can also be turned around in a second, more constitutive way by adopting a "performative" model of agency. On this view, associated especially with post-modernism,[58] there is an important sense in which actors do not preexist actions, but rather are instantiated as particular kinds of subjects at the moment of certain performances. To the extent that they are not separable, actors cannot be said to cause institutional designs, but are instead constituted by them.[59] In international politics the institution of sovereignty provides perhaps the most fundamental example. By acting as the members of sovereign states are expected to act—defending their autonomy, privileging their citizens over foreigners, recognizing the rights of other states to do likewise, and, now, engaging in practices of international institutional design—certain groups of individuals constitute themselves as the corporate actors known as "sovereign states," which have particular powers and rights in international politics. The capacity to engage in these sovereignty-constituting practices is taken as given in this volume, but the point is that if groups of people did not engage in them, there would not "be" sovereign states. To that extent it is problematic to assume that a clear temporal or ontological distinction can be drawn between states and their choices. On the performative view, actor and action are mutually constitutive, not independently existing. Each is what it is by virtue of the other. This suggests that the identity of a state lies not in the state itself, as if it were an object, but in the process by which people who would be a state project themselves into that which they are not.[60] Since this process is continuous, state identity is always an ongoing accomplishment, not ontologically given.[61]

Except for the causal feedback effects of action on beliefs, the causal and constitutive effects of actions on actors are not typically addressed in rationalist scholarship. As such, some might see them as rivals to the rationalist assumption

56. Oatley, this volume.
57. Mitchell and Keilbach, this volume, 906.
58. See especially Ashley 1988; Campbell 1998; and Weber 1998. For critical discussion, see Laffey 2000.
59. For discussion of this distinction, see Wendt 1998 and 1999, 77–88.
60. Wolf 1984, 99.
61. Ashley 1988.

that international institutions are created by a designer. However, my own view is that properly construed, rationalism is compatible with these alternative explanations, and therefore the issue is one of causal depth, not rivalry. To defend this assertion here would take me too far afield; suffice it to say that if rational-choice theory is construed as a useful method rather than as a complete ontology for the study of international life, then it is perfectly legitimate to bracket questions of identity-formation, since these are not the questions the theory tries to answer.[62] Taking certain things as given is a pre-condition for any inquiry and thus something we all do all the time. As such, even though they did not themselves develop hypotheses about the construction of institutional designers, Koremenos, Lipson, and Snidal are perfectly right to justify their procedure by saying that what is taken as exogenous in one perspective can and should be endogenized by another.[63]

That said, it is important to be aware of what we are bracketing. Every time states and other actors make choices about international institutions, they are simultaneously making choices about who is empowered, and not empowered, to make such decisions. This ongoing process of constructing modes of subjectivity matters for at least three reasons.

First, it is part of what is "going on" in institutional design, and therefore a complete understanding of the latter must address it. Doing this would enable us to embed the rational explanation within a larger historical process in which institutional designers are themselves at stake in their practices.

Second, institutional design creates and reproduces political power—since in making choices designers are constituting themselves and others as subjects with certain rights—and as such studying the construction of designers by designs matters normatively. Designing a POW regime helps legitimate the right of states to make war and thus kill members of other states; designing a trade regime helps legitimate states' right to protect private property even if this conflicts with justice; and so on. "We" might want states to have those powers, but then again we might not; and our preference may depend on who is included, and excluded, in this "We." Constituting states and their members as the bearers of sovereign rights is an intensely political issue, and so bracketing it in favor of an assumption of given state subjectivity de-politicizes the design of international institutions to that extent. Calling attention to the effects of designs on designers is a way to ensure the power of the latter remains accountable rather than being taken for granted.

Finally, this issue raises questions about rationality. If part of what institutional designers are doing is choosing future designers, how do we assess the rationality of the choices they make today? The Rational Design framework defines rationality relative to a given conception of Self. This is fine for certain purposes, but what do we do if the Self will change as a result of our choices? Do we factor in the preferences of future, as yet nonexisting, designers, and if so, which ones and at

62. Although it may nonetheless have useful things to say about them; see Fearon and Wendt forthcoming.
63. Koremenos, Lipson, and Snidal, this volume, 768.

what discount rate?[64] Attending to alternatives to the assumption that designers are given in design choices would push these important questions to the fore.

No intentionality?   A second assumption implied by the Rational Design framework is that the features of international institutions are chosen intentionally, by a conscious or deliberate process of calculation. At first glance it is hard to see what a plausible alternative to this would be, since human beings are not automatons. As such, there will always be some intentionality in the process by which institutions are created. However, this does not mean we can automatically conclude that institutions are intended. In social theory a long and sometimes fierce battle has been waged by proponents of a rival, "evolutionary" explanation of institutions, especially Friedrich Hayek and his intellectual descendants, against the design approach (which ironically they term "constructivism").[65] The intensity of the resistance stems not only from a theoretical disagreement about what explains institutions but also from the perceived political implications of those explanations. Evolutionists argue that in fact it is very difficult to intend institutions, and that failure to recognize this has led to over-confidence and some of the most catastrophic design failures in history, namely communism and fascism.[66] As an alternative to "constructivism" they favor trusting instead to processes of trial-and-error learning and natural selection, which operate like an "invisible hand" behind the backs of rational actors. The distinction between these two views is not addressed in this volume, and as I will suggest seems to be explicitly effaced in three of the articles.[67]

Proponents of the evolutionary approach do not necessarily deny that people are intentional beings, that we make rational choices, or even that we should tinker with existing institutions. Many would best be described as "rationalists" themselves. Their concern is rather that even though we may be able to modify institutions incrementally to better realize our ends, the limits of human knowledge and cognitive capacity are so profound that we should not think we can intend successful institutions up front. Even the most deliberately created institutions, like the U.S. Constitution, have been amended repeatedly since their founding. Each amendment to the Constitution was certainly intended at the time it was adopted, but in what sense is the result of those changes intended, and who was doing the intending? Perhaps the Founders, whose "original intent" has guided the evolution of the Constitution, and who also consciously created a mechanism for amending it. But it would be odd to say that the Founders "designed" today's Constitution, since they could not have anticipated the changes that have been made; in many respects it is

---

64. For suggestive treatments of these issues, see MacIntosh 1992; and Stewart 1995.

65. No relation to "constructivism" in IR. For introductions to this debate, see Hayek 1973; Ullmann-Margalit 1978; Prisching 1989; Hodgson 1991; and Vanberg 1994.

66. See especially Hayek 1973; and Scott 1998.

67. Koremenos, Lipson, and Snidal, this volume; Mattli, this volume; and Mitchell and Keilbach, this volume.

clearly an unintended consequence of earlier choices. The assumption that institutional designs are intended, therefore, is ambiguous about whether it refers to the discrete changes made at each step of the way, or to the development over time of the overall structure. Intentionality at the local or micro-level is fully compatible with no intentionality at the global or macro-level. The evolutionist worry about "constructivism" is that would-be institutional designers will generalize from local success to confidence in global success. In the absence of a trans-historical designer, such knowledge is well beyond human reach.

Uncertainty is central to the Hayekian argument, and so the Rational Design project's focus on this factor would seem to put it squarely on the evolutionist side of this debate. Yet the introduction and two of the empirical articles make claims that confuse the issue. Specifically, Koremenos, Lipson, and Snidal argue that even institutions that have evolved very incrementally can be explained by the theory of rational design if their rules have periodically been the object of conscious choice.[68] Their example is sovereignty, the features of which today are the result of many changes made intentionally to the original Westphalian rules. Rational-design theory may shed light on some of the micro-level causes of these changes, but do the editors mean to suggest that sovereignty as we know it today was "intended" in 1648, or that all the individual designers of sovereignty since 1648 add up to a single, trans-historical designer? Presumably not, but in that case then the structure of sovereignty today would require an additional, nonintentional explanation. Similarly, Mattli argues that the development of international private arbitration can be explained by an evolutionary process whose outcome is equivalent to what would have been achieved by a direct effort at rational design.[69] That may be true, but how is it evidence for rational-design theory? The latter assumes rational actors; evolutionary arguments, in contrast, require no such assumption. The decentralized, unintended process Mattli describes is precisely what evolutionists see as a rival to design explanations; it is the structure of the evolutionary process, not the choices at each step of the way, that explains the overall outcome. Finally, in response to the criticism that decision makers may not understand the design problem and as such need to figure things out incrementally, Mitchell and Keilbach suggest that a "trial-and-error process of design, though taking longer, is no less rational or purposive."[70] This again seems to conflate the intentionality of micro-decisions with the intentionality of the macro-result.

Perhaps what these authors are getting at goes back to their functionalism: If, over time, actors make intentional changes to an institution such that the overall result is functional, we can say it was "designed." Yet this seems to introduce a new understanding of "functionalism" from the one underpinning this volume. If micro-intention equals macro-intention, we seem to be saying that subjective rationality equals objective (or "trans-historically subjective") rationality. But that cannot be

68. Koremenos, Lipson, and Snidal, this volume, 766.
69. Mattli, this volume, 923–24.
70. Mitchell and Keilbach, this volume, 906.

right. Incremental changes may cause institutions to evolve in an objectively functional way, but that evolution is more a behind-the-backs process than a purposive one, and as such would have to be explained by the structures in which intentional agents are embedded, not their intentions themselves.[71] If we continue with functionalist imagery, therefore, it may be useful to distinguish two variants: "intentional" functionalism, where outcomes are explained by the expected results of intentional action, and "invisible hand" functionalism, where beneficial outcomes are explained by structural features of a system. Rational-design theory as currently formulated would not explain the latter.

In the meantime, it seems important to distinguish more clearly than this volume does between evolutionary and design explanations, for both positive and normative reasons. With respect to the former, if both planned and unplanned institutions are thought to be explained by rational-design theory by virtue of the simple fact that intentional actors are always involved in making institutions, then it is difficult to determine the boundaries of the theory. This risks trivializing part of what is powerful about its approach, namely the assumption of rational intentionality, and makes it difficult to see what would falsify its claims. Differentiating more clearly between local and global design would help us avoid these problems. Keeping the explanations separate is also important for normative reasons. If decision makers believe they are capable of designing successful institutions, they will be more likely to try. That is great if they are right, but if the critics of "constructivism" are right, it would be better to discourage hopes of design and trust more behind-the-back or laissez-faire processes instead. Blurring the distinction between "local" and "global" does not help us to be clear on this choice.[72]

No choice?   Finally, "design" seems to imply that designers have the freedom to act otherwise, that their designs are "choices." To be interesting this needs to be more than just an existential freedom. Assuming free will, human beings always have the trivial ability to "just say no," even if this means they will be shot. The claim needs instead to be that actors have genuine choices to make, especially if we are going to use the aesthetic term design, which suggests a creative expression of inner desire, where the designer could have done things differently but chose not to.

Some philosophers have questioned whether rational-choice theory is compatible with genuine choice, arguing that its model of man is mechanical and deterministic, reducing actors to unthinking cogs in the juggernaut of Reason.[73] If rational choices are dictated by desires and beliefs, then in what sense do we "choose" them? Rather than pursue this argument, however, I will take at face value the assumption that institutional designers make choices, and focus on how they might be prevented

---

71. For good discussions of these issues, see Ullmann-Margalit 1978; and Jackson and Pettit 1992.
72. For a provocative defense of a more laissez-faire approach to international institutions, see Gallarotti 1991.
73. See Wendt 1999, 126, and the references cited there.

from doing so by structural constraints. The potential effects of such constraints are captured by two alternative explanations, path dependency and teleology.

The implications of path dependency for functional theories of institutional design have been explored in detail by Paul Pierson, and so I will not do much more here than refer the reader to his excellent discussion.[74] Especially when institutions are created piecemeal rather than ex nihilo, would-be designers may face a substantial accumulation of existing norms and practices. Such historical structures facilitate elaboration of existing norms through a logic of "increasing returns,"[75] and inhibit adopting norms that would undo them. The causal mechanism here could be a logic of consequences or of appropriateness. Thus some designs might be instrumentally rational in the absence of preexisting structures, but once history has put things in place, they become too costly to adopt. The future of the Anti-Ballistic Missile Treaty might provide an example: even though the Bush administration thinks the treaty is no longer rational and wants to abandon it, the political cost could be prohibitive. Alternatively, actors might really believe in existing norms and so not want to change them even if they should on purely functional grounds. For example, given the already unwieldy character of EU decision making and the desire to enlarge to the east, allowing a country like Luxembourg to retain its vote seems inefficient, yet abolishing it is normatively unthinkable. Whether for consequentialist or normative reasons, therefore, actors may be constrained by existing structures from making ideally rational choices and as such get locked into a path of institutional "design" that effectively takes away their choice in the matter. This volume's empirical articles do a nice job showing why states might rationally choose institutional designs given certain options, but they do not explore how and why those options, and not others, are on the table in the first place.

The path-dependency perspective suggests a second alternative to the assumption of choice: the teleological view that institutional designers are really just working out the details of some "central animating idea."[76] This could be interpreted in two ways. One version is that the evolution of institutional designs is driven in a counter-rational direction by the unfolding logic of foundational normative principles like equality, democracy, or sovereignty. Once such a principle has been accepted as the basis of a system's constitution, the boundaries within which rational choices will be made are fixed. Subsequent institutional developments will in a macro-sense work out of the implications of that normative logic, even if the eventual result might not be efficient. If the EU continues its current (if halting) institutional evolution in the direction of a federal as opposed to unitary state, for example, then in retrospect one could argue that its core commitment to the principle of state sovereignty contained within it the seeds of the outcome (a federal state being more compatible with sovereignty than a unitary one). At the moment of each

74. Pierson 2000b; see also Pierson 2000a.
75. Ibid.
76. This alternative is raised by Robert Goodin. Goodin 1996, 26.

decision in this evolution actors might have the freedom to make choices, but in the end, at the macro-level, the overall result was pre-ordained. This brings us back to the earlier discussions about the relationship between designs and designers, and design versus evolution. If designers are merely implementing the logic of norms, what really is doing the causal work here: agents or structures? If properly developed, this suggestion might constitute a rival to a functionalist explanation.

However, there is another way to spin a teleological explanation that parallels the volume's functionalist approach, suggesting that the two accounts might be compatible. One could imagine a teleological explanation that took as its central animating idea not substantive principles like sovereignty or democracy, but the principle of instrumental rationality itself.[77] Consider the logic of functionalist explanation: institutional features exist because they serve the purposes of their designers. Now, on the surface this volume is committed only to a subjective rationality, which does not guarantee that institutions really will succeed in serving actors' purposes. However, as we saw earlier in the claim that rational-design theory can even explain institutions that evolve by trial and error or natural selection, some contributors seem to want to go farther, to the proposition that institutions are objectively or trans-historically rational. Thus, even if today's institution of sovereignty was not intended by its founders in 1648, as an outcome of rational tinkering in response to problems over the centuries we could say that its evolution was guided teleologically by the requirements of rationality. Interestingly, precisely this kind of reasoning has been used by some contemporary philosophers of biology to try to resurrect a scientifically respectable form of teleology. These scholars argue on functionalist grounds that organisms have the features they do because they were the most fit by natural selection.[78] This yields a hierarchical explanation in which micro-level mechanisms of competition or (in this case) rational choice are governed at the macro-level by deeper causal logics. Since social scientists tend to be deeply skeptical of teleological explanations, it may be that the authors in this volume would not agree with such a reading of their approach. In that case, however, it seems important to make more clear why rational-design theory, especially in its expansive, objective functionalism variant, is not teleological.

In summary, because the Rational Design project does not engage in a dialogue with alternative explanations, it is difficult to assess fully its own explanation of institutional design. To be sure, we can draw some conclusions from its monological approach. The case studies provide substantial evidence that is consistent with its conjectures and some that is not. Both results are suggestive. Moreover, at this early stage of our knowledge about institutional design there is merit to theoretical "protectionism," taking one theory and seeing how far it can be pushed. But because all observation is theory-laden, in the end we can only evaluate theories against other theories. What I have tried to do, therefore, is begin to map this contrast space

---

77. Cf. Meyer et al. 1997; and Boli and Thomas 1999.
78. See, for example, Wright 1976; and Allen, Bekoff, and Lauder 1998.

of alternative explanations, an exercise that also uncovered some areas where the boundaries of rational-design theory do not seem well defined. Whether the "infant industry" of rational-design theory can survive the competition remains to be seen.

Broadening the Science of Institutional Design

Up to this point I have taken as given that the question we are trying to answer about international institutional design is the positive social science one: What explains the choice of designs? In the rest of this article I raise two questions that are not asked in this volume—about institutional effectiveness and normative desirability— and as such my discussion turns more purely external. In doing so I am conscious that problematizing work for not asking the questions the reviewer happens to be interested in is among the lowest forms of this art, since it fails to consider the work on its own terms. Society needs knowledge about lots of things, and even if there are other questions about institutional design we should ask, we should still ask the explanatory question. Nor need the Rational Design project itself have asked these other questions; it had plenty on its plate already. Yet part of what makes the issue of institutional design compelling is that it does raise big questions beyond the explanatory one. These form another kind of contrast space, the mapping of which will help put the project further into perspective. Moreover, as I began to show in previous sections, the answers to these questions may interact with this volume's explanatory agenda. In my view these interactions should be seen not as mere afterthoughts but as central to what a broader science of institutional design might look like.

Let us assume that we want to contribute to institutional design in the real world, to be "policy-relevant." That already implies a substantial commitment to the premise that we can design institutions. Advocates of an evolutionary approach might protest such "constructivism," but let us bracket their concerns and accept that designing institutions is a problem we want to solve. What should social scientists do to make our study of this issue as useful as possible? In short, what should count as "knowledge" about institutional design?

To answer this it is useful to step back and ask, what kind of "problem" is institutional design? What do we need our knowledge for?[79] There is no single answer, but any satisfactory one should recognize first that making institutions is about what we should do in the future. In contrast, explaining institutions is about what we did in the past. By identifying constraints, explanations of the past may provide some insight into the future, but the connection is not straightforward. Consider the implications if rational-design theory were a perfect, 100 percent true explanation of past institutional designs. In that case it would reveal laws of human behavior with which we can predict institutional choices in the future. That kind of

---

79. Cf. Wendt 2001.

knowledge is great for social scientists, but how does it help institutional designers? They do not need a theory to tell them what they are already going to do. Ironically, rational-design theory seems like it would be more policy-relevant if it were false, since then it could be used normatively to persuade decision makers to be more rational next time. A perfect explanation of past designs would be something of a victim of its own success.

From a practical perspective, in other words, it is not clear what the "problem" is to which rational-design theory is the solution. In fairness, this is not unique to this theory: any theory, rationalist or constructivist, that only explains past choices will be of limited value in making future ones. This stems from a basic assumption of positive social science: that the universe is causally closed and deterministic, and so there must be some set of causes or laws that explains why we had to do what we did. To be sure, the complexity of the social world is such that we can rarely know these laws with certainty, and thus our knowledge will usually be probabilistic rather than deterministic. But this is typically viewed as an epistemological constraint, not an ontological one. I suspect few positive social scientists would say that social life is inherently nondeterministic in the way that quantum mechanics suggests micro-physical reality is;[80] probabilistic laws are simply a function of the limits of our knowledge in a complex world. It is hard to see where human freedom and creativity come into such an ontologically closed picture, except in the "error term." In contrast, the basic premise of real-world design is that the future is open, that we have genuine choices to make, that voluntarism rather than determinism rules the day. This openness means that the question of what will happen tomorrow is to a great extent fundamentally normative rather than positive. If we so choose we can still design institutions solely with reference to explanations of the past, of course, but that would be no less normative a choice, since it would simply privilege the values of the past rather than alternative values.

In short, there is an irreducible ontological and epistemological gap between explaining institutions and making them, rooted in their different orientations toward time, and as the locals will tell you if you are lost in Vermont, "you can't get there from here."[81] Interestingly, this gap between backward- and forward-looking thinking is implicit in E. H. Carr's characterization of the difference between "realism" and "utopianism."[82] As is well known, Carr criticized pure utopianism for "ignor[ing] what was and what is in contemplation of what should be," and thus as being too voluntaristic and dangerous.[83] However, Carr's critique was ultimately not of utopianism per se, but of utopianism untempered by an appreciation for constraints. In his view pure realism was also problematic because it was determin-

80. At least on realist interpretations of quantum mechanics; the Copenhagen interpretation takes a more instrumentalist or epistemological view.

81. On the difference between prediction and forecasting, which are rooted in explaining, and "making" as ways of thinking about the future, see Huber 1974.

82. Carr [1939] 1964.

83. Ibid., 11.

istic and sterile, unable to do anything more than reconcile us fatalistically to the evils of the world. As a result, "sound political thought and sound political life will be found only where both have their place."[84] Which one should be emphasized at a given time depends on historical conditions. While sometimes "realism is the necessary corrective to the exuberance of utopianism, ... in other periods utopianism must be invoked to counteract the barrenness of realism."[85] With the Cold War over, the international community can once again contemplate the utopian side of life, and this volume brings welcome rigor to that impulse. Yet the way it has posed its central question seems still caught up in a realist mentality, oriented toward explaining rather than making, determinism rather than voluntarism.

This does not mean that we cannot or should not explain institutional designs.[86] I am not making an argument against social science or historical research. Explaining the past is essential to society's effort to know and transform itself because it teaches us about constraints. Rather, the point is that because of human freedom and creativity, for the purpose of institutional design in the real world the knowledge produced by such explanations is necessarily incomplete. The different temporalities of explaining and making mean there will always be a gap between a science of the past and a policy for the future. If we want to drive forward rather than just see where we have been, therefore, we need kinds of knowledge that go beyond the causes of institutional design, and we need two in particular: knowledge about institutional effectiveness and knowledge about values.

Institutional Effectiveness

Functionalism assumes that actors will choose those institutional designs that they believe will most efficiently serve their interests. As such, the criterion for whether or not an institution is a rational choice is subjective (at the level of the group), namely that it helps them solve their perceived collective-action problem. Whether it is functional in a more objective sense is not directly relevant. This makes sense if all we are trying to do is explain institutional designs, since what matters is how things seem to actors, not how they actually are.

However, institutions are designed to solve problems in the world, and therefore we will also want to know how well they fit or match the reality toward which they are directed. If institutions perform as their designers expected, there is no problem. Functionalism would then correspond to a Dr. Pangloss situation, the best of all possible worlds. But what if designers' expectations turn out later to have missed the mark? What if an institution has unintended negative consequences of sufficient magnitude that had these been known in advance designers would have made different choices? In short, what if design features are not, in fact, functional? In that

---

84. Ibid., 10; emphasis added.
85. Ibid.
86. I defend the possibility and importance of social science in Wendt 1999, chap. 2.

case institutional choices might have been rational in the subjective sense, but in the objective sense, a mistake.

Of course, what is objectively rational can only be known after the fact and so is not fully available to us. However, by studying institutional effectiveness we can gain some relevant foreknowledge. As with the study of the causes of international institutions, the study of their effects had to await the resolution of the 1990s neorealist-neoliberal debate that institutions "mattered" at all. However, there is now a modest but growing literature on this question, in which Oran Young has been a pioneer.[87] Not surprisingly, it has found that some international institutions work well as intended, while others do not. The factors influencing the depth and scope of these failures are many and still only poorly understood.[88] However, given the Rational Design project's subjective view of rationality, one cause of ineffectiveness that I would particularly emphasize is misperceptions of the true design "problem." At the initial stage of the design process opportunities are rife for mistakes: about what the key issue is, who the relevant parties are, cause-effect relationships, even institutional designers' true interests. If understandings of these issues reflect wishful or otherwise faulty thinking, then even if decision makers choose subjectively rational institutions, they will not be effective. As such, the proper constitution of problems is essential to institutional effectiveness and therefore a crucial step in a functionalist approach to institutional design.

Explaining the effectiveness of institutions poses conventional scientific problems that positivists can really sink their teeth into. As such, the study of effectiveness is a "rearview mirror" activity, concerned with the past. At the same time, however, it is also of considerable relevance for making the future. Rather than explaining why we have chosen the road we have taken, which is only indirectly relevant to where we should go from here, the effectiveness problematique can tell us why some choices worked and some did not, which could directly affect the next ones we make.

In particular, understanding institutional effectiveness helps us make the future in at least two ways. One is by enhancing the objective accuracy with which design problems are defined, and the quality of our means-end calculations. Here we can see a partial dependence of making on explaining/predicting: to be successful the former depends in part on being able to do the latter. For example, knowing how well different institutions work might enable us to choose better between what Philip Pettit calls "deviant-centered" and "complier-centered" designs.[89] To that extent such research would nicely complement this volume's agenda.

However, understanding effectiveness could also have a second, more rival impact. What if it turns out that institutions designed according to the criterion of

87. Young 1994 and 1999. A few of the volume's contributors discuss effectiveness, but this is not their primary focus.
88. For a good discussion, see Young 1999, 108–32; also see Pierson 2000b.
89. Pettit 1996.

maximizing expected utility frequently have significant negative unintended consequences, so that the gap between what seems functional and what really is functional is often large? In some of these cases it might still be best to try to maximize expected utility, in the hopes of getting as close to the optimal outcome as we can. But in other cases, according to the "theory of the second best" we might be better off not doing so and adopting some other decision rule instead.[90] If learning that we are often very poor at predicting design outcomes leads us to approach design in a new way, then the effectiveness problematique would not complement the Rational Design project's research program so much as reconstitute its central concept, rationality. Research into the causes of design choices might then be led to ask a new question, Why do states make such irrational choices?

No doubt the contributors to this volume would readily grant that institutional designs can have unintended consequences, and that the study of effectiveness is an important question. However, if we take into account the kind of "making" knowledge that real-world institutional designers need, then study of institutional causes and effects should not be pursued completely separately. From a scientific point of view the two questions are distinct, but from a policy point of view what counts as knowledge about causes should depend in part on knowledge about effects. This is because to constitute usable knowledge, "functionalism" and "rationality" cannot only be subjective things; they need to have an objective component. In those cases where it turns out that subjectively functional designs are not objectively functional, the assumption that decision makers are rational may not be a good guide to making institutions in the future.

Normative Desirability

Perhaps even more important than knowledge about what works is knowledge about what is right and wrong. After all, institutions are created to advance certain values, and so we cannot design anything until we know what values we should pursue. This knowledge is not considered part of social science as conventionally understood, so some might argue that its production should not take place in IR but over in political theory and normative IR. There is something to this; a division of labor between positive and normative theory is often useful. However, with respect to real-world institutional design their separation is problematic. Given the futural and open-ended character of this problem, a science of design will be more useful if it addresses the relationship between positive and normative in a systematic way.

Assuming that the empirical support for this volume's conjectures holds up, how should we evaluate this result normatively? Is it good that the designers of international institutions are "rational?" Not necessarily—that depends on what their designs are for. The possibility that the institutions set up by the Nazis or Imperial Japanese were rational does not mean they should be repeated. However, from the

---

90. On the design implications of the theory of second best, see Goodin 1995; and Coram 1996.

perspective of the Rational Design framework this normative relativity is not a problem because it defines rationality as purely instrumental. Rationality has to do with means, not ends, and as such does not itself have normative content.

The belief that instrumental rationality has no normative content suggests two points. First, note that this belief treats as exogenously settled many of the most important questions about international institutional design, namely about the constitution of ends. (1) Who should be the designer? In most cases states are the designers. Is this a good thing? What about those affected by international institutions? (2) What values should states pursue in their designs? Wealth? Power? Justice? (3) For whom should states pursue these values? Nations? Civilizations? Humanity? (4) What should be their time horizon? Should states care about future generations, and if so at what discount rate? (5) Should institutional designs focus on outcomes or procedures? In sum, what constitutes "the good" in a given situation to which designers should be aspiring? All of these normative questions are intensely political, and their answers will strongly condition how design problems are defined. There are still interesting normative questions left once ends are decided (some distributional questions, for example), but it is hard not to feel that by the time this volume's rational designers begin their deliberations much of the politics is over.

Second, is it so clear that instrumental rationality has no normative content? One way to raise doubts would be to invoke Jurgen Habermas's concept of communicative rationality, which Thomas Risse sees as an alternative both to rationalism's logic of consequences and the logic of appropriateness emphasized by constructivists.[91] According to Habermas, strategic (a form of instrumental) rationality and communicative rationality exhibit different "orientations toward action," the former being oriented toward success, the latter toward achieving consensus or understanding. An important feature of this difference is that implicit within it are different relationships between Self and Other, which in this case could be one designer to another, or to consumers. Instrumental rationality positions the Other as an object to be manipulated in order to realize the interests of the Self. In this case Self and Other position each other as separate individuals, and power and interest will drive their interaction. Communicative rationality, in contrast, positions Self and Other not as distinct objects but as members of the same community, "team,"[92] or "We." In this case power and individual interest do not matter (or as much), and instead deliberation, persuasion, and the force of the better argument take over. To that extent the difference between the two rationalities may seem to be one of process rather than outcome, which the Rational Design framework seeks to bracket.[93] However, it matters here because (1) it suggests that acting in an instrumentally rational way is itself a constitutive choice about who actors are going to be, which

---

91. Risse 2000.
92. On "thinking like a team," see Sugden 1993.
93. Koremenos, Lipson, and Snidal, this volume, 781.

brings us back to the question of performativity discussed earlier,[94] and as such (2) it is a choice that may have normative consequences, distinct from those of the ends that action seeks to realize. In particular, if instrumental rationality instantiates an individualistic view of the Self, then by acting on that basis institutional designers may unintentionally reproduce that mode of subjectivity and thereby make it more difficult to create a genuine sense of community. This, in turn, raises the possibility that instrumental rationality may come into conflict with ends themselves, thereby giving it normative content.[95]

One paragraph obviously cannot even scratch the surface of this complicated issue. Moreover, the jury is still out on whether the distinction between strategic and communicative rationality even holds up; it may be that a broad-minded rationalism can assimilate the latter.[96] But raising the issue seems important because it suggests that part of deciding how to design rational institutions is deciding what it means to be "rational." This volume offers one answer to this question yet seems to lack a sense that there are alternatives, or that its answer might have normative consequences. This kind of naturalization of instrumental rationality is what critical theorists have long worried about in modernity. Perhaps on balance an instrumental definition of rationality is still the best way to go, but that conclusion should only be reached after discussing the alternatives. One that comes out of the work of Friedrich Kratochwil, among others, is the Aristotelian idea of "practical" reason, a broader conception of rationality that goes beyond calculations of efficiency to include normative concerns.[97] It is certainly desirable that institutional designers know how to calculate, but one would also hope they have wisdom, judgment, and an understanding of the good. These are qualities that a rigid separation of positive and normative theory will do little to cultivate.

Conclusion

A complete, policy-relevant science of institutional design will provide knowledge that answers at least three questions: How and why have design choices been made in the past? What works? And what goals should we pursue? The Rational Design project represents an important step toward answering the first. It addresses the second only implicitly, through the functionalist assumption that states will understand subjectively what is objectively rational. About the third this volume is silent.

These questions are analytically separable, and therefore students of one need not necessarily address the others. Indeed, if what we want knowledge for is only to explain institutions, separating positive from normative may be necessary, since this

94. On different design rationalities as constitutive choices, see Dryzek 1996.
95. Cf. Stewart 1995.
96. See Johnson 1991; and Mitzen 2001, chap. 2.
97. Kratochwil 1989. Also see Haslam 1991.

will protect our findings from personal bias. But if the point of seeking knowledge is to make institutions, then positivists and normativists need to talk to each other, because their concerns interact. In the absence of positive theory, normativists are not forced to confront the realities of the international system and the limits of change to those realities. The result can be utopian prescriptions whose failure may have worse consequences than more realistic "second-best" policies. But in the absence of normative theory, positivists can offer little prescriptive guidance of any kind. Positivists will surely agree that just because actors designed institutions one way in the past is no reason for them to do so again in the future. But if inquiry into institutional effectiveness or normative desirability leads us to question either the definition or value of instrumental rationality, we may be led to ask different explanatory questions than are posed in this volume.

One can fairly ask whether a science that combined all three questions would really be a "science." It probably would not be on conventional understandings of that term. However, one lesson I took away from this volume is that, if we are to make social science relevant to the problems of institutional design facing real-world decision makers (and us, their consumers), we need to broaden our conception of social science to integrate positive and normative concerns—to develop a "practical" understanding of social science, in both its everyday and philosophical senses. Different images of a practical social science can be found in work inspired by Aristotle, Dewey, Buchanan, and Habermas.[98] But with the partial exception of Habermas, these traditions have made little impact on IR, which continues not only to maintain a high wall between positive and normative concerns but also to actively marginalize the latter.

One reason for this marginalization is probably the strong influence of positivism on our discipline, but it has received further impetus from the long theoretical dominance of realism.[99] If international politics is condemned to be a realm of eternal conflict, then the future cannot be different from the past, and normative concerns can be dismissed as "fantasy theory."[100] The third question that a practical science of institutional design should answer—What values should we pursue?—does not come up, since we have no value choices to make. The best we can hope to do is survive, and for that all we need is a positive social science, one that looks to the past to guide our journey "back to the future."[101] In such a closed and deterministic universe the idea of institutional "design" is irrelevant.

Yet this volume's premise is that states do design international institutions, that these choices matter, and (presumably) that social scientists should try to

---

98. See Salkever 1991; Cochran 1999; Buchanan 1990; and Linklater 1998, respectively. Given its rationalist basis, the absence of the Buchanan tradition in this volume, as represented in the journal Constitutional Political Economy, is particularly noteworthy.

99. For a classic discussion, see Wight 1966.

100. Schweller 1999.

101. Mearsheimer 1990.

help make them better. As such, its premise is at least implicitly one of voluntarism and an open future, where things do not have to be done as they have in the past. To fully realize the potential of this premise, however, we need to think harder about the nature of the design problem, its differences from our traditional social scientific concern with explanation, and the implications for the kind of knowledge we seek to produce. Driving may be difficult when it is dark outside, but a science that tries to see the road ahead by using only the rearview mirror makes little sense, especially if we are building the road as we go along. The Rational Design project has performed a valuable service for IR by raising such an interesting problem. Having done so, the hope is that it will lead eventually to a more forward-looking, practical social science.

Rational Design: Looking Back to Move Forward

Barbara Koremenos, Charles Lipson, and Duncan Snidal

Why are international institutions organized in such different ways? Some, like the World Trade Organization (WTO) and the World Health Organization, seek very wide memberships. Others, like the Organization for Economic Cooperation and Development and the Group of Eight, are deliberately restricted. Some, like the UN, cover an extremely broad range of issues. Others are narrowly focused, dealing with a single product (Organization of Petroleum Exporting Countries, OPEC) or a single problem (Convention on International Trade in Endangered Species). Some, like the International Monetary Fund (IMF), perform a variety of centralized tasks and even negotiate sensitive economic policies with member states. Others do little more than organize meetings and collate information, as the Asia-Pacific Economic Cooperation forum does for its members. Most institutions allocate votes equally to all members. But a few of the more important institutions—including the IMF, European Union (EU), and UN Security Council—give large members more votes and effective veto power. Some institutions, like the Outer Space Treaty, are built around rigid promises. Others, like the WTO, allow states to alter their obligations when faced with unusual circumstances.

All these institutions address serious problems of international cooperation, but they are designed in very different ways to cope with them. What explains these differences in institutional design? The Rational Design project has one overriding aim: *to make explicit the connections between specific cooperation problems and their institutional solutions.*[1] To transform this broad goal into a workable research

We thank Jeffrey Smith, Marc Trachtenberg, Deborah Larson, Matthew Baum, Stanley Sheinbaum, the anonymous reviewers, and the editors of *IO*, David Lake and Peter Gourevitch.
    1. In the volume's introduction we define *international institution* broadly enough to include treaties but not so broadly as to include tacit bargaining; Koremenos, Lipson, and Snidal, this volume.

International Organization 55, 4, Autumn 2001, pp. 1051–1082

program, we decomposed the idea of "design" into five measurable dimensions where institutions vary markedly:

MEMBERSHIP   Who is included and excluded?
SCOPE   Which issues are covered?
CENTRALIZATION   How centralized are the main tasks?
CONTROL   Who exerts control within the institution?
FLEXIBILITY   How are changing circumstances accommodated?

The contributors to this special issue of IO have used these dimensions in their articles, allowing us to compare and aggregate the findings. To explain variation in institutional designs, we focused on four independent variables often used to explain the success or failure of cooperation: enforcement and distribution problems, the number of actors involved, and several types of uncertainty. We drew on rational-choice theory to develop a series of testable and refutable conjectures that explain the design characteristics of international institutions in terms of these independent variables; we presented these conjectures in the volume's introduction. Subsequent articles evaluated these conjectures in specific areas of military security, the global economy, and the environment. Finally, Alexander Wendt offered an outside response to these efforts. In this article we provide an overview of the results and discuss the research agenda that lies ahead.

The main aim of the Rational Design project was to develop an explanatory framework and begin to test it against available empirical evidence. We asked the contributors of the case studies to evaluate any and all of our conjectures that related to their cases and to introduce other explanatory arguments as they felt necessary. We did not ask them to evaluate our conjectures against competing theoretical explanations (such as those drawn from realism or constructivism). Indeed, we intentionally departed from the perspective adopted by Alexander Wendt that argues for the need to pit theories against one another. While such "three-cornered fights" have their place, they are neither necessary nor desirable.[2] They are unnecessary because conjectures like ours can be tested against empirical evidence without reference to other theories. Our approach is appropriate because our goal is to understand the world, not to win a hollow victory among theories.[3] Moreover, contests among theories tend to exaggerate the antagonisms among approaches while slighting their complementarities. Indeed, much IR research has implicitly endorsed an erroneous presumption that an argument can only be shown to be right by showing that an alternative argument is wrong. This misses the point: all of our

---

2. Van Evera 1997.
3. We had pragmatic reasons for sticking to a "two-cornered" fight between our conjectures and the evidence. First, we did not want to expend the energies of our contributors on "meta-" and "-ology" debates; we asked them instead to focus on what the rational perspective could accomplish. Second, we did not feel competent to present, for example, the constructivist or realist conjectures about institutional design. If they "lost" such a fight, we would be accused of rigging the contest through our incompetence. While we welcome third parties to join this intellectual effort, we argue below that there is more payoff from doing so as allies than as adversaries.

arguments are incomplete and the alternatives may explain different aspects of the same problem. A more constructive approach is to evaluate each theory on its own terms and to take alternatives seriously by asking what they can explain that others cannot. We adopt this strategy here by using other approaches as guides to the deficiencies of our project and, in a speculative manner, asking whether these defects can be remedied within our framework.

Ours is not the only possible rational-choice approach to institutional design.[4] We focus on actors—usually, but not necessarily, states—trying to solve joint problems at the international level.[5] We emphasize particular problems that play a central role in the rational-choice literature, such as uncertainty, free riding, compliance, and distribution struggles. Alternative rationalist approaches might emphasize actors with different motivations—such as maximizing domestic electoral support or providing "rents" to key groups—and focus on different explanatory variables.[6] Moreover, there is substantial literature in IR rational choice that addresses related points regarding how to make actor preferences endogenous, whether to treat institutions in static or dynamic terms, and what level of aggregation to employ, among others.[7] We do not encompass all of these diverse rational-choice approaches; although, again, we speculate whether some of their insights might be used to improve our analysis. Ours is a rational design framework, not the framework.

Within the rubric of rational choice, we have tried to ensure breadth. Some studies are abstract and deductive; others are more detailed and empirical. Some deal with security issues, others with economic or environmental ones. In principle our conjectures should cover all types of international issues and institutions and all types of international actors. The variety of cases included in this volume is a step in that direction.

We begin with an overview of the findings and an assessment of how the Rational Design conjectures fared. We consider the results on each dependent variable and briefly discuss the independent variables. The results are generally positive, although in a few areas they are mixed or inconclusive. We then turn to the broader implications of our findings, concentrating on several topics directly related to

4. We thank an anonymous reviewer for reminding us of this point.
5. The Rational Design approach can include nonstate actors and does not inherently restrict the autonomous capacity of international institutions. Multinational firms and transnational interest groups can and do act at the international level and sometimes shape specific institutions, as Mattli makes clear. The Rational Design approach can include any type of intentional actor. In practice, however, states shape nearly all important international institutions, and for simplicity we sometimes limit our analysis to them. We also recognize that states can deliberately choose to endow international institutions with more autonomous powers to serve their purposes. According to Andrew Moravcsik, the principal members of the EU have done exactly that. Moravcsik 1998.
6. According to the influential work of George Stigler, Mancur Olson, Douglass North, and others, rent seeking is central to the organization of the state and state-society relations. Their insights about domestic politics could be extended to international cartels, including producer organizations like OPEC, and perhaps to a wider range of international institutions.
7. Many of these issues are taken up in Lake and Powell 1999.

institutional design and its systematic study. We first consider the level of formalization. The main issues here are the trade-offs involved in creating fully deductive models. Second, we conclude that "power" needs to be analyzed more fully and explicitly. Our discussion of control is at least a step in that direction. We also raise questions about how domestic politics affects international institutions. Domestic politics is auxiliary to the Rational Design framework, but we have tried to ensure that, when it is invoked, it is not used in ad hoc ways or as an after-the-fact explanation. Finally, we begin a dialog about how and why institutions change, particularly how they respond to changing preferences, external shocks, and other factors.

Empirical Results

The Rational Design project moves us beyond the question of whether institutions promote cooperation to an analysis of how specific institutional features promote cooperation. By providing an analysis of the importance of institutional design, the project also begins to paint a more detailed picture of how institutions do their work. Before we turn to the specifics, however, three general observations about international institutions stand out in our empirical results.

First, centralization is important. It enables actors to manage the different types of uncertainty they face and eases their cooperation problems when numbers are large. However, centralization is not a matter of "strength" or even of formalization. Instead, it reflects the important roles that central actors play in coordination and communication among participants.

Second, membership is important but operates differently than we anticipated. Its impact does not come by operating as a form of exclusion to address the long-standing IR concern for enforcement; instead, its primary impact is through softer (though not less important) roles in providing information and assurance.

Third, flexibility is one of the most important design features of international institutions. It provides a primary way to deal with the pervasive uncertainty in international politics, as well as a means to address distributional issues.

With this overview in mind, we now consider the specific findings on the conjectures and institutional design variables.

Summary of Results

Table 1 brings together the conjectures and the results of the eight case studies presented in this volume. Not every case study was relevant to every conjecture; we asked contributors to focus only on those conjectures their research spoke to most directly, positively or negatively. Indeed, one of the scope conjectures (S1, SCOPE increases with NUMBER) was not addressed by any of the studies. We also asked the contributors to pay particular attention to conjectures where their cases raised negative findings or where the causal mechanisms differed from those discussed

TABLE 1. Summary of results

Conjecture	Mitchell and Keilbach	Mattli	Oatley	Pahre	Richards	Rosendorff and Milner	Kydd	Morrow
M1: Restrictive MEMBERSHIP increases with the severity of the ENFORCEMENT problem	(−)				(−)			−
M2: Restrictive MEMBERSHIP increases with UNCERTAINTY ABOUT PREFERENCES							+	+
M3: MEMBERSHIP increases with the severity of the DISTRIBUTION problem				+	+			(+)
S1: SCOPE increases with NUMBER								
S2: SCOPE increases with the severity of the DISTRIBUTION problem	+				(−)			
S3: SCOPE increases with the severity of the ENFORCEMENT problem	+							
C1: CENTRALIZATION increases with UNCERTAINTY ABOUT BEHAVIOR		+			(−)			+
C2: CENTRALIZATION increases with UNCERTAINTY ABOUT THE STATE OF THE WORLD		+	+		(−)			
C3: CENTRALIZATION increases with NUMBER				+				+
C4: CENTRALIZATION increases with the severity of the ENFORCEMENT problem	(+)	+	+					−
V1: CONTROL decreases with NUMBER					−			
V2: Asymmetry of CONTROL increases with asymmetry of contributors (NUMBER)			(+)					
V3: CONTROL increases with UNCERTAINTY ABOUT THE STATE OF THE WORLD			+		+			
F1: FLEXIBILITY increases with UNCERTAINTY ABOUT THE STATE OF THE WORLD		+	+		+	+		+
F2: FLEXIBILITY increases with the severity of the DISTRIBUTION problem			+		+	+		−
F3: FLEXIBILITY decreases with NUMBER								+

Note: For full statements of the conjectures, see the introductory article.
Key: Conjecture is supported, +; supported weakly or with qualification, (+); not supported with qualification, (−); not supported, −.

under the conjectures. Thus the "silence" of the empty cells in the table does not indicate missing negative evidence but simply that certain elements of institutional design were either irrelevant to, or outside the focus of, the case study.[8]

8. These silences do raise another issue, however: the potential for selection bias. Results from cases where both the independent variable (X) and the dependent institutional variable (Y) are present might be overinterpreted as suggesting a "sufficient" condition that "X leads to Y." But a "silence" indicates that

In general, the results strongly support the Rational Design conjectures. Nearly 70 percent of the findings are strongly positive, and about 11 percent are strongly negative. (The remaining findings leaned one way or the other and often suggested a modification of the framework.) However, the strength of the results varied across institutional design features, so we consider the implications of the findings on different institutional dependent variables in turn. While we are obviously interested in whether the results speak to the Rational Design framework, we are equally interested in the substantive implications of the results.

Membership

While the overall results are positive, the conjectures on membership held a major surprise for our theoretical expectations. Two of the conjectures—M2, restrictive MEMBERSHIP increases with UNCERTAINTY ABOUT PREFERENCES, and M3, MEMBERSHIP increases with DISTRIBUTION problems—were strongly supported in two of the cases, with no significant contrary evidence. But conjecture M1, restrictive MEMBERSHIP increases with ENFORCEMENT problems, was contradicted in all three cases that addressed it.

We had expected membership to play a significant role in enforcement by operating as a mechanism for excluding noncooperators. This emphasis on membership as an exclusion device followed from our reliance on the logic of public goods that has been prominent in IR theory since hegemonic stability theory. On reflection, our failure to find support for this expectation is reinforced by the stylized observation that states are rarely expelled from international institutional arrangements. This renders enforcement through membership largely irrelevant since deviators are apparently rarely punished in this way.

Instead, the case studies found somewhat different membership mechanisms at play. Ronald Mitchell and Patricia Keilbach find that restricting membership will not help solve the enforcement problem in situations of asymmetric externalities because it misses the whole point of inducing perpetrators to join. If German industry is dumping chemicals in the Ruhr River and the Dutch are suffering downstream, keeping Germany out of any institutional solution hardly solves the problem. Andrew Kydd shows how membership operates as both an informational and an assurance device. Membership criteria not only provide useful signals for selecting good alliance partners but also have a significant impact on levels of trust with third party states. Finally, the support in James Morrow's study for conjecture M3, inclusive MEMBERSHIP increases with the severity of the DISTRIBUTION problem,

X can be present without Y necessarily occurring, so the "sufficiency" claim would be wrong. Ideally, we need to compare across cases to understand what other factors determine when X has the hypothesized effect Y, and when it does not. Although we are not aware of any situations where this problem arises, any interpretation of these results needs to be appropriately bounded in this way. Even with silences, however, a preponderance of positive findings still tells us that a factor does influence institutional design under some circumstances.

requires modification of the argument. Inclusive membership solves the distribution problem in prisoners of war (POW) treaties not by increasing possible trade-offs among a larger number of states but by signaling states' agreement to a set of rules and standards, the heart of the distribution problem. What we have learned from these proposed modifications is that sometimes there are alternative logics of institutional design and that it is essential to pay attention to the details of empirical cases.

These revisions highlight both opportunity and danger for the Rational Design approach. The opportunity is that this approach can handle a wide range of problems and we need not restrict ourselves to public goods or any other model. Reformulating the framework allows it to capture different contexts and nuances and lets empirical anomalies set the stage for progressive theoretical development. The danger, well understood by critics of rational choice, is that models will be modified to fit the data. Our response is to acknowledge the hazards (which are not unique to rational choice) and to emphasize that such "findings" need to be treated more in an exploratory mode than in a confirmatory mode. If the revised conjecture fits across multiple cases, however, we would then argue that it is beginning to acquire significant empirical support.[9]

Finally, since membership questions have been central to discussion in international political economy of multilateralism versus bilateralism and globalism versus regionalism, the relative paucity of findings in the political economy articles is surprising. Instead of being a disapproving silence, however, it reflects the contributors' focus on different design problems. Consider the two articles that do not discuss membership at all. Walter Mattli is concerned with why private actors choose one arbitration forum over another. Limitations on who participates are simply not relevant design features in his analysis. The same is true for Peter Rosendorff and Helen Milner as they develop a two-actor model to examine escape clauses. But to extend their model to larger numbers might require supplementary design features, including membership restrictions. How serious is the noise problem when larger numbers are using escape clauses? How credible are enforcement strategies in large groupings? In other words, would the institutional arrangements be renegotiation proof? The logic of Rosendorff and Milner's model agrees with our membership conjectures, but these findings still need to be worked out in detail.

---

9. Finally, we stress that the Rational Design conjectures were not retrofitted to the findings. We developed the framework before the case studies began. We subsequently refined our terminology, dropped one conjecture where we found its derivation poorly grounded, and dropped another where we found its logic to be identical to one of our other conjectures. Otherwise the conjectures were all derived before the evaluations. The conjecture we dropped on theoretical grounds dealt with the effects of distribution on centralization and had weak empirical support. The other addressed the effect of distribution on control and had strong empirical support. Dropping these conjectures does not affect the overall results.

Scope

The findings strongly support conjecture S2, SCOPE increases with DISTRIBUTION problems, and conjecture S3, SCOPE increases with ENFORCEMENT problems. In their detailed and thorough environmental study, Mitchell and Keilbach find very strong support for these two conjectures. Furthermore, they offer significant extensions of these conjectures by incorporating the impact of symmetry and asymmetry into the analysis and by differentiating positive and negative linkage. For example, when some states pollute and others suffer the consequences, it is impossible to win general agreement for institutions that rely heavily on sanctions. Polluters know that such arrangements will inevitably sanction them and provide few countervailing benefits. Not surprisingly, they try to block them or refuse to join. However, downstream states have an alternative. They can provide side payments to polluters for curbing their ways. This approach has problems of its own—it is rife with collective-action problems and perhaps adverse selection—but it does promise gains for both sides. The actors' heterogeneity leads to a particular institutional design, one that widens issue scope by rewarding good behavior. This potentially opens up wider questions regarding interesting ways to consider facets of "power" within the Rational Design framework. However, though these results confirm the conjectures, they do not resolve questions about generalizability beyond the specific case.

We list John Richards' finding regarding scope in the aviation issue as a qualified "negative," although it could be read either way. He argues that the scope of the Bermuda aviation institutions was determined by states' need to encompass all aspects of aviation competition. This accomplished, aviation already includes what Richards labels extensive "within issue-area" scope, so further external linkage is unnecessary. This recalls the long-standing problem in IR theory of dealing with issue linkage: the definition of issue-areas is itself endogenous.

Centralization

The centralization conjectures received extremely strong support, which draws attention to our conceptualization of centralization. We do not equate centralization with "formal" international organizations. Organizations with headquarters may simply be meeting forums for states that may not delegate anything at all. The International Labor Organization seems to fit this description: In one sense, it is a highly formalized institution, but with respect to substantive tasks performed, it is characterized by relatively low levels of centralization.

The negative findings, though relatively few, provide clues for how to broaden our understanding of centralization. Two of the negative findings come from Richards' analysis of international aviation markets. He argues that these findings are due to an unusual design interaction between centralization and control. Part of the problem in this case study lies in the difficulty of determining empirically whether the Bermuda institutions are centralized. For example, most important decisions—such as routes, entry/exit, and number of passengers—were set by the bilateral agreements and therefore were not centralized. But the International Air Transport Association (IATA) did have centralized fare-setting ability. In particular, the IATA required that all countries unanimously set fares on major routes (both within and between regions), and fares for all smaller routes were based on the agreed price of the major routes. The IATA also added limited centralized monitoring and enforcement in the form of fare inspectors who monitored compliance with agreed-upon fares and issued fines for noncompliance. Despite these centralized mechanisms, Richards argues that the Bermuda institutions substitute control for centralization to overcome problems of uncertainty.

The other negative result is Morrow's finding on conjecture C4, CENTRALIZATION increases with ENFORCEMENT problems. In this case, the source of the enforcement problem lies in the two-level domestic problem between a state and its soldiers. Because the rules for handling POWs must be implemented on the battlefield, national authorities must be able to monitor and restrain their soldiers on the field. Again, Morrow uses an alternative rationalist logic—one that focuses on domestic actors rather than states as the key actors.

Mattli provides confirming evidence for three of the conjectures. For example, he conceives of centralization as an institutional arrangement that coordinates the interaction of two actors, sets procedures, collects information, and serves as the final arbiter. These roles make centralization very useful for resolving both enforcement and uncertainty problems. Enforcement problems arise when firms are no longer going to interact with each other—that is, there is no shadow of the future. Mattli argues that a centralized institution provides procedural safeguards and monitoring to overcome defection problems (conjecture C4). Uncertainty about the state of the world poses another major problem aggravated by the fact that companies are from different areas and their principals often speak different languages. Institutionalized arbitration procedures reduce uncertainty about what rules apply and increase understanding of those rules (conjecture C2, CENTRALIZATION increases with UNCERTAINTY ABOUT THE STATE OF THE WORLD).

One interesting finding revolves around centralization and states' reluctance to delegate power to an international organization. There are two positive findings for conjecture C4, CENTRALIZATION increases with the severity of the ENFORCEMENT problem. However, in neither case are states delegating to an international organization as the focal actor. Mattli's case involves private firms, not states. For Thomas Oatley, the focal actor is essentially the United States. Having a powerful state rather than an international organization play the role of the focal actor is also common in treaty guarantees. Consider the role of the United States in Middle East peace accords.

It is also important to note that centralization of one function does not necessarily serve as a platform for further centralization. Robert Pahre's treatment of "clustered negotiations" in nineteenth-century trade is a good example. Similarly, in the postwar trade regime, bargaining in the General Agreement on Tariffs and Trade (GATT) was clustered, or centralized, for decades before the partners decided to create a more comprehensive institution with dispute panels, a larger staff, and some agenda-setting powers. In the case of POWs, as Morrow shows, states never sought to move beyond multilateral bargaining and the establishment of common rules.

Because our conception of centralization is very broad, an important avenue of inquiry will be to refine this concept into its different components. Centralized tasks may be as mundane as organizing meetings and assembling information provided by member states. But states may also delegate "stronger" centralized tasks, which range from intrusive monitoring to the orchestration of international enforcement. This finer differentiation of tasks is only implicit in our conjectures, and its analysis begs a series of important empirical and theoretical questions.

Finally, contrary to the common presumption that centralized institutions are more effective, more centralization is not always better. States design international institutions to meet specific needs, and decentralized arrangements often serve this purpose more effectively.

Control

The findings on control, though mainly positive, are sparse, so we do not claim too much for them. The two positive findings on conjecture V3, CONTROL increases with UNCERTAINTY ABOUT THE STATE OF THE WORLD, reinforce our general finding that international institutions are important in managing uncertainty—a point we return to later. Oatley's case provides modest support for conjecture V2, asymmetry of CONTROL increases with asymmetry of contributors (NUMBER). The decision-making rule of the European Payments Union (EPU) reflects a compromise between U.S. and European interests. As the source of hard currency, the United States wanted the EPU to exercise substantial control over European governments' macroeconomic policies. The United States established majority rule decision making in the EPU's managing board and wielded additional influence through U.S.-sponsored conditional aid programs. European members, however, had concerns about distribution and uncertainty. These concerns were accommodated by circumscribing the managing board's authority and by providing each European government with a veto over the managing board's decisions in the Organization for European Economic Cooperation. The EPU example illustrates another common feature of control rules: They may need to be quite complex to balance the competing needs of different members.

The one negative result, that states did not give up individual control as numbers increased in the aviation regime, reflects the very high sovereignty costs involved in air transportation during that period for both symbolic and security purposes.

Flexibility

The conjectures on flexibility are very strongly supported. This is gratifying because flexibility as a dimension of institutionalization has not been studied extensively. Our results show that it is a pervasive and important feature of international institutional design—and that the rational approach appears to provide significant insights into it.

If anything, the empirical elaborations show that flexibility is even more important than we anticipated theoretically. Oatley's analysis of European trade and payments after World War II, Richards' analysis of the IATA, and Rosendorff and Milner's analysis of trade agreements all illustrate how flexibility can be designed to permit adjustment within existing institutional arrangements. Provisions in each case allow actors to respond to unanticipated changes in economic circumstances without dismantling the institution. Incorporating such provisions insulates the institutions from shocks that could otherwise threaten their existence.

Flexibility can also be important if actors learn over time about new technologies and tasks. With respect to arbitration rules in rapidly changing industries, Mattli argues that "firms operating at the forefront of new production and exchange methods are likely to prefer a flexible form of dispute resolution."

Importantly, the contributors suggest an expanded definition of flexibility. Oatley argues for one where the rules themselves allow some slack in what would otherwise be a binding constraint. Oatley deals with trade and money, but Morrow reaches similar conclusions about POW rules. His argument is very similar to recent attention given to "soft law" mechanisms that allow states to gain many of the advantages of legalization without being too tightly bound by them.[10] Because the treatment of POWs is so difficult to assess, and responsibility for violations so hard to pin down, some flexibility is essential to avoid mistaken punishments. Flexibility, in other words, helps actors deal with "noise" in the system.[11] If every perceived violation (including nonexistent ones) triggered a response, tit-for-tat feuds would be constant. Rational actors, well aware of the problems arising from erroneous sanctions, have good reasons to design a system with some flexibility.[12] Morrow's analysis suggests an intriguing relationship between flexibility and uncertainty about behavior, a relationship we did not examine in the volume's introduction.

Moreover, while we coded Morrow's finding regarding the relationship between flexibility and distribution (conjecture F2) as negative, it is worth noting that he does indeed uncover some flexibility in the POW treaties that helps solve the distribution problem as he defines it. Importantly, states can file reservations to the treaty at the time of ratification. And, as Morrow states, "they can also make clarifying statements about how they interpret parts of the treaty or object to the membership of another state in the treaty at the time of ratification." Reservations and clarifying statements are forms of flexibility that were not discussed theoretically in the introduction.

10. Abbott and Snidal 2000.
11. Morrow defines noise as "the inability to determine exactly what happened and so to determine precisely the other side's responsibility for the event."
12. The rationale for this kind of flexibility can be found in Downs and Rocke 1990; they argue that in the face of uncertainty about behavior the optimal strategies are often those that specify thresholds that trigger retaliation.

Wendt's comments about flexibility go to the root of the friendly debate in which he engages the Rational Design approach. He proposes that in certain issue-areas, such as human rights or perhaps the environment, "logics of appropriateness" dominate so that states will prefer rigid criteria to govern their behavior.[13] In support, Wendt notes that "there is no exemption for mass murder in the human rights regime."[14] While that particular dramatic example is certainly true, human rights agreements in general are actually much more likely than economic agreements to incorporate escape clauses (24 percent versus 5.4 percent).[15] Thus the preliminary evidence suggests that our hypotheses will also apply to the human rights area.

Still, while we are heartened by the results regarding flexibility, Mitchell and Keilbach are wise to point out that rigidity has benefits as well, which the conjectures on flexibility fail to address. As they argue, states "will eschew such flexibility and accept more binding, specific rules if, as in asymmetric externalities, each side's institutional benefits depend critically on the other side's carrying out the exact terms of the agreed-upon exchange."

Design Alternatives

Design alternatives are important from both a theoretical and an empirical point of view. According to the conjectures, for example, distribution problems can be addressed by membership, scope, and flexibility. Theoretically, we do not offer any arguments that explain when one approach would be used in place of another or when different design combinations might be chosen. It is quite possible that substitutability among the design alternatives weakens our empirical results. For example, if we find evidence for one conjecture (such as C3, CENTRALIZATION increases with NUMBER), we cannot assume that another conjecture addressing the same problem (such as S1, SCOPE increases with NUMBER) would necessarily hold. The (hypothetical) choice of centralization over scope may reflect the differential costs of the alternative design solutions, or it could be the result of reserving scope to address some other problems such as distribution.

Generalizing about design interactions is difficult. Richards finds that states did not create centralized institutions in response to the uncertainty about the state of the world prevalent in aviation markets (conjecture C2). Instead, they relied on strong control mechanisms (conjecture V3). Richards is silent on conjecture C2 because V3 was used to solve the problem. Morrow, however, finds negative results for both conjecture M1, restrictive MEMBERSHIP increases with ENFORCEMENT problems, and

---

13. Wendt, this volume, 1028.
14. Ibid.
15. See Koremenos 2000, which analyzes a random sample of 149 international agreements. Similar results on the flexibility of human rights agreements also emerge when we look at renegotiation provisions, withdrawal clauses, and amendment provisions.

conjecture C4, CENTRALIZATION increases with ENFORCEMENT problems. Since both conjectures address enforcement problems, the logic of substitutability does not seem to be at play.[16]

Independent Variables

Although our primary interest is with the dependent variables of institutional design, some of the "findings" regarding the importance of different independent variables may also provide guidance for future research. Two of the "traditional" explanatory variables in IR—enforcement and number—play only relatively modest roles in the cases. Number appears in only five "tests" of a conjecture in the various cases, although four of those are "confirmations"; enforcement appears eight times, but in half of those cases the conjecture is disconfirmed. By contrast, distribution appears in nine tests, of which seven are confirmations. This provides strong support for the recent movement to bring distributional considerations to the foreground of international relations analysis.

Even more striking is that uncertainty, in its various forms, plays a major role across the conjectures. It appears in fourteen different tests, of which thirteen are confirmations. To be sure, this could be the result of our special interest in uncertainty as a variable leading us to develop more conjectures based on it. Uncertainty has always been central to the study of international politics, especially research guided by recent innovations in game theoretic models. It is instructive to see what role it can play in explaining institutional design and how well those results explain crucial institutional features. This success shows that abstract models can have a significant empirical payoff when translated properly.

Drawing on models also forced us to separate enforcement and uncertainty as independent variables. Our definition of an enforcement problem is therefore quite narrow: given the strategic structure of the cooperation problems, are there incentives for actors to cheat that impede the ability of repeated play to support cooperation? Our analytic choice yielded some important insights. Whereas IR scholarship has tended to clump many things under the rubric of "enforcement problems," our results show that many of these are more precisely characterized as problems of uncertainty. When we do not know what state X is doing, we fear it might be cheating; when we do not know state X's preferences, we fear that it prefers to cheat. Institutions are useful in ameliorating the "enforcement" problems caused by uncertainty, but to solve the enforcement problems as we define them requires changing incentives or even preferences. In no case do we find the latter; Mitchell and Keilbach provide one example of the former.

---

16. An additional problem arises because we do not present an exhaustive set of conjectures. Nor, as we state in the introduction, do the ones presented all flow from one carefully-specified model.

Two broader implications of our definition of uncertainty should be noted. First, we differentiated among types of uncertainty—about preferences, about behavior, and about the state of the world—and showed how a clearer specification of uncertainty is important for developing claims about specific institutional features. In general, whether specificity is achieved through more detailed "verbal" interpretations or through formal derivations, it is essential for the fine-grained institutional approach we advocate.

Second, Wendt correctly points out that we use the conventional conception of uncertainty as equivalent to risk (that is, a probability distribution over known outcomes). This does not address broader conceptions of uncertainty as the truly unknown, where the possible outcomes cannot be enumerated or their probabilities are unknown. The criticism is valid and reflects our decision to focus on dimensions of institutionalization where we could draw most productively on existing rational-choice theory. Although we recognize the danger of letting our analysis be defined in terms of available methodological tools, it would be a greater mistake to let problems we currently cannot solve prevent us from tackling ones we can.

Our more restricted view of uncertainty also makes substantive sense insofar as states do not create extensive institutions in the dark. Indeed, a key aspect of negotiating agreements is replacing uncertainty with shared understandings (or common knowledge) of the problem at hand. For example, the first years of negotiations about global warming centered on achieving such commonality, and institutional progress is closely tied to success on that front. Some aspects of the process of converging to common knowledge may lie outside rational choice, which suggests important complementarities with constructivist and other ideational approaches. How to handle these broader forms of uncertainty is an area of active research both among game theorists and among proponents of alternative decision-making models.[17]

Broader Implications

Level of Formalization

The Rational Design approach has been criticized as both "not formal enough" (by those committed to fully deductive models based on axioms) and "too abstract and formal" (by those who see the rationalist approach as yielding too few concrete, empirically relevant results). Although these complaints are contradictory, we believe each arises for good reasons that should be taken into account.

---

17. Fearon and Wendt point out that parallel critiques of rational choice in terms of bounded rationality (such as Simon's) have since been significantly clarified and narrowed by subsequent work on incomplete information games. See Fearon and Wendt 2001; and Simon 1957. Ongoing game-theoretic work in the evolutionary tradition is exploring the implications of limits to rationality—including ignorance about possible outcomes. Fudenberg and Levine 1998; and Rubinstein 1998.

A comprehensive and precise set of conjectures, formally derived from axioms, is an attractive if rarely achieved goal across the social sciences. Unfortunately, such general models of international institutions are well beyond the reach of current IR scholarship.[18] Our initial conjectures were guided by tightly derived models. But those tended to be partial models of fairly specific circumstances that we had to adapt in a looser fashion to "derive" more general predictions about international institutions. To meet higher standards of rigor, the authors of the formal articles in this volume had to carefully limit their subject matter and remain at a somewhat abstract level. These articles illustrate the possibilities for deepening the larger program of rational institutional design not by building a comprehensive, general theory but by tailoring specific yet connected theories within the larger Rational Design framework. Efforts to bring in domestic politics (discussed later) illustrate the possibilities for expanding our analysis by building on other rational approaches to institutional design; they also show the limitations of formal approaches.

Although a single deductive model is a bridge too far, we hope we have shown how progress can be made with a systematic but less strictly formal approach to the same questions. Our goal was to lay out a consistent and quite general analytic framework and then to derive, by reference to formally established results, a set of conjectures that could be tested against the observed range of institutional design. In doing so, we took seriously the often repeated (and sometimes accurate) charges that rational-choice approaches lack empirical content, have little new to say, and fail to illuminate real-world political processes and outcomes.[19] Our results show, however, that these shortcomings are not inherent to the rational-choice analysis of institutional design.

On the empirical side, we have already discussed the significant findings that came out of the project. While the case studies could surely have been completed without the Rational Design framework, it offered important guidance for the individual articles and, more importantly, provides a systematic way to bring the empirical results together. It enables us to make comparisons across the cases, to see what holds and what does not, and to understand what needs to be modified according to the particular circumstances of individual cases. The results further show that rational-choice empirics need not be ad hoc. The conjectures themselves were clearly falsifiable, and some were shown not to have much support. Proposed modifications to the theory were offered in the spirit of refining and improving its explanatory power, not to armor it against empirical disconfirmation. On the theoretical side, the conjectures are deeply indebted to existing models, and several articles show how the conjectures can be developed further through formal analysis. Rosendorff and Milner's analysis of escape clauses in trade agreements elaborates one of the conjectures on flexibility (F1, FLEXIBILITY increases with UNCERTAINTY ABOUT THE STATE OF THE WORLD) and shows how it can be derived in a somewhat

18. Shubik makes an almost identical argument regarding the application of game theory to explain economic activity. Shubik 1982.
19. Walt 1999.

different way. Their focus on a different type of uncertainty (about domestic politics) shows that the conjectures are more generalizable even as they provide additional depth on the mechanisms underlying the conjecture. This is a good example of how the abstraction of models can bring together different substantive arguments. It also represents a significant "deepening" of the theory by drawing on other rationalist accounts.

Likewise, Kydd's model begins with the basic insight that, in organizations like NATO, membership criteria serve as costly signals to filter out states uncommitted to cooperation. He examines what happens when a nonmember country sees the group as a potentially hostile alliance. This addresses the important policy debate about whether some countries—particularly those once part of the Soviet Union—should not be included in NATO because of the provocative effects on Russia. The formal analysis shows that the more restrictive the membership criteria are, the less provocative expansion is to the outside power. If the criteria are restrictive enough, expansion may actually be reassuring by signaling that the alliance is not expanding as much as it would if it had truly aggressive designs on the outside power. Thus the formal analysis takes us beyond the conventional wisdom to illuminate possibilities not commonly discussed in the policy debate over NATO enlargement.

Several of the empirically oriented articles provide useful feedback on how the framework could be modified to better explain the international experience. Mitchell and Keilbach expand the conceptual basis of scope by differentiating positive versus negative linkages and by considering the existence of asymmetries in externalities. Pahre introduces the notion of clustering as a specific type of centralization that is particularly associated with "most favored nation" status and increases with number of actors. These studies illustrate how a combination of theoretical and empirical results can provide valuable guidance for subsequent theoretical work in the Rational Design framework.

It might seem odd that our "case studies" include two articles that are primarily formal exercises working out the logic of Rational Design-style conjectures in different settings (those by Kydd and by Rosendorff and Milner). Pahre develops a formal analysis as a prelude to a statistical analysis. Yet the inclusion of even purely formal articles is natural for two reasons. First, the conjectures we offered in the introduction represent a beginning (or a continuation) of work in bringing the rational-choice approach to bear on the design of international institutions. As should now be clear, the rational-choice theory applicable to institutional design is rich and complex; to pretend to capture all of the theory's implications even in our large set of conjectures would be hubris on our part. Moreover, as both the empirical and theoretical case studies show, contextual variation matters greatly in determining the design of institutions. The analytic articles represent a first step in showing how the logic of rational design works itself out differently according to these variations.

Second, and perhaps more surprising to some readers, the analytic articles actually contain significant empirical content. Each models a specific problem that has been identified empirically as well as theoretically. Each begins with what are sometimes called "stylized facts," which are widely used by modeling practitioners but often disparaged by empiricists.[20] But good stylized facts have a great deal of empirical content. As a summary, they are not unlike a regression line that conveys the general tendency in a set of data even though it need not pass through (and thus characterize with strict accuracy) any of the individual data points. While they do not capture the details of any single case, such stylized summaries often convey more general information about the set of cases than can any subset of cases. Insofar as models bring together important stylized facts, they provide a possible explanation with significant empirical content. Of course, these are not disconfirming tests in any way, but as guides to the development of better theoretical understandings they bring along substantially more empirical content than is often recognized.[21]

Finally, critics will raise concerns about fitting theory to cases. Those who actually build models will have fewer concerns on this count simply because they know how difficult it is to construct a reasonable model that fits any potential observation. If it were possible, the same would be even truer of verbal theory, since in principle verbal theory subsumes formal theory and much more. Moreover, the explicitness of the assumptions in formal analysis opens it to scrutiny, which makes it easier to weed out implausible assumptions and errors in logic. In fact, by bringing together a wide range of conjectures, the Rational Design framework imposes stronger consistency requirements across different analyses. For example, if different conjectures conflict, the differences must be justified and explained in terms of underlying assumptions.

Power

The fundamental realist critique, beyond its general skepticism of the importance of international institutions, is that institutionalist analyses neglect power.[22] We did not emphasize power in the development of our conjectures because the formal literature does not offer compelling results.[23] However, our conjectures on control do address power relationships within institutions and accord roughly with realist intuitions (in particular, conjecture V2, asymmetry of CONTROL increases with asymmetry of contributors (NUMBER), and to some extent conjecture V3, CONTROL increases with UNCERTAINTY ABOUT THE STATE OF THE WORLD). While we found it

20. A stylized fact is a summary statement of a circumstance or relationship that is observed across a wide range of situations and is taken either as an input into a modeling exercise or as something to be explained through it.

21. Pahre (pers. comm. with Koremenos and Snidal) offers the interesting observation that the more formal articles address only one or two of the conjectures, whereas the nonformal articles address between four and nine conjectures. This reflects the power of formal research in exploring the logic of a particular conjecture and the power of empirical cases in examining evidence on multiple conjectures within a case.

22. Mearsheimer 1994/95.

23. Power is notoriously difficult to conceptualize and theorize—both in the traditional and in the formal literature. An example of the latter is the attempt to treat patience (that is, a low discount rate) as a proxy for power in bargaining models, which we find unpersuasive from a substantive perspective.

surprising that the empirical support for these conjectures is limited, these conjectures nevertheless demonstrate the possibility of incorporating such considerations within the Rational Design framework.

Two articles illustrate alternative ways to bring power into the existing framework. Mitchell and Keilbach's refinement of the scope variable with respect to asymmetric externalities allows a natural extension to power. If the victim is less powerful than the perpetrator, coercion is precluded; hence rewards must be used. If the victim is more powerful, we would expect coercion to be used since it is less costly from the victim's point of view. Their Rhine River pollution example is consistent with this: The weaker victim state, the Netherlands, had to compensate the more powerful perpetrator state, France. Importantly, this analysis can be extended beyond the environmental realm to the security realm, where realists argue that power is most influential. Consider the asymmetric externalities between the United States and North Korea over the latter's "pollution" of the existing nonproliferation system.[24] In this case, the perpetrator is clearly the weaker state; hence, while both rewards and coercion would in principle be possible, we would expect to see coercion. Ultimately, the United States rewarded North Korea with the transfer of light-water reactors. Although this may seem surprising at first glance, closer analysis of the case explains this design choice. North Korea's near autarchy means it is not very vulnerable to coercive tactics such as economic sanctions. As Mitchell and Keilbach argue, "A state's power is thus relational and issue specific, dependent on . . . how vulnerable and sensitive other countries are to the resources it controls."[25] This points out the difficulty of operationalizing power as an explanatory variable.

Power may also play an important role in political economy cases, as Oatley shows with respect to the role of U.S. power in directly affecting the design of the European payments system. Alternatively, power might serve as an intervening variable. For example, during the Bretton Woods negotiations, the U.S. executive used its negotiating power to limit the maximum contribution to the IMF to what Congress would be willing to authorize, thereby ensuring that no other state would have greater control, given weighted voting.[26] This illustrates conjecture V2, asymmetry of CONTROL increases with asymmetry of contributors (NUMBER), that is, power, although the logic is slightly different from what we suggested in the framing article.

Thus nothing in the Rational Design framework precludes power from being incorporated as an additional independent variable. We would expect it to improve our understanding of important dimensions of institutions, especially but not only with respect to security issues. For example, membership decisions during the Cold War were heavily informed by the tight control held by Western powers, which preferred to keep the Communist states out of many international economic

---

24. This example is from Kim 1999.
25. Mitchell and Keilbach, this volume, 898.
26. This example draws on Wheelbarger 1999.

institutions for larger political and ideological reasons. Hence, although we did not emphasize realist power considerations in our framework, we view them as highly compatible with it, especially given that the basic logic of the realist perspective is rational. Thus we do not see the Rational Design project as resolving any of the so-called debates between neoliberal and realist perspectives. Instead, the framework provides an analytical way to bring together their different substantive presumptions in order to evaluate them empirically.

An alternative critique by those who emphasize power considerations is that power interacts in a complex way with other explanatory variables and its inclusion may thereby undermine the entire framework.[27] A simple way to think about the omission of power as an independent variable is through the statistical theory of omitted variables. Omitting an independent variable may bias the estimated impact of the remaining independent variables. But this bias arises only if the included variables are correlated with the omitted one.

In our framework, it is not at all clear that power should be correlated with our independent variables: number, the severity of the distribution problem, the severity of the enforcement problem, and the three kinds of uncertainty. For example, consider the three kinds of uncertainty. State of the world uncertainty tends to be a characteristic of technology or of the natural environment (such as the state of the world when negotiating about global warming) and hence not likely to be correlated with power. With respect to uncertainty about preferences or behavior, perhaps it could be argued that powerful states are better able to conceal information. Yet we also observe today that the most powerful state, the United States, is one of the most transparent. Hence, there is no reason to think that these independent variables would be correlated one way or another.

In any event, this is an issue appropriately addressed by empirical researchers seeking to apply our framework on a case-by-case basis. Our theoretical framework proceeds when all other factors, such as power, are being held constant.

Finally, the explanatory leverage of power may come into play in the substantive terms of the cooperative deal,[28] in other words, "who gets what."[29] Moreover, the goals of the institutions themselves may be affected by the powerful states. Given that we focus on institutions that are created, there may be a nontrivial selection bias operating here.

Domestic Politics

Our framework does not explicitly include—or exclude—domestic politics. The contributors were free to incorporate domestic political considerations to whatever

27. We thank an anonymous reviewer for bringing up this point.
28. This is not meant to denigrate our focus on design. Quite the contrary, design matters if the substantive provisions are going to come into effect and stay in effect.
29. Of course, one of our design features, scope, is substantive in nature. Indeed, the determination of scope may depend on the availability of powerful states to keep items off the agenda (agriculture out of GATT, for example) or to force them on the agenda (services in the WTO, for example).

extent they considered appropriate in explaining their cases. We did not force a particular model of domestic politics on them since there is no widely accepted model available in the literature, and developing one anew was beyond the scope of this project. We did stipulate that domestic politics not be introduced as an ad hoc or post hoc explanation. We also asked the contributors to capture the effects of domestic politics through the variables in our framework whenever possible.

At some level—the claims of structural realism notwithstanding—all international politics has domestic roots. From a rational-choice perspective, states are abstract entities whose preferences can only be understood as a (sometimes problematic) aggregation of other interests.[30] Thus the question is not whether to deal with these considerations but how best to deal with them. In some cases (Mitchell and Keilbach's examination of environmental institutions is a good example), the appropriate response is to follow the longstanding IR tradition that treats states as unitary actors. By treating states as having well-defined preferences over environmental issues, Mitchell and Keilbach produce a convincing explanation of institutional scope without introducing extraneous and complicated domestic political concerns. Kydd, on the other hand, goes part way toward unpacking the domestic "black box" through his discussion of democracy as a signal of benign preferences. But adding in richer domestic detail would complicate his analysis without adding to the explanation.

Among the remaining contributors who did introduce domestic variables into their analyses, we find two broad approaches. The first incorporates key aspects of domestic politics as exogenous factors affecting state preferences or constraints. The second goes part of the way toward endogenizing domestic politics or incorporating them into an overall model of institutional choice. This difference roughly corresponds to the difference between treating domestic factors as determined outside the model and including domestic politics as the second level in a two-level game.

The cases show several ways to incorporate exogenous domestic political factors into institutional design. Some studies highlight a few domestic attributes as invariant characteristics of the environment in which international institutions operate. In Mattli's study of commercial arbitration, for instance, domestic legal environments provide exogenous constraints on arbitral institutions. Both in designing institutions and contesting individual cases, the participants must consider domestic courts. It matters that domestic courts are more responsive to "monitored" arbitration and that courts in some countries, such as India and Singapore, sometimes overrule arbitral awards or block their enforcement.

Other studies incorporate gross domestic characteristics as exogenous explanatory variables. These characteristics affect domestic preferences and, thereby, the existence and design of international institutions. For example, according to Rich-

---

30. We view factors such as a state's position in the international economy or its position with respect to the international distribution of power as constraints and environmental conditions, not as preferences. Over time, of course, the environment may condition state preferences. The Rational Design conjectures, however, are comparative static hypotheses.

ards, domestic commercial interests explain why the United States wanted international aviation institutions to promote competition and the United Kingdom wanted tighter regulation. Because U.S. airlines were more efficient than British ones at the time, they would probably have been the big winners in a more competitive regime. Similarly, Morrow's analysis of the treatment of POWs is based on exogenous domestic preferences in the form of Japanese cultural views of prisoners, German views about Slavic and Western prisoners, and so forth. But it is important not to confuse the role of preferences with the systemic analysis that Morrow's study illustrates. His analysis does not require a theory of how the Germans, Japanese, Americans, or British acquired their preferences regarding POWs, only that they had them. Morrow's specification of interests then plays out in interesting ways within the rational-choice analytic framework, as they do in the other articles that adopt this approach to the incorporation of domestic factors.

An alternative way to think about state preferences is in terms of general goals, such as achieving efficiency or securing reelection or maintaining power more generally. Even approaches that appear to eschew domestic politics incorporate it implicitly this way. Mitchell and Keilbach, for instance, implicitly treat states as having efficiency goals without examining the goals of domestic interest groups more closely. Oatley's article on the payments system after World War II provides a rich depiction of how national preferences vary with domestic political and economic interests. European members had varying employment objectives, which played a central role in determining national preferences over different international payments schemes.

In other cases, domestic politics is conceived of as a source of exogenous shocks to international institutions. In Rosendorff and Milner's article, the designers of trade institutions worry that domestic politics might produce destabilizing shocks. They cope with that possibility by building escape clauses into the institution. The sources of the shocks are not themselves formally modeled but presumably result from changes in the relative economic importance or political influence of various domestic producer and consumer interests. Similarly, in Richards' analysis of how airline deregulation threatened international arrangements, the original "shock" of U.S. deregulation arose from purely domestic considerations.[31] But when the United States moved to deregulate airlines at home, it fundamentally undermined the Bermuda institutions that regulated air travel abroad.

The second broad approach partly endogenizes domestic politics by fleshing out its impact on state preferences. Both case studies of trade adopt this approach. Pahre draws on trade policy models to justify the preferences of the governments in his model. Specifically, he uses an electorally motivated model to derive government preferences for nonzero domestic tariffs and zero foreign tariffs. These preferences inform Pahre's three-state bargaining model from which he derives his main

---

31. Our categories are not intended to pigeonhole each article uniquely. For example, Richards' consideration of domestic factors fits both "gross characteristics" and "exogenous shocks."

theoretical contributions. Likewise, in Rosendorff and Milner's analysis, an informal model of domestic politics underpins their formal model. The government cares about both consumer welfare and firm profits, reflecting the incumbents' concern with reelection.

A blend of the two broad approaches introduces domestic actors into the first-level international game. The studies by Richards and Mattli illustrate this approach by including both states and firms in their international analysis. For simplicity, however, both studies omit any domestic analysis of how firms lobby national governments. In this intermediate case, no domestic bargain is being struck. Instead, the domestic actors have a direct role in striking international bargains, so they are international actors in their own right.

We draw three lessons regarding domestic politics from the articles in this volume. First, rational choice provides several alternative ways to incorporate domestic politics into the analysis of international institutional design. The second concerns the value of theoretical flexibility in incorporating domestic politics. Domestic politics needs to be explicitly addressed to understand some international institutional arrangements but not others. Moreover, when domestic politics is important, the role it plays varies substantially across issue-areas and may be best addressed in different ways. Finally, the analyses here illustrate how these considerations can be incorporated into rational-choice analyses of international relations without requiring a full theory of domestic politics.

Preferences and Preference Change

We did not impose any general assumptions about actors' preferences.[32] Instead, we asked contributors to specify preference configurations in terms of distribution and enforcement problems relevant to their cases. Taking preferences as stable and exogenous is both simple and powerful, which is why it has long been standard in rational-choice modeling. It also avoids the misuse of "revealed preferences," where the preferences themselves are inferred from the very phenomena they are supposed to explain.

Treating preferences as exogenous does not imply they are ad hoc or arbitrary. Several studies develop clear theoretical underpinnings for the preferences they propose. This is clearest in formal articles such as those on trade institutions (Pahre, Rosendorff and Milner), where government objectives are driven by a concern for domestic welfare, distributional effects, and corresponding electoral incentives. Indeed, all the articles specify actors' goals in advance, whether it is to improve the treatment of their captured soldiers (Morrow) or to improve their external monetary balance while achieving other domestic economic goals (Oatley). Such assumptions are typically based on any existing empirical and theoretical consensus in the field in combination with more focused knowledge of the issue at hand.

---

32. For an in-depth discussion of related issues, see Lake and Powell 1999, especially the introduction and the chapters by Peter Gourevitch and Jeffry Frieden.

This clear specification of actor preferences is one of the prime virtues of any rationalist framework. Doing so also invites serious inquiry into the correctness of alternative specifications—for example, does vote maximizing or the pursuit of economic efficiency provide a better explanation of trade policy?—as well as into how preferences change (either exogenously or endogenously) and how institutions might change correspondingly, a topic we consider in the next section.

The relationship between "bedrock" preferences and constraints provides a guide to an empirical analysis of preference change. Bedrock preferences are fundamentally stable preferences, but composite actors or actors operating under constraints may sometimes be usefully modeled as if they had preferences that depend on the particular decision context. Consider the two-level setting discussed earlier, where one level is diplomatic relations among states and the other involves domestic politics within each state. The impact of one level on another can be thought of in terms of the constraints that one level imposes on the other. In this two-level arrangement, the executive has to negotiate an international agreement subject to the constraint of domestic ratification. An alternative conceptualization is to treat the two levels as one—component parts of a unitary actor—and treat the outcome of domestic bargaining as a change in preferences. An extreme example would be a successful trade regime that strengthens free-trade interests and severely weakens protectionist forces.[33] The cumulation of this process would forge "trading states" with very different goals from their mercantilist predecessors.[34]

Viewed this way, Rosendorff and Milner's escape clauses can be interpreted as states designing institutions for the possibility that they will have different preferences (instead of the same preferences but different domestic constraints) at some point in the future. Similarly, we often speak of rich and poor countries having different preferences over some issue (for example, environmental quality), but this difference in preferences could alternatively be expressed in terms of different constraints (for example, levels of development). While it might be desirable to express all of these relationships in terms of bedrock preferences and different constraints, it is sometimes empirically useful to sacrifice some of that generality in favor of more context-specific preferences (implicitly incorporating constraints). This allows us to specify plausible preferences using empirical knowledge of specific cases and to identify preference "change" within the cases.

One example of an empirically identifiable preference change is when a state becomes democratic (or communist or fascist). The assumption is that we can impute different (international) preferences to domestic leaders operating under the different constraints imposed by alternative regime types. This allows us to trace the impact of preference changes but does not account for the change itself, which remains exogenous.

---

33. Rogowski 1989.
34. Rosecrance 1986.

A related source of change—here in beliefs rather than preferences—occurs within the actors as they learn how the world works and therefore shift their informational constraint. Institutional flexibility facilitates this type of learning by lowering the risks of agreement while states discover how an agreement works.[35] Reassurance in security affairs illustrates another type of learning: states develop insights into one another's preferences and likely behavior, as Kydd's analysis shows. When such learning occurs at the collective level, it can generate an alternative and superior equilibrium that states achieve partly by designing appropriate institutions. This perspective captures the understanding that security communities are, above all, groupings of states that have developed common expectations about one another's pacific behavior—expectations that then change their individual and hence collective behavior. In this sense, our framework captures the important idea that "anarchy is what states make of it" and shows how rational purpose and institutions play a central role in constructing alternative equilibria.[36]

Another way that preferences can change is when different actors (with different preferences) become involved. Membership rules, for example, determine which actors are included in an institution and thus which preferences must be accommodated in its design. As membership increases, the heterogeneity of the group will typically increase. Admitting nongovernmental organizations or other private actors, for example, can add valuable expertise and information, but it also adds new voices and new preferences. Moreover, while we have not addressed international organizations as actors, they clearly have that role in certain situations. Some, such as the EU, are major players that operate with substantial independence and authority—their preferences have a major impact on issue outcomes.

Even if the actors remain the same, their preferences may change endogenously. Participation within international institutions, for example, may alter the participants' goals and the trade-offs they make. Successful international economic relations typically increase states' interests in pursuing deeper forms of economic cooperation. The steady development of the GATT/WTO framework is a good illustration. So, too, is the construction of a single European currency. These changes are really in "derived" preferences, that is, preferences over actions conditional upon the constraints imposed by other actors' behaviors and by the institutional environment. Hence, bedrock preferences are constant—a hallmark assumption and limitation of the rational-choice approach.

This discussion of preferences illustrates possible limitations to the Rational Design framework, but these limitations do not diminish its value. Rather, they point out challenges for theory development and testing. In some cases, rational-choice theory will have to be augmented by auxiliary and even competing theories. One source will be other rationalist accounts of the more detailed processes and mechanisms of preference formation, as in our earlier discussion of domestic

35. Koremenos 2001a.
36. Wendt 1992.

politics. Another source will come from outside rationalist approaches as suggested by Wendt's discussion of the logic of appropriateness. One of the continuing debates about the logics of consequences and appropriateness concerns the extent to which these are truly independent logics—as we believe they are in part—versus the extent to which they are deeply intertwined. Surely one reason we have seen the emergence of a "nuclear taboo," of human rights regimes, and of a delegitimization of bribe-paying is because of their consequences. Yet these changes also reflect fundamental changes in preferences that go beyond such direct effects.

Dynamics of Institutional Change

Throughout this volume, we have treated institutions as components of equilibria. They are designed to address specific problems and are supported, in turn, by those who benefit from the resulting equilibrium. This approach allows us to understand why institutions have their specific features, and comparing across equilibria (comparative statics) provides insights into how institutions adapt to different circumstances. Although the strength of the empirical results supports both our strategy and our view of institutions, the equilibrium assumption only indirectly addresses questions about institutional change.

Equilibrium analysis can also provide stronger guidance for a more dynamic analysis. Understanding how the components of an equilibrium fit together helps identify the circumstances under which an equilibrium becomes unstable and when a new equilibrium will emerge.[37] When a change in one or more of the basic parameters of a game, such as the number of players or the degree to which players value the future, invalidates the equilibrium, then the players are in the same position as they were when they originally negotiated the equilibrium: they must establish a new equilibrium. Often change is not so dramatic; the old equilibrium continues to be sustainable while new equilibria emerge.[38] Whether or not states exploit resulting opportunities is at least partly a function of the original institutional design. For example, planned review conferences and opportunities for renegotiation may facilitate Pareto-superior shifts.[39] Importantly, however, once an institution is formed, a subset of players can use opportunities for equilibria shifts to exploit other players.[40] Again, the possibility of such redistributive moves depends on the original design—in particular, the control rules.

Generally speaking, change is most interesting when there are multiple equilibria, including potential ones that depend on new institutional arrangements. Since different equilibria may favor different actors, choosing among them is politically charged. More is at stake here than technical shifts induced by changing circum-

37. Calvert 1995.
38. Koremenos 2001b.
39. Koremenos 1999b.
40. See Knight 1992; and Gruber 2000.

stances. Rather, exogenous changes set the table for tough political bargaining over which institutional equilibrium to pursue.

Changing an institutional equilibrium is often difficult because those who benefit from current arrangements resist change. This conservative bias is reinforced by other factors. The first is transaction costs—a dead weight that lessens or even eliminates the gains from changing equilibria. Second, many international actors are risk-averse and so are reluctant to gamble on untested solutions. Finally, the institution viewed as an actor may have an interest in defending its associated equilibrium, even if that is inefficient. This tendency may be offset by the availability of institutional mechanisms that promote nonthreatening change within the institution. Ultimately, of course, such resistance is bounded by the ability of states to abandon inefficient institutions.

Institutional stability means that existing institutional arrangements are determined not simply by existing conditions (the focus of comparative static analysis) but also by the historical development of the institution ("path dependence"). Because existing institutions reflect their development, they differ significantly from what might be created de novo. An important example is that the voice of rising powers is likely to be underweighted, and the voice of former powers overweighted, in long-standing institutions compared to how they would be weighted in brand new institutions. Because of institutional "stickiness" and path dependence, institutional design will be hotly contested since the choices persist and are not easily undone.[41]

Institutional stickiness generates a "stability/instability" paradox of institutions. The stability of institutions is central to their value since it allows actors to pursue their objectives, including plans to update the institutions themselves. Indeed, if institutions were highly malleable, they would have no impact in solving the problems states face. Yet this stickiness also means that over time institutions can deviate significantly from the collective goals of states and not effectively address current needs. Thus the very stability that gives institutions their value also allows them to build up instability-generating pressure as external conditions change. Therefore, one of the greatest challenges in institutional design is to find the optimal trade-off between stickiness and flexibility. Here we can usefully distinguish between two kinds of institutional change, one aimed at creating new institutional equilibria, the other at sustaining an existing equilibrium in the face of changing external circumstances.[42]

Many historic junctures of international institutionalization have entailed substantial interstate deliberations in search of arrangements that can better states' interactions. This is especially apparent in this volume's more historically oriented studies. Oatley, for instance, traces institutional change from a network of bilateral

---

41. A highly instructive example is the long-standing difficulty that states have had in agreeing on televisions standards—even though all would benefit from a common standard—because of future implications for competitiveness. See Austin and Milner 2001; and, more generally, Abbott and Snidal 2001.

42. This echoes Krasner's change of regime and change within a regime. Krasner 1983.

trade agreements into the multilateral European Payments Union. Similarly, Richards analyzes how the development of the Bermuda institutions was driven by change in aircraft technology and postwar market characteristics and suggests that the regime's breakdown was the result of changing state interests. Change is also relevant in the more formal articles, as exemplified by Kydd's discussion of the importance of the dynamics of reassurance to the expansion of NATO. Such institutional innovations begin with a clear understanding that it is impossible to predict all future contingencies and that outcomes are path-dependent. Indeed, institution designers are often repairing problems that emerged during the failure and breakdown of earlier institutions. Therefore, they try to anticipate the effects of institutions, to block bad paths and facilitate good paths, and to create institutional mechanisms to deal with what they cannot anticipate.

Several of the Rational Design dimensions of institutionalization—flexibility, control, and centralization—address how institutions can be designed to adapt to changing circumstances, including those that could never be fully anticipated in the original design. The flexibility conjectures, in particular, describe how institutions accommodate the unforeseen changes represented by uncertainty. Here, individual actors are empowered to adapt their behaviors to new circumstances but must do so in ways that respect and maintain the stability of the institutional arrangement. The centralization and control dimensions suggest ways where the institution itself is empowered to adapt its rules to deal with new and unanticipated circumstances. Thus a secretariat may be authorized to implement the goals of an organization in a particular operational activity, or a dispute panel may interpret a rule over which members disagree. For important issues, the members sometimes act directly by voting on some new activity or rule.

Thus the Rational Design understanding of how institutions develop departs somewhat from the view held by Robert Axelrod and Robert Keohane, who recognize but de-emphasize the prospects for rational institutional design. They characterize the construction of international regimes as "groping," whereby states rely on "experimental, trial-and-error efforts to improve the current situation based on recent experience."[43] We agree that evolutionary selection (or groping) is an important aspect of dynamic change, but we emphasize self-conscious rational design as central to the creation, maintenance, and further development of international institutions. Furthermore, we believe that Wendt's emphasis on the opposition of evolutionary models to rational design obscures important complementarities in practice. Rational design can take advantage of evolutionary good fortune by consciously reinforcing and imitating successful designs. More proactively, policymakers sometimes experiment with alternative designs and select "winners" while letting "losers" go. Although parallel experiments are usually limited to small projects (by operational organizations, for instance, like the World Bank or the Food and Agriculture Organization), many international institutions have been shaped by

---

43. Axelrod and Keohane 1986, 251.

"experiments" implicit in their past operations. Rational designers learn by experience. They stick with arrangements that work and modify ones that do not. This is not to deny the relevance of unplanned events, but good institutional design encompasses centralization, flexibility, and other features designed to address and take advantage of the unanticipated.[44]

Rational design is even relevant to cases where institutional formation has been "spontaneous." Consider sovereignty and the states-system itself. Although these relationships emerged spontaneously around interstate practices, states have subsequently formalized and ratified the implicit rules that emerged. The same has happened with customary law more generally. It has been codified to make it more precise and to ensure that the expectations it entails are widely understood. In response to changes such as those in communications, transportation, the environment, and military technology, formal negotiations have been used to modify and update international law, including the rules of sovereignty.

Furthermore, institutions that have any centralized capacity will themselves become adaptive agents. Their institutional goals are not identical to those of states, but they must attend to states' interests to further their own goals. International organizations like the World Bank and the IMF that need continuing support and funding from states must respond to their needs and increasingly to the needs of nongovernmental organizations that are able to pressure states.

Finally, we disagree with Wendt's assertion that rational design cannot address what he calls "invisible hand" functionalism, where beneficial outcomes are explained by structural features of a system. Wendt's view seems to be rooted in an insistence that rational design must directly govern the behavior of actors all the way down to the microlevel. This is not necessary: Rational design often concentrates on creating macro structures that operate primarily by channeling decentralized behavior. Many of the best designs lay out only broad parameters and allow the details to be filled in by the individual actors. The familiar example, of course, is the market. Markets often emerge spontaneously, but when they do not, they may be promoted by institutional design in terms of the creation of property rights and arrangements to facilitate exchange. Institutional design can also be used to break down barriers to markets that may have emerged for other reasons or to serve certain vested interests. The development of the GATT/WTO can be seen partly in this light, whereas the effort to introduce tradable pollution-emission rights into the Kyoto Protocol is an explicit effort at "invisible hand" design. Again, rather than try to separate invisible-hand design from rational-design explanations, we believe it is more important to understand their interaction.

In summary, although equilibrium analysis focuses on prevailing circumstances, it provides important insights into change as well. Pressure for change can be understood in terms of the shortcomings of existing equilibria; the resolution of

---

44. For an overview of the complementarities and tensions between rational choice and evolutionary approaches, see Kahler 1999.

these pressures may lie in movement toward a new equilibrium. Of course, equilibrium analysis is hardly sufficient for a complete understanding of institutional transformation and change. But we cannot fully understand them without it.

Conclusion

Our research program, though ambitious, is far from comprehensive. Wendt identifies several significant gaps in our analysis. We close by discussing two that we agree with—the need to evaluate the effectiveness of institutions and the value of normative analysis—and one that we think is severely misplaced—the notion that we have been looking in the rearview mirror.

Institutional Effectiveness

Wendt correctly observes that even if institutions are designed according to rational-design principles, in practice these principles might themselves be flawed. We agree that evaluating institutional designs for their effectiveness is an important task that should be closely related to ongoing work on institutional design. This topic was controversial at the conferences leading up to this volume. We decided to bracket considerations of effectiveness to concentrate on the design variables. Nevertheless, our ability to explain regime design based on the assumption of effectiveness does provide indirect support for the assumption itself.

The case studies report at least indirectly on effectiveness. For example, Mattli shows that the growth of international commercial arbitration has occurred precisely because it provides a more effective way for private parties to resolve certain types of disputes. Mitchell and Keilbach explain how the Rhine chloride convention was effective in obtaining French and German support for Dutch efforts to limit pollution. Oatley shows how the specific institutional arrangements of the European Payments Union were tied to its effectiveness in solving distributive problems among its member states. Indeed, the empirical discussions of design features in practice must ultimately entail some evaluation of the effectiveness of the institutional arrangement. Nevertheless, we agree that more detailed study of effectiveness—including an analysis of whether states change designs when effectiveness is inadequate—would be a valuable adjunct to our analysis.

The study of effectiveness will be especially interesting in situations where alternative designs are available to address a problem. For example, an enforcement problem might be addressed by membership restrictions, issue scope, centralization, or some blend of these institutional features. But theory alone cannot tell us which combinations will be chosen. Thus the empirical study of effectiveness goes directly to the more complex questions of design interactions—both as substitutes and complements—that our simple bivariate conjectures do not capture.[45] Moreover, effectiveness raises the issue of whether there are design "traps" whereby a sub-optimal institutional design equilibrium is sustained even though an alternative and superior design is available. Such research requires not just further intensive comparative analysis of institutions but also the study of institutional development over time as actors rearrange designs to better address the problems they face.

Finally, Wendt's implication that rational design is not relevant when we do not understand either the "objective" world or our "true interests" (his terminology) is unwarranted. As we argue in the introduction, one of the key purposes of creating more centralized institutions is to reduce uncertainty about the "state of the world" (conjecture C2). International organizations, for example, sponsor international research and information exchange to promote learning about problems. International conferences and soft law processes are often aimed at promoting more general understandings not only of problems but of the common interests of the participants.[46] Thus rational design can address the issues of uncertainty that Wendt and we agree are so central to international institutionalization.

Normative Considerations

With respect to Wendt's emphasis on the need to broaden our analysis to address normative considerations, he is correct that any rational-design approach implicitly includes a normative element—through the goals of the designers, through the interests to which they must attend, and perhaps through its very orientation toward action. All merit serious consideration. Rational design focuses on incentives (though not necessarily material ones) for solving problems such as collective action. But it is essentially silent on the sources of preferences that underlie these incentives, and on the development of collective values that might guide institutional design. This is not a problem of rational design per se but of the general issue of linking positive and normative analysis. Rational design is no more handicapped in this than are other approaches, and, we argue, it brings some advantages to normative analysis.

In several places Wendt suggests that the logic of appropriateness is more closely attuned to normative issues than is our rational logic of consequences. While normatively attractive notions of "right" (or legitimacy, duty, fairness, and so on) may provide the basis for logic of appropriateness, the reverse need not hold. Slaveholders, Gestapo members, and colonial powers all act "appropriately" in terms of their own identities but not in terms of at least some normative criteria. Similarly, rational design can be motivated by normatively attractive goals—fairness, equity, altruism—but it also can be motivated by morally reprehensible

---

45. For a fuller discussion, see the volume's introduction.
46. Abbott and Snidal 1998 and 2000. At a more technical level, Wendt misconstrues the implications of the "theory of the second best." Second best theory does not recommend that we stop trying to "maximize expected utility." Instead, it provides guidance on certain pitfalls in doing so.

goals. So we agree with Wendt that rational design is valuable and perhaps even necessary for achieving normatively attractive goals, but it is not sufficient.

Wendt overlooks another potentially important link between rational and normative analysis. Efficiency is a core value of rational design and it carries substantial normative weight of its own. Whatever our specific goals, rational design can help us achieve them better. In this limited sense, the positive connotation of "rational" is not accidental.[47] Moreover, if a normative theory of international institutions is to be practical, it must deal with the issues covered by rational design. Normative considerations should guide what we design our institutions to accomplish, but that design must also take into account the incentives of the actors within those institutions.

Rational Design Is Inherently Forward Looking

Finally, we reject Wendt's suggestion that rational design is akin to "driving with the rear view mirror." We would characterize the Rational Design research program as using past experience along the road—augmented and informed by theory—not only to look ahead but also to plan for unforeseen conditions around the next curve and over the next hill.

Wendt argues that "any theory ... that only explains past choices will be of limited value in making future ones." But since we cannot yet validate our theories against future choices, we have no better alternative. A well-validated theory gives us some confidence in our understanding and justifies projecting the results to novel circumstances. Wendt is correct that under his most extreme form of uncertainty— knowing literally nothing about the future—rational design will not be of much help (beyond proposing institutional arrangements to reduce our ignorance). But neither will anything else. Fortunately, many of the problems we face display enough continuity and similarity to past problems that the insights will transfer. Rational choice provides a good vehicle for this transference.

Moreover, a number of the institutional features we introduce—notably, centralization, control, and flexibility—are fundamentally geared toward managing various types of uncertainty about the future. Although we derive our conjecture about them in terms of uncertainty viewed as risk, these same institutional features would likely be valuable for handling the "deeper" types of uncertainty that Wendt suggests. If we do not know exactly what lies around the next curve, we should choose the driver or the institutional arrangements that have been shown to be most able to adapt and respond to unanticipated circumstances.

To ask that a design be forward looking is not to suggest that its designers be omniscient. To say that the American Founders did not anticipate today's U.S.

47. In fact, one of the exciting areas of research in international relations has been on the role of normative factors in affecting international outcomes through persuasion and direct action. Margaret Keck and Kathryn Sikkink make the important point that normative actors must act strategically and take into account issues of institutional design if they are to achieve their goals. In short, normative actors need good designs. Keck and Sikkink 1998.

Constitution is not to imply that their design was not considerably better than the alternatives (such as the Articles of Confederation) or that their design did not have a profound impact. The brilliance of the U.S. Constitution, and the reason for its wide emulation, is that it solved a number of fundamental problems facing the country in the late eighteenth century. It also proved effective and durable enough that later generations were unwilling to abandon it even when it failed to meet all their needs. It remains an important institution because it contains provisions for interpreting and adjusting it to new conditions. Indeed, one of the key points of rational design is precisely that, because we cannot anticipate the future, we must design institutions capable of managing the problems that arise down the road.[48]

Finally, a significant tension within rational choice is explaining why, if a superior institutional arrangement is possible, actors have not already adjusted to it. Why study rational design except to document what has already been achieved? But this misinterprets a central contribution of rational-choice theory: demonstrating that rational individuals in collective decision-making settings do not automatically achieve their optimal outcomes. The reasons are several—including multiple equilibria, path dependence, and error. But perhaps the most important reason is the existence of a hidden informational constraint: actors do not know which institutional designs will solve particular problems.[49] The learning process in international relations has been uneven precisely because neither state leaders nor scholars fully understand institutional design—witness, for example, the tragic failures of Versailles and the League of Nations and the imperfect achievements of the UN. But compare these with the successes, like the WTO, NATO, and the EU—from which practitioners and scholars can draw lessons for future designs.

The best way to incorporate these empirical lessons is by combining them with a strong theoretical understanding. This has been the imperfect design of this project. We look forward to having this volume in the public discourse so that other scholars can evaluate the results and continue to test whether our initial conclusions hold.

---

48. For similar reasons, there is no need to presume that institutional designs must be all embracing. The best designs, like property rights in the market, often establish broad parameters within which individual actors determine specific outcomes through their actions.

49. Townsend 1988.

References

Abbott, Kenneth, and Duncan Snidal. 1998. Why States Act Through Formal Organizations. *Journal of Conflict Resolution* 42 (1):3–32.

———. 2000. Hard and Soft Law in International Governance. *International Organization* 54 (3):421–56.

———. 2001. International "Standards" and Governance. *European Journal of Public Policy* 8 (3):345–70.

Abbott, Kenneth, Robert Keohane, Andrew Moravcsik, Anne-Marie Slaughter, and Duncan Snidal. 2000. The Concept of Legalization. *International Organization* 54 (3):401–20.

Abreu, Dilip, David Pearce, and Ennio Stacchetti. 1986. Optimal Cartel Equilibria with Imperfect Monitoring. *Journal of Economic Theory* 39:251–69.

Adler, Emanuel, and Michael Barnett, eds. 1998. *Security Communities.* Cambridge: Cambridge University Press.

Aggarwal, Vinod K. 1985. *Liberal Protectionism: The International Politics of Organized Textile Trade.* Berkeley: University of California Press.

Akerlof, George A. 1970. The Market for "Lemons": Quality Uncertainty and Market Mechanism. *Quarterly Journal of Economics* 84 (3):488–500.

Aksen, Gerald. 1991. Ad Hoc Versus Institutional Arbitration. *ICC International Court of Arbitration Bulletin* 2:12.

Albright, Madeleine. 1998. NATO Enlargement: Advancing America's Strategic Interests. *U.S. Department of State Dispatch* 9 (March):13–18.

Allen, Colin, Marc Bekoff, and George Lauder, eds. 1998. *Nature's Purposes: Analyses of Function and Design in Biology.* Cambridge, Mass.: MIT Press.

Amini, Gitty M. 1997. A Larger Role for Positive Sanctions in Cases of Compellance? Working Paper 12. Los Angeles: Center for International Relations, UCLA.

Andersen, K. B. 1958. Political and Cultural Development in Nineteenth-Century Denmark. In *Scandinavian Democracy: Development of Democratic Thought and Institutions in Denmark, Norway, and Sweden,* edited by Joseph A. Lauwerys, 150–59. Copenhagen: Universitets-Bogtrykkeri.

Andresen, Steinar. 1989. Science and Politics in the International Management of Whales. *Marine Policy* 13 (2):99–117.

Arkin, Harry. 1987. International Ad Hoc Arbitration. *International Business Lawyer* 15 (1):5–9.

Arnaldez, Jean-Jacques, Yves Derains, and Dominique Hascher, compilers. 1997. *Collection of ICC Arbitral Awards 1991–1995.* The Hague: Kluwer Law International.

Asbeek-Brusse, Wendy. 1997. *Tariffs, Trade, and European Integration, 1947–1957: From Study Group to Common Market.* New York: St. Martin's Press.

Ashley, Richard K. 1988. Untying the Sovereign State: A Double Reading of the Anarchy Problematique. *Millennium* 17 (2):227–62.

Ashworth, Tony. 1980. *Trench Warfare, 1914–1918: The Live and Let Live System.* New York: Holmes & Meier.

Asmus, Ronald D., Richard L. Kugler, and F. Stephen Larrabee. 1996. What Will NATO Enlargement Cost? *Survival* 38 (3):5–26.

Asmus, Ronald D., and F. Stephen Larrabee. 1996. NATO and the Have-Nots: Reassurance After Enlargement. *Foreign Affairs* 75 (6):13–20.

Asmus, Ronald D., and Robert C. Nurick. 1996. NATO Enlargement and the Baltic States. *Survival* 38 (2):121–42.

Auerbach, Jerold S. 1983. *Justice Without Law?* New York: Oxford University Press.

Augier, Charles. 1906. *La France et les traités de commerce: Étude sur les tarifs des douanes de la France et de l'étranger.* Paris: Librairie Chevalier et Riviere.

Austin, Marc, and Helen Milner. 2001. Strategies of European Standardization. *Journal of European Public Policy* 8 (3):411–31.

Axelrod, Robert. 1984. *The Evolution of Cooperation.* New York: Basic Books.

Axelrod, Robert, and Robert O. Keohane. 1986. Achieving Cooperation Under Anarchy: Strategies and Institutions. In *Cooperation Under Anarchy,* edited by Kenneth Oye, 226–54. Princeton, N.J.: Princeton University Press.

Bagwell, Kyle, and Robert W. Staiger. 1999. Multilateral Trade Negotiations, Bilateral Opportunism, and the Rules of GATT. NBER Working Paper 7071. Cambridge, Mass.: National Bureau of Economic Research.

Bailey, Joseph P. 1997. The Economics of Internet Interconnection Agreements. In *Internet Economics,* edited by Lee W. McKnight and Joseph P. Bailey, 155–68. Cambridge, Mass.: MIT Press.

Bailey, Ronald H. 1981. *Prisoners of War.* Alexandria, Va.: Time-Life Books.

Baker, C. S., and S. R. Palumbi. 1994. Which Whales Are Hunted? A Molecular Genetic Approach to Monitoring Whaling. *Science* 265:1538–39.

Baldwin, David A. 1971. The Power of Positive Sanctions. *World Politics* 24 (1):19–38.

———. 1979. Power Analysis and World Politics: New Trends Versus Old Tendencies. *World Politics* 31 (2):161–94.

Baldwin, Richard. 1987. Politically Realistic Objective Functions and Trade Policy. *Economics Letters* 24 (3):287–90.

Barker, A. J. 1975. *Prisoners of War.* New York: Universe Books.

Barry, Brian. 1979. Is Democracy Special? In *Philosophy, Politics, and Society,* edited by Peter Laslett and James Fishkin, 155–96. New Haven, Conn.: Yale University Press.

Bartov, Omer. 1985. *The Eastern Front, 1941–45, German Troops, and the Barbarization of Warfare.* Basingstoke, Hampshire: Macmillan.

———. 1991. *Hitler's Army: Soldiers, Nazis, and War in the Third Reich.* New York: Oxford University Press.

Barzel, Yoram. 1989. *Economic Analysis of Property Rights.* Cambridge: Cambridge University Press.

Bates, Robert H. 1997. *Open-Economy Politics: The Political Economy of the World Coffee Trade.* Princeton, N.J.: Princeton University Press.

Bazant, Johann von. 1894. *Die Handelspolitik Österreich-Ungarns 1875 bis 1892 in ihrem Verhältnis zum Deutschem Reiche und zu dem westlichen Europa.* Leipzig: Verlag von Duncker und Humbolt.

Bean, Robert W. 1948. European Multilateral Clearing. *Journal of Political Economy* 56 (5):403–15.

Beckert, Jens. 1996. What Is Sociological About Economic Sociology? Uncertainty and the Embeddedness of Economic Action. *Theory and Society* 25 (6):803–40.

Bendor, Jonathan, and Dilip Mookherjee. 1987. Institutional Structure and the Logic of Ongoing Collective Action. *American Political Science Review* 81 (1):129–54.

———. 1997. Comparing Centralized and Decentralized Institutions: A Reply to Schwartz and Tomz. *American Political Science Review* 91 (3):695–97.

Benedick, Richard Elliot. 1991. *Ozone Diplomacy: New Directions in Safeguarding the Planet.* Cambridge, Mass.: Harvard University Press.

Bennet, P. G., and M. R. Dando. 1982. The Arms Race as a Hypergame: A Study of Routes Towards a Safer World. *Futures* 14 (4):293–306.

Benson, Bruce L. 1989. The Spontaneous Evolution of Commercial Law. *Southern Economic Journal* 55 (3):644–61.

Berg, A. J. van den. 1981. *The New York Arbitration Convention of 1958: Towards a Uniform Judicial Interpretation.* Deventer: Kluwer Law and Taxation.

Berle, Beatrice Bishop, and Travis Beal Jacobs, eds. 1973. *Navigating the Rapids: From the Papers of Adolf A. Berle, 1918–1971.* New York: Harcourt Brace Jovanovich.

Bernauer, Thomas. 1995. The International Financing of Environmental Protection: Lessons from Efforts to Protect the River Rhine Against Chloride Pollution. *Environmental Politics* 4 (3):369–90.

———. 1996. Protecting the Rhine River Against Chloride Pollution. In *Institutions For Environmental Aid: Pitfalls and Promise,* edited by Robert O. Keohane and Marc A. Levy, 201–32. Cambridge, Mass.: MIT Press.

Bernauer, Thomas, and Peter Moser. 1996. Reducing Pollution of the River Rhine: The Influence of International Cooperation. *Journal of Environment and Development* 5:389–415.

Bernauer, Thomas, and Dieter Ruloff. 1999a. Introduction and Analytical Framework. In *The Politics of Positive Incentives in Arms Control,* edited by Thomas Bernauer and Dieter Ruloff, 1–46. Columbia: University of South Carolina Press.

Bernauer, Thomas, and Dieter Ruloff, eds. 1999b. *The Politics of Positive Incentives in Arms Control.* Columbia: University of South Carolina Press.

Bernheim, B. D., and Michael D. Whinston. 1990. Multimarket Contact and Conclusive Behavior. *RAND Journal of Economics* 21 (spring):1–26.

Bernstein, Lisa. 1992. Opting Out of the Legal System: Extralegal Contractual Relations in the Diamond Industry. *Journal of Legal Studies* 21 (1):115–57.

Best, Geoffrey. 1994. *War and Law Since 1945.* New York: Oxford University Press.

Biermann, Frank. 1997. Financing Environmental Policies in the South: Experiences from the Multilateral Ozone Fund. *International Environmental Affairs* 9 (3):179–218.

Birnie, Patricia, ed. and compiler. 1985. *International Regulation of Whaling: From Conservation of Whaling to Conservation of Whales and Regulation of Whale-watching.* New York: Oceana Publications.

Black, C. E. 1943. *The Establishment of Constitutional Government in Bulgaria.* Princeton, N.J.: Princeton University Press.

Blank, Stephen. 1998. Russia, NATO Enlargement, and the Baltic States. *World Affairs* 160 (3):115–25.

Boli, John, and George M. Thomas, eds. 1999. *Constructing World Culture: International Nongovernmental Organizations Since 1875.* Stanford, Calif.: Stanford University Press.

Braumoeller, Bear F., and Gary Goertz. 2000. The Methodology of Necessary Conditions. *American Journal of Political Science* 44 (4):844–58.

Brauneder, Wilhelm, and Friedrich Lachmayer. 1980. *Österreichische Verfassungsgeschichte.* 2d ed. Wien: Manzsche Verlags- und Universitätsbuchhandlung.

Broches, Aron. 1979. The "Additional Facility" of the International Centre for Settlement of Investment Disputes (ICSID). *Yearbook of Commercial Arbitration* 4:373–79.

Brown, Laura Ferris. 1993. Arbitral Institutions Active in International Commercial Arbitration. In *The International Arbitration Kit: A Compilation of Basic and Frequently Requested Documents,* 4th ed., edited by Laura Ferris Brown, 387–95. New York: American Arbitration Association.

Brown, Michael E. 1995. The Flawed Logic of NATO Expansion. *Survival* 37 (1):34–52.

Brown, Michael E., Sean M. Lynn-Jones, and Steven E. Miller, eds. 1996. *Debating the Democratic Peace.* Cambridge, Mass.: MIT Press.

Buchanan, James M. 1965. An Economic Theory of Clubs. *Economica* 32:1–14.

———. 1990. The Domain of Constitutional Economics. *Constitutional Political Economy* 1 (1):1–18.

Buchanan, James M., and Gordon Tullock. 1962. *The Calculus of Consent: Logical Foundations of a Constitutional Democracy.* Ann Arbor: University of Michigan Press.

Buckley, Peter, and Malcolm Chapman. 1997. The Perception and Measurement of Transaction Costs. *Cambridge Journal of Economics* 21 (2):127–45.

Bueno de Mesquita, Bruce, James D. Morrow, Randolph M. Siverson, and Alastair Smith. 1999. Policy Failure and Political Survival: The Contribution of Political Institutions. *Journal of Conflict Resolution* 43 (2):147–61.

Bühring-Uhle, Christian. 1996. *Arbitration and Mediation in International Business: Designing Procedures for Effective Conflict Management.* The Hague: Kluwer Law International.

Bull, Hedley. 1977. *The Anarchical Society: A Study of Order in World Politics.* New York: Columbia University Press.

Burley, Anne-Marie. 1993. Regulating the World: Multilateralism, International Law, and the Projection of the New Deal Regulatory State. In *Multilateralism Matters: The Theory and Praxis of an Institutional Form,* edited by John Gerard Ruggie, 125–56. New York: Columbia University Press.

Burley, Anne-Marie, and Walter Mattli. 1993. Europe Before the Court: A Political Theory of Legal Integration. *International Organization* 47 (1):41–76.

Busch, Lutz-Alexander, and Barbara Koremenos. 2001a. Negotiating the Bargaining Agenda. Unpublished manuscript, University of California, Los Angeles.

———. 2001b. Just How Dark is the Shadow of the Future? Unpublished manuscript, University of California, Los Angeles.

Butler, William E. 1992. The Hague Permanent Court of Arbitration. In *International Courts for the Twenty-First Century*, edited by Mark W. Janis, 43–53. Dortrecht: Martinus Nijhoff Publishers.

Calvert, Randall L. 1995a. Rational Actors, Equilibrium, and Social Institutions. In *Explaining Social Institutions*, edited by Jack Knight and Itai Sened, 57–93. Ann Arbor: University of Michigan Press.

———. 1995b. The Rational Choice Theory of Social Institutions: Cooperation, Coordination, and Communication. In *Modern Political Economy*, edited by Jeffrey S. Banks and Eric A. Hanushek, 216–67. New York: Cambridge University Press.

Campbell, David. 1998. *Writing Security: United States Foreign Policy and the Politics of Identity*. Rev. ed. Minneapolis: University of Minnesota Press.

Canavan, Christopher, and B. Peter Rosendorff. 1997. How the EMU Killed the ERM: International Regimes with Temporary Relief Clauses. Unpublished manuscript, University of Southern California, Los Angeles.

Caron, David D. 1995. The International Whaling Commission and the North Atlantic Marine Mammal Commission: The Institutional Risks of Coercion in Consensual Structures. *American Journal of International Law* 89 (1):154–74.

Carr, Edward Hallett. [1939] 1964. *The Twenty Years' Crisis, 1919–1939*. New York: Harper and Row.

Carter, Barry E., and Phillip R. Trimble. 1991. *International Law*. Boston: Little, Brown.

Casella, Alessandra. 1996. On Market Integration and the Development of Institutions: The Case of International Commercial Arbitration. *European Economic Review* 40 (1):155–86.

Cass, Ronald A., Richard D. Boltuck, Seth T. Kaplan, and Michael Knoll. 1997. Antidumping. USC Law School Working Paper Series, 97-15. Los Angeles: USC Law School.

Cates, Armel, and Santiago Isern-Feliu. 1983. Governing Law and Jurisdiction Clauses in Euroloan Agreements. *International Financial Law Review*, 28–36.

Chan, Steve. 1997. In Search of Democratic Peace: Problems and Promise. *Mershon International Studies Review* 41 (1):59–91.

Chayes, Abram, and Antonia Handler Chayes. 1995. *The New Sovereignty: Compliance with International Regulatory Agreements*. Cambridge, Mass.: Harvard University Press.

Clapp, Jennifer. 1997. The Illegal CFC Trade: An Unexpected Wrinkle in the Ozone Protection Regime. *International Environmental Affairs* 9 (4):259–73.

Clark, William Roberts. 1998. Agents and Structures: Two Views of Preferences, Two Views of Institutions. *International Studies Quarterly* 42 (2):245–70.

Coase, Ronald. 1960. The Problem of Social Cost. *Journal of Law and Economics* 3:1–44.

Cochran, Molly. 1999. *Normative Theory in International Relations: A Pragmatic Approach*. Cambridge: Cambridge University Press.

Coe, Jack. 1997. *International Commercial Arbitration: American Principles and Practice in a Global Context*. Irvington-on-Hudson, N.Y.: Transnational Publishers.

Coleman, James S. 1990. *Foundations of Social Theory*. Cambridge, Mass.: Belknap Press.

Collie, Melissa P. 1988. Universalism and the Parties in the U.S. House of Representatives, 1921–80. *American Journal of Political Science* 32 (4):865–83.

Columbia Journal of Law and Social Problems. 1970. Rabbinical Courts: Modern Day Solomons. *Columbia Journal of Law and Social Problems* 6:49–75.

Connolly, Barbara, and Martin List. 1996. Nuclear Safety in Eastern Europe and the Former Soviet Union. In *Institutions for Environmental Aid: Pitfalls and Promise*, edited by Robert O. Keohane and Marc A. Levy, 233–79. Cambridge, Mass.: MIT Press.

Conybeare, John A. C. 1980. International Organization and the Theory of Property Rights. *International Organization* 34 (2):307–34.

Cooter, Robert, and Janet T. Landa. 1984. Personal Versus Impersonal Trade. *International Review of Law and Economics* 4 (1):15–22.

Copeland, Dale C. 2000. *The Origins of Major War*. Ithaca, N.Y.: Cornell University Press.

Coppa, Frank J. 1970. The Italian Tariff and the Conflict Between Agriculture and Industry: The Commercial Policy of Liberal Italy, 1860–1922. *Journal of Economic History* 30 (4):742–69.

———. 1971. *Planning, Protectionism, and Politics in Liberal Italy: Economics and Politics in the Giolittian Age.* Washington, D.C.: The Catholic University of America Press.

Coram, Bruce Talbot. 1996. Second Best Theories and the Implications for Institutional Design. In *The Theory of Institutional Design,* edited by Robert E. Goodin, 90–102. Cambridge: Cambridge University Press.

Coulson, Robert. 1993. The Practical Advantages of Administered Arbitration. *National Institute for Dispute Resolution (NIDR) Forum* (winter):41–43.

Covo, Jacques. 1993. Commodities, Arbitrations, and Equitable Considerations. *Arbitration International* 9 (1):57–66.

Cowhey, Peter F. 1990. "States" and "Politics" in American Foreign Economic Policy. In *International Trade Policies: Gains from Exchange Between Economics and Political Science*, edited by John S. Odell and Thomas D. Willett, 225–51. Ann Arbor: University of Michigan Press.

Cowhey, Peter F., and John Richards. 2000. Comparative Institution Building in International Service Markets. Unpublished manuscript, University of California, San Diego.

Craig, W. Laurence, William W. Park, and Jan Paulsson. 1990. *International Chamber of Commerce Arbitration.* New York: Oceana Publications.

Crampton, R. J. 1997. *A Concise History of Bulgaria.* Cambridge: Cambridge University Press.

Curtin, Philip D. 1984. *Cross-Cultural Trade in World History.* Cambridge: Cambridge University Press.

Curzon, Gerard, and Victoria Curzon. 1976. The Management of Trade Relations in the GATT. In *International Economic Relations of the Western World 1959–1971*, vol. 1., *Politics and Trade,* edited by Andrew Shonfield, Gerard and Victoria Curzon, T. K. Warley, and George Ray, 143–286. London: Oxford University Press for the Royal Institute of International Affairs.

Cutler, A. Claire. 1995. Global Capitalism and Liberal Myths: Dispute Settlement in Private International Trade Relations. *Millennium* 24 (3):377–97.

Dam, Kenneth W. 1970. *The GATT: Law and International Economic Organization.* Chicago: University of Chicago Press.

D'Amato, Anthony, and Sudhir K. Chopra. 1991. Whales: Their Emerging Right to Life. *American Journal of International Law* 85 (1):21–62.

David, René. 1985. *Arbitration in International Trade.* Boston: Kluwer Law and Taxation Publishers.

Davidson, Paul. 1991. Is Probability Theory Relevant for Uncertainty? A Post-Keynesian Perspective. *Journal of Economic Perspectives* 5 (1):129–43.

Davis, John R. 1997. *Britain and the German Zollverein, 1848–66.* New York: St. Martin's Press.

Deardorff, Alan V. 1984. Testing Trade Theories and Predicting Trade Flows. In *Handbook of International Economics,* vol. 1, edited by Ronald W. Jones and Peter B. Kenen, 467–517. Amsterdam: Elsevier Science Publishers.

Deardorff, Alan V., and Robert M. Stern. 1992. Multilateral Trade Negotiations and Preferential Trading Arrangements. Discussion Paper No. 307. Ann Arbor: University of Michigan Institute of Public Policy Studies.

Dempsey, Paul Stephen. 1978. The International Rate and Route Revolution in North Atlantic Passenger Transportation. *Columbia Journal of Transnational Law* 17:393–449.

———. 1987. *Law and Foreign Policy in International Aviation.* New York: Transnational Publishers.

Demsetz, Harold. 1969. Information and Efficiency: Another Viewpoint. *Journal of Law and Economics* 12 (1):1–22.

Dennett, Carl P. 1919. *Prisoners of the Great War: Authoritative Statement of Conditions in the Prison Camps of Germany.* Boston: Houghton Mifflin.

Dequech, David. 1997. Uncertainty in a Strong Sense: Meaning and Sources. *Economic Issues* 2 (2):21–43.

DeSombre, Elizabeth R. 2000. *Domestic Sources of International Environmental Policy: Industry, Environmentalists, and U.S. Power.* Cambridge, Mass.: MIT Press.

Deutsch, Karl W., Sidney A. Burrell, Robert A. Kahn, Maurice Lee, Jr., Martin Lichterman, Raymond E. Lindgren, Francis L. Loewenheim, and Richard W. Van Wagenen. 1957. *Political Community in the North Atlantic Area: International Organization and the Light of Historical Experience.* Princeton, N.J.: Princeton University Press.

Dezalay, Yves, and Bryant G. Garth. 1996. *Dealing in Virtue: International Commercial Arbitration and the Construction of a Transnational Legal Order.* Chicago: University of Chicago Press.

Diebold, William. 1952. *Trade and Payments in Western Europe: A Study in Economic Cooperation, 1947–51.* New York: Harper and Brothers.

Dierikx, Marc L. J. 1992. Shaping World Aviation: Anglo-American Aviation Relations, 1944–1946. *The Journal of Air Law and Commerce* 57 (3):795–840.

Dion, Doug. 1998. Evidence and Inference and the Comparative Case Study. *Comparative Politics* 30 (2):127–45.

Doo, Leigh-Wai. 1973. Dispute Settlement in Chinese-American Communities. *American Journal of Comparative Law* 21 (4):627–63.

Dorn, A. Walter, and Andrew Fulton. 1997. Securing Compliance with Disarmament Treaties: Carrots, Sticks, and the Case of North Korea. *Global Governance* 3 (1):17–40.

Dow, Alexander, and Sheila Dow. 1985. Animal Spirits and Rationality. In *Keynes' Economics: Methodological Issues,* edited by Tony Lawson and Hashem Pesaran, 46–65. Armonk, N.Y.: M. E. Sharpe.

Dower, John W. 1986. *War Without Mercy: Race and Power in the Pacific War.* New York: Pantheon.

Downs, George W., and David M. Rocke. 1990. *Tacit Bargaining, Arms Races, and Arms Control.* Ann Arbor: University of Michigan Press.

———. 1995. *Optimal Imperfection? Domestic Uncertainty and Institutions in International Relations.* Princeton, N.J.: Princeton University Press.

Downs, George W., David M. Rocke, and Peter N. Barsoom. 1996. Is the Good News About Compliance Good News About Cooperation? *International Organization* 50 (3):379–406.

Downs, George W., David M. Rocke, and Randolph Siverson. 1986. Arms Races and Cooperation. In *Cooperation Under Anarchy,* edited by Kenneth Oye, 118–46. Princeton, N.J.: Princeton University Press.

Dresner, Martin, and Michael W. Tretheway. 1988. The Changing Role of IATA: Prospects for the Future. *Annals of Air and Space Law* 13 (1):3–23.

Drezner, Daniel W. 2000. Bargaining, Enforcement, and Multilateral Sanctions: When Is Cooperation Counterproductive? *International Organization* 54 (1):73–102.

Dryzek, John S. 1996. The Informal Logic of Institutional Design. In *The Theory of Institutional Design,* edited by Robert E. Goodin, 103–25. Cambridge: Cambridge University Press.

———. 1999. Transnational Democracy. *Journal of Political Philosophy* 7 (1):30–51.

Dunoff, Jeffrey L., and Joel P. Trachtman. 1999. Economic Analysis of International Law. *Yale Journal of International Law* 24 (1):1–59.

Eichengreen, Barry J. 1993. *Reconstructing Europe's Trade and Payments: The European Payments Union.* Ann Arbor: University of Michigan Press.

Ellickson, Robert C. 1991. *Order Without Law: How Neighbors Settle Disputes.* Cambridge. Mass.: Harvard University Press.

Esty, Daniel C. 1994. *Greening the GATT: Trade, Environment, and the Future.* Washington, D.C.: International Institute for Economics.

Eyal, Jonathan. 1997. NATO's Enlargement: Anatomy of a Decision. *International Affairs* 73 (4):695–720.

Farrell, Joseph. 1987. Cheap Talk, Coordination, and Entry. *Rand Journal of Economics* 18 (1):34–39.

Farrell, Joseph, and Robert Gibbons. 1989. Cheap Talk Can Matter in Bargaining. *Journal of Economic Theory* 48 (1):221–37.

Fearon, James D. 1994. Domestic Political Audiences and the Escalation of International Disputes. *American Political Science Review* 88 (3):577–92.

———. 1998. Bargaining, Enforcement, and International Cooperation. *International Organization* 52 (2):269–305.

Fearon, James D., and David D. Laitin. 1996. Explaining Interethnic Cooperation. *American Political Science Review* 90 (4):715–35.

Fearon, James D., and Alexander Wendt. 2001. Rationalism and Constructivism in International Relations Theory. Paper presented at PIPES workshop, University of Chicago, May.

———. Forthcoming. Rationalism Versus Constructivism? A Skeptical View. In *Handbook of International Relations,* edited by Walter Carlsnaes, Thomas Risse, and Beth Simmons. Los Angeles: Sage Publications.

Finlayson, Jock A., and Mark W. Zacher. 1983. The GATT and the Regulation of Trade Barriers: Regime Dynamics and Functions. In *International Regimes,* edited by Steven D. Krasner, 273–314. Ithaca, N.Y.: Cornell University Press.

Finnemore, Martha. 1996a. *National Interests in International Society.* Ithaca, N.Y.: Cornell University Press.

———. 1996b. Norms, Culture, and World Politics: Insights from Sociology's Institutionalism. *International Organization* 50 (2):325–48.

Fisk, George M. 1903. German-American "Most Favored Nation" Relations. *Journal of Political Economy* 11 (2):220–36.

Frieden, Jeffry A. 1999. Actors and Preferences in International Relations. In *Strategic Choice and International Relations,* edited by David A. Lake and Robert Powell, 39–76. Princeton, N.J.: Princeton University Press.

Friedman, James W. 1971. A Non-cooperative Equilibrium for Supergames. *Review of Economic Studies* 38 (1):1–12.

Friedman, Kenneth S. 1980. Analysis of Causality in Terms of Determinism. *Mind,* n.s., 89 (356):544–64.

Friedman, Philip. 1978. An Econometric Model of National Income, Commercial Policy, and the Level of International Trade: The Open Economies of Europe, 1924–1938. *Journal of Economic History* 38 (1):148–80.

Fritz, Stephen G. 1995. *Frontsoldaten: The German Soldier in World War II.* Lexington: University Press of Kentucky.

Fudenberg, Drew, and David K. Levine. 1998. *The Theory of Learning in Games.* Cambridge, Mass.: MIT Press.

Fudenberg, Drew, and Eric Maskin. 1986. The Folk Theorem in Repeated Games with Discounting or with Incomplete Information. *Econometrica* 54 (3):533–54.

Gaddis, John Lewis. 1998. History, Grand Strategy, and NATO Enlargement. *Survival* 40 (1):145–52.

Galanter, Marc. 1981. Justice in Many Rooms: Courts, Private Ordering, and Indigenous Law. *Journal of Legal Pluralism and Unofficial Law* 19:1–47.

———. 1993. Reading the Landscape of Disputes. *UCLA Law Review* 31:4–71.

Gallarotti, Giulio. 1991. The Limits of International Organization: Systematic Failure in the Management of International Relations. *International Organization* 45 (2):183–220.

Garrett, Geoffrey. 1992. International Cooperation and Institutional Choice: The European Community's Internal Market. *International Organization* 46 (2):533–60.

Garrett, Geoffrey, and George Tsebelis. 1996. An Institutional Critique of Intergovernmentalism. *International Organization* 50 (2):269–99.

Garrett, Richard. 1981. *P.O.W.* Newton Abbot [Devon]: David and Charles.

Garthoff, Raymond L. 1997. NATO and Russia. *The Brookings Review* 15 (2):8–11.

Genschel, Philipp. 1997. How Fragmentation Can Improve Co-ordination: Setting Standards in International Telecommunications. *Organization Studies* 18 (4):603–22.

Gentinetta, Jörg. 1973. *Die Lex Fori Internationaler Handesschiedsgerichte.* Bern: Verlag Stämpfli.

Glaser, Charles L. 1994. Realists as Optimists: Cooperation as Self Help. *International Security* 19 (3):50–90.

———. 1997. The Security Dilemma Revisited. *World Politics* 50 (1):171–201.

Goldgeier, James M. 1998. NATO Expansion: the Anatomy of a Decision. *Washington Quarterly* 21 (1):85–102.

Goldstein, Judith. 1993. Creating the GATT Rules: Politics, Institutions, and American Policy. In *Multilateralism Matters: The Theory and Praxis of an Institutional Form,* edited by John Gerard Ruggie, 201–32. New York: Columbia University Press.

Goodin, Robert E. 1995. Political Ideals and Political Practice. *British Journal of Political Science* 25 (1):37–56.

———. 1996. Institutions and Their Design. In *The Theory of Institutional Design,* edited by Robert E. Goodin, 1–53. Cambridge: Cambridge University Press.

Gourevitch, Peter Alexis. 1999. The Governance Problem in International Relations. In *Strategic Choice and International Relations,* edited by David A. Lake and Robert Powell, 137–64. Princeton, N.J.: Princeton University Press.

Graving, Richard J. 1989. The International Commercial Arbitration Institutions: How Good a Job Are They Doing? *The American University Journal of International Law and Policy* 4 (2):319–76.

Gray, Christine, and Benedict Kingsbury. 1992. Inter-State Arbitration Since 1945: Overview and Evaluation. In *International Courts for the Twenty-First Century,* edited by Mark Janis, 55–83. Dordrecht: Martinus Nijhoff Publishers.

Green, Edward J., and Robert H. Porter. 1984. Noncooperative Collusion Under Imperfect Price Information. *Econometrica* 52 (1):87–100.

Greif, Avner. 1992. Institutions and International Trade: Lessons from the Commercial Revolution. *American Economic Review* 82 (2):128–33.

Greif, Avner, Paul Milgrom, and Barry R. Weingast. 1994. Coordination, Commitment, and Enforcement: The Case of the Merchant Guild. *Journal of Political Economy* 102 (4):745–76.

Grieco, Joseph M. 1988. Anarchy and the Limits of Cooperation: A Realistic Critique of the Newest Liberal Institutionalism. *International Organization* 42 (3):485–507.

Grossman, Gene M., and Elhanan Helpman. 1994. Protection for Sale. *American Economic Review* 84 (4):833–50.

———. 1995. Trade Wars and Trade Talks. *Journal of Political Economy* 103 (4):675–708.

Gruber, Lloyd. 2000. *Ruling the World: Power Politics and the Rise of Supranational Institutions.* Princeton, N.J.: Princeton University Press.

Gruson, Michael. 1982. Legal Aspects of International Lending. In *Handbook of International Business,* edited by Ingo Walter and Tracy Murray, 27:3–21. New York: John Wiley and Sons.

Guerin-Calvert, Margaret E., and Steven S. Wildman. 1991. *Electronic Services Networks: A Business and Public Policy Challenge.* New York: Praeger.

Güth, Werner, and Hartmut Kliemt. 1994. Competition or Co-Operation: On the Evolutionary Economics of Trust, Exploitation, and Moral Attitudes. *Metroeconomica* 45 (2):155–87.

Haanappel, Peter P. C. 1978. *Ratemaking in International Air Transport: A Legal Analysis of International Air Fares and Rates.* Amsterdam: Kluwer.

———. 1980. Bilateral Air Transport Agreements, 1913–1980. *The International Trade Law Journal* 241–67.

Haas, Ernst B. 1980. Why Collaborate? Issue-Linkage and International Regimes. *World Politics* 32 (3):357–405.

Haggard, Stephan, and Beth A. Simmons. 1987. Theories of International Regimes. *International Organization* 41 (3):491–517.

Hall, Peter A., and Rosemary R. Taylor. 1996. Political Science and the Three New Institutionalisms. *Political Studies* 44 (5):936–57.

Hansen, Wendy L., and Thomas J. Prusa. 1995. The Road Most Taken: The Rise of Title VII Protection. *World Economy* 18 (2):295–313.

Hardin, Garrett. 1968. The Tragedy of the Commons. *Science* 162:1243–48.

Hardin, Russell. 1982. *Collective Action.* Baltimore, Md.: Johns Hopkins University Press for Resources for the Future.

Hargreaves-Heap, Shaun. 1989. *Rationality in Economics.* Oxford: Blackwell.

Harris, Bruce, Michael Summerskill, and Sara Cockerill. 1993. London Maritime Arbitration. *Arbitration International* 9 (3):275–302.

Hasenclever, Andreas, Peter Mayer, and Volker Rittberger. 1997. *Theories of International Regimes.* Cambridge: Cambridge University Press.

Haslam, Nick. 1991. Prudence: Aristotelian Perspectives on Practical Reason. *Journal for the Theory of Social Behaviour* 21 (2):151–69.

Hata, Ikuhiko. 1996. From Consideration to Contempt: The Changing Nature of Japanese Military and Popular Perceptions of Prisoners of War Through the Ages. In *Prisoners of War and Their Captors in World War II,* edited by Bob Moore and Kent Fedorowich, 253–76. Oxford: Berg.

Hayek, Friedrich A. 1973. *Law, Legislation, and Liberty.* Vol. 1, *Rules and Order.* Chicago: University of Chicago Press.

Heiner, Ronald A. 1983. The Origin of Predictable Behavior. *American Economic Review* 73 (4):560–95.

Henderson, W. O. 1984. *The Zollverein.* 3d ed. London: Frank Cass.

Hillman, Arye L., Ngo Van Long, and Peter Moser. 1995. Modeling Reciprocal Trade Liberalization: The Political-Economy and National-Welfare Perspectives. *Swiss Journal of Economics and Statistics* 131:503–15.

Hirschman, Albert O. 1970. *Exit, Voice, and Loyalty: Repsonses to the Decline in Firms, Organizations, and States.* Cambridge, Mass.: Harvard University Press.

Hirshleifer, Jack, and John G. Riley. 1992. *The Analytics of Uncertainty and Information.* Cambridge: Cambridge University Press.

Hodgson, Geoffrey M. 1991. Evolution and Intention in Economic Theory. In *Evolutionary Theories of Economic and Technological Change,* edited by P. Paulo Saviotti and J. Stanley Metcalfe, 108–32. Philadelphia: Harwood Academic Publishers.

Hoekman, Bernard M. 1989. Determining the Need for Issue Linkages in Multilateral Trade Negotiations. *International Organization* 43 (4):693–714.

———. 1993. Multilateral Trade Negotiations and Coordination of Commercial Policies. In *The Multilateral Trading System: Analysis and Options for Change,* edited by Robert M. Stern. Ann Arbor: University of Michigan Press.

Hoekman, Bernard M., and Michel M. Kostecki. 1995. *The Political Economy of the World Trading System from GATT to WTO.* Oxford: Oxford University Press.

Hoekman, Bernard M., and Michael P. Leidy. 1989. Dumping, Antidumping, and Emergency Protection. *Journal of World Trade* 23 (5):27–44.

Hoel, Alf Håkon. 1993. Regionalization of International Whale Management: The Case of the North Atlantic Marine Mammals Commission. *Arctic* 46 (2):116–23.

Hoellering, Michael F. 1994. The Institution's Role in Managing the Arbitration Process. In *Arbitration and the Law,* 151–61. Irvington-on-Hudson, N.Y.: Transnational Juris Publications.

Hogan, Michael J. 1987. *The Marshall Plan: America, Britain, and the Reconstruction of Western Europe, 1947–1952.* Cambridge: Cambridge University Press.

Holmes, Richard. 1985. *Acts of War: The Behavior of Men in Battle.* New York: Free Press.

Holt, Sidney. 1985. Whale Mining, Whale Saving. *Marine Policy* 9 (3):192–213.

Hosli, Madeleine O. 1993. Admission of European Free Trade Association States to the European Community: Effects on Voting Power in the European Community Council of Ministers. *International Organization* 47 (4):629–43.

Howe, Anthony. 1997. *Free Trade and Liberal England 1846–1946.* Oxford: Clarendon Press.

Huber, Bettina J. 1974. Some Thoughts on Creating the Future. *Sociological Inquiry* 44 (1):29–39.

Hufbauer, Gary Clyde, and Howard F. Rosen. 1986. *Trade Policy for Troubled Industries.* Washington, D.C.: Institute for International Economics.

Hunter, Martin, Jan Paulsson, Nigel Rawding, and Alan Redfern. 1993. *The Freshfields Guide to Arbitration and ADR.* Boston: Kluwer Law and Taxation Publishers.

Iklé, Fred Charles. 1961. After Detection—What? *Foreign Affairs* 39 (2):208–20.

International Committee of the Red Cross (ICRC). 1948. *Report of the International Committee of the Red Cross on its Activities During the Second World War (September 1, 1939–June 30, 1947).* Vols. 1–3. Geneva: ICRC.

International Convention for the Regulation of Whaling (ICRW). 1946. ICRW (2 December 1946) T.I.A.S. No. 1849, 161 U.N.T.S. 72.

Jackman, Henry. 1999. We Live Forwards but Understand Backwards: Linguistic Practices and Future Behavior. *Pacific Philosophical Quarterly* 80 (2):157–77.

Jackson, Frank, and Philip Pettit. 1992. Structural Explanation in Social Theory. In *Reduction, Explanation, and Realism,* edited by David Charles and Kathleen Lennon, 97–131. Oxford: Oxford University Press.

Jackson, Joseph, Jr. 1991. The 1975 Inter-American Convention on International Commercial Arbitration: Scope, Application, and Problems. *Journal of International Arbitration* 8 (3):91–99.

Jarvin, Sigvard, and Yves Derains. 1990. *Collection of ICC Arbitral Awards 1974–85.* Deventer: Kluwer Law and Taxation Publishers.

Jarvin, Sigvard, Yves Derains, and Jean-Jacques Arnaldez. 1994. *Collection of ICC Arbitral Awards 1986–1990.* Deventer: Kluwer Law and Taxation Publishers.

Jervis, Robert. 1976. *Perception and Misperception in International Politics.* Princeton, N.J.: Princeton University Press.

———. 1978. Cooperation Under the Security Dilemma. *World Politics* 30 (2):167–214.

Johnson, Derek Kirby. 1991. *Institutional Commodity Arbitration.* London: Lloyd's of London Press.

———. 1993. Commodity Trade Arbitration. In *Handbook of Arbitration Practice,* edited by Ronald Bernstein and Derek Wood, 257–85. London: Sweet and Maxwell.

Johnson, James. 1991. Habermas on Strategic and Communicative Action. *Political Theory* 19 (2):181–201.

Jones, W. Glyn. 1970. *Denmark.* London: Ernest Benn Limited.

Jones, William C. 1958. An Inquiry into the History of the Adjudication of Mercantile Disputes in Great Britain and the United States. *The University of Chicago Law Review* 25 (3):445–64.

Jönsson, Christer. 1987. *International Aviation and the Politics of Regime Change.* New York: St. Martin's Press.

Kahler, Miles. 1999. Evolution, Choice, and International Change. In *Strategic Choice and International Relations,* edited by David Lake and Robert Powell, 165–96. Princeton, N.J.: Princeton University Press.

Kamminga, Menno T. 1978. Who Can Clean Up the Rhine: The European Community or the International Rhine Commission? *Netherlands International Law Review* 25 (1):63–79.

Kamp, Karl-Heinz. 1998. NATO Entrapped: Debating the Next Enlargement Round. *Survival* 40 (3):170–86.

Kaplan, Jacob J., and Gunther Schleiminger. 1989. *The European Payments Union: Financial Diplomacy in the 1950s.* Oxford: Clarendon Press.

Kasaba, Reşat. 1988. *The Ottoman Empire and the World Economy: The Nineteenth Century.* Albany: SUNY Press.

Kasper, Daniel M. 1988. *Deregulation and Globalization: Liberalizing International Trade in Air Services.* Cambridge, Mass: Ballinger.

Keck, Margaret E., and Kathryn Sikkink. 1998. *Activists Beyond Borders: Advocacy Networks in International Politics.* Ithaca, N.Y.: Cornell University Press.

Kenen, Peter B. 1995. *Economic and Monetary Union in Europe: Moving Beyond Maastricht.* Cambridge: Cambridge University Press.

Keohane, Robert O. 1983. The Demand for International Regimes. In *International Regimes,* edited by Stephen D. Krasner, 141–71. Ithaca, N.Y.: Cornell University Press.

———. 1984. *After Hegemony: Cooperation and Discord in the World Political Economy.* Princeton, N.J.: Princeton University Press.

———. 1990. Multilateralism: An Agenda for Research. *International Journal* 45:731–64.

Keohane, Robert O., and Joseph S. Nye, Jr. 1989. *Power and Interdependence: World Politics in Transition.* 2d ed. Glenview, Ill.: Scott Foresman.

Kerr, Lord Justice. 1987. Arbitration Versus Litigation: The Macao Sardine Case. *Arbitration International* 3 (1):79–87.

Kim, Jaegwon. 1971. Causes and Events: Mackie on Causation. *Journal of Philosophy* 68 (14):426–41.

Kim, Kunsan. 1999. 1994 U.S.–North Korean Nuclear Agreement: Environmental Solutions for International Security. Unpublished manuscript, University of California, Los Angeles.

Kindleberger, Charles P. 1981. Dominance and Leadership in the International Economy: Exploitation, Public Goods, and Free Rides. *International Studies Quarterly* 25 (2):242–54.

King, Gary, Robert O. Keohane, and Sidney Verba. 1994. *Designing Social Inquiry.* Princeton, N.J.: Princeton University Press.

Knight, Frank Hyneman. 1921. *Risk, Uncertainty, and Profit.* New York: Houghton-Mifflin.

Knight, Jack. 1992. *Institutions and Social Conflict.* Cambridge: Cambridge University Press.

Knorr, Klaus. 1975. *The Power of Nations: The Political Economy of International Relations.* New York: Basic Books.

Koremenos, Barbara. 1998. Constructing International Agreements in the Face of Uncertainty. Unpublished manuscript, UCLA, Los Angeles, Calif.

———. 1999a. A Model of the Duration and Renegotiation Provisions of International Agreements in a Changing Environment. In On the Duration and Renegotiation of International Agreements. Ph.D. diss., University of Chicago.

———. 1999b. On the Duration and Renegotiation of International Agreements. Ph.D. diss., University of Chicago.

———. 2000. Bending But Not Breaking: Flexibility in International Financial and Monetary Agreements. Working Paper 1.73. Berkeley: Center for German and European Studies, University of California.

———. 2001a. Loosening the Ties that Bind: A Learning Model of Agreement Flexibility. *International Organization* 55 (2):289–325.

———. 2001b. Leadership and Bureaucracy: The Folk Theorem and Real Folks. Unpublished manuscript, University of California, Los Angeles.

Kramer, Mark. 1999. Neorealism, Nuclear Proliferation, and East-Central European Strategies. In *Unipolar Politics: Realism and State Strategies After the Cold War,* edited by Ethan B. Kapstein and Michael Mastanduno, 385–463. New York: Columbia University Press.

Krammer, Arnold. 1979. *Nazi Prisoners of War in America.* New York: Stein and Day.

Krasner, Stephen D. 1983. Structural Causes and Regime Consequences: Regimes as Intervening Variables. In *International Regimes,* edited by Stephen D. Krasner, 1–21. Ithaca, N.Y.: Cornell University Press.

———. 1991. Global Communications and National Power: Life on the Pareto Frontier. *World Politics* 43 (3):336–66.

———. 1999. *Sovereignty: Organized Hypocrisy.* Princeton, N.J.: Princeton University Press.

Krasner, Stephen D., ed. 1983. *International Regimes.* Ithaca, N.Y.: Cornell University Press.

Kratochwil, Friedrich V. 1989. *Rules, Norms, and Decisions.* Cambridge: Cambridge University Press.

Kreps, David M. 1990. *A Course in Microeconomic Theory.* Princeton, N.J.: Princeton University Press.

Kronman, Anthony T. 1985. Contract Law and the State of Nature. *Journal of Law, Economics, and Organization* 1 (1):5–32.

Kydd, Andrew. 1997. Game Theory and the Spiral Model. *World Politics* 49 (3):371–400.

———. 2000a. Trust, Reassurance, and Cooperation. *International Organization* 54 (2):325–57.

———. 2000b. Overcoming Mistrust. *Rationality and Society* 12 (4):397–424.

Laffey, Mark. 2000. Locating Identity: Performativity, Foreign Policy, and State Action. *Review of International Studies* 26 (3):429–44.

Lakatos, Imre. 1970. Falsification and the Methodology of Scientific Research Programmes. In *Criticism and the Growth of Knowledge,* edited by I. Lakatos and A. Musgrave, 91–196. Cambridge: Cambridge University Press.

Lake, David A. 1988. *Power, Protection, and Free Trade: International Sources of U.S. Commercial Strategy, 1887–1939.* Ithaca, N.Y.: Cornell University Press.

———. 1996. Anarchy, Hierarchy, and the Variety of International Relations. *International Organization* 50 (1):1–34.

Lake, David A., and Robert Powell. 1999. International Relations: A Strategic-Choice Approach. In *Strategic Choice and International Relations,* edited by David A. Lake and Robert Powell, 3–38. Princeton, N.J.: Princeton University Press.

Landa, Janet T. 1981. A Theory of the Ethnically Homogeneous Middleman Group. *Journal of Legal Studies* 10 (2):349–62.

Lawson, Tony. 1993. Keynes and Conventions. *Review of Social Economy* 51 (2):174–200.

Lazer, David. 1999. The Free Trade Epidemic of the 1860s and Other Outbreaks of Economic Discrimination. *World Politics* 51 (4):447–83.

Legro, Jeffrey. 1996. Culture and Preferences in the International Cooperation Two-step. *American Political Science Review* 90 (1):118–37.

LeMarquand, David G. 1977. *International Rivers: The Politics of Cooperation.* Vancouver, B.C.: Westwater Research Centre, University of British Columbia.

Lepgold, Joseph. 1998. NATO's Post–Cold War Collective Action Problem. *International Security* 23 (1):78–106.

Lessig, Lawrence. 1999. *Code and Other Laws of Cyberspace.* New York: Basic Books.

Levi, Margaret. 1997. *Consent, Dissent, and Patriotism.* Cambridge: Cambridge University Press.

Levy, Marc A. 1988. Leviathan's Leviathan: Power, Interests, and Institutional Change in the International Whaling Commission. Unpublished manuscript, Harvard University, Cambridge, Mass.

———. 1993. European Acid Rain: The Power of Tote-Board Diplomacy. In *Institutions For The Earth: Sources Of Effective International Environmental Protection,* edited by Peter M. Haas, Robert O. Keohane, and Marc A. Levy, 75–132. Cambridge, Mass.: MIT Press.

Lindberg, Anders. 1983. Småstat mot Stormakt. Beslutssystemet vid tillkomsten av 1911 års svensk-tyska handels och sjöfartstraktat. In *Bibliotheca historica Lundensis* vol. 55. Lund: CWK Gleerup.

Linderman, Gerald F. 1997. *The World Within War: America's Combat Experience in World War II.* New York: Free Press.

Linklater, Andrew. 1998. *The Transformation of Political Community: Ethical Foundations of the Post-Westphalian Era.* Columbia: University of South Carolina Press.

Lipson, Charles. 1985. *Standing Guard: Protecting Foreign Capital in the Nineteenth and Twentieth Centuries.* Berkeley: University of California Press.

———. 1986. Bankers' Dilemmas: Private Cooperation in Rescheduling Sovereign Debts. In *Cooperation Under Anarchy,* edited by Kenneth A. Oye, 200–25. Princeton, N.J.: Princeton University Press.

Lohmann, Susanne. 1997. Linkage Politics. *Journal of Conflict Resolution* 41 (1):38–67.

Lowenfeld, Andreas F. 1993. *International Litigation and Arbitration.* St. Paul, Minn.: West Publishing.

Lowenfeld, Andreas F., ed., 1981. *Aviation Law: Cases and Materials.* New York: Mathew Bender.

Lupia, Arthur, and Mathew McCubbins. 1994. Who Controls? Information and the Structure of Legislative Decisionmaking. *Legislative Studies Quarterly* 19 (3):361–84.

Macaulay, Stewart. 1963. Non-Contractual Relations in Business: A Preliminary Study. *American Sociological Review* 28 (1):55–67.

MacIntosh, Duncan. 1992. Preference-revision and the Paradoxes of Instrumental Rationality. *Canadian Journal of Philosophy* 22 (4):503–29.

MacKenzie, S. P. 1994. The Treatment of Prisoners of War in World War II. *Journal of Modern History* 66 (3):487–520.

Mackie, J. L. 1965. Causes and Conditions. *American Philosophical Quarterly* 2 (4):245–64.

———. 1974. *The Cement of the Universe: A Study of Causation.* Oxford: Clarendon Press.

Maggi, Giovanni. 1999. The Role of Multilateral Institutions in International Trade Cooperation. *American Economic Review* 89 (1):190–214.

Mahaim, E. 1892. La politique commerciale de la Belgique. *Handelspolitik* 1:197–238.

Maitland, Frederic William. 1936. Trust and Corporation. In *Selected Essays,* edited by Harold D. Hazeltine, Gaillard T. Lapsley, and Percy H. Winfield, 141–222. Cambridge: Cambridge University Press.

Mandelbaum, Michael. 1995. Preserving the New Peace: The Case Against NATO Expansion. *Foreign Affairs* 74 (3):9–13.

March, James G., and Johan P. Olsen. 1989. *Rediscovering Institutions: The Organizational Basis of Politics*. New York: Free Press.

———. 1998. The Institutional Dynamics of International Political Orders. *International Organization* 52 (4):943–69.

Marchionatti, Roberto. 1999. On Keynes' Animal Spirits. *Kyklos* 52 (3):415–39.

Marsh, Peter T. 1999. *Bargaining on Europe: Britain and the First Common Market, 1860–1892*. New Haven, Conn.: Yale University Press.

Martin, Gene S., Jr., and James W. Brennan. 1989. Enforcing the International Convention for the Regulation of Whaling: The Pelly and Packwood-Magnuson Amendments. *Denver Journal of International Law and Policy* 17 (2):293–315.

Martin, Lisa L. 1992a. *Coercive Cooperation: Explaining Multilateral Economic Sanctions*. Princeton, N.J.: Princeton University Press.

———. 1992b. Interests, Power, and Multilateralism. *International Organization* 46 (4):765–92.

———. 1994. Heterogeneity, Linkage, and Commons Problems. *Journal of Theoretical Politics* 6 (4):73–93.

Martin, Lisa L., and Beth Simmons. 1998. Theories and Empirical Studies of International Institutions. *International Organization* 52 (4):729–58.

Matis, Herbert. 1973. Leitlinien der österreichischen Wirtschaftspolitik. In *Die Habsburgermonarchie, 1848–1918. Im Auftrag der Kommission für die Geschichte der Österreichisch-Ungarischen Monarchie*, vol. 1, edited byAdam Wandruszka and Peter Urbanitsch, 29–67. Vienna: Österreichischen Akademie der Wissenschaften.

Mattli, Walter. 1999. *The Logic of Regional Integration: Europe and Beyond*. Cambridge: Cambridge University Press.

———. 2000. Sovereignty Bargains in Regional Integration. *International Studies Review* 2 (2):149–80.

Mattli, Walter, and Anne-Marie Slaughter. 1995. Law and Politics in the European Union. *International Organization* 49 (1):183–90.

———. 1998a. The Role of National Courts in the Process of European Integration: Accounting for Judicial Preferences and Constraints. In *The European Court and National Courts—Doctrine and Jurisprudence: Legal Change in Its Social Context*, edited by Anne-Marie Slaughter, Alec Stone Sweet, and J. H. H. Weiler, 253–76. Oxford: Hart Publishing.

———. 1998b. Revisiting the European Court of Justice. *International Organization* 52 (1):177–209.

McCubbins, Mathew, and Thomas Schwartz. 1984. Congressional Oversight Overlooked: Police Patrols Versus Fire Alarms. *American Journal of Political Science* 2 (1):165–79.

McGillivray, Fiona, Iain McLean, Robert Pahre, and Cheryl Schonhardt-Bailey. 2001. Tariffs and Modern Political Institutions: An Introduction. In *International Trade and Political Institutions*, edited by Fiona McGillivray, Iain McLean, Robert Pahre, and Cheryl Schonhardt-Bailey, 1–28. Cheltenham, UK: Edward Elgar.

McGinnis, Michael D. 1986. Issue Linkage and the Evolution of International Cooperation. *Journal of Conflict Resolution* 30 (1):141–70.

McKnight, Lee, and Joseph P. Bailey, eds. 1997. *Internet Economics*. Cambridge, Mass.: MIT Press.

McMillan, John. 1991. *Dango:* Japan's Price-Fixing Conspiracies. *Economics and Politics* 3 (3):201–18.

Mearsheimer, John J. 1990. Back to the Future: Instability in Europe After the Cold War. *International Security* 15 (1):5–56.

———. 1994/95. The False Promise of International Institutions. *International Security* 19 (3):5–49.

Mentschikoff, Soia. 1961. Commercial Arbitration. *Columbia Law Review* 61 (5):846–69.

Meyer, John, John Boli, George M. Thomas, and Francisco O. Ramirez. 1997. World Society and the Nation-State. *American Journal of Sociology* 103 (1):144–81.

Miles, Edward L., and Arild Underdal, eds. 2000. *Explaining Regime Effectiveness: Confronting Theory with Evidence*. Cambridge, Mass.: MIT Press.

Milgrom, Paul R, Douglass C. North, and Barry R. Weingast. 1990. The Role of Institutions in the Revival of Trade: The Law Merchant, Private Judges, and the Champagne Fairs. *Economics and Politics* 2 (1):1–23.

Milner, Helen V. 1988. *Resisting Protectionism: Global Industries and the Politics of International Trade.* Princeton, N.J.: Princeton University Press.

———. 1997. *Interests, Institutions, and Information: Domestic Politics and International Relations.* Princeton, N.J.: Princeton University Press.

Milner, Helen V., and B. Peter Rosendorff. 1996. Trade Negotiations, Information, and Domestic Politics: The Role of Domestic Groups. *Economics and Politics* 8 (2):145–89.

———. 1997. Democratic Politics and International Trade Negotiations: Elections and Divided Government as Constraints on Trade Liberalization. *Journal of Conflict Resolution* 41 (1):117–46.

Milward, Alan S. 1984. *The Reconstruction of Western Europe, 1945–51.* London: Methuen.

Mingst, Karen A. 1981. The Functionalist and Regime Perspectives: The Case of Rhine River Cooperation. *Journal of Common Market Studies* 20 (2):161–73.

Mitchell, Brian R. 1979. *European Historical Statistics 1750–1950.* New York: Columbia University Press.

Mitchell, Ronald B. 1994. *Intentional Oil Pollution at Sea: Environmental Policy and Treaty Compliance.* Cambridge, Mass.: MIT Press.

———. 1999. International Environmental Common Pool Resources: More Common than Domestic but More Difficult to Manage. In *Anarchy and the Environment: The International Relations of Common Pool Resources,* edited by J. Samuel Barkin and George E. Shambaugh, 26–50. Albany, N.Y.: SUNY Press.

———. 2001. Quantitative Analysis in International Environmental Politics: Toward a Theory of Relative Effectiveness. Unpublished manuscript, University of Oregon, Eugene.

Mitchell, W. 1904. *An Essay on the Early History of the Law Merchant.* Cambridge: Cambridge University Press.

Mitzen, Jennifer. 2001. Toward a Visible Hand: The International Public Sphere in Theory and Practice. Ph.D. diss., University of Chicago.

Mnookin, Robert. 1994. Creating Value Through Process Design. *Journal of International Arbitration* 11 (1):125–37.

Mnookin, Robert, Jean-Pierre Méan, and Eric Robine. 1994. Panel Discussion: Geneva Global Arbitration Forum (21 October 1993). *Journal of International Arbitration* 11 (1):138–45.

Montreal Protocol. 1987/1990. Montreal Protocol on Substances that Deplete the Ozone Layer, as Amended in London, June 1990 (16 September 1987) 26 I.L.M. 1541 (1987); and 29 June 1990, reprinted in 30 I.L.M. 539 (1991).

Moravcsik, Andrew. 1991. Negotiating the Single European Act: National Interests and Conventional Statecraft in the European Community. *International Organization* 45 (1):19–56.

———. 1998. *The Choice for Europe: Social Purpose and State Power from Messina to Maastricht.* Ithaca, N.Y.: Cornell University Press.

———. 2000. The Origins of Human Rights Regimes: Democratic Delegation in Postwar Europe. *International Organization* 54 (2):217–52.

Morgenthau, Hans J. 1993. *Politics Among Nations: The Struggle for Power and Peace.* Brief ed. Revised by Kenneth W. Thompson. New York: McGraw-Hill.

Morrow, James D. 1991. Alliances and Asymmetry: An Alternative to the Capability Aggregation's Model of Alliances. *American Journal of Political Science* 35 (4):904–33.

———. 1994a. Alliances, Credibility, and Peace-Time Costs. *Journal of Conflict Resolution,* 38 (2):270–97.

———. 1994b. *Game Theory for Political Scientists.* Princeton, N.J.: Princeton University Press.

———. 1994c. Modeling the Forms of International Cooperation: Distribution Versus Information. *International Organization* 48 (3):387–423.

———. 1997. Strategy, Victory, and the Laws of War. Paper presented at the 93rd Annual Meeting of the American Political Science Association, Washington, D.C.

———. 1999. The Strategic Setting of Choices: Signaling, Commitment, and Negotiation in International Politics. In *Strategic Choice and International Relations,* edited by David A. Lake and Robert Powell, 77–114. Princeton, N.J.: Princeton University Press.

Mueller, Dennis C. 1989. *Public Choice II.* Cambridge: Cambridge University Press.

Mundell, Robert. 1962. The Appropriate Use of Monetary and Fiscal Policy for Internal and External Stability. *IMF Staff Papers* (April):70–79.

Mustill, Michael, and Stewart Boyd. 1989. *Commercial Arbitration.* London: Butterworths.

Myers, James J. 1991. Could Arbitration Be Made a More Effective Method of Resolution of Construction Disputes? *International Business Lawyer* 19:313–19.

Nadelmann, Ethan A. 1990. Global Prohibition Regimes: The Evolution of Norms in International Society. *International Organization* 44 (4):479–526.

Nash, John F., Jr. 1950. The Bargaining Problem. *Econometrica* 18 (2):155–62.

NATO. 1995. NATO Study on Enlargement. Available at ⟨www.nato.int⟩ (accessed 16 July 2001).

Neill, Brian T. 1988. High Tech and Dispute Resolution I: The Challenge of Presenting Technical Evidence. *International Business Lawyer* 16 (5):233–36.

Nimmo, William F. 1988. *Behind a Curtain of Silence: Japanese in Soviet Custody, 1945–1956.* New York: Greenwood.

North, Douglass C., and Robert Paul Thomas. 1973. *The Rise of the Western World: A New Economic History.* Cambridge: Cambridge University Press.

North, Douglass C., and Barry R. Weingast. 1989. Constitutions and Commitment: The Evolution of Institutions Governing Public Choice in 17th-Century England. *Journal of Economic History* 49 (4):803–32.

O'Halloran, Sharyn. 1994. *Politics, Process, and American Trade Policy.* Ann Arbor: University of Michigan Press.

Oatley, Thomas, and Robert Nabors. 1998. Redistributive Cooperation: Market Failure, Wealth Transfers, and the Basle Accord. *International Organization* 52 (1):35–54.

Olson, Mancur. 1965. *The Logic of Collective Action.* Cambridge, Mass.: Harvard University Press.

Olson, Mancur, and Richard Zeckhauser. 1966. An Economic Theory of Alliances. *The Review of Economics and Statistics* 48 (3):266–79.

Organization for European Economic Cooperation (OEEC). 1952. *Europe—The Way Ahead: Towards Economic Expansion and Dollar Balance.* Paris: OEEC.

Osborne, Martin J., and Ariel Rubinstein. 1994. *A Course in Game Theory.* Cambridge, Mass.: MIT Press.

Ostrom, Elinor. 1990. *Governing the Commons: The Evolution of Institutions for Collective Action.* Cambridge: Cambridge University Press.

Overy, Richard. 1997. *Russia's War: A History of the Soviet War Effort, 1941–1945.* New York: Penguin.

Oye, Kenneth A. 1992. *Economic Discrimination and Political Exchange: World Political Economy in the 1930s and 1980s.* Princeton, N.J.: Princeton University Press.

Oye, Kenneth A., ed. 1986. *Cooperation Under Anarchy.* Princeton, N.J.: Princeton University Press.

Pahre, Robert. 1994. Multilateral Cooperation in an Iterated Prisoners' Dilemma. *Journal of Conflict Resolution* 38 (2):326–52.

———. 1998. Reactions and Reciprocity: Tariffs and Trade Liberalization from 1815 to 1914. *Journal of Conflict Resolution* 42 (4):467–92.

———. 1999. *Leading Questions: How Hegemony Affects the International Political Economy.* Ann Arbor: University of Michigan Press.

———. 2001. Is MFN Better for Spreading? Unpublished manuscript, University of Illinois at Urbana-Champaign.

Pamuk, Şevket. 1987. Commodity Production for World-Markets and Relations of Production in Ottoman Agriculture, 1840–1913. In *The Ottoman Empire and the World-Economy,* edited by Huri İslamoğluInan, 178–202. Cambridge: Cambridge University Press.

Park, William W. 1995. *International Forum Selection.* Boston: Kluwer Law International.

———. 1997a. The Relative Reliability of Arbitration Agreements and Court Selection Clauses. In *International Dispute Resolution: The Regulation of Forum Selection,* edited by Jack L. Goldsmith, 3–35. Irvington-on-Hudson, N.Y.: Transnational Publishers.

————. 1997b. When and Why Arbitration Matters. In *The Commercial Way of Justice,* edited by G. M. Beresford Hartwell, 72–100. The Hague: Kluwer Law International.

Patterson, Gardner, and Judd Polk. 1947. The Emerging Pattern of Bilateralism. *Quarterly Journal of Economics* 62 (1):118–42.

Paulsson, Jan. 1993. The Role of Institutions in Arbitration. In *Handbook of Arbitration Practice,* edited by Ronald Bernstein and Derek Wood, 427–57. London: Sweet and Maxwell.

Perlman, Lawrence, and Steven C. Nelson. 1983. New Approaches to the Resolution of International Commercial Disputes. *The International Lawyer* 17 (2):215–55.

Perlmutter, Amos, and Ted Galen Carpenter. 1998. NATO's Expensive Trip East: The Folly of Enlargement. *Foreign Affairs* 77 (1):2–6.

Peterson, M. J. 1992. Whalers, Cetologists, Environmentalists, and the International Management of Whaling. *International Organization* 46 (1):147–86.

Pettit, Philip. 1995. The Virtual Reality of *Homo Economicus. The Monist* 78 (3):308–29.

————. 1996. Institutional Design and Rational Choice. In *The Theory of Institutional Design,* edited by Robert E. Goodin, 54–89. Cambridge: Cambridge University Press.

Pierre, Andrew J., and Dmitri Trenin. 1997. Developing NATO-Russian Relations. *Survival* 39 (1):5–18.

Pierson, Paul. 2000a. Increasing Returns, Path Dependence, and the Study of Politics. *American Political Science Review* 94 (2):251–67.

————. 2000b. The Limits of Design: Explaining Institutional Origins and Change. *Governance* 13 (4):475–99.

Platt, D. C. M. 1968. *Finance, Trade and Politics in British Foreign Policy 1815–1914.* Oxford: Clarendon Press.

Plous, S. 1985. Perceptual Illusions and Military Realities: The Nuclear Arms Race. *Journal of Conflict Resolution* 29 (3):363–89.

Pogge, Thomas W. 1997. Creating Supra-national Institutions Democratically: Reflections on the European Union's "Democratic Deficit." *Journal of Political Philosophy* 5 (2):163–82.

Posner, Eric A. 1999. A Theory of Contract Law Under Conditions of Radical Judicial Error. John M. Olin Law and Economics Working Paper No. 80 (2D Series). Chicago: The University of Chicago Law School.

Powell, Walter W., and Paul J. DiMaggio, eds. 1991. *The New Institutionalism in Organizational Analysis.* Chicago: University of Chicago Press.

Preeg, Ernest H. 1995. *Traders in a Brave New World.* Chicago: University of Chicago Press.

Price, Richard. 1995. A Genealogy of the Chemical Weapons Taboo. *International Organization* 49 (1):73–103.

Prisching, M. 1989. Evolution and Design of Social Institutions in Austrian Theory. *Journal of Economic Studies* 16 (1):47–62.

Putnam, Robert D. 1988. Diplomacy and Domestic Politics: The Logic of Two-Level Games. *International Organization* 42 (3):427–60.

Rae, Douglas W. 1969. Decision-Rules and Individual Values in Constitutional Choice. *American Political Science Review* 63 (1):40–56.

Raiffa, Howard. 1982. *The Art and Science of Negotiating.* Cambridge, Mass.: Harvard University Press.

Rawls, John. 1971. *A Theory of Justice.* Cambridge, Mass.: Harvard University Press.

Redfern, Alan, and Martin Hunter. 1991. *Law and Practice of International Commercial Arbitration.* 2d ed. London: Sweet and Maxwell.

Reisman, W. Michael, and Chris T. Antoniou, eds. 1994. *The Laws of War: A Comprehensive Collection of Primary Documents on International Laws Governing Armed Conflict.* New York: Vintage.

Reiter, Dan. 2001. Why NATO Enlargement Does Not Spread Democracy. *International Security* 25 (4):41–67.

Richards, John. 1999. Toward a Positive Theory of International Institutions: Regulating International Aviation Markets. *International Organization* 53 (1):1–37.

Riker, William H., and Steven J. Brams. 1973. The Paradox of Vote Trading. *American Political Science Review* 67 (4):1235–47.

Risse, Thomas. 2000. "Let's Argue!": Communicative Action in World Politics. *International Organization* 54 (1):1–39.

Risse-Kappen, Thomas. 1996. Collective Identity in a Democratic Community: The Case of NATO. In *The Culture of National Security,* edited by Peter J. Katzenstein, 357–99. Ithaca, N.Y.: Cornell University Press.

Rittberger, Volker, and Michael Zürn. 1990. Towards Regulated Anarchy in East-West Relations: Causes and Consequences of East-West Regimes. In *International Regimes in East-West Politics,* edited by Volker Rittberger, 9–63. London: Pinter.

Rochester, J. Martin. 1986. The Rise and Fall of International Organization as a Field of Study. *International Organization* 40 (4):777–813.

Rogowski, Ronald. 1989. *Commerce and Coalitions: How Trade Affects Domestic Political Alignments.* Princeton, N.J.: Princeton University Press.

Rosecrance, Richard. 1986. *The Rise of the Trading State.* New York: Basic Books.

Rosendorff, B. Peter. 1996. Voluntary Export Restraints, Antidumping Procedure, and Domestic Politics. *American Economic Review* 86 (3):544–61.

———. 1999. Stability and Rigidity: The Dispute Settlement Procedure of the WTO. Unpublished manuscript, University of Southern California, Los Angeles, Calif.

Rubinstein, Alvin Z. 1998. NATO Enlargement Versus American Interests. *Orbis* 42 (1):37–48.

Rubinstein, Ariel. 1998. *Modeling Bounded Rationality.* Cambridge, Mass.: MIT Press.

Ruggie, John Gerard. 1982. International Regimes, Transactions, and Change: Embedded Liberalism in the Postwar Economic Order. *International Organization* 36 (2):379–415.

———. 1993. Multilateralism: The Anatomy of an Institution. In *Multilateralism Matters: The Theory and Praxis of an Institutional Form,* edited by John Gerard Ruggie, 3–47. New York: Columbia University Press.

Ryan, Reade H., Jr. 1982. Defaults and Remedies Under International Bank Loan Agreements with Foreign Sovereign Borrowers—A New York Lawyer's Perspective. *University of Illinois Law Review* 1982:89–132.

Salkever, Stephen G. 1991. Aristotle's Social Science. In *Essays on the Foundations of Aristotelian Political Science,* edited by Carnes Lord and David K. O'Connor, 11–48. Berkeley: University of California Press.

Sampson, Anthony. 1984. *Empires of the Sky: The Politics, Contests, and Cartels of World Airlines.* New York: Random House.

Sanders, Pieter. 1996. Arbitration. In *International Encyclopedia of Comparative Law.* Vol. 16, *Civil Procedure,* edited by Mauro Cappelletti, ch. 12. Dordrecht: Martinus Nijhoff Publishers.

Sandler, Todd. 1993. The Economic Theory of Alliances: A Survey. *Journal of Conflict Resolution* 37 (3):446–83.

Schelling, Thomas C. 1955. American Foreign Assistance. *World Politics* 7 (4):606–26.

———. 1960. *The Strategy of Conflict.* Cambridge, Mass.: Harvard University Press.

Schimmelfennig, Frank. 1998/99. NATO Enlargement: A Constructivist Explanation. *Security Studies* 8(2/3):198–234.

———. 2001. The Community Trap: Liberal Norms, Rhetorical Action, and the Eastern Enlargement of the European Union. *International Organization* 55 (1):47–80.

Schott, Jeffrey J. 1994. *The Uruguay Round: An Assessment.* Washington, D.C.: Institute for International Economics.

Schotter, Andrew. 1981. *The Economic Theory of Social Institutions.* New York: Cambridge University Press.

Schrader, Dorothy. 1996. *Intellectual Property Provisions of the GATT 1994: "The TRIPS Agreement."* Doc. 94-302A. Washington, D.C.: Congressional Research Service, Library of Congress.

Schwartz, Edward P., and Michael R. Tomz. 1997. The Long-run Advantages of Centralization for Collective Action: A Comment on Bendor and Mookherjee. *American Political Science Review* 91 (3): 685–93.

Schwartz, Eric A. 1995. Resolution of International Construction Disputes. *International Business Lawyer* 23 (4):149–58.

Schweller, Randall L. 1998. *Deadly Imbalances: Tripolarity and Hitler's Strategy of World Conquest.* New York: Columbia University Press.

———. 1999. Fantasy Theory. *Review of International Studies* 25 (1):147–50.

Scott, James C. 1998. *Seeing Like a State: How Certain Schemes to Improve the Human Condition Have Failed.* New Haven, Conn.: Yale University Press.

Sebenius, James K. 1983. Negotiation Arithmetic: Adding and Subtracting Issues and Parties. *International Organization* 37 (2):281–316.

Sell, Susan. 1996. North-South Environmental Bargaining: Ozone, Climate Change, and Biodiversity. *Global Governance* 2 (1):97–118.

Shaw, Stanford J., and Ezel Kural Shaw. 1977. *History of the Ottoman Empire and Modern Turkey.* Vol. 2, *Reform, Revolution and Republic: The Rise of Modern Turkey, 1808–1975.* Cambridge: Cambridge University Press.

Shea, Donald. 1955. *The Calvo Clause: A Problem of Inter-American and International Law and Diplomacy.* Minneapolis: University of Minnesota Press.

Shepsle, Kenneth A. 1983. Institutional Equilibrium and Equilibrium Institutions. Paper presented at the 79th Annual Meeting of the American Political Science Association, Chicago.

———. 1989. Studying Institutions: Some Lessons from the Rational Choice Approach. *Journal of Theoretical Politics* 1 (2):131–47.

Shubik, Martin. 1982. *Game Theory in the Social Sciences.* Vol. 1, *Concepts and Solutions.* Cambridge, Mass.: MIT Press.

Sigvaldsson, Herluf. 1996. The International Whaling Commission: The Transition from a 'Whaling Club' to a 'Preservation Club.' *Cooperation and Conflict* 31 (3):311–52.

Simon, Herbert A. 1957. *Administrative Behavior: A Study of Decision-Making Processes in Administrative Organization.* 2d ed. New York: Macmillan.

Slate, William. 1996. International Arbitration: Do Institutions Make a Difference? *Wake Forest Law Review* 31:41–64.

Slater, Richard. 1982. Syndicated Bank Loans. *The Journal of Business Law* (May):173–99.

Smit, Robert H. 1994. An Inside View of the ICC Court. *Arbitration International* 10:53–76.

Smith, Alastair. 1995. Alliance Formation and War. *International Studies Quarterly* 39 (4):405–25.

Smith, Michael Stephen. 1980. *Tariff Reform in France 1860–1900: The Politics of Economic Interest.* Ithaca, N.Y.: Cornell University Press.

Snidal, Duncan. 1979. Public Goods, Property Rights, and Political Organizations. *International Studies Quarterly* 23 (4):532–66.

Snidal, Duncan. 1985a. Coordination Versus Prisoners' Dilemma: Implications for International Cooperation and Regimes. *American Political Science Review* 79 (4):923–42.

———. 1985b. The Limits of Hegemonic Stability Theory. *International Organization* 39 (4):579–614.

———. 1991. Relative Gains and the Pattern of International Cooperation. *American Political Review* 85 (3):701–26.

———. 1994. The Politics of Scope: Endogenous Actors, Heterogeneity, and Institutions. *Journal of Theoretical Politics* 6 (4):449–72.

———. 1997. International Political Economy Approaches to International Institutions. In *Economic Dimensions in International Law: Comparative and Empirical Perspectives,* edited by Jagdeep S. Bhandari and Alan O. Sykes, 477–512. Cambridge: Cambridge University Press.

Snyder, Glenn H. 1984. The Security Dilemma in Alliance Politics. *World Politics* 36 (4):461–95.

Sochor, Eugene. 1991. *The Politics of International Aviation.* Iowa City: University of Iowa Press.

Spence, A. Michael. 1974. *Market Signaling: Informational Transfer in Hiring and Related Screening Processes.* Cambridge, Mass.: Harvard University Press.

Spruyt, Hendrik. 1994. *The Sovereign State and Its Competitors: An Analysis of Systems Change.* Princeton, N.J.: Princeton University Press.

Srinagesh, Padmanabhan. 1997. Internet Cost Structures and Interconnection Agreements. In *Internet Economics,* edited by Lee McKnight and Joseph P. Bailey, 121–54. Cambridge, Mass.: MIT Press.

Stedman, Bruce. 1990. The International Whaling Commission and Negotiation for a Moratorium on Whaling. In *Nine Case Studies in International Environmental Negotiation,* edited by Lawrence E. Susskind, Esther Siskind, and J. William Breslin, 151–75. Cambridge, Mass.: MIT-Harvard Public Disputes Program.

Stein, Arthur A. 1980. The Politics of Linkage. *World Politics* 33 (1):62–81.

———. 1983. Coordination and Collaboration: Regimes in an Anarchic World. In *International Regimes,* edited by Stephen D. Krasner, 115–40. Ithaca, N.Y.: Cornell University Press.

Stern, Robert M. 1997. Constituent Interest Group Influences on U.S. Trade Policies Since the Advent of the WTO. RSIE Discussion Papers 416. Ann Arbor: Research Center in International Economics, University of Michigan.

Steward, Margaret G. 1986. Forum Non *Conveniens:* A Doctrine in Search of a Role. *California Law Review* 74 (4):1259–1324.

Stewart, Hamish. 1995. A Critique of Instrumental Reason in Economics. *Economics and Philosophy* 11 (1):57–83.

Stipanowich, Thomas. 1996. Beyond Arbitration: Innovation and Evolution in the United States Construction Industry. *Wake Forest Law Review* 31:65–182.

Stockholm Chamber of Commerce (SCC). 1988. *Rules of the Arbitration Institute of the Stockholm Chamber of Commerce.* Stockholm: SCC.

Stoett, Peter J. 1997. *The International Politics of Whaling.* Vancouver, B.C.: University of British Columbia Press.

Streit, Christian. 1993. Partisans—Resistance—Prisoners of War. In *Operation Barbarossa: The German Attack on the Soviet Union, June 22, 1941,* edited by Joseph L. Wieczynski, 260–75. Salt Lake City, Utah: Charles Schlacks, Jr.

Sugden, Robert. 1993. Thinking as a Team: Toward an Explanation of Nonselfish Behavior. *Social Philosophy and Policy* 10 (1):69–89.

Summerskill, Michael. 1993. Maritime Arbitration. In *Handbook of Arbitration Practice,* edited by Ronald Bernstein and Derek Wood, 347–96. London: Sweet and Maxwell.

Sykes, Alan O. 1991. Protectionism as a "Safeguard." *University of Chicago Law Review* 58 (1):255–305.

Taneja, Nawal K. 1980. *U.S. International Aviation Policy.* Lexington, Mass: Lexington Books.

Tannenwald, Nina. 1999. The Nuclear Taboo: The United States and the Normative Basis of Nuclear Non-Use. *International Organization* 53 (3):433–68.

Taylor, Michael. 1969. Proof of a Theorem on Majority Rule. *Behavioral Science* 14 (3):228–31.

Thucydides. 1954. *History of the Peloponnesian War.* Translated and with an introduction by Rex Warner. Baltimore, Md.: Penguin Books.

Tollison, Robert E., and Thomas D. Willett. 1979. An Economic Theory of Mutually Advantageous Issue Linkage in International Negotiations. *International Organization* 33 (4):425–49.

Tonnessen, J. N., and A. O. Johnsen. 1982. *The History of Modern Whaling.* Translated by R. I. Christophersen. Berkeley: University of California Press.

Toope, Stephen J. 1990. *Mixed International Arbitration: Studies in Arbitration Between States and Private Persons.* Cambridge: Grotius Publications.

Townsend, Robert M. 1988. Models as Economies. *Economic Journal* 98 (390):1–24.

Trebilcock, Michael J., and Robert Howse. 1995. *The Regulation of International Trade.* London: Routledge.

Trenholme, Russell. 1975. Causation and Necessity. *Journal of Philosophy* 72 (14):444–65.

Triffin, Robert. 1957. *Europe and the Money Muddle: From Bilateralism to Near Convertibility, 1947–1956.* New Haven, Conn.: Yale University Press.

U.S. Department of State. 1947. *Foreign Relations of the United States.* Vol. 3. Washington, D.C.: U.S. Government Printing Office.

————. 1948. Outline of European Recovery Program, Draft Legislation and Background Information, submitted by the Department of State for the use of the Senate Foreign Relations Committee, 19 December 1947. Y4.F76/2: Eu 7/4. Washington, D.C.: U.S. Government Printing Office.

————. 1950. *Foreign Relations of the United States.* Vol. 3. Washington, D.C.: U.S. Government Printing Office.

Ullmann-Margalit, Edna. 1978. Invisible-Hand Explanations. *Synthese* 39 (2):263–91.

UN Environment Program (UNEP). 1991. Ad Hoc Working Group of Legal Experts on Noncompliance with the Montreal Protocol. Third Meeting. Indicative List of Measures that Might Be Taken by a Meeting of the Parties in Respect of Non-Compliance with the Protocol. UNEP/Ozl.Pro./WG.3/L.7. Nairobi: UN Environment Program.

Vagts, Detlev. 1987. Dispute-Resolution Mechanisms in International Business. *Recueil Des Cours* 203:17–93.

Van der Beugel, Ernst H. 1966. *From Marshall Aid to Atlantic Partnership: European Integration as a Concern of American Foreign Policy.* Amsterdam: Elsevier.

Van Evera, Stephen. 1997. *Guide to Methods for Students of Political Science.* Ithaca, N.Y.: Cornell University Press.

————. 1999. *Causes of War: Power and the Roots of Conflict.* Ithaca, N.Y.: Cornell University Press.

van Zandt, J. Parker. 1944. *Civil Aviation and Peace.* Washington, D.C.: Brookings Institution.

Vanberg, Viktor. 1994. Cultural Evolution, Collective Learning, and Constitutional Design. In *Economic Thought and Political Theory,* edited by David Reisman, 171–204. Boston: Kluwer Academic Publishers.

Vance, Jonathan F. 1994. *Objects of Concern: Canadian Prisoners of War Through the Twentieth Century.* Vancouver, B.C.: UBC Press.

Vercelli, Alessandro. 1995. From Soft Uncertainty to Hard Environmental Uncertainty. *Economie Appliquee* 48 (2):251–69.

Victor, David G. 1998. The Operation and Effectiveness of the Montreal Protocol's Non-Compliance Procedure. In *The Implementation and Effectiveness of International Environmental Commitments: Theory and Practice,* edited by David G. Victor, Kal Raustiala, and Eugene B. Skolnikoff, 137–76. Cambridge, Mass.: MIT Press.

Vigrass, B. W. 1993. The Role of Institutions in Arbitration. In *Handbook of Arbitration Practice,* edited by Ronald Bernstein and Derek Wood, 461–76. London: Sweet and Maxwell.

Viner, Jacob. 1924. The Most-Favored-Nation Clause in American Commercial Treaties. *Journal of Political Economy* 32 (1):101–29.

Walsh, Virginia. 1999. Illegal Whaling for Humpbacks by the Soviet Union in the Antarctic, 1947–1972. *Journal of Environment and Development* 8 (3):307–27.

Walt, Stephen M. 1987. *The Origins of Alliances.* Ithaca, N.Y.: Cornell University Press.

————. 1997. Why Alliances Endure or Collapse. *Survival* 39 (1):156–79.

————. 1999. Rigor or Rigor Mortis? Rational Choice and Security Studies. *International Security* 23 (4):5–48.

Waltz, Kenneth N. 1979. *Theory of International Politics.* Reading, Mass.: Addison-Wesley.

Watson, Joel. 1999. Starting Small and Renegotiation. *Journal of Economic Theory* 85 (1):52–90.

Weatherford, Roy. 1982. *Philosophical Foundations of Probability Theory.* London: Routledge and Kegan Paul.

Webb, Michael. 1991. International Economic Structures, Government Interests, and International Coordination of Macroeconomic Adjustment Policies. *International Organization* 45 (3):309–42.

Weber, Cynthia. 1998. Performative States. *Millennium* 27 (1):77–95.

Weingast, Barry R. 1979. A Rational Choice Perspective on Congressional Norms. *American Journal of Political Science* 23 (2):245–62.

Weiss, Edith Brown, and Harold K. Jacobson, eds. 1998. *Engaging Countries: Strengthening Compliance with International Environmental Accords.* Cambridge, Mass.: MIT Press.

Weitowitz, Rolf. 1978. *Deutsche Politik und Handelspolitik unter Reichskanzler Leo von Caprivi 1890–1894.* Düsseldorf: Droste Verlag.

Wendt, Alexander. 1992. Anarchy Is What States Make of It: The Social Construction of Power Politics. *International Organization* 46 (2):391–425.

———. 1998. On Constitution and Causation in International Relations. *Review of International Studies* 24 (special issue):101–18.

———. 1999. *Social Theory of International Politics.* Cambridge: Cambridge University Press.

———. 2001. What Is IR For? Notes Toward a Post-Critical View. In *Critical Theory and World Politics,* edited by Richard Wyn Jones, 205–24. Boulder, Colo.: Lynne Rienner.

Werner, Yvonne Maria. 1989. Svensk-tyska förbindelser kring sekelskiftet 1900. Politik och ekonomi vid tillkomsten av 1906 års svensk-tyska handels och sjöfartstraktat. In *Bibliotheca historica Lundensis,* vol. 65, edited by Eva Österberg and Göran Rystad. Lund: Lund University Press.

Wetter, J. Gillis. 1995. The Internationalization of International Arbitration: Looking Ahead to the Next Ten Years. *Arbitration International* 11 (2):117–35.

Wheelbarger, Kathryn. 1999. The Bretton Woods Institutions: How and Why States Cooperated to Organize the International Monetary Agreement. Unpublished manuscript, University of California, Los Angeles.

Wight, Martin. 1966. Why Is There No International Theory? In *Diplomatic Investigations,* edited by Herbert Butterfield and Martin Wight, 17–34. London: Allen and Unwin.

Wilkinson, Dean M. 1989. The Use of Domestic Measures to Enforce International Whaling Agreements: A Critical Perspective. *Denver Journal of International Law and Policy* 17 (2):271–92.

Williams, Judith Blow. 1972. *British Commercial Policy and Trade Expansion 1750–1850.* Oxford: Clarendon Press.

Williams, Michael C., and Iver B. Neumann. 2000. From Alliance to Security Community: NATO, Russia, and the Power of Identity. *Millennium* 29 (2):357–87.

Williamson, Oliver E. 1975. *Markets and Hierarchies: Analysis and Antitrust Implications.* New York: Free Press.

———. 1983. Credible Commitments: Using Hostages to Support Exchange. *American Economic Review* 73 (4):519–40.

———. 1985. *The Economic Institutions of Capitalism: Firms, Markets, Relational Contracting.* New York: Free Press.

Wilson, Robert A. 1994. Causal Depth, Theoretical Appropriateness, and Individualism in Psychology. *Philosophy of Science* 61 (1):55–75.

Winham, Gilbert R. 1986. *International Trade and the Tokyo Round Negotiations.* Princeton, N.J.: Princeton University Press.

Winter, Eyal. 1996. Voting and Vetoing. *American Political Science Review* 90 (4):813–23.

Wolf, Fred Alan. 1984. *Star Wave: Mind, Consciousness, and Quantum Physics.* New York: MacMillan.

Wood, Philip. 1980. *Law and Practice of International Finance.* London: Sweet and Maxwell.

Wright, Larry. 1976. *Teleological Explanations: An Etiological Analysis of Goals and Functions.* Berkeley: University of California Press.

Yablokov, Alexey V. 1994. Validity of Whaling Data. *Nature* 367 (6459):108.

Yarbrough, Beth V., and Robert M. Yarbrough. 1986. Reciprocity, Bilateralism, and Economic "Hostages": Self-enforcing Agreements in International Trade. *International Studies Quarterly* 30 (1):7–21.

———. 1992. *Cooperation and Governance in International Trade: The Strategic Organizational Approach.* Princeton, N.J.: Princeton University Press.

Young, Oran R. 1979. *Compliance and Public Authority: A Theory with International Applications.* Baltimore, Md.: Johns Hopkins University Press.

———. 1989. *International Cooperation: Building Regimes for Natural Resources and the Environment.* Ithaca, N.Y.: Cornell University Press.

———. 1994. *International Governance: Protecting the Environment in a Stateless Society.* Ithaca, N.Y.: Cornell University Press.

———. 1999. *Governance in World Affairs.* Ithaca, N.Y.: Cornell University Press.

Zacher, Mark W., with Brent A. Sutton. 1996. *Governing Global Networks: International Regimes for Transportation and Communications.* New York: Cambridge University Press.